D1268955

CONDITIONS OF
WORLD ORDER

CONDITIONS OF
WORLD ORDER

EDITED AND WITH AN INTRODUCTION
BY STANLEY HOFFMANN

BRIAR CLIFF COLLEGE
LIBRARY

SIOUX CITY, IOWA

A CLARION BOOK

PUBLISHED BY SIMON AND SCHUSTER

A Clarion Book
Published by Simon and Schuster
Rockefeller Center, 630 Fifth Avenue
New York, New York 10020
All rights reserved
including the right of reproduction
in whole or in part in any form
Copyright © 1966, 1968 by
the American Academy of Arts and Sciences

Reprinted by arrangement with Houghton Mifflin Company

First Clarion printing 1970

SBN 671-20748-2
Manufactured in the United States of America

The essays in this book appeared in *Daedalus*,
the Journal of the American Academy of Arts and Sciences.
"The Anarchical Order of Power" by Raymond Aron is
reprinted with the permission of Encyclopedia Britannica.

JX
1395
.C66
1965

CONTENTS

71584

STANLEY HOFFMANN

Introduction

THE AMERICAN ACADEMY OF ARTS AND SCIENCES has, in recent years, been increasingly concerned with the shape, prospects, and problems of the world's future. For the first time, the world lives a common history. The disruptions of two world wars, the technological revolution that has immeasurably shrunk distances, developed communications, and "accelerated history," the world-wide sweep of ideologies have made of this planet an echo chamber. While the Academy's Commission of the Year 2000 tries to investigate the major trends that will characterize and transform our societies, Stephen Graubard, the editor of *Dædalus*, and Raymond Aron, whose writings on industrial society, international relations, and ideology have shown such passionate and disciplined concern with the possibilities, the limits, and the moral imperatives of social change, decided to call a conference on "Conditions of World Order." Under what conditions would this world of rapid change, rising threats, and huge disparities be, if not peaceful and stable, at least tolerable and manageable? It was hoped that a discussion of this subject by men of various disciplines and from all continents would, if not provide an answer to a vital but sprawling problem, at least prove interesting, tolerable, and manageable.

Dr. Graubard, in issuing invitations to the Conference, described its purpose as follows:

Professor Raymond Aron of the University of Paris, who will be Chairman of the Seminar, has suggested that we may be witnessing the beginning of an "Age of Universal History"—for the first time nations and peoples form a single world system—yet the old cultural diversities persist, new sources of conflict have appeared, and these very conditions constitute the major factors influencing world order. The persistence of these diversities we consider to be inevitable; homogeneity will not soon prevail. Consequently, the problem is to be understood, first, how and whether such diversities imperil international stability, and, secondly, how it is possible to organize so that there can be peaceful coexistence between societies which remain fundamentally different. This is the key question for which the Seminar is convened, and it will form the background of our discussion. The foreground will be occupied by a host of questions more limited in scope which must be dealt with in pursuit of the larger concerns.

In addressing ourselves to a "stable world order" members of the Seminar will, it is hoped, discuss problems of international relations as something more than relations between states. The military, political, and economic rivalries of great powers, while unquestionably important, are not the only significant determinants of international order or disorder. We must look at the various political systems and at the peoples themselves —their numbers, diversities, cultures, economic levels, and ideologies —to discover how these factors affect international stability. In other words we must analyze all the various types of disparities which are dangerous yet likely to persist.

Thus, at the Villa Serbelloni in Bellagio, Italy, where the Conference met, thanks to the hospitality of the Rockefeller Foundation, and in the papers subsequently published in *Dædalus* (Spring, 1966), the issues underlying all the topics under discussion can be described as follows. First, in the present race between equalization and unevenness that characterizes the world (equalization through science and technology—that is, what is being called modernization, development, or rationalization; the unevenness of political and economic regimes, of ideological, ethnic, and power conflicts, of levels of development, of cultural traditions), which force will prove to be the stronger? Second, what are the factors that, today and tomorrow, will tend to create or to reinforce stability, harmony, or at least coexistence?

I have tried to summarize the discussions of the Conference in the report that follows. The papers themselves show both the extent to which the authors have remained in disagreement, and the vast scope of their search for order. The first part of the volume examines the state of the international system and the prospects of and obstacles to world order in the realm of world politics. The second part deals with the impact of science and material progress on the social order. Without being so complete as one might ideally have wanted it to be (for instance, without providing a thorough analysis of the impact of technological change), this set of essays not only raises important issues, but gives a more positive and unpessimistic answer than the

Introduction

papers on world politics. Finally, the last three essays discuss some of the spiritual conditions of world order.

Most of the essays in this volume were prepared for the Conference in Bellagio, which was sponsored by the Congress for Cultural Freedom, with a grant from the Ford Foundation and the American Academy of Arts and Sciences. The papers by Mr. Godfried van Benthem van den Bergh, Professor Mus, and myself were written later and published in the Summer, 1966, issue of *Dædalus*, as were the papers by Professor Dyckman, who was at Bellagio, and Mr. Scrimshaw, who was not. I wish to express my thanks to them, as well as to the other contributors to this volume, and to those participants in the Conference who did not write essays, but took an active part in our discussions: Ambassador Jamal Muhammed Ahmed of the Sudan, Professor Masao Maruyama of Tokyo, Dr. Robert S. Morison of Cornell University, Mr. Pitambar Pant of India, Ambassador Pietro Quaroni of Italy, and Professor Adul Wichiencharoen of Thammasat University in Thailand.

One more note of thanks—last but not least—to Raymond Aron, whose contribution as chairman of the Conference supplied the foundations, the cement, and the roof to whatever bricks the other participants brought so as to build a livable "house of many mansions" for a world in search of order.

CONDITIONS OF
WORLD ORDER

STANLEY HOFFMANN

Report of the Conference on Conditions of World Order—
June 12-19, 1965, Villa Serbelloni, Bellagio, Italy

I. *A Working Definition of World Order*

UNDER THE chairmanship and guidance of Raymond Aron, the
twenty-one men who met at Bellagio from June 12 to June 19 in
order to define conditions of World Order participated in a double
experiment. One was intellectual—the attempt to discuss both the
chances for and the obstacles to world order as they appear in
1965. It is this aspect of the seminar that will be covered primarily
in this report. The other experiment was really an enterprise in
collective psychology—a psychodrama of sorts. How would men
coming from different countries, from different cultural and
ideological backgrounds, from different professions and disciplines
interpret the subject, lock horns, join issues, and reach conclusions?
Would the meeting be a succession of monologues or a successful
seminar? I will make some remarks about this aspect at the end.

Inevitably, the first session was devoted to a succession of
monologues: each member was asked to state how he saw the
problem of world order, the chairman hoping that the main themes
would arise from those statements. Not only did the main themes
arise, but what happened was like the beginning of a symphony in
which all the themes of the piece are introduced, so that the rest
of the symphony merely adds developments and variations, but no
fresh theme. The metaphor breaks down in one respect only:
those developments and variations were added not simply because
of the skills of the various members of the group—composers capable of refining their themes, if not of inventing new ones—but
because of the conductor's subtle and energetic interventions.
Aron's leadership prodded the seminar into giving depth and complexity to ideas all of which had appeared by the end of the
first session.

Indeed, his first intervention provided the composers with a
key for their symphony. They had not all used the term "world
order" in the same way. Aron distinguished five possible meanings

1

and suggested that the seminar concern itself with one of those. Two of the meanings were purely descriptive: order as any arrangement of reality, order as the relations between the parts. Two were analytical—partly descriptive, partly normative: order as the minimum conditions for existence, order as the minimum conditions for *co*existence. The fifth conception was purely normative: order as the conditions for the good life. Aron proposed that the conference forget about the last—for it could lead the members only to platitudes or to an acrimonious reproduction of the conflicts of values that exist in the world—and examine the fourth. "Conditions of world order" would thus mean: under what conditions would men (divided in so many ways) be able not merely to avoid destruction, but to live together relatively well in one planet.

If "order" was thus defined, "world" remained a bit fuzzy. Obviously the consequences for the meeting were less disastrous than if "order" had been kept in confusion: after all, there are limits to the planet, and everybody agreed that for the first time the planet was living a single history. But some ambiguity subsisted on two points. One, what are the factors and events that affect that single history? Does the new unity of the planet, does "le monde fini" serve as an echo chamber for *all* that happens within its component parts, or for some aspects or forces only? We all agreed that "world order" means more than interstate relations: world order is affected by domestic structures and transnational phenomena; but we never rigorously defined which domestic and transnational circumstances have an impact on world order and which do not. Secondly, Mr. Waddington remarked that there was not so much *a* world order, as *a set* of world ordering systems—different kinds of relations between groupings of varying natures (nations, industrial organizations, races, religions, and so forth). The point, a sound one, was not pursued much further. This is much to be regretted, for the conference rather single-mindedly concentrated on whatever was assumed by some to work for peace, harmony, and unity—with the dissenters trying to show why the millennium would not come—instead of looking at the ways in which ineradicable diversity could be made constructive, and inevitable conflicts manageable. It might have been better, although far more difficult, to discuss the chances of multiple improvements, instead of alternatively throwing up and shooting down grand solutions or wild hopes.

As for "conditions," there remained throughout the conference some ambiguity here also. Perhaps because of the meaning of order proposed by Aron, the seminar concerned itself more with analyzing and assessing the conditions already making for world order than with defining conditions that would assure such order in the future—perhaps also because, as we shall see, many participants thought that the present conditions were both necessary and to a large extent sufficient. In any event, the minority who thought that this was not the case was not homogeneous: some were concerned with finding ways of going beyond what existed now or what might come out of a mere continuation of present trends, while others were more interested in showing critically why those trends were far from reassuring.

The order of the sessions that followed the first was anything but rigid and linear. The themes announced in the symphony's prelude were not developed one by one. If anything, the composition was cyclical. This report will not, however, try to follow the order of the meeting. It will deal with the three main themes that emerged; two concerned the conditions of order discerned by all the participants, and which can, with some flippancy, be called peace and prosperity; the third theme—rather unexpected, given the subject-matter of the conference, but not at all surprising given the professional composition of the seminar—dealt with the relations between thought and action, a problem that was in part epistemological and methodological, in part a turn toward the fifth definition of order.

II. *Order in Interstate Relations*

The basic problem, here, can be defined as follows: is the nation-state a form of social organization that is likely to persist? Is it an obstacle to world order? If so, how can it be overcome?

It became obvious from the start that description and prescription are hard to separate: our values shape our knowledge. A man convinced that the nation-state is the greatest threat to peace and must be superseded will find ways of showing that in the present world the nation-state is already on the way out. And yet, for clarity's sake, I will try to keep the three questions more separate than they were in the discussions.

Fate of the nation-state. Perhaps because of the scrambling of analysis and judgment, the issue of the nation-state's fate and solidity was not fully discussed, even though (to a student of international relations, at least) it may not be indifferent for world order to know whether the present mushrooming of nation-states represents a last orgiastic gasp before death and transfiguration, or means that any kind of world order will have to be based on a type of unit whose flaws have not exactly gone unnoticed. Evaluation and prescription somehow overshadowed straightforward diagnosis. Hoffmann suggested that the nuclear stalemate in particular, the increase in the costs of the use of force in general, had given a new lease on life to nation-states, even to those that may appear artificial or unviable; indeed, material as well as nuclear interdependence, while removing the states' incentives to madness, also remove their incentives to suicide. The only conceivable mutation of world politics is a "mutation at the brink," should a local holocaust convince the surviving powers that the uncertainties of a radically new system of relations are less frightening than the perpetuation of traditional interstate politics. Aron agreed that the future of world politics would in all likelihood consist of a "muddling through" of states, for he saw no sign of a mutation in world affairs. The reason that the issue was not directly discussed further may have been that few participants believed either that the nation-state would disappear (Lord Gladwyn, the chief prosecutor of the nation-state, still envisages for 1985 a world in which four of the five expected "poles" would be nation-states: the U.S., the U.S.S.R., China, and India) or that the nation-state would remain unaffected by trends and institutions that have already changed the substance if not the form of sovereignty.

Defense and indictment of the nation-state. That the nation-state may nevertheless be a threat to world order was denied by nobody. Indeed, the charges against it were formidable and varied. First, there was Lord Gladwyn's often repeated blanket critique of the nation-state as a factor of anarchy whose tendency toward unlimited sovereignty had to be curbed in the interest of survival. Secondly, there were a number of detailed references to the dangers created by contemporary nation-states. One was the analysis of the limits of the nuclear stalemate. Although the restraints imposed on the states by the peril of annihilation were recognized by all the participants, some tried to show that these restraints remain fragile and that the stalemate, a necessary precondition of order in the nuclear age, was however not a sufficient guarantee. Aron reminded his listeners that if total war was no longer "the continuation of politics by other means," the *threat* of

4

war and certain *kinds* of war were another matter altogether. Hoffmann insisted on the persistence of various social functions of war even in the nuclear age, on the prospects of dangerous crises among the major nuclear powers (due in particular to the role of third parties and to revolutionary wars), on the perils of nuclear proliferation. He and Mr. Fourastié showed that the very restrictions on the use of force tend to perpetuate unsolved problems and acute tensions in various parts of the world. Aron and Kissinger thought that proliferation might lead to local wars, not to a major nuclear war: global world order would be preserved at the cost of a fragmentation of the international system. Yet Aron himself recognized that there was more magic than necessity in one crucial restraint observed until now by the nuclear powers—their abstention from any aggressive use of nuclear weapons—and Kissinger confessed that the experience of a local nuclear war among small powers without cataclysmic effects could erode the restraint, based on horror, that has marked great power behavior until now.

Kissinger himself introduced another line of attack against the contemporary nation-state. In a systematic analysis of the impact of domestic structures on foreign policy, he showed the absence of any common legitimacy today, due to the heterogeneity of the leaders who have to coexist for the first time in a single international system, and whose range extends all the way from America's bureaucratic leadership to the rulers of the new countries for whom "the future is more real than the present." He spoke of the contrast and clash of the political and of the prophetic style of leadership, of the tensions created by some nations' desire for absolute security, of the rigidities introduced by the heavy bureaucracy of the larger states. He denounced the perils for peace that stem from the insecurity of most leaders, in search of immediate successes; he discussed the dangers resulting either from the excessive sense of identity of some states, engaged in an overbearing manipulation of others, or from the insufficient sense of identity of other states which compensate for its absence by engaging in external adventures. Hoffmann remarked that the picture was perhaps too somber, since those conflicting visions and policies have to interact in an international system that leaves its members with little more freedom than prisoners in a chain gang, that tends to thwart prophets and to tame ambitions; but nobody denied that even the decline of force and the deterrence of ideological expansion would still not mean the reconciliation of ideologies or the harmony of interests. As Professor Gadamer observed, the way in which the mass media help leaders manufacture the general will and the game of mirrors between leaders and masses do not contribute to peace.

Still another line of criticism of the contemporary nation-state dealt with the heterogeneity of nation-states in the present world. Professor O'Connell emphasized the differences between the new African states and the model nation-state of the West. This heterogeneity explains in part the present incoherence of international law, whose concepts have been both suddenly extended to and challenged by new states eager to borrow Western notions of the sovereign state but not Western rules for restricting the state.

Against those charges, there were some attempts at defending not so much the nation-state as nationalism, or rather at suggesting distinctions among nationalisms. Mr. Pant and Mr. Jaguaribe—an Indian and a Brazilian—revived Mazzini's celebration of liberal nationalism, a necessary spring of action and a force for self-respect and dignity. They contrasted it either with the evil nationalism that entails an assertion of superiority or with the lack of national feeling in countries run by oligarchies and dominated by foreign imperialism. Mr. Málek asserted that cooperation among East European states, despite the difficulties created by their very different levels of development, shows that nationalism can be curbed without abolishing the nation-states. But Kissinger and Aron reminded the group that no clear line separates once and for all good and bad nationalisms. Moreover, nationalism is not the only possible poison carried by the nation-state: ideological claims pushed by it can make conflicts even more intense, and, as Kissinger remarked, states, whether national or not, necessarily breed conflicts due to the fragmentation of power and to the competition of interests in the world.

"Comment s'en débarrasser" (or, shall we overcome?). When it came to proposals for going from the present danger to future stability, unanimity collapsed. There was disagreement about methods, about specific suggestions, and about their prospects.

On methods, whereas many members, and Lord Gladwyn in particular, expressed an interest in institutional solutions, others pressed for different directions. Professor Waddington, intrigued by the nuclear stalemate (and praised by Aron as the first natural scientist willing to celebrate its virtues), was interested in seeing whether one could set up more automatic feedback systems like it, in which each part would depend for its very existence on its relations with the other parts. Mr. Málek denied the possibility of an institutional solution at this stage of history, but pressed for a functional approach—not in the sense of functional agencies but in the sense of an analysis of the functions that could already be carried out cooperatively at the world level; the promotion of world order implies the promotion of those functions.

On the whole, however, the discussion took place along familiar institutional lines. Very little—surprisingly—was said about the U.N.; Hoffmann's skepticism about a U.N. police force was not really challenged. Nor was his critique of disarmament, which he deemed hopeless because it goes against "the operation of uncertainty in the international state of nature"—that is, nations prefer familiar uncertainties to thoroughly unfamiliar leaps in the dark. As for international law, despite some nuances in the interpretation of the causes, scope, and originality of its present disarray, O'Connell, Aron, and Hoffmann tacitly recognized that it could itself progress only if world order progresses, rather than contribute directly to world order in the crucial areas of war and peace. Consequently, two kinds of schemes received more attention. On the one hand, Professor Morison paid a glowing tribute to the functional agencies of the U.N., and suggested that they be made more independent of politics, that is, both of the states and of the U.N., a suggestion whose practical chances and likely effects were assessed skeptically by others. On the other hand, the seminar engaged in more than one great debate about the virtues and prospects of regionalism, championed by Lord Gladwyn with the undiscouraged enthusiasm worthy of a true believer.

Lord Gladwyn's case was a two-stage construction. The first stage was an analysis of, and praise for, the movement of European integration. He saw in the supranational method an admirable invention for superseding the nation-state, and in European integration (once Britain is included) a way of removing one of the main sources of tension in the world, by allowing for the disengagement of both superpowers from Europe and for the reunification of Western and Eastern Europe (without Russia). A number of objections were presented (and left Lord Gladwyn unperturbed). Ambassador Quaroni and Hoffmann stressed the limits and difficulties not yet overcome by the "Monnet method," especially in the

7

areas of foreign policy and strategy. Others showed the discrepancies between the various advantages different advocates of European integration have claimed for their cause: was the purpose of the movement to put an end to wars among Europeans? Was it to ease tensions between the non-European superpowers? Or the end of power politics among European nations? Or, on the contrary, the acquisition of more power for Europe through a fusion of nations separately too weak? Not only are those arguments quite different, but each one is debatable—and was debated, especially by Kissinger, Quaroni, and Aron. Whereas Lord Gladwyn presented European integration as a sure blessing, Hoffmann and Kissinger remarked that an institutional structure cannot be judged *in abstracto*: a collectively impotent United States of Europe, or else a federated Europe that would define its identity only in sharp opposition to the U. S., might be a curse.

The second stage of Lord Gladwyn's analysis was a plea for extending to other parts of the world the benefits of regionalism, borrowing from the European example. He was aware of the difficulties, particularly in Africa (where nationalism is still the only alternative to tribalism). But he was confident both about the feasibility of such schemes and about the unlikelihood of regional groupings becoming and behaving merely like enlarged nation-states. In order to assure harmony among the four large poles mentioned before, Europe as the fifth pole, and the other regions of the world, he suggested the creation of a World Council of limited membership. Professor Tinbergen supported Lord Gladwyn by referring to the economic advantages of regionalism and to the impact of European economic integration on other areas which begin to imitate Europe. Aron also gave a *préjugé favorable* to the concept, while suggesting a further study of the effects of regional groupings on nonmembers and on big-power conflicts. However, once again, objections multiplied. Hoffmann and Pant challenged the significance of regional contiguity in a world in which many problems can be tackled only on an international basis. Kissinger, Málek, Jaguaribe, and Hoffmann showed that the transplantation of the European experience outside Europe runs into considerable difficulties, such as the heterogeneity of élites and states in most regions or the divisive role played by the superpowers which try to preserve their domination of or their influence in an area.

In the final analysis, the discussion of the so-called remedies, or solutions, remained inconclusive. Hoffmann presented the picture of a world relying on the fragile hope of self-restraint by the nations; they would remain the basic units, despite a growing and tightening net of functional and regional agencies that would tend to untie the Gordian knot which presently ties so many different functions around the nation-state. Since he himself expressed reservations about the effectiveness of those agencies, and doubts about the permanent triumph of self-restraint in a world of revolutions, unsolved tensions, and nuclear spread, his picture was, as Aron put it, "rather depressing"—like an abdication before reality. But when it came to defining what ought to be done in order to improve reality, the seminar was not able to go beyond Lord Gladwyn's controversial plan and Jaguaribe's praise of certain schemes for the gradual reduction of tension among the superpowers. It is interesting, and perhaps a bit disturbing, that the problem of the relations among those powers, implicitly or explicitly recognized as decisive for international order by most participants, was not discussed frontally. And so, the sum total of the variations and developments of the first theme amount to: "The nuclear stalemate plus . . . ."

III. *Development and Rationality*

If the first theme led only to a somewhat tentative conclusion, due to the small number among the participants of what Aron called "active optimists" about world politics, active optimism asserted itself much more with respect to the second theme: the contribution to world order of the efforts made, by scientists and economists particularly, in order to overcome poverty and disease and to promote development. Here again, it is possible to divide the discussions into three subjects: a description of the ways and means of such progress, an assessment of their over-all achievements, a prescription for their triumph.

The ways and means of material progress. The seminar included a significant number of men associated with or in charge of economic planning in their respective countries. It was not surprising to hear planning celebrated as a method capable of eliminating poverty, of projecting material progress into the future, and of laying the foundations for international (not merely national) order. Messrs. Pant, Dyckman, Fourastié, and Tinbergen, in various ways, stressed that we now had enough knowledge of the regularities of the material world, of the trends and rules of large-scale behavior, of the desirable rates of growth for various categories of nations, in order both to set goals acceptable by most groups in a population and to solve the technical problems of various sectors (health, population). International organizations help to make different plans compatible and to coordinate efforts on a world or regional basis. Those assertions, presented most lyrically by Mr. Pant, were not left unchallenged. Aron pointed out that not all the results attributed to planning were caused by it, and reminded the group of a French economist's unflattering reference to Chantecler in connection with the French plan; Jaguaribe and Hoffmann remarked that planning, a possible condition of world order, was itself possible only when certain essential political and social requirements existed already in a country—a basic consensus on goals, a minimum of compatibility between masses and élites, a modicum of efficiency. Kissinger doubted that planning could be useful when the objectives themselves are in question, or provides criteria for their selection. Even the planners did not all deny the blemishes: Dyckman wondered whether planners had succeeded in creating a sense of purpose, and he noticed that our understanding of social systems was far from sufficient; Fourastié observed that the causes of economic progress remain often misunderstood in the new countries, where people tend to cling to a magic conception of economic power, seen as a kind of stock that belongs to the wealthy nations who got it through some unfair mystery, and from whom it should be taken away. In other words, as Aron put it, planning entails not merely the application of techniques, but a change of civilization; economic progress is not a gift but a painful process.

And yet, those reservations did not seem to disturb most of the participants. The achievement of planning, in which scientific knowledge gets applied to the production of goods, was seen as only one example of the increasing practical importance of science in improving living conditions. Morison and Málek celebrated the rise of a community of scientists—capable of solving problems "according to their own criteria," said the former, and numerous enough, by comparison with past communities of scientists, to effect a real qualitative change for mankind, said the latter. Such men are all linked by the responsibilities they have not only toward science but toward society. Thus we came to the notion of the progress of "operational rationality" in the modern world.

History and "operational rationality." The injection into history of scientific rationality—experimental, questioning, anti-authoritarian, as Pant put it—the prevalence of a "rational model" based on faith in progress, formed the core of Professor Jaguaribe's argument, which would have warmed the hearts of the Enlightenment *Philosophes* as well as of Auguste Comte. According to Jaguaribe, the antinomies that have blocked world order were, first, the clash between the requirements of rationality and those of power politics or of the power motivations of politicians and, secondly, the contrast between men's rationality in the area of means and the nonrational character of the selection of ends. Those antinomies could now be overcome at last: our achievements in the realm of operational rationality have effected a decisive change in the process of appropriation of wealth, influence, and power. Appropriation through spoliation has ceased to pay (an idea expressed by Aron some years ago); history stops therefore being a zero-sum game. It becomes a game over nature—for organization, not over man—for domination. Rationality is cumulative: the higher the level of the rationality of means, the more the selection of ends itself will tend to become rational.

This seductive presentation and prognosis ran into some objections. Aron, Gadamer, and Hoffmann questioned the assumption of a necessary "spillover" of rationality from the realm of means to the realm of ends. They pointed out that the process of appropriation was far from smooth and could still imply revolutions and expropriations. Hoffmann said that the final use of supposedly rational means still depended on the ends selected by the men in power—that the translation of rationally discovered "truths" into political and social forms could still lead to conflicting polities; or, as Aron put it, where the application of scientific reason brings no demonstrably certain results, relativism persists. Nicol observed that the scientists still get their funds from national sources. Kissinger remarked that the key issue of today was not appropriation but administration: the progress of bureaucracy leads to the alienation of the masses. Thus, while nobody challenged the notion of a rising level of rationality of means, which contributes to world order as defined by Aron for the seminar, there was no general acceptance of Jaguaribe's philosophy of history.

Material advancement as common goal. Jaguaribe had presented material advancement as the driving force of modern history. Professor Waddington proposed to reach much the same result—a world united by material progress—in a different way: by suggesting it not as a historically determined end, but as a deliberately chosen goal. All other "world-ordering systems," based on spiritual elements (ideology, culture, religion), had been divisive and failed to provide for the kind of order he was looking for, and which he calls "homeorhesis": an order which is not static, which does not prevent disturbances but allows for the return to stability after disturbances (a dynamic notion taken from biology but obviously essential to a social scientist). Therefore, what the world needs is an ordering system based on a sufficiently inclusive value, which can only be material development; since disparities in wealth are the ultimate cause of disorder (if not the immediate cause), the adoption of such a value would take the heat out of other sources of disturbances. Once again, as Aron pointed out, the recognition of the new mutual advantage in common development was being used as a thread and a springboard: the experience of dialogue between East and West over rates of growth had indeed led to "mutual instruction," in Aron's words, if perhaps not quite to the convergence discerned by Tinbergen.

Two lines of argument arose out of Waddington's reflections. One, developed in particular by Kissinger, challenged the assumption that most tensions are ultimately due to disparities in wealth and the assumption that material advancement would thus reduce tension: many conflicts arise because leaders have goals that have nothing to do with development, and development may well lead to instability domestically and internationally (one nation's progress being interpreted by another as a threat). Fourastié produced a similar argument; he quoted Ben Bella's statement about "Algerians willing to eat grass," listed the many drives that move men, besides the drive for material progress, and stressed the importance of random phenomena in history. The other line of argument focused on the ambiguity of the "single value" prescribed by Waddington, and therefore on its unifying force. Mankind, said Hoffmann, had never been able to settle for a single goal: the notion of material advancement was either insufficient to create a strong enough bond, or too full of potential conflicts if it includes (as Waddington had hinted) a reference to the "good life"; moreover, (supposing a single goal could prevail) the enforcement of material development would still be quite susceptible of leading to fragmentation, given the diversity of techniques and institutions that would promote this goal. Two kinds of replies were presented to this objection. One was made by Waddington and Dyckman: world order assuredly requires many bonds, not only material advancement; but the latter goal would be a powerful link, and an agreement on means among systems disagreeing on ends could be most useful. In other words, as Aron put it, even if ends keep diverging, material advancement could now become accepted by all as the necessary means. The other reply went further: it presented material progress not just as a common set of means, or as one end among others, but as an end that inevitably drags other common ends along with it. Pant mentioned the case of the Indian economy: the solution of material problems cannot be separated from that of problems like corruption, education, peace. Tinbergen spoke of the "ethics of planning." Waddington himself stated his belief that material advancement, taken as a serious value, implies a concern for human dignity. The discussion that followed, about the relation between human dignity and material advancement, established both that there was, at present, a link in the mind of many and that the link was anything but clear (nations, as Aron and others pointed out, have often preferred independence to immediate material progress). To Mr. Adul's rather sharp questioning of the meaning of human dignity, Aron replied that it could be defined only negatively—it is the rejection of certain, no longer tolerable, relations among men. But the variability of the notion shows that, as the chairman put it, man is "a dissatisfied being whose dissatisfactions are necessary for history to go on."

As one can see, the discussion failed to produce the kind of "community" that Waddington had hoped to collect around his central value. But if there was dissent about the degree of world order which this value could create, there was none about the positive contribution material advancement as a common goal had already made and could make. Moreover, the discussion on material advancement and the dispute on the scope of its contribution to world unity served as the passageway to the seminar's examination of the relevance of values to world order, and to the assessment of the ways in which different sorts of intellectuals can promote world order.

IV. *Thought and Action*

The "third theme" of the seminar is more a third dimension

than a unified theme. Its coherence comes from what Aron, in *Paix et Guerre*, has called praxiology—the questioning of the original hypotheses and the discussion of one's ability to overcome the basic antinomies of the subject-matter. One could have had a debate on the values required for world order without a debate on the contributions of social or natural scientists in particular and intellectuals in general—and vice versa. And yet, the two discussions were very closely linked.

Values and world order. Aron, as we have seen, had warned that any attempt at defining world order as "the good life" would lead to platitudes or to recriminations. However, the problems of whether a world order was possible without a common system of values and whether such a system was possible in the near future never ceased coming up, in the interstices and at the outcome of debates on other subjects.

The assertion of the need for a common system of values was made most strongly by Professor O'Connell. For him, the incoherence of the modern world, the intransigence of the sovereign states, the collapse of international law (deprived of its normative elements by political scientists and fragmented by constitutional lawyers) proceed from the decline of the rational "metaphysic of human order" that had existed in the Middle Ages, and survived until recently. It was obvious from his remarks (and he made it quite explicit in the course of the discussion) that he did not think science could provide a substitute: the scientific method of hypothesis and verification aims at *knowing* the behavior of *things*. What he was concerned with was the *control* of *human* behavior by a "regime of oughtness": what world order requires (as Professor Gadamer confirmed, with a reference to the Greek *dikaion* that served as the basis of Roman Law) is a set of moral norms, not merely a net of empirical norms.

O'Connell's approach was diametrically opposed to that of some other members of the seminar, who both believed in a return to (or progress toward) the unity of values and thought that science was providing those values. Waddington introduced the concept of "arising ends," purposes that come out of the nature of a system. Morison was more explicit, and claimed a great deal: for him, science is capable of defining and solving problems of general importance, possesses techniques for producing agreement, and plays an ethical role, for instance by suggesting (thus, often, helping us rule out) the likely results of certain courses of action (such as nuclear war). Restraints on states could therefore be expected not from the obsolete precepts of natural law, but from the order of nature. Indeed, science has progressed only through and since the demise of the old metaphysic. Both Morison and Jaguaribe celebrated the advent of a new humanism, shaped by the universal progress of science or, as Jaguaribe put it—again in Comtian terms —by the passage from a world based on the notion of salvation to a world based on the idea of culture, from the transcendence of God to the transcendence of man.

The optimistic drive of "scientisme" did not conquer all the other participants (not to mention O'Connell). It was not only that, as Kissinger implied, there was a metaphysic hidden behind that drive. It was also because the contribution of the scientific method to the unification of values was not above debate. First, as Aron indefatigably observed, no clear system of ethics can be derived from nature: universal progress is a purpose given by man, not by nature; in other words, the so-called arising ends are a matter of human choice, not of scientific dictation; they do not guarantee our future; or, as Kissinger put it, we can do (technically) whatever we want, but do not always know what we want. Secondly, cultural systems, and in particular religions, have shown great resilience and, far from being "folkloric residues," continue to influence behavior. It was Professor Mus's role in the seminar to trace the complex, continuing impact of Buddhism on the modes of thought and action of Asian states and to remind his listeners of the divergent conceptions of world order represented by different Asian religions. Between China's brand of universalism, which led to a relatively centralized empire, and India's universal order, which covered South-East Asia with self-centered kingdoms, on the one hand, and the respective behavior of China and India today, on the other, the lines of continuity could be seen, barely hidden behind Professor Mus' allusive erudition, and put into strong light by Mr. Adul.

The rejection of the scientific (or scientistic) pretense of a gradual unification of values through science would have led to the relativism lamented by Professor O'Connell, if everybody had agreed that there can be no world order without a harmony of values. This was, however, not the position taken by Aron. For him, the cultural and religious diversity of the world is the inevitable corollary of the fact that mankind lives in the first truly global international system. Moreover, the old metaphysical conception of a true, rational order that preexists man and history and which men-in-history ought to approximate and reproduce is dead: today, reason is indeed defined by science and has, therefore, a very different meaning from the one it had in the old conception. Nevertheless, the demise of the traditional sense of order and the heterogeneity of the single system do not condemn the world to disorder, or man to hopeless relativism: it is possible to find a minimum of order common to diverse social systems because of the beginning of certain universal trends—for instance, the diversity of economic systems leaves room for comparisons and conclusions reached as a result of the notion of a generalized economy. Thus the admittedly precarious shoots of a new world order are growing neither out of a metaphysic nor out of scientific requirements alone, but out of a historical experience which suggests lines of evolution. Indeed, our present notion of order is evolutionary: we no longer believe in a fixed order, but view order as creation, the product of man in history. The old conception was adequate for stagnant societies. Our societies are changing and acutely aware of change, and they breed the notion of an order to be achieved. The diversity of conceptions, that is, of value preferences, concerning the ultimate directions and purposes accounts for the fragility of our order; the existence of common directions accounts for its possibility. As Mr. Graubard put it, we ask today not whether what we do and think coincides with what was laid down in the past, but what will be the consequences of our thoughts and acts.

It would have been interesting to pursue those lines of analysis and, following Aron's lead, to investigate the nature and origins of the universal trends he discerned. Some are undoubtedly due to the rise of "operational rationality," to the "necessary means": material advancement, as well as to the nuclear situation; for instance, the trends which the proliferating new international law of world technology exemplifies are due not to common "arising purposes," but to the rising needs of reciprocity and predictability in an ever more interdependent world. But the discussion did not go any further.

Sciences, social sciences, and action. It went quite far, however, on another subject: the contribution the various disciplines can make to the promotion of world order. Those who saw such an order arising out of "operational rationality" were particularly anxious—sometimes almost like crusaders—to introduce more of it into the world, and in a more systematic and foresighted fashion; a generalization of planning, so to speak, was their wish and their request. On the other side were those who had some doubts both about the extent to which the rising rationality of means suffices to assure world order and about man's capacity to control and plan his future.

The outlines of the argument appeared, of course, in the first session. Waddington had suggested that world order ought to be like the order of a body or that of a population, not that of a crystal; the order of a population is based on differences among parts, it includes just a few relations among individual elements, and it allows for chance processes. Hoffmann and Aron pointed out, first, that this gives one no idea of what the substance of the order would be—precisely the bone of contention with regard to world order—and, second, that world order has to take into account not mere differences but conflicts. The reciprocal relations of the parts of a body, said Aron, rule out something that is perfectly conceivable in world order, that is, the extermination of one part of the system by another. This early discussion about the notion of order suggested already the subsequent main lines of opposition about the chances and types of scientific control.

On one side were the natural scientists and most of the economists. Proud of the degree to which they have been able to control their subject-matter (in the sense both of accumulating knowledge and of applying it to the solution of problems), they kept summoning the other social scientists who were not economists to reach the same state of development and in particular to engage in what came to be called "political planning." Mr. Fourastié was the most constant advocate of projections of a "future without war," capable of polarizing minds in the same way that Mr. Monnet has captured the Frenchmen's imaginations by projecting an economic future of progress for postwar France. To be sure, he recognized that political planning would have to be more "ideal" (or, as Mr. Gadamer put it, more abstract) than economic planning. But he thought that the confrontation of various representations of the future and the deliberate choice of some possibilities would be useful, if only a greater number of intellectuals and civil servants devoted themselves to long-range thinking and if techniques such as simulation were applied. Already, planning for large-scale enterprises (which requires the consideration of their relations with other such enterprises and with the state) approximates political planning. Fourastié was supported by Tinbergen, who regretted that political scientists should go on thinking about shorter intervals of time than economists, and by Pant, who gave constitution-making as an example of domestic political planning and asked for international political planning against war and poverty.

The political scientists, on the other side, picked up the challenge by trying to show why the notion of political planning was unsatisfactory, especially in world affairs. Hoffmann and Kissinger stressed that planning is hardly possible when the ends are in doubt or in contest, when intentions regularly fail to lead to expected results, when gaming techniques only confirm the hypotheses or implicit theories that originally inspired the players. The element of uncertainty, said Kissinger, is far greater in the political than in the economic realm: in foreign policy, judgments depend on assessments that cannot be proven at the time when the judgments must be made, and the scope of decision is greatest when certainty is smallest. A truly effective constitution, said Hoffmann, presupposes a modicum of consensus and is capable of transforming political forces; but this is not always the case domestically, and it is even less so in the world, where consensus is sharply limited and where the Charters of world agencies must take the existence of nation-states as a rather fixed necessity. Aron developed almost a general theory of the differences between economic and political planning. The latter is hampered by our limited knowledge of the rules and trends of the political system: economic planning is based on the notion of growth, but the concept of political development is purely metaphorical since we do not know the direction of political systems and must realize that there are different possible directions. Political planning is hampered by the impossibility of quantifying the values implied in a political system. It is hampered, finally, by the conflictual nature of political systems: planning politics would mean planning the loss of power of some groups to the benefit of others and would thus reduce or eliminate the neutrality of the planners. All these obstacles explain why the political scientists' "time horizon" is lower than the economists': deprived of the assumption of growth, the former cannot fail to have a much shorter "optimal distance."

This discussion on various kinds of planning reflected a disagreement about the general possibilities and advantages of scientific control. Natural scientists and economists were looking forward to a planned and controlled future, in which the methods of their disciplines would have been adopted universally. The objecting political scientists tried to show, on the one hand, that the problems involved in manipulating reality were completely different in the world of science (and economics, where planners work toward goals set or accepted by the men in power) and in the world of politics (where control and planning would require both the manipulation of the leaders and the knowledge by the leaders of the laws of successful manipulation of social reality): we do not know enough to control much, and we are not in a position to control what we know. They also stressed, on the other hand, that manipulation in social affairs can lead to repulsive results (such as brainwashing); moreover, such results have been achieved also when science itself was manipulated by leaders with evil purposes. The social scientist thus has excellent reasons for modesty. But this does not mean that he is a pure analyst or critic without practical influence. Social science may not be directly operational, in the sense of controlling events, but it is indirectly operational, as Aron and Fourastié asserted, by influencing minds (cf. the importance of contemporary strategic doctrine); as Fourastié put it, given the historical efficiency of arbitrary wills undetermined by reality, it is of crucial importance to affect those wills. It was again Aron who presented a typology of the ways in which ideas can influence action: either through knowledge—here social and political science are far behind economics and the natural sciences—or through the creation of conceptual frameworks that affect our way of acting—here political science holds its own—or through representations of the future—in which social science (rarely value-free even in its first two modes of influence) combines with ideological, cultural, or religious values.

The role of the intellectuals. Aron's last category suggested that the creation of utopias—the representations of an ideal future—remains the function of intellectuals, even if they have only limited means of guaranteeing their utopias' advent. Inevitably, a seminar engaged in a quest for order and composed of intellectuals was going to raise the question of their role in the establishment of order.

The most ambitious statement was made by Jaguaribe. It is to intellectuals that he entrusted the sacred task of promoting the triumph of operational rationality and of the "humanistic *paideia*" which inspires science and which science demonstrates. The word sacred is put here without irony, for Jaguaribe described intellectuals as a new priesthood, whose faith is in the achievement of rational knowledge by objective methods, and whose action would indeed lead to a rising rationality of ends since they are by essence the critics of Caesar and the censors of power. Morison approved and reasserted the need for the intellectuals to be as independent from the world of power as the priests had been in the sixth and seventh centuries; he stated that the world of thought could thereby hope to set some limits on the world of power. Whereas Comte, who carried the idea of the new priesthood to its logical consequences, had wanted the intellectuals to have a set of dogmas, Jaguaribe and Morison rebelled against any dogmatism for their technical humanism, except the dogmatism of scientific method and of the search for truth.

The seminar did not receive the notion of the new priesthood too well. Kissinger pointed out that, in any priesthood, the requirements of insight fight against those of organization, and that inspiration is always thwarted by its institutionalization. As Waddington put it more brutally, a priesthood would consecrate the mediocrities and penalize the creators. Even apart from that somewhat artificial notion, there were serious objections to the Jaguaribe-Morison view of the role of the intellectual. First, many participants challenged the idea, implicit in this view, of a kind of natural unity of the servants and practitioners of scientific rationality. As Aron reminded his listeners, intellectuals in the past have often been the carriers of discord, and in the long run conscience is the dissatisfied part of mankind. The present emergence of a community of scientists is not an innovation; it is merely a return to a past tradition which the cold war had interrupted. Hoffmann said that the nationalization of the intellectuals by the states was as possible as the internationalization of the world by the intellectuals; the fierce debates among atomic scientists were a chilly denial of Jaguaribe's optimism. Professor Maruyama quoted Pasteur: science has no boundary, but scientists do: they are rarely capable of transcending the reality in which they live; they are often committed or bound to the value system of their society. Second, even if the intellectuals showed more solidarity than they have exhibited so far, their capacity to tame the world of power was assessed with skepticism by many of the conferees. Aron remembered how often intellectuals had been the justifiers of power. Kissinger listed the permanent contradictions between policy-making and intellectual performance—the intellectual asks about the truth of a proposition, works at the pace of the mind, tends to criticize the attainable because it is not the ideal, while the policy-maker is concerned with the consequences of action, has problems thrust on him, and must approach them by stages. Today's wave of Caesarism-cum-technocracy reduces the capacity of any group to operate as an effective conscience. Aron pointed out that the community of scientists can perfectly well coexist with violent conflicts in the world.

Thus the hopes of some that the concept of the good life could emerge from science, be propagated by the intellectuals, and become operational because of science's control of reality were far from shared by all the participants.

V. *Thoughts on Thoughts on World Order*

It is now time for me to do to the seminar what the seminar ultimately did to world order—question the basic postulates and pass some kind of judgment.

Any exercise like this conference is necessarily unfinished. One goes into it not knowing what will come out of it, and one leaves it with a set of general impressions and of reactions to individual statements or performances, not with a clear-cut sense of accomplishment. However, two general remarks should be made.

The first one may appear somewhat discouraging. The conference revealed a double kind of fragmentation that contrasted rather sardonically with its theme—how to coexist in one world. The most frequently noticed was the fragmentation of knowledge. As this report has tried to show, the gaps between disciplines were revealed rather starkly, not only by analyses that threw light on the differences between their methods and their effects, but also by the difficulty for the specialists of one discipline to enter into the universe of discourse of another. As Graubard put it, the world trend may be toward a decline of parochialism, but the professional parochialisms are intense indeed. The only mind that seemed able to transcend them all, to understand both the essence and the limits of each, and to see how they can be concerted was that of the Chairman, whose prolonged exercise in creative catalysis was indispensable to the success of a meeting which would, without him, have sagged into the proverbial soufflé that fails to rise. He managed to reduce the damage to a shaky start and a saggy close, but everything in between was so to speak carried and lifted by his brilliant, yet diplomatic, definitions, interpretations, and *relances*.

Another kind of split was equally evident, if less discussed: the split between what might be called the builders and the critics, between minds primarily devoted to the creation of a system or the advocacy of a method or the proselytizing of an idea, and minds primarily concerned with the analysis of reality, with the dissection (or vivisection) of systems, utopias, and theories. The battle lines here did not separate disciplines so much as personalities. True, the natural scientists were all, or so it seemed, on the "constructive" side, and so were most of the economists—but not all, and not unqualifiedly. The political scientists were mostly on the other side, but again with a significant exception (Jaguaribe). It should be added that this kind of a division has nothing to do with the division between optimists and pessimists, on which the conferees tended at times to hypnotize themselves. A critical mind is not necessarily a pessimist—if he is a good analytical intellectual he will rather be neither a permanent optimist nor a permanent pessimist—whereas a "constructor" may well be deeply pessimistic about what would happen if his theory or utopia were not realized (cf. Lord Gladwyn).

The second remark has to do with the balance of achievements and failures of the meeting. We agreed on the importance of the nuclear stalemate and on the continuing dynamics of development as the bases of world order. We disagreed about the degree to which international relations would be transformed by those forces, as well as on the extent to which the new forms of interdependence would create not only the "minimum conditions of co-existence" but also a genuine community of values and of power—one world in the sense of philosophical agreement on "the good life" and political harmony. This, in my eyes, suggests that the conference reflected quite well the present state of affairs in the world despite occasional flings into utopianism. It suggests that the seminar demonstrated, on its own scale, the truth of Marx's proposition—that mankind raises only those problems it can solve. For what was omitted entirely, or barely mentioned, or left undeveloped was precisely those issues that nobody knows how to tackle yet. We do not know yet how the development and the power rise of Red China will affect the relations between the superpowers and the future of the nuclear stalemate. We do not know yet, for the single international system in which we live is still too recent, what kinds of domestic problems and upheavals will have a direct impact on world order: hence our neglect of an impressive list of issues raised at the last session by Dyckman, such as migrations, communications, access to information and to scarce resources, what Graubard called the problems of mass (including those of the city). We do not know how to control the population explosion, which remained as absent from our discussions as Red China. Finally, despite the hopes and prophecies described before, we do not really agree on philosophical and political values; therefore, the conference, moved by the same desire for survival and development as the world at large, carefully avoided exposing the ideological differences that remain, and refrained from defining the "good life" in a single world. We used the word democracy rather than the word freedom, and we all politely mentioned Hitler whenever we wanted to blast villainy or to blame irrationality. In a world in which the regime of Spain could still prevent a Spanish professor from coming to our meeting, our wisdom may have been cowardice. But whether our *pudeur* was tantamount to abdication is not so certain: for one could argue that the very possibility of discussing world order meaningfully, that is, without platitudes even while leaving out ideological antagonisms, is in itself evidence of a "demise of the ideological age." To hear a Czech Marxist speak for a "functional analysis of the state and of world order" came as a welcome surprise, and could have been used as partial evidence by those who saw in nuclear and material solidarity resilient and dynamic forces toward order. Whether the failure to discuss the "good life" should be applauded also is far less sure, but it too reflected deep (though disturbing) trends in the world. For if scientists believe that the world of nature and technology sets its own "arising ends," it may well be because the truly normative functions of man suffer an eclipse—as a result of the collapse of old metaphysics or because of a lazy or tired resignation to the kind of life that the necessities of modern economics and techniques, the methods of science, and the delicate dictates of nuclear survival seem to shape—so that the quality of life is more determined than planned, more foisted upon man than willed by him, perhaps even without distinction of culture, religion, or ideology. Thus, it is difficult to forecast moral unification around a new humanism not only when philosophical and political splits persist, but also when one feels impotent to impose one's vision or one's dreams on a world whose necessities are felt too compelling, or when one feels complacently confident that those necessities bring with them the best of all possible worlds. The seminar's avoidance of the somewhat overwhelming subject of education in a "monde fini," despite Málek's and Gadamer's references to its importance, is both understandable and symbolic.

I have mentioned Marx's dictum. I must also mention Kant's

prophecy. His tantalizing essay on universal history had predicted that the world of nations would unite as a result of the negative process of increasingly costly wars and the positive process of increasing material interdependence. The Seminar showed that Kant's account remains the most likely theory of world order. The increasing disutility of war and the rising tide of development are both the products of science. The former, which takes the strategic form of mutual deterrence, that is, a system of mutual denials and frustrations, merely prevents disasters; the latter exploits the possibilities thus created, in order to bring to mankind the satisfactions which science and its applications provide. Whether the continuing divisions of mankind, in the form of rival nation-states as well as of domestic powderkegs, will ultimately destroy the negative process (without which the positive one could not function), as only a few of us seemed to dread; whether these divisions will, even without destroying our fragile peace, delay, dilute, or distort the positive process of development, as some of us continued to fear; whether on the contrary both processes would interact so as to overcome the divisions of mankind and replace its present forms of organization with more "rational" ones, as many of us hoped, was obviously not something which the Seminar could decide. Kant's philosophy of order—like the philosophy that underlies, despite their denials, the projections and certainties of our "*scientistes*"—presented as necessary something which is only possible. We did not agree that it was indeed necessary. But we agreed that the possibility appeared likelier than ever and that, if a "homeorhetic" world order emerges, it will be along those lines. It would have been premature and presumptuous to say more: as the one professional philosopher among us—Gadamer—remarked, we should not require of the future so much more (or better) than we have received in the past. Or should we?

RAYMOND ARON

The Anarchical Order of Power

MEN CONTINUE to belong to political units pretending to independence. Hence, there is no "planetary society" or "human society" comparable to Pueblo or French society, or to the society of the United States or the Soviet Union.

The examples just given intentionally illustrate the diversity of the "political units" or "societies" of which the state claims to be the sovereign expression. A historian of the school of Spengler or Toynbee would contrast "national societies," naively proud of their originality, with the "intelligible field" that makes up a whole "civilization," such as ancient civilization or Western Christian civilization.* An ethnologist would reply that the truly intelligible field lies below and not above politically organized society. A state such as the Soviet Union encompasses many ethnic groups or cultural communities whose past, customs, and even creeds remain different in many respects.

We shall, nonetheless, take the multiplicity of legally sovereign states (according to the Charter of the United Nations) as the characteristic trait of the "a-social society" or the "an-archical order" of mankind. The former expression goes back to Kant; the latter borrows the notion of anarchy from the banal critique of the system of rival sovereignties. Both seek to emphasize the *essential imperfection* of "human society," to assume the existence of a "society" of all mankind, in the sense that the city-states and empires of the ancient world and the nation-states of Europe constituted one.

This essential imperfection is not corrected by the growth of commercial transactions between countries and continents alone. It is in vain that telecommunication satellites transmit words and

* Toynbee prefers to use the term society in designating these "intelligible fields."

images instantaneously; it is in vain that scholars and intellectuals meet in conventions. However useful relations transcending national borders among private individuals may be—whether in the domain of sports, science, tourism, religion, or business—and whatever influence these individual relations may exert over a long term on the "reserved domain" of relations between states, those relations still remain today what they have been throughout history: they have not entirely left the stage of the law of the jungle. A sovereign collectivity is one which makes its own laws, and whose leaders acknowledge obedience to no one else in certain matters—those affecting so-called vital interests—and in certain circumstances— those involving the choice between war and peace. The state is not solely, but it is at the very least and in any case, that institution which possesses the monopoly of legitimate violence. Now this monopoly must be effective and not merely legal. What army would be capable of fulfilling for the whole of mankind the function entrusted to the police force in nation-states? All civilizations (or societies, in Toynbee's use of the word) have known a violent history motivated mainly by the relations between states. Modern civilization, while planetary in its technico-economic dynamism, has not eliminated, or even touched morally, interstate relations, which continue, despite our individual condemnations of their cruelty and our desire to shake off their yoke, ruthlessly in their unreasonable rationality to forge our common destiny.

"A-social society," "an-archical order," "unreasonable rationality" —these apparently contradictory expressions are not dictated by a love of paradox or literary affectation. The society of states is by essence a-social, since it does not outlaw the recourse to force among the "collective persons" that are its members. Order, if there be one, in this society of states is an-archical in that it rejects the authority of law, of morality, or of collective force. In an anarchical society, why would any individual give up to someone other than himself the concern for his security? On the other hand, when one thermonuclear bomb alone has more power of destruction than all the bombs or shells used during World War II, is it not unreasonable to risk a war whose sole possible benefits would be derisory when compared to the certain costs?

It is easy to elicit enthusiasm by contrasting the spirit of science with the parochial unenlightened spirit. Jets fly at over 500 miles per hour; tomorrow supersonic planes will fly at Mach 2 or 3; ballistic missiles cover nearly 10,000 miles in an hour; and customs officials continue to guard borders; armies, incapable of protecting populations, consume resources that would be better used in the struggle against hunger or underdevelopment. How long will the contradiction between the universal diffusion of technology and the survival of traditional diplomacy persist?

The whole planet is alone scaled to the technology of the twentieth century: the conquest of outer space testifies to this even more than thermonuclear bombs. It does not necessarily follow that the continuation of traditional diplomacy is merely a "survival"—or at least before pronouncing facile condemnations, we must attempt to understand the anarchical order of the international system, as it has been for millennia and remains today (though not without substantial modifications due to changes in thought and events).

Man is a *naturally* social animal (the word nature here being understood in the meaning given to it by biologists). Human young depend on their mothers for a long period; the family by itself is weak and threatened. The species can only evolve toward the full realization of its potentials in and through societies, capable of preserving what preceding generations have acquired, and thus of promoting the further accumulation of knowledge and power. The so-called archaic societies that came into being before the neolithic revolution were narrow. Each placed itself spontaneously at the center of a universe that it interpreted both arbitrarily and intelligibly at once: defined or constituted by a system of values, a way of life, indeed a world-view, each tended to regard the others as foreign and, therefore, strange, though this strangeness did not necessarily provoke hostility. To this extent, Bergson is wrong in affirming that collectivities are like wolves to one another (*homo homini lupus*), while members of the collectivities are like gods to one another (*homo homini deus*). The most closed societies were not devoid of internal conflicts, and were not perforce dedicated to a struggle unto death with near-by or far-off societies. So long as the strictly political organization—borders, laws, central power—is imperfect, the limits of the societies themselves do not appear clearly, and one hesitates often over the meaning of the words used to designate its groupings (family, clan, village, tribe, and so forth). But these uncertainties of vocabulary, reflecting ambiguities inscribed in reality itself, do not eliminate the major fact: mankind began by division and not by unity; every human society grew conscious of its originality in developing a culture—it established

27

RAYMOND ARON

itself by distinction from the others, proud, and not anxious, to discover itself different from others.

The interstate relations that one observes throughout the several thousands of years of major history—that of so-called higher civilization—are a work of culture, and, as such, they may be called artificial if one equates the nature of man or of societies with their initial state. Even biologists would resist such an equation: man is an animal species which, being organized in stable groups, has a history. This history does not mark the end of the biological evolution of the species, but it is not any less evident than that evolution. The history of civilizations and the evolution of the species react upon one another, whatever be the interpretation that one proposes for this duality in terms of metaphysics or religious beliefs.

The conflicts between states, more or less regulated by tradition, custom, or laws, form an integral part of civilizations; they belong not to the biological order, but to the human order. This proposition is not in contradiction with the formula, common among the classic philosophers, according to which the relations between states are still in the *state of nature*. The latter stood in contrast to the *civil society (l'état civil)*, and both sprang from culture, not from animal nature. The concept of nature, in this sense, is ambiguous because it contrasts at times with convention, at other times with civil society, and most times with both together. In contrast to conventions, the state of nature is characteristic of man *quā* man, leaving aside the infinite and arbitrary diversity of mores. Hence, natural laws are universal laws—those applying to all men, irrespective of the norms to which an individual is subject by virtue of his membership in a particular society. In contrast to civil society, the state of nature excludes a supreme authority, a tribunal entitled to render verdicts, a police authorized to enforce them: therefore each man is responsible for his own security, free in his decisions, including the decision to take up arms.

The concept of the state of nature represented an interpretation of the behavior appropriate to historical man, a pessimistic or optimistic metaphysics. Some philosophers described the state of nature as the war of all against all; others, on the contrary, depict man as peaceful and kindly outside of society. Some proclaim that the state of nature knows no other law than that of might; others, claiming that man by himself tends toward the fulfillment of his reasonable nature, placed natural laws above the positive laws of civil society. But all maintained the discrimination between the state of nature where each man, separate or sovereign, can count only on himself, and civil society where law reigns, where justice is rendered by tribunals, where the police suppress violence.

This distinction does not at all suggest that the present style of interstate relations represents the survival of a primordial situation of individuals or societies—the war of all against all: archaic societies were not all bellicose, and the struggles in which they engaged were often ritualized to the point of being closer to our competitive games than to the death struggles of the industrial age. Nor does this distinction imply that interstate hostilities derive, through the mysteries of the collective unconsciousness, from the enmity that primitive man attributed spontaneously to the foreigner: it is simply the product of historic experience, confirmed by the study of all civilizations. City-states and empires alike were established through violence; the maintenance of peace was the first task of those in power within politically organized units, but peace among these units was never imposed by the same method. All international systems have been an-archical, in the strict sense of the term: they have not been subjected to an *archē*. Once an *archē* is recognized, the political units are deprived of their constitutive principle—auto-nomy, in-dependence, the ability of taking by themselves the decisions engaging their destiny.

This distinction in essence does not exclude a similarity in the realm of practice. Within states, too, individuals and groups rival one another, and there is a permanent risk of recourse to violence. And it is true that there is not a single state which has not been established by violence, from narrower collectivities of differing cultures. The homogeneity of a people has always been the work of centuries, meaning most often, the work of force. Only the United States of America has a slightly different history. Leaving aside the wars against the Indians, then against Mexico and Spain, American nationality was forged by a constitutional law established for nearly two centuries. Millions of immigrants freely decided to join this *Commonwealth*, that is, this community.

In short, the philosophical distinction between the state of nature and civil society expresses a permanent fact of history: men live in society, but there have always been many societies and not one society. Every historic society has been particular and in more or less regular relation with other societies. Within each of them, the rival ambitions of individuals or groups, ethnic heterogeneity, and opposition of interests created a permanent risk of illegitimate violence. Between societies, recourse to armed force was legitimate since, in the absence of civil authority, each could count only on itself to ward off all perils and to survive.

It is scarcely necessary, in order to explain the endemic character of wars, to endow man with greater aggressiveness than that of other primates: the conditions, constant throughout history, of the political organization of mankind suffice to explain the precariousness of peace and the frequency of wars. Peace could be safeguarded only, and always temporarily, by the balance of rival powers or the victory of the strongest and the establishment of an empire.

The specificity of interstate relations (legitimacy of recourse to force), as confirmed by historical experience, imposes no conclusion regarding the future of human society; it merely prohibits an illusory extrapolation. The passing from many sovereignties to one sovereignty is neither logically nor materially impossible, but it would be *essentially* different from the passing from city-state to empire. Empires eliminated or integrated sovereign states; they did not eliminate all external sovereignty. United under one sovereignty, mankind would no longer have any enemy—unless it be on another planet. This would be a mutation of history itself and not a mutation within history.

A world state is not in contradiction with the biological or social nature of man, as it has been revealed across the centuries. If Rome was able to spread out to the British Isles and to Byzantium at a time when legions traveled by foot, modern techniques for movement on land, on sea, and in air make a planetary empire materially possible. What excludes such an empire today and for the foreseeable future of the next decades are the historic actors. By historic actors I mean the politically organized collectivities, the minorities governing them, and perhaps the peoples themselves. Heads of state hold fast to sovereignty—that is, to their freedom of action internally and externally, of which the term sovereignty represents the juridical or ideological expression. Peoples respond to the call for "national independence," some because they have barely left behind the colonial regime, and others because the official ideology depicts classes and states engaged in a death struggle.

If we use the word *nationalism* here to indicate the will of politically organized collectivities, established on a territory and subject to a state, to maintain vis-à-vis other similar collectivities a liberty theoretically total and at least equal to that of others, then we shall say that the planetary expansion of technology and the modern economy does not result in a universal state. Peoples or states act on the stage of history like individuals who *refuse* to submit to a master and *do not know how* to submit to a common law.

The obstacle to the setting up of a universal state is the same as the obstacle involved in maintaining it. In order to establish a universal state, in the absence of consent, it would be necessary to break the resistance of states, as the resistance of the feudal barons was broken by the armed force of the kings, as that of the Greek city-states or of Macedonia was broken by Roman legions. But the monarchic precedent has no value as an example so long as a universal sovereignty must encompass heterogeneous peoples; the Roman precedent might serve as a model, but it inspires terror. At what price and with what consequences would unity be arrived at through the defeat of all the pretenders to empire save one?

But let us suppose that the universal state has been established: it could survive only by the effective monopoly of legitimate violence. It would have to possess enough weapons to prevent provincial groups from resorting to force or, at least, to prevent the extension of conflicts, if these groups conserved an army. But could the army of the universal state succeed in *constraining* local armies by the threat of nuclear weapons alone (supposing that there were a monopoly of the universal state)? Or are we to imagine the ex-states reduced to the level of administrations, virtually disarmed? Under this hypothesis, one requires of these administrations (ex-states) a confidence in the loyalty of its people (ex-citizens) of which our period provides few examples. In both cases, one assumes that the main problem has been solved, namely, the consent of the peoples and the states to surrender to a universal state a portion of their autonomy that has been held essential over the centuries. But all indications are that they do not fear the nuclear apocalypse enough to abdicate.

Lord Russell gave mankind a deadline of a few decades, until the end of the century, to choose between a world-state and annihilation. At the end of the second decade of the atomic age, a third path appears.

History has more imagination than wise men do. It has thus far refused to choose between collective suicide and the abdication of states. It has gradually brought a certain order out of the anarchy common to all international systems, an order favoring the limitation of armed conflicts, subject to an oligarchy camouflaged by democratic phraseology.

This order results in the first place from a quasi-regulation of interstate violence—a regulation as novel as the historic conjuncture itself. There are three sorts of weapons available today, corresponding to three combat methods: let us say, symbolically, the submachine gun, the tank, and the atomic bomb—the first instrument being adapted to guerrilla warfare, the second to regular army fighting, the third to thermonuclear exchanges (or push-button warfare, to adopt the terminology of science fiction). In terms of power of destruction, there is nothing in common between the guerrilla fighter, the tank-driver, and the crew of the minuteman missile, any more than there is anything in common between a wrench used by a garage mechanic, a conveyer belt in an automobile factory, and the equipment of an atomic plant. But more recent techniques, while they may be most characteristic of the present age, do not eliminate former techniques, and this for two reasons. Automation (where it is possible and profitable) is so expensive that it can only be partial and take place gradually. Large sectors of the economy continue to remain refractory to automation, and the mechanic's wrench, in the form of the shovel and the pick, will continue to remain symbolic. Similarly, the thermonuclear bomb and the ballistic missile will eliminate neither the machine gun of the guerrilla fighter nor the coolie who transports on his back the rice and munitions of the combatants.

The individual weapon—light, effective in short-term operations, in ambushes, and in man-to-man fighting—was the response of the colonized peoples to the colonial domination of the European states. The white man had imposed his domination on the peoples of Asia and Africa thanks to the superiority of his technology and science, thanks also to his prestige. Once that prestige had been destroyed by wars or defeats, domination tended to have no foundation besides force. The Vietnamese, Indonesians, or Congolese could not defeat the regular armies of France, Holland, or Belgium, but they could foster insecurity. Provided that they benefit by the sympathy and complicity of the masses, a few thousand guerillas are able to eliminate all desire of the rich peoples to rule. In the twenty years since the explosions of Hiroshima and Nagasaki, the machine guns of guerrillas have changed the map of the world much more than tanks or atomic bombs. At Dien Bien Phu, these guerrillas had become soldiers organized in divisions, who dealt a final blow to an expeditionary force, worn out after seven years of struggle against elusive combatants.

Wars, all limited and local, between regular or quasi-regular armies, have all ended since 1945 in armistices that have not been followed by peace treaties. The demarcation lines consecrate the accidental results of combat operations at the time of the cease-fire: such is the case of the border between India and Pakistan in Kashmir, between Israel and the Arab states in the Near East, between North and South Korea after three years of fighting.

The contrast is striking between the victory of the rebels over the Dutch or the French in Indonesia or Viet-Nam, and the draws or armistices without peace treaties at the conclusion of hostilities between regular armies.

Need we add that the reason for this contrast is more political than military. The machine gun is not irresistible, and the tank is not ineffective. The guerrillas won nearly everywhere because the "imperialists," morally and materially weakened by World War II, no longer believed in their mission, and because Empire becomes too costly when it entails economic obligations toward conquered peoples. The Israeli tanks could have gone on to Cairo. If there had been enough of them, American tanks could have reached the Yalu. The Great Powers of the international system wanted, above all, to arrive at a compromise when they confronted one another directly or through satellites interposed prudently; most times they stopped military operations between second-power states; they prevented weapons from fulfilling their secular function of deciding otherwise insoluble questions. By their intervention, they have maintained situations that, in other times, one would have deemed absurd: the division of Jerusalem or of Kashmir. The limitation of hostilities seemed to be the prime objective of the Great Powers of the system, if not of the interested parties, during this period.

Is the guerrilla a vestige of the past who will disappear with the disappearance of underdevelopment itself? To be sure, when one observes the relations between Israel and the Arab states, the punitive expeditions undertaken by units of the regular Israeli army in response to operations by the *fedayis*, one is tempted to draw a sort of correlation between the level of development and the nature of weapons, between the type of society and the mode of combat. This correlation is indeed linked to particular circumstances, without being entirely accidental. As soon as guerrillas have won the war, driven out the colonialists, and founded a state, the state seeks

33

to create a regular army equipped with heavy weapons, tanks, fighter planes, and bombers. Each new state does so because other states that have preceded it in the career of independence have done so before it. Concern for prestige? Not exclusively. A regular army protects the state against other guerrillas that would be recruited among the veterans or among those who expected that the end of domination would usher in a new era, a sort of golden age. It is also of use in the border disputes that threaten to break out after the end of colonialism and hence of anticolonialist solidarity. Finally, it must not be forgotten that even in industrialized countries, during times of oppression, there have been snipers and guerrillas.

In truth, the guerrilla belongs to our age, as he belongs to most ages of human history; but he takes a novel form in the industrial age. He incarnates the anti-technical to the extent to which he defies the instruments of massive destruction developed by science, but he utilizes weapons and means of communication that have also been forged by industry, and he has likewise developed rationally his methods of action. If technology refers not only to the material objects made by machines, but also to a form of thought, a sort of rationality in action, guerrilla warfare, as taught by the Chinese after long experience, is henceforth conducted according to precise rules. These entail a technique of organization, a technique for the psychological manipulation of the masses, playing on terror and on hope. To be sure, the guerrilla is, more often than the soldier in uniform, left to his own devices; he must therefore be capable of initiative, and retain in solitude the sense of his own responsibility, as well as the consciousness of a solidarity with his dispersed and innumerable comrades. But, the more guerrilla warfare becomes organized, the more the guerrilla resembles the soldier. The discipline he is subject to will never have the same physical presence as in regular armies, but its distant and diffused character are compensated by its ruthless sanctions. Leaders are nowhere, but they are everywhere. There is, so to speak, no longer any question of *degree* either in the crime or in the punishment. The differences between guerrillas and soldiers remain; the tendency toward their rapprochement grows out of a like desire for effective techniques.

As an isolated volunteer, the guerrilla seems superior to the soldier in human qualities. Although heroic, he is not necessarily fighting the holy war: all depends on the cause for which he sacrifices his rest or his life. Since 1940, the guerrilla has symbolized the struggle against the Nazis, then against the "colonialists." He has benefited from the sympathy of progressivist opinion despite the cruelty, often inevitable, of his means. He has been the "resistance," David against Goliath, the Pekinese or Kabyle peasant, bare-handed against planes or tanks, the soldier in the shadows destined more for martyrdom than for glory. Should this same guerrilla serve a doubtful cause, or the population for the most part be against his cause, or should the victory bring to power a detested regime, he will become again, in the eyes of all defenders of the established order, whether Occidentals or Afro-Asians, what he has been in other times—the outlaw, closer to the bandit than to the soldier, the man who kills unexpectedly and often randomly, the man who introduces the reign of suspicion, who confuses the essential distinction between peace and war, between law and violence. When faced with mechanical monsters, he incarnates the grandeur of the resistant, rebel, or heretic. When faced with the norms of civilized existence, he incarnates the aggressivity—animal or human, primitive or permanent—that society must control in order to live.

The triad of the submachine gun, the tank, and the ballistic missile with a thermonuclear warhead, of the guerrilla, the soldier, and the crew of the ballistic missiles buried in silos, will have tomorrow, as today, a historic significance. The complex dialectic linking each of these three types of weapons to the two others will continue symbolically, at least until mankind substitutes the rule of law for the rule of violence. Each of these three weapons, each of the three methods of combat will preserve its meaning. Nuclear weapons prohibit the repetition of the total wars that prevailed during the first half of the twentieth century. Regular armies remain the guarantee of internal peace in all states that cannot do without the possible recourse to force. At the same time, they provide strategists with a means of avoiding the alternative of all-or-nothing, of passivity or the apocalypse. States aspiring to play leading roles on the world scene can no more do without nuclear weapons than without conventional weapons. The guerrilla rebellion, the supreme response, and often a desperate response, to injustice, poses an ironical challenge to the omnipotence of machines.

Does the dialectic of the three weapons constitute an international order? During the postwar period it has been the principle of what has come to be called variously the *cold war* or *bellicose peace, precarious order* or *endemic disorder*. Contemporaries have denounced this constant ambiguity; there is no outbreak of major war, but true peace is neither imposed by a victor nor arrived at together by rivals. In retrospect, the historian tends to place a more balanced judgment on the first two decades of the atomic age, and indeed even to hope secretly that this ambiguous conjuncture, this limitation of violence should continue.

For twenty years, from 1945 to 1965, there have been only two states worthy of the title of nuclear powers. Great Britain, while possessing nuclear weapons, has not conducted an independent diplomacy. France and Communist China have exploded atomic bombs, but do not yet possess the combination of bombs, missiles to carry them, and a network of alert and communication, without which the weapons alone cannot really be effective military or diplomatic arms. At the time of the Korean War, the United States had only a limited stock of nuclear weapons, including neither thermonuclear bombs nor tactical nuclear weapons. From 1953 on, as Stalin's successors perfected and completed their weapons, they spoke more and more willingly of peaceful coexistence. They were tempted, between 1958 and 1962, to obtain a modification of the *status quo* in Berlin through threat of force, under the protection of intercontinental missiles. They never risked carrying out their threat. When they were constrained by an American ultimatum to withdraw their intermediate-range ballistic missiles from Cuba, they immediately gave up their Berlin operation. The two major powers —thermonuclear duopolists—became aware of their common interest not to be involved in a war of annihilation, or, in other words, they understood that none of the stakes of their conflict was worth the cost of a war in which nuclear weapons would be used. Let us consider the terminology borrowed by rational strategists from economics: they compare cost and profit—that is, the losses in lives and goods that a war would entail on the one hand, and the possible fruits of victory on the other (the latter being appraised on the basis of a coefficient calculated in terms of the uncertainty of the outcome). The higher the losses, the fewer the advantages of victory, even if the risk of defeat is slight, and the more the rational strategist is inclined to prefer the certainties of peace to the risks of war.

On the whole, the optimistic argument based on "peace through fear" remains true, no matter how many nuclear powers there are. States producing these weapons will discover at the same time both their power and their impotency, the capacity they have acquired to destroy and the vulnerability of their own population and cities.

Nothing prevents conjecturing the spread of wisdom alone with the proliferation of nuclear weapons.

It would nonetheless be imprudent to overlook the circumstances that have favored the reasonable use that the two major powers have made of their nuclear weapons. In the first place and above all, both the United States and the Soviet Union were victors in the war, satisfied, having neither a defeat to avenge nor territory to conquer. The Soviet Union, seizing the opportunity to exploit its victory, had subjected 100 million Europeans to Marxist-Leninist law. The United States, despite the call for a *roll-back,* resigned itself to the *fait accompli* and confined itself to preventing any further advance of the Soviet armies in Europe. The success of containment was acceptable to both of the major powers, since each could interpret it as a success: the Americans because they had achieved the goal that they had set out, and the Russians because they had never wanted to do more than consolidate their empire over Eastern Europe, including East Germany.

To be sure, despite the fact that the stakes of their rivalry were not *national* in the narrow sense of the term (neither begrudged the existence and the territory of the other), the two major powers still remained enemies in that their ideologies each claimed to be universally valid. In certain cases, the most inexpiable struggles are those involving the confrontation not of so-called national interests (a province, a border line), but rather this nonmaterial good—the glory of preeminence, the power, at last uncontested, of no longer having a rival at one's side. No one can say whether, in the absence of nuclear weapons, the victors of World War II would have resolved their conflict by force. There is little doubt that these weapons contributed to imposing a preference for peaceful settlements.

In many respects, the duopoly is a less unpredictable situation than a conjuncture involving numerous actors. The situation was all the more stable as long as each of the duopolists exercised virtually uncontested power within its own camp. The United States and the Soviet Union avoided direct confrontation as much as possible. West Germany, the state least satisfied by the *status quo,* has no autonomous diplomacy vis-à-vis Pankow or Moscow. In Asia, until the schism between the Soviet Union and Communist China, the leaders of the Kremlin, alone capable of balancing an American nuclear force, retained, in case of crisis, a means of influencing the decisions of the North Koreans and the Chinese. Thus, the two major powers acquired imperceptibly the habit of pursuing their politico-ideological rivalry, while keeping the risks of the "unthinkable" war at a minimum.

The technico-strategic precautions reinforced political prudence. Analysts in institutes and universities set forth the conditions under which war involving the use of nuclear weapons might break out without having been desired by either side. American statesmen, especially, did their utmost to take precautions in order to attenuate these dangers. Security mechanisms were developed either to prevent the accidental explosion of a bomb, or to prevent an officer, no matter what his grade, from making the decision to utilize nuclear weapons without having received an order from the President of the United States (the latter alone has the legal authority to make such a decision and, thanks to electronics, these weapons are for the most part physically impossible to use without that decision), or finally to prevent the escalation to extreme measures if, by some misfortune, an atomic bomb should be set off despite all (the hotline).

These refined technico-political precautions are the expression of a strategic concept that is not so much new as renewed. The two major wars of the twentieth century had been, from a certain point of view, total wars: World War I, having broken out over an obscure conflict in the Balkans and spread through the alliance system, had, to the surprise of most of the generals and statesmen, lasted over four years, thanks to the improvised mobilization of all able-bodied men in combat units and factories. Entire societies had at once industrialized and mobilized, as if to illustrate the close relationship between the military and industrial spheres foreseen by certain sociologists at the beginning of the nineteenth century. The diplomatic system of Old Europe, the center of the world system, crumbled under the weight of the war and the revolutions it brought with it. World War II was still more total, since the Japanese attempt at empire had accompanied that of the Third Reich, and the mere existence of the sovereignty of the defeated states had been suspended for a period that the victors themselves reserved the right to determine.

Public opinion and statesmen themselves were haunted by the specter of these total wars, prisoners of the alternative of peace or war—the illusory evidence was provided still more by the events of 1914 than by those of 1939. Since 1945, because of thermonuclear bombs, the efforts of strategic thinking, the Cunning of Reason, those responsible for world politics have finally understood the lesson of Clausewitz: absolute war—one resulting from the escalation to extremes—is not a model, but a menace, a menace that can be warded off as long as the means of force remain in the service of policy, the "intelligence of the state." It falls to this intelligence to weigh the risks that must be run or the sacrifices that it is legitimate to accept to attain a goal.

On the one hand, the blurring of the distinction between war and peace has brought about the *bellicose peace:* the permanent mobilization of the nuclear apparatus, the limited use of military force here and there throughout the world, the qualitative race for armaments, with each of the major powers devoting billions and billions of dollars to the development of bombs, missiles, planes, and more highly perfected conventional weapons. It has also made total war less probable—that monstrous and absurd war in which thermo-nuclear powers heap upon one another, as in an orgy of destruction, all the means of destruction at their disposal. The strategy of the flexible response has become a fact at times of crisis—the strategy of all nuclear powers, despite the fact that in periods of calm certain states still proclaim the doctrine of massive retaliation, futile talk so long as the hour of reckoning does not sound.

In point of fact, for twenty years, nuclear weapons have con-stantly been placed at the service of a defensive strategy, conceived as a supreme recourse. The very term *deterrent* suggests this de-fensive use. To deter someone is to prevent him from taking certain action under threat of sanctions. Why would the sanction be neces-sarily or immediately unlimited? For ten to fifteen years, the ob-session over the preceding wars, the confusion over nuclear weapons and the strategy of deterrence was such that the weapons them-selves were called a deterrent, as if *any weapon* were not, in certain cases, a force of deterrence in the hands of a determined man. Neither of the two nuclear powers has ever tried, up until now, to obtain a modification of the *status quo* at the expense of the other, or to obtain the surrender of a non-nuclear power by the threat of using these weapons. In Cuba, the United States restored the *status quo ante;* in Berlin, the Soviets finally accommodated themselves to the military presence of the West in West Berlin.

Circumstances have likewise favored limitations on the use of conventional weapons. The nuclear powers alone possessed large stocks of them, and after the Korean campaign they feared to use them wherever there was a possibility of escalation. Elsewhere, the states involved in conflicts possessed relatively few weapons. The

United Nations served as an intermediary between the two major powers and the states involved, standing behind the peace efforts made by one or another of the major powers, or even by the member-states as a whole.

Finally, the submachine gun has been widely used, and wars of liberation have, for the most part, ended in the victory of the guerrillas. There have been exceptions, however—in the Philippines and in Malaysia. But these wars have tended to result in the independence of countries subject to colonial domination. Now American and Soviet opinion were in agreement with that of the Afro-Asian countries in condemning *en bloc*, on principle, the governing of colored peoples by white men (even though the same condemnation did not extend to the governing of Asian peoples by the Russians). The Europeans never became totally invested in these struggles. The French, who fought from 1946 to 1954 in Indochina, from 1954 to 1962 in Algeria, never attacked the logistical basis of the guerrillas in China, in Tunisia, or in Morocco. In one case, they did not have the indispensable military resources; in the other, they were paralyzed by a guilty conscience and the opposition of their allies and of a segment of French opinion. Nonetheless, in 1962, thanks to the fortified lines along the borders, the isolation of Algeria had succeeded in choking out the guerrillas. The French government consented to Algerian independence not because the guerrillas had won on the battlefield, but because, politically, no other solution was feasible in the long run.

From the moment that wars of liberation take on as their objective not the winning of independence from a colonial state, but the installing of a regime identified by American public opinion with communism, the guerrilla ceases, in the eyes of that opinion, to be the freedom fighter and becomes instead the perhaps sincere but blind militant of a despotic party, and the rules by which wars are fought are and will be changed. Already, North Viet-Nam has borne witness to the horrors of bombings because it supports the action of the Vietcong.

The dialectic of the three weapons has, for twenty years, maintained peace among nuclear powers, favored decolonization without diplomatic upheaval, restrained the use of conventional weapons. Will this dialectic play the same role in the decades ahead?

As far as thermonuclear weapons are concerned, there are three sets of conditions necessary to the prolongation of "peace through fear": technical—the maintenance of the balance of terror; strategic —the acceptance by all heads of state of the so-called graduated response doctrine, of progressive retaliation; and political—the nature of the conflict and the stakes.

The concept of the graduated response, the cool head during a period of crisis, requires that nuclear weapons be sufficiently dispersed or protected so that a first strike cannot eliminate the capacity for retaliation by any one of the states involved. This kind of stability depends therefore on the qualitative armaments race so far as the major powers are concerned, and on the acquisition of a nuclear apparatus (weapons and delivery vehicles) by new members of the atomic club.

The two major powers of the years 1945-1965 are both hostile to the "proliferation of atomic weapons"—the United States, with an ostentatious passion, the Soviet Union more discreetly. According to probabilities, does not the danger of an explosion increase along with the number of bombs—or even more, with the number of states possessing them? This is irrefutable reasoning on an abstract plane, but without contact with reality: it supposes the problem resolved— in other words, that other states have decided to leave to two, three, or four among them the exclusive possession of weapons that are supposedly decisive or glorious.

In theory, according to strict Machiavellian logic, the United States and the Soviet Union could have or even should have opposed at all costs the development of a Chinese nuclear capability. However, the Russo-American alliance against the atomic threat does not suffice to eliminate the politico-ideological enmity. And still more: just as the nuclear powers have never used their supreme arms offensively to compel the surrender of a state without such arms by imposing a choice between submission and annihilation, so too they have never attempted through such a threat to prevent the development of a new atomic force. All indications are that they respect the sovereignty of states—whether out of weakness or because of their political antagonism—and resign themselves to an evolution contrary to their common interest.

Proliferation probably will not stop with the present fifth nuclear power (China), but this does not mean that it will be unlimited, at least in the foreseeable future. Switzerland and Sweden would use such weapons to protect their neutrality—in other words, they will remain outside the major game. India will one day follow the lead of China, Israel that of France or Switzerland. This proliferation will not be without risks: one would have to be blind or to believe in the rationality of all statesmen to deny this. But the error of too many specialists is to confuse these numerous and diverse threats with the probability of the unthinkable war. The threat is probably smaller for the superpowers of today than for less important countries, who will have entered the atomic club without sufficient resources.

Under what conditions is peace through fear most stable? Where the forces of reprisal are least vulnerable, the states have both the will and the means to apply the doctrine of graduated response, and the disproportion between the cost and the stakes is enormous. All these conditions favoring peace through fear are met in the case of the relations between the United States and the Soviet Union. Short of an improbable technical break-through, they will persist during the decades ahead. They will not be met to the same extent elsewhere, in Asia or the Near East. But the United States and the Soviet Union will not allow themselves to be dragged unwillingly into a war of annihilation. The dissemination of nuclear weapons increases, to a degree impossible to pin down, the danger that, one day or another, nuclear weapons will be used militarily on some battlefield or other. At least for the next twenty or thirty years proliferation should not overturn the military foundation of the present order—the existence of arms so terrifying that even those who possess them keep them on reserve to be used only as a supreme recourse, in order to prevent certain initiatives or the extension of limited conflicts. The greatest threat to mankind, despite what one hears, is not that a few more states should come to possess nuclear weapons, but that statesmen should make a different use of their weapons in the diplomatic game.

The foundation of the present order of power, this anarchical order that tends toward the limitation of violence, is in the final analysis *psychological*. One reads in a report made to UNESCO nearly fifteen years ago that war begins in the minds of men. Such a formula is more false than true in our times, when it has been said that the citizens of one state detest those of another state because they have fought or are fighting them rather than vice versa. If diplomatic conditions require a reversal of alliances, a well designed propaganda campaign is sufficient to overcome collective passions or to give them another goal. On the other hand, when some states possess means of destruction against which all the others cannot protect themselves, and which they cannot respond to either, the essential focus lies predominantly in the minds of the group of men responsible for the diplomacy or strategy of the nuclear powers.

The strictly defensive or deterrent use of atomic weapons is dictated by a certain logic. It has been rightly said that the very limitless nature of these weapons renders their effective utilization difficult. It has been rightly said that there is no comparison between the capacity to destroy and the ability to convince, between *strength* as it is measured according to strictly military potential, and the *power* of a state to obtain the submission or consent of other states. It has rightly been said that never before have states so superior in strength to others as the United States and the Soviet Union been defied with impunity by dwarf states like Albania and Cuba. It has been rightly said that, from now until the end of this century, no state will even come close to attaining the economic and military potential of either of the superpowers. China and India, both larger in population, have not even transcended the first phase of industrialization. All the other states either have a much smaller population (and among industrialized countries, the Soviet Union and the United States have a relatively high demographic rate of growth) or a much lower per capita income. An American writer created a scandal in 1964 by declaring that, at the end of the century, the two superpowers of today would outstrip their potential rivals even more plainly than today. The statement was nonetheless incontestable, under two conditions: that the Soviet Union and the United States maintain the same internal coherence and political will within their borders, and that potential resources be identified with military strength and diplomatic power.

In reality, what ought to have provoked the scandal was not the very plausible prediction of a continued or enlarged separation between the resources at the disposal of the two major powers and those of other states, but rather the sequence from resources to power and strength. At the beginning of the 1960's, observers were struck by the disintegration of the blocs, by the impunity of the small states, by the apparent uselessness of nuclear weapons in daily relations or even in struggles for national liberation. It is desirable that this disproportion between the power of destruction and the power of persuasion should be prolonged and enlarged, but it is not determined solely by the nature of weapons or by the dialectic of the three weapons. For the time being, happily, statesmen are paralyzed by the "atomic taboo." The atomic weapon, like the gold reserves used to back currency, is buried in the ground, and accumulated in stockpiles, although always ready to be used. To paraphrase Clausewitz, one might say that nuclear weapons allow firm commitments to be honored and credit operations to be paid in cash. But nuclear weapons are not employed physically, any more than gold is removed from the storage vaults. The crisis—with its exchanges of threats and messages, and dialogue of affirmations of will—is the equivalent of what Clausewitz called commitment.

The true question concerning the future thus involves the continuation of this fragile order, founded at once on a strategic doctrine expounded gradually and spontaneously by the actors in history, and on prohibitions arising out of the depths of the human conscience—or perhaps, one might say, out of the collective unconsciousness. Will the superpowers respect the imperative of the exclusively deterrent use of nuclear weapons? Will not the inclusion of new members in the atomic club push them to reestablish, thanks to the defense against the ballistic missile and civil defense, the margin of superiority that the progress of the Chinese and Europeans threatens to penetrate? Will the smaller nuclear powers be capable of the same moderation if their so-called retaliatory force is vulnerable? Will not the states that have reduced their conventional weapons to a minimum in order to acquire a nuclear force be driven some day to the choice between passivity (that is, defeat) or a violation of the atomic taboo?

Finally, and above all, a question that one hesitates even to pose can hardly fail to haunt the minds of those who reflect upon the future. As long as war is and remains an act of violence in which one collective person attempts to compel another collective person, the offensive use of the nuclear threat is morally and even materially difficult: if the person that one is bent on bringing to surrender remains indifferent to the warning shots, if "Ruritania" allows first one, and then two of its cities to be destroyed rather than surrender, what choice do the superpowers have, if not to recognize once again, in ending the course of destruction—more futile even than monstrous—that man is a human being capable of preferring his reasons for living over his very life. The order of power in the atomic age is thus founded on the *atomic taboo*, the rational strategy of the major powers, and the courage of historic man. But what might happen the day when the states involved are no longer comparable to "collective persons" each seeking to obtain the submission of the other, but to a Hitler bent on exterminating an entire race deemed to be a noxious animal species?

Heaven forbid that a statesman might exist who would dream that nuclear weapons could not only be deterrent weapons—that is, instruments to be used in human dialogue—but also arms of extermination.

An anarchical order is normally inegalitarian to the extent to which, in the absence of a common law or an impartial police, the powerful prevail over the weak. Thus, Plato's Callicles deemed natural—in conformity with nature—the domination of the most powerful. Thus, according to Spinoza and Hobbes, in the absence of civil society, power determines rights. Philosophers did not ignore the fact that at least a principle of equality exists between individuals. The weak man is still able, in certain circumstances, to kill the strong man. Man does not act as man when he kills his fellow man as the hunter kills his prey: the essential quality of victory is lost when the defeated is no longer present to recognize his defeat.

The anarchical order of the international system has always been inegalitarian. In the most complex system, that of the Greek city-states or of the European states prior to 1914, the great powers constituted a closed club with membership reserved to sovereigns possessing a minimum of military strength. The question attributed to Stalin during the last war: "The Pope! How many divisions does he have?" roughly translates a traditional doctrine. A great power deemed itself injured if it was not consulted when an important affair was discussed. Eventually, the great powers settled the affairs involving lesser powers among themselves; sometimes they imposed a status (neutrality) or borders upon smaller states solely to avoid or to settle their own conflicts.

Nuclear weapons have not decisively modified this customary order of power. The present order is both more and less inegalitarian than international orders of the past. It is less so for two reasons. The first is the egalitarian design of modern civilization. The likening of "political units" to "collective persons" is suggested by the language we use, by the reigning ideology, by the anticolonialist passion. No distinction is made between the liberation of peoples and the liberation of individuals (or rather, the latter is placed before the former). The separation of ethnic groups, as we have seen, is a means of eliminating inequalities among individuals belonging to one or another of them. The old principle of European *Ius Gentium* (international law), implying a certain equality between states—an equality arising out of the recognized sovereignty of all states—is reinforced and enlarged by the egalitarian design of our period. The international law of the last century did not exclude the protectorate, foreign concessions (so-called unequal treaties), or the managing of certain public services in an independent state by bureaucrats from other countries representing the so-called community of civilized nations. Again, following World War I, the mandate formula implied a hierarchy among states, in that the mandatory states were by this very fact recognized worthy of administering "dependent peoples," of working for their welfare and development. The liquidation in two decades of almost all colonial administrations consecrated the triumph of the egalitarian idea on the world level, but at the same time it increased the real inequalities between states that were juridically equal, at least in their sovereignty, and it enlarged the divergence between the legal theory espoused by the United Nations and the realities of international politics.

The elimination of protectorates, mandates, or colonies, the equal footing of "Ruritania" and the United States in voting in the United Nations General Assembly consecrates the triumph of the egalitarian ideal in our century. But this has not been the sole agent of that historic revolution. The unarmed member of the resistance, or the one armed with a submachine gun, Gandhi and Giap, forced the Europeans to recall the ideal that they proclaimed in Europe; and nuclear weapons at first promoted the revolt of the colored peoples because the two states that possessed them had no colonies in the ordinary meaning of the term (although the Soviet Union maintains a multinational empire carved out by great sweeps of the sword, while Latin Americans denounce American hegemony, if not Yankee imperialism). But nuclear weapons by themselves do not suffice to found an empire. The guerrilla resists the strength of industrialized states, thereby limiting the reign of technology or, perhaps more precisely, inventing a technique that does not require the instruments forged by the technology of the rich peoples.

This double equalization—in refusing a hierarchy between ethnic groups or states and in the dialectic of the submachine gun and skilled weapons—is likewise a function of the heterogeneity of the international system, whose members are held to be equal, while from all points of view (extent of territory, volume of population, per capita income, degree of development) they have never been so unequal in any of the systems of the past. We observe the dénouement of this paradox every day: a combination of formal democracy and real oligarchy, to borrow our nouns from the Greeks and our adjectives from Marx. The two major powers, and especially the United States, possess all means of force—both conventional and nuclear weapons; they can mobilize immense resources to back their foreign policy. They are the main characters in the drama.

Anarchy continues to exist because there are two of them, and they cannot even agree to prevent the proliferation of nuclear weapons. The authority exercised by each of the major powers on its bloc is directly related to the fear aroused by the other. The consolidation of peaceful coexistence produces as a consequence the loosening of the blocs. Elsewhere, in the developing countries (*le Tiers-Monde*), the will of the major powers meets with the revolt of the masses and the submachine gun of the guerrilla.

The power of the two oligarchs is neither assured nor unlimited. Between now and the end of the century, two evolutions —the one probable, and the other as certain as a historic evolution can be—will tend to curtail that power. Nuclear weapons are not used militarily but, without them, the Chinese Nationalists would not retain Quemoy and Matsu, and American bombers would not be attacking North Viet-Nam. The United States owes its freedom of action in Asia and even in Africa to its nuclear supremacy. It is probable that the military distance between the first-rate nuclear powers and the second-rate nuclear powers will decrease within the next decades and, by virtue of this, the planetary system will be less unified than it is today. Even though they may not be capable of striking American territory, the Chinese nuclear force will exercise a certain deterrence on American diplomacy. The superpowers will have to resign themselves to giving up their presence in the four corners of the globe.

The almost certain evolution is the rise of China, which will almost certainly bring about the dissociation of the Soviet camp, and the "nationalization" of the Marxist-Leninist party-religions. It is permissible to speculate on the consequences of this factor of prime importance, on the realignments that it will provoke, on the relative weight of East and West, of Asia, America, and Europe in the world of the year 2000. But such is not within the scope of this article.

Our objective was more modest. The order of power—that is, the interstate order—has always been anarchical and oligarchical: anarchical because of the absence of a monopoly of legitimate violence, oligarchical (or hierarchic) in that, without civil society, rights depend largely on might. We inquired how this traditional order had been adapted to technological civilization. Our conclusion is that this order has been transformed, but not overturned. Pessimists prophesy the collective suicide of mankind failing a kind of historic mutation such as would be denoted by the renunciation of military sovereignty by states. Optimists believe in peace through fear, in the end of the domination of peoples by peoples, since domination does not pay.

We have no grounds to decide in favor of one or the other. Mankind has always lived dangerously. The dangers are no longer the same, but they have not disappeared. One mankind, united under one sole rational administration in order to exploit natural resources, would correspond to one possible end of the human adventure. The adventure is still far from this final state, conforming not to *the* logic of history but to *a* partial logic that fascinates because it at once attracts and repels. Would man achieve fulfillment or perdition if he were to arrive at the Promised Land of the world-state of technology?

This material is excerpted from a major article commissioned from M. Aron by the editors of *Encyclopaedia Britannica*. In view of the importance of the conference on the Conditions of World Order, and of M. Aron's contribution to it, *Britannica* has waived its usual precedents in order to grant special permission for this publication.

D. P. O'CONNELL

The Role of International Law

Introduction

A JURIST who discusses "order" has in mind a particular and fairly restricted concept of order. Unlike the natural or social scientists, he is not concerned with problems of hypothesis and verification, or limited to describing events and analyzing tendencies. His is a discipline concerned with the control of human behavior, and it is therefore normative. In a colloquium on "world order" it is therefore important that the jurist insist that the normative element be retained in the discussion, for, if he fails to do so, he abandons his claim to keep his study discrete from politics. He may well consider that the activities of the political scientists or economists or experts on international relations are properly concerned with no more than the ascertainment of trends and the prediction of consequences. His own discipline requires something more, and that is the element of value. Other parties to the colloquium may, with much cogency, argue that this serves only to import into the debate a conflict of ideas that can never be resolved and will only distract. Distract it certainly will; but if there is no solution to the problem of value then the role that law can play in producing the "conditions of world order" is seriously restricted.

International law is, of course, not the only, or even the most significant, factor making for world order, but that it is a factor cannot be denied. The point for consideration is the extent to which it is a factor, and the extent to which a basic intellectual disagreement about its nature, function, and importance inhibits it in this respect. The nuclear deterrent, schemes of technical aid, or regional association may assist in stabilizing international relations, and may therefore be described as "conditions of world order."

Their very existence, and the resistance they offer to tendencies of disorder, may be productive of rules of law. But it is unsatisfactory to have no other base for order than factual circumstances so ephemeral and so vague. Therefore, the jurist who demands autonomy for his subject must contend that it has objective standards, and these in themselves are conditions of world order. In this contribution to the colloquium an attempt is made to demonstrate that, because international lawyers are in disagreement on questions of value, and are unclear as to the criterion for isolating their subject from other areas of study, the subject is in disarray; and it is in disarray because the conflict of ideas in philosophy, carried over into jurisprudence, has not been resolved. This is merely a fact which the colloquium should note.

The international lawyer also has a contribution to make on the issues of the sovereign state as an impediment to world order, and organization as a factor in world order, because he is especially concerned with the nature of sovereignty and the problem of organizational links between sovereign states. This paper will seek to demonstrate that the concept of the national, sovereign state is more viable in the newer areas of the world than it has ever been, and that the optimism expressed with respect to its demise is unwarranted. A system of world law must accept the fact that states act as if independence implied untrammeled liberty. New states sometimes pretend to reject the values upon which the traditional legal structure rests; but in their claims they depend on a theory of the state that is a Western export. It is important that the paradox be pointed out, because analysis of the concept of the sovereign state, which has preoccupied many contributors to the colloquium, is thereby assisted. There is, also, not much optimism that the jurist can bring to the discussion on regional organization. One state has even taken the extreme step of withdrawing from the United Nations, and this is only one of many examples in history of an irrational tendency toward national suicide.

As long as there is a common sense of values and a common goal to be achieved, the sovereign state will be prepared to restrict its will. Therefore it is possible to deal with specific international problems by embodying in regulatory form an agreed minimal solution, and thus, piecemeal, to restrict the areas of conflict and disagreement. Here the lawyer has an important role to play, and has been remarkably successful in recent years as, for instance, in many aspects of the utilization of the oceans. But the point not to be overlooked is that, while the legislative process grows daily in volume and complexity, the jurist finds himself less intellectually equipped than he has ever been for the task of creating a regime of international justice. Much of his activity is pragmatic in character and technical in detail, and the discipline of international law in the wider sense is increasingly being deprived of the philosophical underpinning which will enable it to act as a solvent of those international problems—and they are the great problems—which escape from and defy the legislative technique. Deprived of the concept of order in its philosophical or value sense, the jurist finds the struggle to systematize the complex and incongruous world society ever more frustrating and exhausting.

Within the past fifteen years a vast new international universe has emerged which calls for regulation, and hence for rules of international law. The problems of outer space, problems concerning the passage of space vehicles, the damage caused by them, the use of the physical elements of space for the purposes of telecommunication are only the most obvious of a host of novel questions. At the more mundane level, the human community is threatened by problems of disposal of nuclear and industrial waste, pollution of the seas and waterways, and the exhaustion of common resources in fisheries—all issues which escape from the regulatory confines of the state and can be settled only internationally. Vast political changes in the structure of the world, resulting from the dissolution of the imperial systems, the rapid fusion and equally rapid dismemberment of territories in unions and federations, and the growth of supranational economic, and even political, groupings such as the Common Market, threaten the stability of institutions and channels of commerce and investment. And over and above these technical questions remain the profoundly challenging issues of aggression, self-defense, equality, and immunity of states. The rate at which multilateral conventions are contracted and modified accelerates every year, and a vast new technical edifice has been erected, upon which the existing patterns of human intercourse are perilously sustained.

Not surprisingly, international law in this generation has acquired a new aspect and an ever-increasing complexity. The international lawyer has become an indispensable technician in the operation of a variety of government departments, international organizations, and private corporations. In his hands international law, as a technical system, works in a relatively mechanical way;

and the skepticism with which the uninitiated contemplate the subject is unwarranted. Every day, countless decisions are made pursuant to rules laid down in treaties, agreements, or the decisions of the courts. States thereby adapt their behavior to a regime of law, at least in those matters which fall within the routine patterns of international intercourse.

It is not with respect to the machinery of international law, effective or ineffective as it may be in its details, but with respect to the subject itself that these remarks are addressed. From time to time it is necessary for practitioners of a discipline to stand back from its enmeshing complexities and look at it as a discipline. In the case of international law this has become very difficult for two reasons: in the first place, the details have accumulated so rapidly and in such quantity that the subject has escaped from the grasp of all its exponents; it has ceased to be a discipline in the traditional sense because it can be examined critically and intensively only in a fragmentary fashion. The study of the operations of some sixty or more international organizations has itself become more than a full-time occupation—indeed, keeping abreast of the workings of the United Nations is completely preoccupying—and there is serious danger that this branch of knowledge will be detached from the context of traditional international law, on which it nonetheless has a catalytic impact. This problem of magnitude and diversity, of course, bedevils all contemporary scholarship and imperils established disciplinary boundaries, but in the case of international law especially it is aggravated by the second difficulty to which reference must be made, and that is that the very integrity of the subject is at issue for want of any consensus of views on its theoretical basis.

It may be paradoxical that, at a point in time when rules of international law are multiplied to the extent that even most foreign offices cannot keep them in perspective, the subject is more deprived of the guidance of theory than ever before. At one end of the scale it has been annexed by the political scientists, and has become a mere aspect of international relations; as such it has tended to lose its juristic character, and hence its claim to autonomy. At the other end of the scale it has been transformed by the constitutional lawyers into an annex of their subject, into what in the United States has been called "foreign relations law"; and in the process, while remaining juristic in nature, it has lost its cosmopolitanism, and hence its claim to be international. There is, needless to say, every justification for the student of international relations to include in his conspectus the study of international law, for without consideration of the legal factors problems of international relations are likely to be distorted. There is, too, an obvious need for the domestic lawyer to be an exponent of international law, for rules of international law interlock with constitutional law in many various ways, and influence the solution of purely domestic legal problems. Realism demands that international law be seen as only one feature of a complex international mechanism, and perhaps a somewhat defective one at that, just as it forbids us to propose that every international problem is soluble by legal means, or should be solved by legal means. But this is not the point: the juristic integrity of international law is impeached when the political scientist utilizes its features in his analysis of international relations, while remaining incompetent to bring to bear on the analysis the critical standards of the lawyer; and it is no less impeached when the constitutional lawyer applies to his problem the standards of his own legal system and neglects the universal horizon of the rules he is utilizing.

Two examples will suffice: the international relations expert will hardly do justice to a study of the relations of the United States or of France with Communist China if he does not take into account the recognition problem; but his investigation of the proposal of the "Two Chinas" as the solution of the problem is likely to be defective if he fails to analyze in a lawyerlike fashion the profound juristic impediments that exist to this solution—and have, though in an inarticulate fashion, operated in world politics to make the problem apparently quite intractable. At the same time, the domestic lawyer who seeks to solve the problem of enforcement of the confiscatory legislation of a foreign state by applying to it the guillotine of the "act of State doctrine," without appreciating that this prescinds from the problem of full faith and credit in the public law of the United States, and is therefore peculiar and local, is likely to betray the cause of international law by diminishing the horizon of the problem.

There are countless instances of both types of misappropriation of international law; the political scientists have emasculated international law by withdrawing from it its normative element, and reducing it to a system of logic giving form to international problems without influencing their content; and the constitutional lawyers have solved litigious issues with international elements by the importation into alien legal environments of technical solutions manufactured in domestic legal systems—as happened in English law when the American doctrine of "act of State" was imported to solve the problem of recognition of foreign confiscatory legislation, though English law affords an inhospitable context for the doctrine.

International law, except in the field of regulation by treaty and action by international organizations, is thus in danger of falling between two stools, and this is mainly due to the fact that it is theoretically adrift. The problem is not so much that its philosophical foundations have been questioned; it is, rather, that the question is not even being posed. There is now so much international law writing in the world—the number of journals and reports in the field is sufficient already to occupy fifty pages of bibliography, leaving aside books and monographs—that no one can digest it. But very little of it rises above the descriptive and the anecdotal; much of it is repetitious, most of it is ephemeral, and in its sum it adds to the systematic exposition of international law in only a fragmentary and disconnected fashion. It prescinds from the hypothesis that international law is the "practice of States," but the practice which is examined is that of one, or at best, a few states, and when aggregated often discloses, not symmetry, but incongruity. By what philosophical trick such an aggregation of what is, after all, mere fact is transformed into a system of "oughtness," is unclear; and the existence of this problem has probably never occurred to the vast majority of writers and researchers in the field of international law. In fact, the content of international law owes much less to a record of how states have acted than to juristic speculation; and despite the emphasis that has, quite rightly, been placed on precedent and empirical techniques, the subject has been systematized by the processes of legal elaboration. At the present time, when the "general principles of law" are being increasingly resorted to for such purposes as the protection of foreign investment, international law is taking on the aspect of an intellectual construction which it possessed in the seventeenth and eighteenth centuries; but it remains enmeshed in empirical techniques. A discipline is imperiled when its systematic character and the hypothesis on which scholarship is based cease to correspond. To make clear the increasing irrelevance of the hypothesis of state practice at the present time, but the reason that the hypothesis remains unquestioned, it is necessary briefly to trace, in the history of the subject for the past three centuries, the persistent tension between the theoretical exposition of international law and the examination of its precedents.

International law owes its disciplinary origin to the speculations of Renaissance philosophers and moralists on the problems that arose from the fragmentation of medieval Christendom, and in the Age of Reason it acquired a structural unity and an intellectual integrity by virtue of the elaboration of universally accepted and unchallenged axioms and general principles. Its normative character derived from the intersection of law and morality which medieval metaphysics had made possible, and which a sense of universal order had sustained. It superimposed itself on princes and nations, less by virtue of their tolerance of its precepts than by virtue of the cogency of its systematic exposition; in short, it was law because jurists possessed a common insight into the regime of justice between peoples, and because justice was thought to derive from fundamental human rights and liberties that were discoverable in nature.

This edifice was demolished when the capacity of the mind to know objective truth, and hence metaphysical order, was questioned in the latter half of the eighteenth century. The mind might construct principles of behavior, but these would remain in the realm of "oughtness," quite detached from the realm of actual conduct. This left the theory of justice to the speculations of the moralist, and law to the analysis of the technician. Formal origin in the organs of state legislation became the touchstone by which law was isolated as a category, and this had the effect of endowing the concept of the national sovereign, which throughout the Age of Reason had been confined by the concept of the primordial nature of man, with a novel ascendancy and irresponsibility. Since there was now no formal source of law above the will of the sovereign, and an unbridgeable gulf had opened between law on the one hand and morality, and justice as an aspect of morality, on the other, international law lost the intellectual cogency that had made it possible. John Austin relegated it to the domain of "positive morality," denying it the description "law," and so depriving it of normative content as to debase it to the intellectual order of social convention. No doubt to Austin it did not thereby suffer in authority, and, indeed, he may even have expected that authority to be enhanced. However, as a system it now came increasingly to depend, as the law of the state had come to depend, on analysis of practice, on description of what states do—in other words, on positivist techniques. Inevitably it lost its speculative character and became an area of empirical methodology confined only by the problems with which it dealt, and not by the "nature" of the international community.

Whatever views one has on nineteenth-century political philosophy, one must acknowledge that it retained an acute awareness of the self-consistency and dogmatic character of theories of law, and hence of theories of international law. Even the relevance of international law, once the abstraction of sovereignty had been carried to its logical end and the world had become a congeries of mutually competitive sovereign states, was itself the subject of systematic consideration. And if much of this was destructive of the moral authority which Austin and Kant, and even Hegel, had left to international law, much of it conserved that authority. Jellinek's impressive doctrine of the state, although it derived from the theory of the sovereign will, found a place for international law in a new intellectual order of things by virtue of the notion of "autolimitation," according to which states fall under the regimen of international law through a process of self-abnegation. Even if to the modern cynic there is something specious about this type of construction, it was intrinsically liberal in tendency, and it gave German international law doctrine a vitality and coherence which it has never lost.

Compared with the situation before 1914, international law today is intellectually anarchic. It is, of course, not the only intellectual activity to suffer from the incoherence of the contemporary world, but in its case the disability is compounded by the lack of theory to render congruous what is, in so many respects, factually incongruous. "State practice" is today the practice of a large number of states, many of them immature, and impatient, and many of them arraigned in power blocs in a way that threatens the stability of traditional legal institutions. And the "practice" derives sometimes from political decisions in which the legal factor has played no role at all, or has been discounted, and, sometimes from legal advice that is unsound, based on defective analysis of the problem, on resort to the wrong books or to books that are out of date, and frequently given under pressure and in too brief a form. Such "practice" may be valueless as a precedent. What value, then, lies in the collection of records of attitudes struck by states from time to time, or of actions taken by them? Unless the precedents can be evaluated and compared critically the investigation cannot be raised above the anecdotal level; yet, it is precisely with respect to the canons of evaluation and criticism that contemporary international legal scholarship is barren. Evaluation implies judgment and judgment implies reason, not choice or will. If international law is to possess autonomy, therefore, its rational and speculative character must be conceded, but the imperative theory of law, and the whole philosophical environment of the sovereign state, denies it this character. Here is the central problem of international law, and it is a problem scarcely adverted to in all the vast literature to which reference has been made.

These comments are not mere philosophical ax-grinding. They go to the heart of the question of the role that international law plays in the conditions of world order. Just as world order cannot be discussed effectively until the philosophical differences concerning what is meant by "order" have been exposed, so international law as a system of ordination cannot be examined until differences in the nature of law, its origin and its purpose, have been clarified. If the subject's discreteness is threatened through its absorption into wider and less specific areas of study, its role in the scheme of world order will be seriously affected. Therefore the first requirement is to investigate the claims of international law to autonomy, and its capacity to co-ordinate; and this is a requirement, it is necessary to repeat, more neglected now than ever before in the subject's history.

Two important impediments to the effectiveness of international law derive from this philosophical instability, both of them affecting the "community" nature of the discipline. The first impediment is the argument that international law, being the product of imperialism and Western statecraft, cannot bind new states that have been emancipated from this environment. The second, and the more philosophically consistent, argument is the Communist thesis that the content of international law derives from the principles of peaceful coexistence. Both these impediments emanate from views on human society that stand in marked opposition to the metaphysics of community which generated international law in the seventeenth century.

The proposition is found, not infrequently, in contemporary academic writings that newly emergent nations cannot be bound by an international law that reflected the acquisitive ambitions and the political philosophies of the European and American states. The authors offer no better rationalization of this view than the argument that continued subjection to this alien imposition is inconsistent with accession to sovereignty. The argument is thus founded upon the philosophical abstraction of sovereignty, and thus upon a view of political organization which is antiquated and subversive of the order of modern society. If the argument were sound, one would expect it to be equally valid when applied to the emergence of new entities anywhere in the world, as a result of revolution, or as a result of political reconstruction. In fact the argument was not employed when Panama seceded from Colombia, Cuba from Spain, or Finland from Russia, although these events occurred at the time when the abstraction of sovereignty was most complete. Neither has it been employed in cases such as the formation and dissolution of the United Arab Republic, though in form this involved the disappearance of one sovereignty and the substitution therefor of another.

The argument of emancipation is reserved, then, for the cases of emergence of dependent peoples; yet the only criterion of its validity, namely the absoluteness of sovereignty, is one not inherently so restricted. This makes the argument, in a dialectical sense, seriously suspect. However, that is not the point to emphasize when considering the issue raised by it for the effectiveness of a world rule of law. The real point is that the argument superimposes the sovereign state on the structure of international relations instead of integrating it in that structure. It repudiates by implication all metaphysical character in the human community, and reduces the latter to Hobbes' state of nature, from which Vattel in the eighteenth century rescued it. It bases law on will, not on subjection to a rational order of behavior, and is to this extent inherently anarchic. Furthermore, the argument is devoid of internal consistency. The sovereign state is an intellectual artifact; its character, its form, and its qualities derive from a theoretical exposition of political organization which is nothing if not Western, and has its roots in the Age of Reason as much as has international law. New states can hardly claim the privileges and faculties of states and yet repudiate the system from which these derive; yet this is precisely what the argument involves. It overlooks that a state, when it commences to exist as a state, does so in a structural context which gains its form from law, just as a child when born into a society becomes subjected to it by virtue of the order of being in which it is integrated.

Superficially the argument of emancipation is attractive to new states who are security conscious, jealous of new liberties, in peril of losing them, and hence fearful of unknown commitments. There is, in view of the plastic and uncertain content of international law, some justification for caution before conceding such commitments. Also, the new states, through their own influence on usage, can contribute to the change and adaptation of rules of law to suit their new environment. But these are arguments of a pragmatic character. They do not justify a thesis of universal emancipation, for the result of that thesis would be to precipitate the disintegration of the structure of international relations. In fact, law enhances the liberties, the security, and the dignity of new states, and it enables them to preserve the structure of trade, co-operation, and investment throughout the process of political change. Not surprisingly, it would be very difficult indeed to find any statement emanating from a government of a new state which would give comfort to the thesis of emancipation, which has been propounded by academics and remains academic. On the contrary, new states quickly become very conscious of the advantages to them of the existing legal order, and it would do less than justice to their intelligence and sense of responsibility to suppose that they are all bent on a libertarian course in their international behavior.

One of the primary achievements of any system of law is continuity and institutional stability throughout the process of change. In this highly complex international society the need for continuity and stability is more necessary than ever before, and the emphasis is, accordingly, thrust on the maintenance of the legal universe. Referring to the structure of relations achieved by multilateral treaty-making, the Assistant Director-General of the International Labour Organization has written that, without it,

international law would have lost all contact with reality in an industrialized world community drawn together by economic and strategic need and the development of a common material civilization, but held asunder by the clash of political and ideological forces.

And going on to discuss the problem of continuity of this fabric throughout the process of independence, he says:

The obligations of multipartite legislative instruments are not, however, badges of continuing servitude; they are a necessary part of full co-operation in the international community and participation in them must therefore be regarded as one of the hallmarks of emancipation.

It is found that the technical advisers to new states, on the whole, examine the obligations imposed by international law in an objective and serious fashion, and that their governments want to be told straight out what the lawyer's view is, so that this can be a factor to be taken account of in the formulation of policy. There is little evidence that new states want to scrap existing rules and manufacture their own; they have gone to immense lengths to maintain continuity in their internal legal system, and they are only too aware of the implications of tearing up the traditional fabric of international law.

The relativism that permeates international law in the Western and non-aligned camps is matched by the deliberately contrived relativism of Communist theorizing. Professor Tunkin, a leading Soviet international lawyer, has explained the dogmatic character of this relativism as follows: He distinguishes between the coexistence of states in previous orders of being from coexistence as understood by the Marxist, which is "coexistence of States belonging to two diametrically different economic systems." In other words, it is the maintenance in being as facts of two utterly contradictory orders, and it is therefore not an order in itself integrating them in the interests of a common end, as it was to the fathers of international law. The "general principles of law," which in traditional Western thought comprise the normative precepts mediating between speculative philosophy and actual rules of law, to Tunkin are no more than the aggregation of positive rules actually existing in various legal systems.

General principles of law which may be found in the legal systems of States belonging to those two systems, though sometimes containing technically similar rules, are of different juridical and class nature, i.e. are different as legal norms. There are therefore no general principles "common to all States." There may be common legal notions reflecting general features of legal phenomena, but not common legal norms.

It follows from this that Communist doctrine conceives of no means of forming rules of law save through the consent of states, and of each and every state. "To become a norm of international law of universal application," Tunkin says of a rule, "it should be recognized by all States." The imposition of majority will, like the imposition of the general principle, "is in complete contradiction with the fundamental universally recognized principles of international law, and especially with the principle of equality of States." Here is a doctrine with its roots in the "state of nature" thesis of the eighteenth century, which envisaged states as isolated beings coexisting in an unordered condition, and ordered, like the individuals who make the social contract, by an act of continuous consent. The sovereignty of states derives largely from the sovereignty of man in isolation, and it is not the least of the paradoxes of Marxism that it utilizes this rank individualism as the cornerstone of a system of collectivism. The paradox is most evident in the Marxist theory of international society, and this goes far to explain the devious and uncertain doctrines of interstate relations propounded in the Soviet during the past forty years.

The Communist thesis perpetuates the cleavage between justice and law which derives from the "state of nature" epoch. "To say that international law should live up to the precepts of international morality and to say that international law flows out of morality are two completely different assertions," says Tunkin. "Morality or a notion of justice do not constitute the 'basis' of international law." He reverses the order of priorities, proceeding from "the facts of international life to ideas," instead of from ideas to the facts. The formula *ubi societas ibi jus* is erroneous, because law is the creation of the will of the ruling class. "There was a society which did not know law, and there will be a society which will have no law, and, of course, no international law as well." It follows that international law is a feature of the epoch of contradiction. The economic structure of society is the basis on which all other social phenomena develop, and international law as a social phenomenon derives its content from the conjunction of wills of the ruling classes in contradictory systems. The principles of peaceful coexistence reflect this unstable juxtaposition of rival systems, and their content is modified by the pressures which tend to tilt the construction one way or another. But, since the historical pressure is consistently in the direction of tilt toward socialism, these principles are constantly being modified as the class expression of the socialist countries begins to predominate.

When propagated as a code, the principles of peaceful coexistence assume the character of grandiloquent moral propositions—the sovereignty of states must be respected, intervention is illegal, aggression is outlawed. And many Western lawyers have been deceived into believing that the content of these principles is the same as the content of traditional international law; and that hence there is a stable basis of world order in the shared convictions of East and West. When the Communist international lawyers, however, specify the conclusions which they believe to emanate from the principles of peaceful coexistence, the unstable political character of the latter becomes obvious. And what is, perhaps, more intriguing is that the emanating rules are apt to provoke serious quarrels among the Marxist international lawyers themselves. There is no better way of establishing this point than by linking the Communist view of international law as it applies to new, and non-willing, states with the view that new states are emancipated from international law.

In 1962 there appeared in East Germany under the auspices of the *Akademie für Staats—und Rechtswissenschaft "Walter Ulbricht"* a dissertation on the rules of succession of new states to the obligations of the old. This purports to be based on the principles of peaceful coexistence, and the deduction is made that in the period of transition from capitalism to socialism the rule is one of universal succession. This is not, however, the universal succession of the old regime. In that period universal succession implied complete succession; now it implies a complete succession only with respect to those rights and obligations which do not aim to produce a new world war, enslave or plunder other peoples, or harm the socialist camp, which alone aims at the preservation and strengthening of peace. One of the principles of peaceful coexistence is the "peaceful working together of states." This principle must not be negatived by change of sovereignty. But what lies behind the principle? The answer given consists in a quotation from a declaration of representatives of Communist and workers' parties in Berlin in November 1960: "With peaceful coexistence favourable conditions are created for the extension of the class war in capitalist countries and the national freedom movements of peoples in colonial and dependent lands."

The dialectical character of this thesis becomes clear from the context. While the German Democratic Republic is unrecognized by most of the world it can claim participation in the various international organizations only as long as it can maintain its identity with the *Reich*, or its succession to it. The first alternative is excluded by the necessity for the Soviet to maintain diplomatic relations with the Federal Republic of Germany, as well as with the German Democratic Republic; and the logical position has been taken of contending that both of these entities are separate states, and hence new states. This makes the Democratic Republic's participation in international organizations—which is regarded as the index of its status—conditional on legal continuity.

In the historic drift toward socialism, continuity of international law is a necessary step in gaining for new socialist states a foothold in the existing structure, from which further advances can be made. But new states which have been emancipated from imperialist and capitalist domination are in a different position. They gain a foothold in the direction of socialism by repudiating the existing structure. Therefore, it becomes clear, the concept of sovereignty is a double-edged weapon; it is a shelter behind which states can be immunized from legal rules which derive from the epoch of exploitation; and it can be, by virtue of the concept of equality of states which emanates from it, a guarantee of the benefit of these rules in the epoch of transition from capitalism to socialism. It then becomes apparent that the rules of international law are objective only if one concedes the inevitability of the march to socialism; otherwise they are intolerably subjective and unstable, and there is no possibility of discourse between Western and Soviet lawyers on their content. As it happens, Soviet lawyers are increasingly retreating from this system of extreme relativism, conceding the restrictive pressures of juristic reasoning, and becoming aware that a real stability in international behavior, and not mere preservation of vantage points, is necessary for the new way of life that is emerging in Communist countries. For this reason, they have been privately critical of the East German thesis. They concede the necessity for the thesis in the case of East Germany, but they recognize that it has dangers for the Soviet's own struggle to draw the teeth from the class-war concept.

Some Western international lawyers, observing the division of the world into cultural and political complexes in marked antagonism with each other, have raised the question whether it is correct to speak of an international community at all; whether, on the contrary, it may not be correct to say that there are two or more communities sharing differing legal convictions, and hence producing more than one system of international law for governing the relationship between their constituent political entities. The question misapprehends the nature of community. Man as man transcends political divisions and participates in community by virtue of human, not class, coexistence. The "urge" to law follows as a matter of course. Law then has its starting point in man, and this is true no less of international law than it is of the law of the state. The point has never been better made than by Suarez in 1612:

the human race, no matter into how many different peoples and kingdoms it may be divided, always preserves a certain unity. Every State, when viewed in relation to the human race, is a member of that universal society, for States, when standing alone, are never so self-sufficient that they do not require some mutual association and intercourse, at times for their own greater welfare and advantage, but at other times because of some moral necessity or need.

It thus becomes evident that when a lawyer is called on to contribute a discussion on the conditions of world order he is unlikely to advance the question very far unless he takes a stand on the ultimate issue of the point of intersection between law and philosophy; unless, in other words, he apprehends the intellectual horizons of the concept of order and its concomitant concept of community. Order, unlike the state, is not an artifact, any more than is community. Both concepts, order and community, are imposed on the mind by the metaphysical notion of man; and if this notion be questioned order is reduced to a mere state of fact, which is inconstant and may even be terminated altogether. The technique of establishing the machinery of world order by recording the practice of states is inhibited by the presupposition that the will of the state is a preeminent source of law, and moral pressures are irrelevant. A rational approach to state practice will thrust the emphasis on positive manifestations of the need for order and stability to be discovered in regular solutions devised by states in their day-to-day practice; an imperative approach will thrust it on the formal divergencies and discrepancies in this practice. The two approaches tend respectively toward affirmation and denial. Ultimately, then, the problem is one of the jurist's conviction of his function. If he sees this function as one of channeling the normative pressures in society and their organization in rubric form he is committing himself to a concept of order which will be different from that yielded by an imperative theory of the state. A positive approach from the position of fact is essential for verification of the pressures, but a positive approach alone cannot make the facts of state usage congruous, or raise the analysis above the anecdotal. The jurist at the present time is bewildered by the difficulties that modern philosophy, accompanied by modern technology and sociology, places in the way of all his efforts to bridge the gap between what states do and what they ought to do. Incoherence of practice is thus both occasioned by and compounded by incoherence in theory and to this extent the conditions for world legal order are imperilled.

Conclusion

The other papers in this issue of *Dædalus* have been concerned with the ascertainment of trends toward or against world order. Necessarily they have been analytical and descriptive. This paper has, perforce, raised wider issues that are at bottom philosophical. It would hardly be contested that international law is an important adjunct of international diplomacy, and is, therefore, a factor in promoting stability and order in the behavior of nations. However, as a discipline it has lost much of its coherence, and hence much of its independent influence in the world of today, because of basic disagreements concerning its nature and functions. There is, first, the disagreement between socialist and nonsocialist lawyers, which prescinds from a disagreement about the nature of society, and ultimately about the nature of man. There is, secondly, the disagreement between lawyers of new countries and lawyers of old ones, which prescinds from the political notion of nationalism, and reflects a nineteenth-century philosophy of the state. And there is, finally, the disagreement between the lawyers who treat international law as if it were a branch of constitutional law, and the political scientists who treat it as an aspect of international relations—the one derogating from the subject's universality, the other from its normativity. These disagreements, which overlap each other, are facts to be taken into account in any discussion on world order; and since they betray a basic conflict of values they are very relevant in assessing what are the chances of a world, or even regional, system of behavior, the basic principles of which will command universal assent.

LORD GLADWYN

World Order and the Nation-State—A Regional Approach

THERE IS no doubt that the nation-state is still the   only unit in international relations which has any real political, as opposed to economic, significance. By this I mean that no conventional alliance, from N.A.T.O. downwards, can speak on all occasions with one voice, still less organizations like the Afro-Asian group, the Organization of American States, the Arab League or even (now) the E.E.C. Since World War II, the number of nation-states has greatly increased—there are now one hundred and seventeen members of the United Nations with a possible twenty or thirty to come—and many of those recently created are even more conscious of their so-called "independence" than the more historical ones. Nowhere since 1945 has the absolute sovereignty of the nation-state been questioned, still less restricted, save only in two areas, Eastern and Western Europe. In Eastern Europe, as a result of Soviet occupation, the various nation-states were subjected to a form of centralized control exercised by the Communist Party in Moscow; in Western Europe between 1950 and 1965 some of the nation-states came together voluntarily in an effort to achieve a supra-national entity. This was largely due to the experiences of a war in which all of them had been at some stage totally defeated. In the East, however, it now looks as if the nations concerned are recovering a good deal of their independence, if not of their central sovereignty, while in the West the whole idea of a supra-national entity has now been challenged by the open and declared hostility of the present French government to any such notion.

Elsewhere in the world it must be admitted that efforts to achieve federations or their equivalents among the so-called "emergent" nations have all failed. For instance, the United Arab Republic is now united only in name. The Arab League exists only as a sort of discussion forum. The proposed association of Kenya, Tanzania, and Uganda has not materialized. It is questionable whether the Federation of Nigeria will survive. The Federation of Rhodesia has already collapsed. There is little hope that the unification of the Maghreb in North Africa will be achieved. Unfortunately, little progress has been made in South America toward any real association of the various states under the auspices of the Organization of American States. Further afield, the prospect of a united India as a continuation of the old Raj broke down in 1946. Even the newly formed Federation of Malaysia has already partially collapsed, and that in South Arabia is encountering the most grievous difficulties. In North America it is true that Canada and the United States may be coming closer together in a general way, though even here we are faced with a rise of nationalist feeling in the Province of Quebec.

Must we then assume that any attempt to limit the complete independence of the nation-state, which varies in size from the 600 million of China to the 200 thousand of the Maldive Islands, is the only possible basis for the construction of the new world order, and that all efforts to produce a more rational, indeed a less dangerous, international structure are inevitably doomed? But first let us try to define the nation-state in its international significance.

Perhaps we can say that it is a collection of people, usually though by no means always consanguineous and monoglot, accustomed to being governed from one center, who regard themselves as possessing virtues and qualities that must at all costs be preserved, and who are not disposed to allow their collective power to be shared with any other nation. It will be observed that any collection of people who wanted to run their own affairs would come under this definition, including quite a number which would like to be nation-states if they could; but in practice we must say that any such collection is a nation-state only if it is generally recognized as independent and capable of membership in the United Nations. It then becomes an entity whose defense against aggression is in principle assured. (China is, of course, so recognized as a state; it is only the representative character of the government that is disputed.)

Clearly such a nation-state can be merged in another state either by its own desire or (if the United Nations does not function) by some act of force. Wales, or Ireland before the rebellion, or even to some extent Scotland, are examples of amalgamation by force. Other potential nation-states, such as Bavaria, are now part of a German whole. The Kingdom of Savoy and other Italian states were eventually merged in the Kingdom of Italy. If historical precedent is any guide, it is quite possible that some existing nation-states may in the future be merged in larger entities, perhaps by extreme economic pressure, perhaps even by war. It is equally possible that some existing nation-states may break up, perhaps especially those that are in effect the remains of empires, containing as it were "submerged" nations that are racially and linguistically distinct. But, with the emergence of some world order based on the United Nations, actual suppression of a nation-state except by its own volition, or as a result of internal disruption, is becoming increasingly difficult. Even the smallest states can now depend to some degree on a collective guarantee against aggression.

Naturally, since the beginning 450 years ago of this strange system, which nevertheless did not prevent an extraordinary cultural period, countless learned men and even some statesmen produced schemes to end a suicidal and dangerous anarchy. None had the slightest effect. The League of Nations, between the two wars, was the one which came nearest to curbing the nation-state, but even that collapsed because of its evident inability to control in any way the actions of its members, not only Italy and Japan, but even to some extent the U.S.S.R. After World War II, it is now evident that the United Nations, in default of some major political settlement between East and West, is in much the same position. Anarchy prevails in the world. The nation-state's freedom of action is limited only by its power. Worse than that, it is often enabled to pursue what it imagines to be its own individual interests at the expense of its neighbors because of an inability of the larger powers to impose their will, owing to the necessity of preserving the only existing guarantee of peace, namely, the nuclear Balance of Terror. Tension therefore is only too likely to accumulate, and one day there will be a war of some kind, which may well spread, even if we manage, through sheer fright, to avoid a general nuclear explosion.

It is of course evident that sovereign nation-states can and do enter into alliances and indeed into international associations under which they agree to abide by common rules, drawn up in the interests of the group as a whole. There is thus in effect often some temporary restriction on their complete freedom of action. But in all such alliances or organizations it is possible for a nation-state to resign in the last resort, and, therefore, there is no ultimate obligation to have regard for any decision taken in common if such a decision is not deemed to be in accordance with the interests of the nation-state concerned. And, as most of them like being independent, there is now less compulsion or desire to merge with some group than there was at the end of World War II. This tendency applies even to the United Nations itself, from which one large state has resigned already. The United Nations, it is true, has power to overrule the declared will of a nation-state, though this applies only to the majority of the international community and not to the five permanent members of the Security Council. However, it is true that if these five members are in agreement it is possible now to put legal sanctions behind any action taken against any nation-state which may be thought to be acting against the interests of the world generally. The only instance since the war of nation-states voluntarily taking the enormous jump from total independence into some kind of supra-national entity occurred when six European countries ratified the Treaty of Rome, but it is by no means certain as yet that this Treaty will still apply when there is no further means of escaping from its evident supra-national implications.

It might consequently be supposed that, except for some slight control exercised in theory by the World Organization, the chances are that the various nation-states of the world will continue to have complete freedom of action and will join one alliance or another, as it seems in their interest. If world peace is maintained at all, in such circumstances, it will have to be on the basis of some constantly changing world balance, in which there will necessarily be a strong element of instability. It may even be argued that the very balance of terror between the two superpowers, or giants, of the modern world in itself encourages the dissolution of alliances and therefore actually encourages the tendency of the nation-states to insist on complete independence. Regrettable though this may be, it is a fact that the authority of the superpowers can only with difficulty be exercised over allies who do not accept the ideas of the most powerful section of their own group and prefer to take an independent line. If the balance rests on the impossibility of either the one superpower or the other committing an act of aggression against any member of the opposing side, then it is clear that there is no danger for any of the smaller powers since *ex hypothesi* their own leader cannot exercise more than a certain pressure on them if he does not want them actually to desert and go over to the other side. This is clearly a position which can be and is exploited, though it is rather difficult to see what a rebellious ally can gain from the operation except psychological satisfaction.

Finally, if one considers the arguments in favor of retaining the nation-state, there is that of "plus ça change plus c'est la même chose." If indeed we succeed in merging various nation-states, especially in Europe, where their existence has given rise to so many and so great disasters in the past, what is there to prevent the new potential superpower from behaving as irrationally as any other nation-state and thus increasing rather than diminishing world tension and the risk of nuclear war? It can indeed be pleaded in refutation of this that a united Europe would not have those national ambitions which characterize a divided one, and, further, that if a World Balance resulted from unification there would be that much less possibility of some European dictator emerging. But all these are legitimate arguments which must be answered by those who believe in the gradual tempering of international anarchy by the building up of an effective and lasting World Authority.

Nevertheless the case against the maintenance of the nation-state in its historical integrity, and certainly against the disruptive, nationalistic tendencies now at work in that cradle of war, which is Western Europe, is very strong. We must, of course, consider the integrating influence of the industrial system of the latter part of our century. Whatever the arguments in favor of the maintenance of the nation-state, it is, economically speaking, becoming increasingly difficult for the latter to preserve its complete independence unless it is very large or (paradoxically) very primitive. The great "automated" factories of our age require huge "home markets" if they are to sell their goods at a profit. In the long run the maintenance of tariff barriers around medium-sized states can produce only unemployment and economic distress. But if customs unions are formed then more and more "integration" becomes inevitable. The nation-states concerned may try to resist this process; but the only choice in front of them, assuming the process of industrialization continues, is between union among themselves or absorption by one of the existing super-states.

Should they choose union the way is now less difficult than it was. For it is no longer a straight choice between hegemony, conquest, or federation. The new techniques of the Treaty of Rome have clearly demonstrated their efficacity and their suitability for the ancient historical nation-state which is in no-wise prepared to lose its integrity or its "personality." Within the framework of the Commission, the Council, and the European Parliament there is scope for the continuation of genuine national identities and thus for the constitution of a supra-national entity in which the dreaded "loss of sovereignty" would come, as it were, unawares. It is only the atavistic urge which stands in the way of such a development, and it is doubtful if even that can stand in its way for very long. As soon as the embodiment of past glories is removed from the scene, the real forces of the future will take over; and though these may be "communistic" (in the sense of directed economies) it seems likely that they will at least not be nationalistic. France, it is true, has the ability to build herself up into a self-sufficient neutralist state if she so desires; but, if no other Western European state follows her example, what then? Would she really be prepared to be a Soviet satellite forever?

The position therefore is that even if the E.E.C. of the Six achieves political unity—which it cannot in practice do on a non-supra-national basis because the Germans will not accept the hegemony of France—the two giants will continue to glare at each other over the Elbe and the position will remain unstable. If nationalism prevails and the E.E.C. breaks up, the position will be much the same, except that it will be even more unstable than under the first hypothesis. Only if Britain joins will it be possible to create a situation which in the long run may enable the Americans and the Russians to disentangle themselves from the Continent by agreement and to prepare for the peaceful reunification of Germany, perhaps at first in the sense of an association of the various Germans within a larger democratic and politically inoffensive whole. After this has been done relations with Eastern Europe could be gradually improved, though no doubt the West will continue to look primarily toward Washington and the East toward Moscow. In a real sense there is a community of interest between the United States and Western Europe. But it is possible to imagine the emergence of a Europe which will gradually acquire an individuality of its own, and which could, not from the nuclear (because that would be absurd even if it were possible) but from every other point of view, be something equivalent to Russia and America. And I maintain that this would be the best of all possible stabilizing factors.

It seems thus on the whole probable that the present bipolar World Balance itself will be slowly transformed by the emergence of a regional *bloc* in Western Europe. If it is not, and if the nation-state endures, then the chances of World War III would probably be considerably greater and it would in any case be difficult to conceive of any advance toward the achievement of a World Order involving some reduction of international tension. Nationalism may indeed represent the "live forces" making for change, and in a non-nuclear world there is no doubt that constant and violent struggles between nations would gradually produce a synthesis of some kind. But modern weapons are so horrifying that to a large extent this logic is no longer applicable; and if it does not apply, then what are the alternatives before us? Are we really to eliminate reason in our concept of the development of human events? Assuming that reason does prevail and that some sort of regional bloc does emerge in Western Europe (which is the only district in which the nation-state may be to any noticeable extent modified in present conditions), what consequences would flow from the point of view of the construction of an eventual World Authority?

Clearly the general situation would be substantially altered by the creation of another "pole." The bipolar world that has virtually existed from 1945 until now has already been changed to some degree by increasing restiveness on the part of the superpowers' allies on both sides of the Iron Curtain and by the explosion of the first Chinese nuclear device. The formation of a political community in Western Europe (which might eventually embrace some Eastern European states as well) would create a new World Balance, even if Europe did not attempt to become a nuclear power on a scale emulating Russia and America. For it is clear that once a united Europe has been achieved by peaceful means the whole international situation changes. If the two superpowers no longer confront each other on the line of the Elbe, they will be free to indulge in common policies toward the Third World, and notably, of course, toward China. Thus a "climate of peace" may gradually be established in the Northern Hemisphere, and the eventual admission of China to the U.N. might facilitate some long-term peaceful solution of the difficulties of that great country, for it is indeed hard to see how the Chinese could in such circumstances successfully pursue any territorial claims they may have on the Soviet Union. We ought therefore to arrive at a situation in which North America, associated perhaps with Australasia and enjoying friendly relations with a united Western Europe, would find herself in a world embracing also some equivalent power in Russia and eventually even in China, which themselves would, no doubt, have close relations with the Middle East and South East Asia respectively. There would thus be three nuclear poles (or five, in the unlikely event that Europe and Japan would begin large-scale production of nuclear weapons) but not more than five in the sense of great regional politico-economic *blocs*. Naturally, if Japan ever made common cause with China that would alter the entire world balance for the worse, but it does not look, at the moment, as if there is any chance of such a development during the next twenty or thirty years.

Can we then conceive of any further politico-economic entities of the same sort of importance? Clearly there is another potential one—the Indian subcontinent. But as far as can be seen at present it looks as if India and Pakistan—or rather the Hindus and the Muslims—will be unable during the next twenty years or so to settle their differences; nor is it even certain that India will not break up into her component parts during this period. Still, it cannot be denied that there is a certain chance if not of the Indian subcontinent, at any rate of India becoming a world power during the period contemplated; and it is not to be excluded that if it does so it will possess some kind of nuclear capability, though probably not of the first order and hardly on a level with that of Europe or (conceivably) of Japan.

Elsewhere in the world there seems little prospect of many positive supra-national entities emerging out of the welter of nation-states which now exists. In the Middle East it is true that there is a common Muslim sentiment that extends from Casablanca across North Africa (if the heretic Shias are included) to the frontier of the Pakistani-Indian border, and within this area there is the more limited Arab League. It is not to be denied that there is a possibility that the Arab League, which, after all, rests to some extent on a common language, will become more united during the next twenty years or so; at the moment, however, the rivalries between its component parts are so great that this seems on the whole to be unlikely. The other three world "regions" are clearly South East Asia, South America, and Africa south of the Sahara. Here also everything suggests that no definite supra-national entity will emerge. There is indeed talk of some "Malayan" coming together which would include Indonesia, Malaysia, and the Philippines; but the structure of such a huge conglomeration is clearly not present and could hardly be built up in the time available. There may indeed be some vague political association which, it is to be hoped, would come more under Western than under Eastern influence. In the north of the region all the countries have been at one stage in history under the domination of China or, alternatively, of India. The hope would surely be that, exposed to the pressure of surrounding great powers, these states could eventually work out some scheme for friendly association with the one great power or the other. If the whole area is to avoid becoming a battlefield, this clearly will have to be done.

In Latin America much would seem to depend on whether the United States can come to terms with the revolutionary regimes which will probably come into power in some of the countries during the next twenty years. If it does, it should be possible to achieve greater cohesion between some of them than has proved possible up to now. If the Organization of American States continues—as is devoutly to be hoped—this could also be used for encouraging greater unity. Here again, it seems unlikely that anything equivalent to an international entity will emerge either in the whole of Latin America or in parts of it. Perhaps the most unlikely ground for the emergence of any new region is Africa south of the Sahara, where the tendency probably would be toward a disruption of the present "nation-states" (which are really colonial artifacts) and a reversion to tribalism of some kind, which will result in new nations emerging over a period of time.

Assuming that things work out more or less along the lines suggested, it will thus be seen that a world balance replacing the present "bipolar" system will have to be achieved through some World Authority in which the United States, the Soviet Union, China, and probably Japan, and (we must hope) a European Community, will be sitting as the permanent members, with perhaps one representative chosen from the still separate nation-states of the Arab world, the Indian subcontinent, South East Asia, South America, and Africa south of the Sahara sitting with them. Such a World Authority ought after a period of time to be able to act on some basis of majority rule. It would of course be a world *authority* and not a world *government*, since clearly the idea of direct elections to a world parliament would be inconceivable at any rate before the end of this century.

All this is only the vaguest of outlines, but provided we do succeed in setting up some supra-national authority in Europe it seems to be at least possible that this is the general way in which the world is going to evolve. The emergence of a supra-national authority in Europe might serve as an example which would encourage other areas less disposed toward a general supra-national conception to look upon it more favorably. In any case the great advantage of regionalism is that international disputes can be solved to a large extent regionally, and that the problems confronting a World Authority would simply be those concerning any clash of interest between the superpowers or the organized "regions" concerned. It could be in such circumstances that there would no longer be any real need for the General Assembly of the United Nations, though clearly it will be desirable to maintain and to reactivate the International Court. Even if this should be considered an ideal dream, what is the alternative conception for the establishment of a World Order and the construction of a real political basis for enduring peace? As I have suggested above, the principle of each for himself and the devil take the hindmost might well have worked after World War II, as indeed it worked after the Napoleonic Wars, were it not for nuclear weapons, which in themselves make any such principle a simple recipe for suicide. I can only hope that the general idea of regionalism will be examined by experts with greater academic qualifications than my own, but in the meantime we must all advance toward the unification of Europe and the eventual construction of some Atlantic Society.

Contemporary Nationalism in the Western World

I. *An Exploration*

UNTIL VERY recently the subject of contemporary nationalism in the Western world was considered more or less dead. It seemed as if the mature democracies of the West were moving slowly but surely to establishing the institutions necessary to cope with their mutual dependence. Differences arose not between nationalists and internationalists, but between federalists and functionalists, between regionalists and universalists, or between "Europeans" and "Atlanticists." Nationalism was considered a thing of the past, linked to the unspeakable atrocities committed in its name. Nationalism had to be transcended to build a new world, so it was better to believe it no longer existed.

This was made easier by the fact that nationalism is a very vague concept. It does not imply a precise reference to a phenomenon in the real world. There are as many definitions of nationalism and its object, the nation, as there are writers about nationalism.[1] Nationalism has manifested itself in many historical forms, and the consequences of nationalist strivings have been both beneficial and disastrous. The evaluation of nationalism as a social force is therefore difficult and often determined by the specific forms and consequences with which the observer has come into contact. To give a contemporary example: if the United States government could have established, beyond doubt, that Ho Chi Minh's nationalism would prove stronger than his communism—thus making Viet-Nam a buffer against China's dominance in South East Asia—his nationalism might have been applauded as vigorously as the nationalism of de Gaulle is detested.

Some more specific reasons can be given for the postwar belief that nationalism in the Western world was a negligible factor. In the first place there was a tendency to identify nationalism with the aggressiveness of Nazi Germany, Fascist Italy, and Militarist

Japan. The rational and enlightened democracies could almost by definition not be nationalist. Sentiments which by any objective standard should be called nationalist were thought of as being only patriotic.

Second, a historicist belief in the inevitability of the development of larger units than the nation-state was prevalent. It was thought that it was in the logic of historical development that both those and universal international organizations would arise in response to the functional needs of the modern industrialized and democratized world. The nationalism of the developing countries did not contradict this belief. It was thought that the phase of nation-building and the accompanying nationalism were necessary to give the cohesion to heterogeneous societies that modernization and economic development demanded. Modernization, in turn, would lead to a more rational appreciation of functional needs and to an attitude toward nationalism similar to the attitude in the West. These beliefs were not often made explicit, but they are implicit in much of the writing on regional and international integration.[2] This might also explain why the United Nations, Atlantic cooperation, and European integration were until recently all equally supported by the political élites of the Western world, without much thought being given to the possibility that these might be or become conflicting objectives.

General de Gaulle has forcibly brought nationalism into the limelight again. Although the above-mentioned historicist belief has led some commentators to call his nationalism "anachronistic," others have tried to describe it as neo-nationalism. Both descriptions stem from the idea that nationalism in the Western world has all but disappeared.

But was that idea correct? There is in any case one social scientist who never had any illusions about the disappearance of nationalism in the Western democracies. Gunnar Myrdal, in his book *Beyond the Welfare-State,* has, on the contrary, analyzed the model: "The Welfare-State is nationalistic."[3]

In the pre-World War I period the process of national integration—implying "spatial and social mobility as between regions and classes, equalisation of opportunities, cultural homogenisation and an increasingly perfected political democracy"—proceeded in a partial world community of the rich countries. Between them labor, capital commodities, and services flowed freely. Since then a series of international crises and the great depression have led to increasingly nationalistic economic policies. These, in turn, have contributed to further international disintegration, which led to even more nationalistic policies. This process is an illustration of Myrdal's well-known idea of circular causation: each change is both the cause and the effect of the other changes, with the result that the changes cumulate.

Although after World War II some effective countermeasures in the field of trade and payments were taken in the context of regional organizations within the zone of the rich countries, the trend toward national economic integration is continuing with "unabating force." In each of the rich countries economic progress is taken more or less for granted; education is continuously being improved; social mobility and sharing in the national culture increase, facilitated by better means of transportation and communication. This has made a further development of the democratic political system possible, so that it now works to bring the economic system into accord with the ideals of liberty and equality of opportunity for all.

The role of the state in economic and social life has become more and more important. From "nightwatchman" or "oppressor" the state has changed into a "provider," into the Welfare or Service state. This development has been accompanied by a modicum of national planning which has "for many reasons, almost by necessity, an autarchic tendency." Economic policies become directed "towards welfare and equality at home, full employment and stability of the national economy, without much thought being given to international integration."

But this process does not operate only at the economic level. Living in a democratic national Welfare state tends to turn people's interests inwards. Their expectations focus on the particular groups and organizations that articulate their interests and take part in the process of collective bargaining by which the decisions in the Welfare state are taken. In this way the Welfare state "builds, ever firmer, its own psychological foundations in people's valuations and expectations." And, "A growing identification with the nation-state, and with all the people within its boundaries, is thus a natural result of the development of the democratic Welfare state." Human solidarity is thereby confined to the boundaries of the nation. When international relations seem to threaten his prosperity or security, the citizen is tempted to assume a nationalistic outlook: "to avoid viewing the international development in a world perspective and from the viewpoint of his ideals of liberty and equality as applied to mankind at large, but instead to narrow his vision so as to make it easier for him to put the blame on the foreigners." "In particular," Myrdal adds, "the cold war opens the opportunity to escape responsibility by attributing all threats to a single origin, the world communist conspiracy."

According to Myrdal we must face squarely the fact that "Our democratic Welfare state in the richer countries is protective and nationalist." His remedy is not to eliminate the Welfare state, but to pose the goal of a Welfare world as the logical complement of the Welfare state and to demonstrate that the realization of this goal would be to the advantage of the existing Welfare states.[4] The great merit of Myrdal's analysis is that he focuses our attention on the structural characteristics of the modern nation-state and demonstrates how conducive these are to nationalist behavior and attitudes. The only objection one can make to Myrdal's treatment of nationalism is that he refrains from giving a description of what he understands nationalism to be. Implicit in his analysis, though, is a very broad view of nationalism as both policies and attitudes which are nation-centered, based on a narrow and short-term definition of the national interest. He defines nationalism, one might say, as thinking, attitudes, or behavior which takes the interests of *national* society rather than those of *human* society at heart. Nationalism, in Myrdal's view, contains an element of hypocrisy: it is the application of values held to be universal in a limited "national" framework. He is concerned mainly with *economic* nationalism.

But one can point to a similar process of circular causation with respect to defense. *National survival* is still held to be the ultimate goal of defense,[5] and as long as there is no immediate prospect of a World Order, which can guarantee survival, nation-states will want to defend themselves. Also, because defense implies mobilizing military power, one state's defense is often perceived as a threat to another state's survival. Nuclear weapons have as yet not changed the psychological mechanisms leading to perceptions of threat. As a statement of fact, John Herz is surely right when he points to the extreme "permeability" of the territorial state in the nuclear age.[6] Knowledge of this fact, however, has not only failed to provide us with a solution for the creation of a world-wide institutional framework capable of maintaining peace by having a monopoly of force; it has even seriously hampered defense integration on a regional scale.[7] Nuclear power has not led to the "demise" of the territorial state; it has instead provided a new symbol of national prestige for the nation-state. And the nuclear stalemate, while being a constraint for the superpowers, has provided new opportunities for independent action by the smaller ones.

This shows us that a government does not have to be guided by an explicit nationalist ideology or by specific nationalistic aims tc behave in a nationalistic manner. The structure of the Welfare state and the intractabilities of security may promote nationalistic behavior even by the most internationalist of statesmen.

But the structure of the Welfare state and the security dilemma do not exhaust the catalogue of factors contributing to nationalist attitudes and behavior. The nation-state has developed as, or from, a "national culture society,"[8] as a unit distinguished by "the complementarity or relative efficiency of communications among individuals."[9] These theoretical statements by distinguished researchers of nationalism point to the extremely complicated clusters of feelings, emotions, symbols, ideologies, role perceptions, historical experiences, and patterns of economic, social, and political communication for which the concept "nation" might be considered a shorthand description. In all nation-states nationalist ideologies are still "available": they may be picked up and used again or their premises may still be so self-evident that political issues, or political goals, may derive from them. The nation-state is commonly identified with the fatherland, with "home" in a larger sense, and for this reason commands the self-evident loyalties of its inhabitants. Individual identity and self-respect are, with few exceptions, still related to the image of their own nation and the respect it can command at home and abroad. Probing deeper than ordinary conversation, one will find in nearly every individual a shifting balance of pride and doubt about the qualities of the nation to which he belongs. Indifference about nationality is rare.

With these complexities in mind, the following descriptions of specific instances of nationalism have been written with the purpose of trying to isolate the "nationalist" aspects of the behavior, ideologies, and attitudes of a number of countries in the Western world. The emphasis is different in each: the ideology of a great actor (de Gaulle); historical experience and Welfare state nationalism (Britain); a specific historical problem (Germany); the experience and social structure of a small country (the Netherlands); attitudes (European nationalism); and the historical experience of a country which suddenly found itself a world power (the United States). The common denominator of all these aspects of nationalism is that they focus on ideas, attitudes, and behavior which presume that the nation-state is and will continue to be the most important unit of human organization. The descriptions may sometimes seem slightly one-sided, but that is a result of the perspective taken. Their purpose is to explore the varieties of contemporary nationalism in the Western world, not to give a comparative theory; yet some conclusions will be advanced.

II. *The Nation as Person and Idea: The Nationalism of General de Gaulle*

It cannot be denied that the nationalism of de Gaulle—his policies and ideology—has been beneficial for France itself. After the thirties, full of discord and feuds between the different political and social groupings, marked by an "orgy of self-laceration and doubts";[10] after the humiliation of the quick defeat by Germany; after Vichy and the occupation; after the disastrous colonial wars, Diem Bien Phu, Algeria, and the threat of civil war unleashed by the OAS, France needed someone or something to return to her a certain measure of self-respect, pride, and national cohesion. One has to admit that Stanley Hoffmann is right when he says that the "confident nation" of de Gaulle is better than the "confused and bitter" nation of the thirties and the postwar period.[11]

This judgment, however, implies a view of de Gaulle's nationalism as a means to heal the wounds of the past and as an instrument to make of France a stable, established nation-state.[12] If this were so, would the excessive nationalism characterizing de Gaulle's foreign policy have been necessary? Would it have had to be so dogmatic with respect to supranational forms of organization? It would be misleading to explain de Gaulle's nationalism purely as a pedagogical instrument in which he does not really believe. De Gaulle's nationalism is an essential and deeply ingrained part of his personality and view of the world.

De Gaulle sees himself as having been called to lead France to its destiny. He is able to perceive this destiny by the grace of his special intuition: "Toute ma vie je me suis fait une certaine idée de la France" is the first sentence of the memoirs of de Gaulle. He goes on: "The emotional side of me tends to imagine France, . . . as dedicated to an exalted and exceptional destiny. . . . But the positive side of my mind also assures me that France is not really herself unless she is in the front rank . . . . In short, to my mind, France cannot be France without greatness."[13] It would be wrong to say that de Gaulle identifies himself with France in the sense that he wants to use France for his own greatness. He sees himself as the inspiration of France, as the executor of her destiny. This gives him the right to speak for France, as he did in 1940 in London without being the "official" representative of his country: "Devant la confusion des âmes françaises, moi, Général de Gaulle, soldat et chef français, j'ai conscience de parler au nom de la France."

De Gaulle's belief in the destiny of nations implies a view of the nation as some kind of organic entity with a distinct personality. It is not this particular biological metaphor, however, which has influenced de Gaulle's thinking, but the biological metaphysics contained in the philosophical writings of Bergson. This becomes clear from de Gaulle's early and, for his political philosophy, most illuminating book, *Le Fil de l'Epée*.

For de Gaulle the nation is the only constant and immutable unit in history. Ideologies go, but nations remain: "Je me refuse à entrer dans une discussion valable sur le sujet de la querelle idéologique entre Pekin et Moscow. Ce que je veux considérer ce sont *les realités profondes qui sont humaines, nationales et par conséquent internationales.* L'étendard de l'idéologie ne couvre en realité que des ambitions."[14]

The nation is a human entity which is also superhuman because it has "duration" (Bergson's concept of time) and forms a continuous stream of life. By belonging to a nation, the individual can participate in a life transcending his own lifetime. He is thus admitted to the continuity of life, to the flow of time.

The nation, like every living being, is a center of action—not of a fixed (determined) amount of action, but of a quantity of potential action. To exhaust these potentialities fully or at least as far as possible gives the nation "grandeur" and leads her on to achieve "gloire." The intellect cannot grasp this truth; the will to "grandeur" finds its source in intuition. Intuition will guide the individual inevitably toward identification with the nation, if he wants to partake of the stream of life. The life-force (élan vital) must lead to national greatness. But national greatness is not achieved by prosperity. Prosperity is a useful result of intellectual effort, but, if prosperity and personal happiness are posited as the ends of life, stagnation and inaction are the undesirable outcome. Alfred Grosser says that for de Gaulle: "The lot of the French is not an end, but a means to improve the destiny of France."[15]

What should be the goals of the leader of France? Because the world consists of a number of nations—with different destinies and interests—foreign policy must reign supreme. As Grosser has written: "A nation may be regarded as a human entity which acts in a world made up of other such entities. In this perspective, foreign policy is the only true policy. The sole aim of internal policy is to assure order and unity, and to develop an influence to be used abroad."

The first necessity is to give the nation the maximum of "puissance": "Le profond ressort de l'activité des meilleurs et des forts est le désir d'acquérir la puissance."[16] But the nationalism of de Gaulle is not warlike or aggressive. De Gaulle's conception of the role of France has much in common with his ideas on leadership.[17] To the nations which accept France's leadership, the leader is benevolent. But France must be able to raise her voice in the concert of nations—and be listened to—because she is destined to lead. But what France does for her own greatness also serves the world. The mission of France is universal.

Apart from the leader, the nation needs an instrument of authority: the state. But the state is subordinated to the will to greatness of the nation as interpreted by the leader.[18] The state therefore should not be "une juxtaposition d'intérêts particuliers dont ne peuvent sortir jamais que de faibles compromis," but "une institution de *décision, d'action, d'ambition,* n'exprimant et ne servant que l'intérêt national."[19] Above all else, the nation needs an instrument of power: "la situation de la France a profondément changé. Ses institutions nouvelles la mettent en mesure de *vouloir* et *d'agir.* Son développement intérieur lui procure la prospérité et *la fait accéder aux moyens de la puissance.*" The only instrument of power which gives a nation rank in this age is a nuclear force. The "force de frappe" is therefore above all a necessary attribute of the nation, to be acquired by the nation with her own means. Without her own nuclear force, France would not be able to follow her destiny, because she would be hampered in the exercise of her free will by the will of others. Without a nuclear force, France cannot be really independent: "We would no longer be a European power, a sovereign nation, but simply an integrated satellite."[20]

The nation is for de Gaulle thus both the highest value and the most profound reality ("une realité profonde, qui est humaine"). Every nation has a special destiny and therefore specific interests. Human reality is "nationale et par conséquent internationale"; it is

structured on the nation-state. Federalism and supranational institutions—composed of bureaucrats and technocrats, trying to represent a fictitious common interest instead of the only real, the
national, interest—are unnatural and therefore pernicious. Integration is a bad word: nations cannot merge, for they have different
destinies and interests. If their interests coincide, they can cooper-
ate and coordinate their policies. That this is a necessity in the age
of industrialization and development is very well realized by de
Gaulle. But, in his conception, there are definite limits to the possibilities of international cooperation. There must be as little institutionalization as possible, and, when international institutions are
necessary, the final say has to remain with intergovernmental institutions. Cooperation and coordination must be based on the autonomy of the participating nations. To integrate the French nuclear force in an Atlantic defense "partnership" or "federation"
would be a crime against France, for the destinies and interests of
Anglo-Saxons and French cannot remain identical over a longer
period. This is the basis of de Gaulle's attitude, and all arguments
for the "force de frappe" based on strategic hypotheses (even
though they may be rational within their own context) are rationali-
zations of his overriding concern with "la France."

What kind of foreign policy goals have followed from de
Gaulle's type of explicit nationalist ideology?

Defenders of the Gaullist position regarding the necessity of
ending American hegemony in the Atlantic framework have often
based their defense on de Gaulle's "Europeanism." It can indeed be
said that de Gaulle is also a European "nationalist": he thinks that
Europe, as "mère de la civilisation," has a special destiny and that
Europe's great past ensures her great future. Stanley Hoffmann
has, because of this, written that "Europeaniser les Européens"
should be considered one of the most important goals of de Gaulle.[21]
But the form of the United Europe de Gaulle has wanted to create
has given sufficient foundation to the suspicions of his partners in
the Six that his European purpose was but a cover for his desire to
impose a French instead of an American hegemony on them.

De Gaulle's "Europeanism" has thus suffered from a fatal ambivalence and from considerable confusion. The relations between
French nationalism and European nationalism have never been
made clear. The only "Europe" that would be able to fulfill
de Gaulle's desire for independence from the United States is a
Europe de Gaulle cannot imagine. His insistence on the necessity

of an independent French "force de frappe" has made it much more difficult to defend his version of a political union of the Six. He could probably have attracted more support if he and his ministers had not made it absolutely clear that the French "force de frappe" can become "European" only as a protecting umbrella spread out by France over the Six, but remaining under the exclusive jurisdiction of France.

But de Gaulle's aims for Europe have not been determined solely by his European nationalism. De Gaulle's view of human reality as founded on the continuity and persistence of nations implies that lasting peace can be achieved only by some sort of "equilibrium." It is possible to explain de Gaulle's European policy and his attitude toward the United States and NATO as an attempt to hasten the change from one system of world equilibrium—the bipolar system, which cannot last because it is based on ideological rather than national solidarities—to another system in which France (and Europe) will be able to play a more important role. This has been done in a one-sided, but lucid, and very illuminating book, *L'Europe de l'Atlantique à l'Oural*, written by the theoretical economist and former president of the French European movement, René Courtin.[22]

Courtin believes that the clue to de Gaulle's foreign policy goals can be found in the seemingly elusive formula "Europe from the Atlantic to the Urals," which de Gaulle has used time and time again.[23] He thinks this implies a view of the future world equilibrium as being based on the coexistence of three great powers: in the West, the group of Anglo-Saxon nations; in the East, China; and, in the center, a reconciled greater Europe. This means that Russia must again have replaced the Soviet Union. Marxist ideology cannot change the essential qualities of the Russian nation. Russia is a "nation blanche d'Europe, conquérante d'une partie de l'Asie ... en face de la multitude jaune qu'est la Chine, innombrable et misérable, indéstructible et ambitieuse."[24] China will make claims to Siberia, the Algeria of Russia. The Urals have been chosen not only because they are the traditional geographical border of Europe, but also because the real, the white Russia stops there. The Atlantic Alliance will have to disappear: it was anyway but a consequence of the mistakes of Yalta and Potsdam, not a permanent framework in which France would find her destiny.

Courtin thinks that de Gaulle wanted to use the Europe of the Six, led by France as the only nuclear power, as a counterweight to Russia in the great European confederation to be. Germany would be lured in because it could be reunified. The attractiveness of this scheme for Russia would lie in the recognition of existing borders, the withdrawal of American troops and weapons from the continent, the dissolution of NATO, and a German pledge never to acquire nuclear weapons. The task of the great European confederation would then be the coordination of foreign policy toward the Anglo-Saxons, China, and the developing world.

Courtin even believes that de Gaulle already saw a chance to achieve this at the time he broke off the negotiations between the EEC and Britain, but that his scheme misfired completely. It seems more probable, however, that de Gaulle, in January 1963, wanted only to explain his vision of the future to the Russians to see whether they had any interest in this conception—and was rebuffed. But it is entirely plausible that de Gaulle indeed considers the kind of world equilibrium described by Courtin as the ideal situation for France to play an important role in a stable world of nation-states. De Gaulle's style of politics, and the fact that only *he* determines foreign policy, makes it possible for him to entertain both long-term objectives and goals which are intermediate from the point of view of the long-term objective, but have direct advantages in the transitory period. For example an independent "force de frappe" provides France with diplomatic and bargaining power both in the Atlantic Alliance and in the great European confederation of the future; a political union of the Six on de Gaulle's terms would enhance the power of France, could become a focus of attraction for other European countries, and could serve eventually as a counter-weight against Russia in the great European confederation. But, as it is not certain how long the thawing of the Soviet Union and the reassertion of the Russian nation will take, the transitory period might last a long time. This means that one should always provide oneself with fall-back positions; a position of leadership in the "tiers monde," good relations with Eastern Europe, the Soviet Union, and even China. Nevertheless, it seems that there is less emphasis on "Europe" now in French foreign policy than before. De Gaulle's ambitions for Europe have been frustrated, and the new world equilibrium is, in any case, distant. It seems that de Gaulle has given up wanting to change the international system and has fallen back on a policy which tries to maximize French prestige and influence in the existing international environment.

The Europe of the Six is now considered useful only as a means to give France some economic advantages. The supranational ambitions of the EEC, until recently acquiesced in because the Six might have developed into the independent political unit de Gaulle wanted it to become, must now disappear. If the European Commission were to become the strong political body which it could and if the EEC were to develop further along the lines of the Treaty of Rome, France might find itself severely limited in its liberty of action. The role of the Commission must therefore be curtailed for both ideological and practical reasons.

De Gaulle's provocation of the 1965 crisis in the Common Market[25] provides a severe test for the theory of supranational integration, which is based on the conception of a process which moves forward until the supranational and national arenas of decision-making have become inextricably linked, and which acquires its dynamism from the rewards which the participants receive.[26] The interest groups in France behave according to this theory, that is, they disapprove of de Gaulle's actions. But it is now doubtful whether the economic rewards of the supranational method—which leaves unresolved the crucial questions of human identity and solidarity which nationalism answers—will prevail over the socio-psychological rewards of nationalism from which de Gaulle derives his power.

III. *British Nationalism: "The Lion, the Ostrich and the Gentleman"*[27]

The British empire could not have been built—and certainly not maintained—if its growth had not been accompanied by the awakening of the nation and of nationalism. But, in Britain, nation and state were contained within "natural borders." British insularity is an important determining factor of the character of British nationalism. The security of the insular position has contributed to the relative smoothness with which the British political system could evolve gradually toward tolerance, freedom, and democracy. The Puritan revolution was too early to upset continuity as much as the French revolution did, and it gave Britain a national ideology: the messianic belief in the British mission to bring religious freedom and political liberty to the world. In the nineteenth century this ideology was put forward in a secularized form by John Stuart Mill, who considered the British nation to be the most suited to spread his ideas "on liberty" to the other peoples of

Europe. If British influence in the world were weakened, the cause and practice of freedom would be weakened too.[28]

A revolution was not required, however, for the political emancipation of the British people, but evolution instead of revolution has lent the British establishment its peculiar conservative and octopus-like character. This characteristic of the British social structure might have led to the complacency which made Arthur Koestler compare the British nation in peacetime with an ostrich taking its head out of the sand only in wartime to change miraculously into a lion.

Most of the British empire was built before the heyday of nationalism in the period 1870-1914. British parliamentary government, even before the French revolution, was admired and misinterpreted by Montesquieu as the "trias politica" model for France to follow. Britain led the industrial revolution: it had in London the first world financial center and the first big modern navy; it was also the first world policeman. Britain was already a *status-quo* power in the nineteenth century.

For these reasons British nationalism has never been rancorous or shrill: it has always been confident, dignified, and a bit arrogant.[29] The British are not conscious of being nationalists. A gentleman is a patriot, not a nationalist.[30]

After 1945 the lion quickly calmed down. Was it the lion or the ostrich that elected Labour? It is difficult to say: Certainly, the king of lions was deposed, but do ostriches like to experiment with nationalization? In any case, the fact that Britain was the only allied country in Europe not occupied during the war (on the Continent the resistance played an important role in the development of the European idea) made British political opinion much less inclined to see the future in terms of becoming part of a supranational entity, of a European federation. On the contrary, Britain still aspired to an independent role in world politics which over the years has been defined in different ways: as leader of the Commonwealth; as junior, but diplomatically more experienced, partner of the United States; or as mediator in the Cold War. It was much more difficult for Britain to admit decline than it was for the Continental powers, which had to start from scratch after 1945. The early decision to build a separate nuclear force was indicative of British aspirations. There were, of course, also more rational reasons[31] for the British search to remain one-up on Europe, but plain nationalism has certainly been an important cause. British hostility to supranational integration had manifested itself before the days of the Schuman plan. In the Council of Europe, itself a compromise between British pressure (the Committee of Ministers) and federalist ideas (the Consultative Assembly), the British were the leaders of the "functionalists" as opposed to the "federalists." The nationalism of the Welfare state, as referred to in the first part of this article, heavily influenced the attitude of the Labour government. According to Northedge: "There was concern in Labour Party circles lest the postwar mood in western Europe revolt against national sovereignty should sweep Britain into supranationalist arrangements at the moment when the main levers of her economy were being brought, for the first time in peace, under state control at home." Northedge mentions two other reasons for Britain's attitude toward Europe: Britain as a member of a united Europe "might be wholly unable to influence the larger forces outside Europe which were coming to shape the world as a whole" and "it was hard to believe that the Europeans . . . really had the political ability to make a fundamentally constructive advance."

Both Welfare-state nationalism and a traditional nationalist desire to keep "rank" and play a prestigious role in world politics were thus behind Britain's refusal to have anything to do with the integrative efforts undertaken on the "European Continent." The Schuman Plan, the abortive European Defense Community, and the European Economic Community were equally opposed by Britain because of their supranational ambitions. Attlee declared, for example, apropos of the Schuman Plan, "We on this side were not prepared to accept the principle that the most vital forces of this country should be handed over to an authority that is utterly undemocratic and responsible to nobody."[32] The fact that Britain had to remain "independent" was taken so much for granted by Labour and Conservative alike that serious debate on the question of joining Europe started only after the government had already taken the decision to apply for membership in the EEC.[33]

On the other hand, it is perhaps not quite fair to attribute British opposition to forming a part of a federated Europe only to stubborn nationalism. Many Britons would not object to becoming part of an Atlantic federation and some would not even mind if Britain were to become the fifty-first state of the United States.[34] As John Mander remarks: "Frenchmen are foreigners: Americans are not. It is irrational that Englishmen feel this way, but they do."[35] It is not only joining a *supranational* Europe that Britain objected to, but also joining *Europe*. But there is a certain difference between Labour and Conservative in this respect. The Conservative government took the decision—mainly defended on economic grounds, and without spelling out the political implications—to link Britain to Europe, but Macmillan went out of his way to save the formal independence of the British deterrent at the ill-fated conference at Nassau. And Conservative defenders of the "independent" British deterrent often sound exactly like Gaullists, although they claim to want the "extra diplomatic weight" that the bomb insures mainly to sit in on disarmament negotiations. Labour, on the other hand, was much more ready to give up the independence of the British deterrent—in return for more influence on American decision-making. But, with respect to Europe, Labour has been —no doubt also for domestic political reasons—more nationalistic than the Conservatives. In a speech given at the Labour Party Conference in October 1962 Gaitskell commented that Britain's entry into EEC might be "the end of Britain as an independent nation" and that "as a province of Europe" Britain could not remain the "mother country" of the Commonwealth. To join EEC "would mark the end of a thousand years of history."[36] As Nora Beloff rightly remarks: "The European issue had muddled things up."[37]

The new Labour government at first conformed to the predictions of those Europeans opposed to British entry into the EEC by deciding on the 15 per cent surcharge on imports without prior consultation, not even with its EFTA partners. This "nationalistic" behavior—apart from violating EFTA—was considered contrary to the postwar European code of economic policy. How could a government like that understand the "community method"? But it seems that the Labour government has now made a more realistic assessment of the future of British relations with Europe. And there are no indications that Britain might want to follow the pattern of de Gaulle's nationalist policies, that is, exploit the international constellation for its own ends. The 1961-1962 debate has in any case had the healthy effect of making the alternatives for Britain much clearer.

IV. *The Seduction of the Nation-State: Nationalism in Germany*

The unification of Germany in 1870-71 was supported by popular German nationalism, but brought about by Bismarck with the interests of the Prussian state in mind. On the basis of the linguistic definition of the German nation—the ideal model of the nation according to Rupert Emerson[38]—however, the German nation-state did not come into being before Hitler's "Grossdeutschland" in 1938. Only then were all those settlements considered as German (the German-speaking part of Switzerland being an obvious exception) caught within German borders. But, as Lemberg remarks, precisely that solution demonstrated that a German nation-state comparable with the French or Spanish nation-states did not belong to the realm of possibilities.[39] It did in any case last only seven years. But the idea of the German nation-state lived on.

Immediately after World War II, however, every German of good will was consciously anti-nationalist. This feeling was so strong in the younger generation that it prohibited any identification with Germany and, therefore, also with the society in which these young Germans had to live. "Ohne mich" (without me) was a widespread answer to a past for which they felt the German nation as a whole should be held responsible. European unification therefore had a particular significance for Germany. On the one hand, "Europe" could be welcomed by many Germans as a new fatherland; on the other hand, because the supranational principle made it possible for Germany to be accepted as an equal partner in the new European organizations, the Germans could feel that "Europe" was not forced upon them. "Europe" not only provided the Germans with a new focus of identification, but also returned to them some self-respect *as Germans*. The enthusiasm for Europe has for these reasons been very strong in Germany.

But it was difficult for Germany to enter Europe without any qualms. Germany was burdened with an old-fashioned nineteenth-century problem that also had to be solved. According to nationalist doctrine, state and nation should coincide: and, since Germany was divided, "reunification" was both morally and politically desirable and necessary. West Germany was an unnatural state, and the G.D.R. did not even exist. Adenauer once declared (during his visit to Moscow): "The division of Germany is abnormal. It is against human and divine law and nature."[40] This nationalist assertion seems so self-evident that most Germans would be reluctant to consider reunification a nationalist issue.

The German national problem has regrettably been intensified by the ideological struggle and by the kind of regime the G.D.R. had to suffer. It was furthermore both symbolized and intensified by the divided former capital, Berlin. But the successive German governments have not given priority to "reunification." They have tried—within the framework of tight relationships with the movement toward European integration and narrow Atlantic relations—to let the political goals of the Atlantic allies coincide with those of Germany.[41] But, they have not seriously tried to dispose of the "nationalist" problem by replacing the goal of "reunification" by the goal of achieving for the East Germans an existence worthy of human beings.[42] On the contrary, even in German trains, one can still read that there are parts of Germany—of which the borders of 1937 are drawn—"zur Zeit unter Fremdverwaltung" (temporarily administered by foreigners).

But "reunification" has been promoted more by words than by deeds. German foreign policy should, according to its makers, not only be a "reaction to the behavior of the environment . . . but also a reaction to the German past."[43]

Given the definition of "reunification" as at least to a large extent the nationalist problem of recreating a German nation-state, it is possible to use reunification as a thermometer to measure German nationalism: when public and political concern about reunification increases, the temperature of German nationalism rises. That this is in fact the case can, apart from the results of recent public opinion polls, also be concluded from the efforts of German politicians to make nationalism respectable again.[44] To give one example of many: Defense Minister Von Hassel declared that he would like to see an increase of "Heimatliebe" (love of the fatherland) and added: "How open the world may be and how far the free nations may go in their cooperation, only the soil of the fatherland can give the solid basis for personal uprightness and political behavior. The abstract idea does not have the power to bring men and peoples together."[45]

To the desire for reunification and the need for a new German self-respect, as forces which might lead to a resurgence of nationalism, should the influence of the example of de Gaulle on German political thinking be added? "Why shouldn't Germany start pursuing a more active foreign policy directed mainly to the defense of her own interests?" One finds this attitude primarily among the politically interested of the young generation.[46] The so-called German "Gaullists," however—their most important representatives being Strauss and zu Guttenberg—do not defend a nationalist policy in this sense. They do not advocate German behavior modeled on de Gaulle's foreign policy, but they want what they conceived of as a Gaullist Europe, politically and militarily strong and less dependent on the United States. But one cannot separate this desire from their criticism of the United States. They think that the United States, by wanting to maintain a détente in its relations with the Soviet Union, will be forced to accept the *status quo* of a divided Germany and so act against the German national interest, which they interpret as reunification.[47] The successive German governments, however, have certainly not been led by a nationalist ideology. On the other hand, German policy toward the EEC has often been hesitant, and the German government has— as have all the other member governments—usually held back from widening the powers of the European Commission. To conclude: German nationalism after the war has understandably been very weak, but there are disconcerting danger signals. (Mr. Strauss's raising of the spectre of a new Hitler if Germany were not treated as equal in the nuclear field has been a recent addition.) The future of German nationalism will very much depend on the evolution of domestic politics and the treatment by the German government and political parties of the reunification issue.

V. *The Nationalism of Small Nations: Dutch Nationalism*

There is a qualitative difference between the position of nations which, because of the nature of their nationalism, their history, their geographic position, and their power potential, are able to fulfill—or to aspire to—an independent role in world politics and nations which are forced to link their destiny to a large whole.[48] It is, therefore, necessary to give at least one example of the latter category, for which I have chosen a country with which I am reasonably familiar.

It can be—and has been—maintained that Great-Netherlands (including most of Belgium and part of the Northwest of France) is a more "natural" nation than the Netherlands. The well known historian Pieter Geyl, after a polemic against the "Belgian" historian Henri Pirenne, published in 1930 the first volume of his *Geschiedenis van de Nederlandse Stam*, which, although "stam" means literally "tribe," can best be translated as "History of the Netherlands Nation."[49] (Geyl could, of course, not use the word "nation" because it would seem as if he had written a book about the Netherlands, whereas with "stam" he meant the area where

Dutch was spoken.) Geyl tried to demonstrate that the links between North and South had been much stronger—politically, culturally, and economically—than was commonly supposed and that the separation had been due to accidental, mainly strategic circumstances. The implication was that the "real" nation still existed, but did not coincide with the state boundaries.

The fact that this was written as late as 1930 demonstrates that irredentist nationalism has been extraordinarily weak in the Netherlands. There has never been strong support for the Flemish movement in the Netherlands. During World War I the Flemish "activists" turned in desperation to Germany for support—which was repeated by the "Flemish National League" (VNV) during World War II. In the Netherlands only historians, writers—one of the best prewar literary journals was called *Groot Nederland* ("Great Netherlands")—and national-socialist and fascist groups showed interest in the Flemish cause.[50] Why? Apart from the historical development as described by Geyl, a possible answer to this question may be found in the Dutch social structure. Dutch society is characterized by the phenomenon of pillarization:[51] the whole of social and political life is still organized on the basis of religious and quasi-religious affiliations. But this phenomenon is the consequence of the struggle for emancipation of three religious and political-ideological movements: Catholics, Workers (Socialists), and Orthodox-Protestants against the Liberal-Protestant patrician establishment. I would suggest that all the energies of the emancipating groups, which otherwise could have turned to "nationalist" causes, were consumed in this struggle, whereas the patrician establishment could not care less about the Catholic peasants of the Flemish provinces of Belgium.

In its foreign policy, the Netherlands followed a policy of strict neutrality from 1830 until 1940. Even Hitler could not change that. In 1939, the majority of the Dutch population, including government and political élite, still believed that the Netherlands would be able to keep out of the war.[52] Dutch nationalism therefore took the form of moral complacency, of the feeling that Dutch peacefulness was due to moral virtue and a superior governmental and legal system. The Netherlands has a famous tradition of international law based on the excellent legal faculties of the Dutch universities, but has no tradition of political science or the study of international relations.

After 1945, the break with the past was complete. The Dutch

foreign minister, van Kleffens, declared in the plenary session of the United Nations preparatory conference in San Francisco:

We are ready to accept certain limitations of that more or less complete freedom of action which hitherto has characterized a sovereign State. We should like to see those limitations accepted in the same measure by all States, great and small. If this cannot be obtained at once, and if, together with the other medium and smaller states, we are to set an example in this respect, we shall be proud to do it.[53]

In the Dutch constitution a provision has subsequently been enacted which makes it possible for the Dutch government to give by agreement legislative, executive, and judicial competences to supranational or international organizations (art. 67). Thereafter, the Netherlands has consistently supported (and stimulated: the Messina Conference) European integration, Atlantic cooperation, and international organization.

But the advent of General de Gaulle on the European political scene has brought the Dutch government into serious difficulties. The Dutch do not see Europe as a new fatherland, but conceive of a functional relation between European integration and Atlantic cooperation as two means of achieving a closer bond between the nations of the Western world (of which Atlantic cooperation should have—at least in the near future—priority). But the nationalist de Gaulle has awakened nationalist feelings in the Netherlands too. It is easily acceptable to see one's future as part of a supranational Europe, with ample guarantees for being able to influence the decision-making process, or as part of an Atlantic defense federation led by the benevolent giant on the other side of the ocean. But the prospect of being part of a European political union, dominated by an old-fashioned nationalist or maybe later by a Germany hungry for reunification, makes the Dutch think—and sometimes say—"over our dead bodies." In defense of the Dutch position, "balance of power" arguments sometimes turn up: The leading newspaper *Nieuwe Rotterdamse Courant* wrote, for example, after Labour won the British elections, that this would not have to influence the negative Dutch attitude with respect to a political union of the Europe of the Six, "because it has always been and still remains a Dutch interest, that our country maintains a certain balance in its relation with the three surrounding big states" and "even a supranational Europe should have an internal equilibrium." This attitude comes close to that of de Gaulle but is in absolute opposition to his political goals, because the parts of the desired equilibrium are different. But precisely for Gaullists it should be easy to understand how deep Dutch opposition to a Gaullist Europe goes.

VI. *European Nationalism: Supra-nationalism or Anti-Americanism?*

Whether or not it will be possible to call a European federation into being without a nationalism based on the idea of a nation "Europe" is still an open question. But such a nationalism does not exist at the moment. There is no widespread political movement which has as its main goal the making of a new national state out of "Europe." This fact is, no doubt, connected with the difficult problem of the geographical delimitation of "Europe." The Europe of the Six, in any case, "are not—they are not even in the process of becoming—a national community."[54] It seems difficult to conceive of the Europe of the Six as a prospective nation. Stanley Hoffmann discusses the postulate "that Europe is not only a geographical expression but an entity capable of overcoming its divisions . . . ." Although he later speaks of the need for "a sort of collective European nationalism," he does not mention the postulate of a European nation.[55] The explanation for this omission can again be only the arbitrary geographical delimitation of the Europe of the Six.

But it is possible to speak of European nationalism in a negative sense: as an attempt to consolidate the uniqueness and superiority of Europe as "mère de la civilisation" (de Gaulle) and to return to the European countries as a united Europe the power "which it deserves" by making Europe militarily and diplomatically independent of the United States. This type of European nationalism is negative because its only content is the postulate of European distinctiveness from the United States, which turns but too easily into outright anti-Americanism. In fact, anti-Americanism more often than not contains a reference to Europe rather than to the separate nations, perhaps because it is felt that only the resources of superiority of the whole of Europe can justify anti-American assertions.

The first phase of European nationalism in the form of anti-Americanism occurred in the immediate postwar period, when it was demonstrated that Europe could not recover without the aid of the United States. As Max Beloff says: "We must admit that

much of the early propaganda for the European idea had a definitely anti-American flavour and that the idea of resisting 'Ameri-
canization' [was] part of it."⁵⁶ Europeans asserted that political
and economic power do not determine the *real* value of a country:
spiritual and cultural achievements are much more important.⁵⁷
Americans were gum-chewing barbarians, bad-mannered, rude, and
materialistic. Everything that embellishes life and makes it worth
living comes from Europe. The Americans were also considered
politically naive and diplomatically inexperienced: these do-
gooders had much to learn from the Europeans. In this way both
right and left could partake of anti-Americanism. The left had
the added reason of holding the Americans largely responsible
for the cold war. The right disapproved of American support for
independence movements in the colonies and became livid when
the United States opposed the Suez adventure of Britain and
France. Anti-Americanism has been particularly strong in France,
according to Michel Crozier, partly because "America, whose
universalistic ideal is so close to the French, seemed in the process of taking over what used to be the glory of French culture."⁵⁸

The European idea has, over the years, been fed by the compensation ideology which I have called European nationalism. A
typical nationalist instrument is also the rewriting of history, which,
for Europe, has been done by scholars like Henri Brugmans and
Denis de Rougemont. Nationalist attitudes without a nation to
refer to is perhaps the best description of current European nationalism. Although Hallstein might go a little too far when he says
"Everything that has been done in the field of European unification
is in the last analysis based on the objective to return to Europe a
role in accordance with its traditions, possibilities and self-
respect,"⁵⁹ it is certainly true that many "Europeans" cherish not
only the idea of a European federation, but also the ideal of a
powerful Europe.

VII. *American Nationalism: The Power Without Glory*

American nationalism has, for obvious reasons, not been able to
refer itself to the attributes of the nation used by the various nationalisms in Europe: a grandiose history and culture, common
ancestors and language, and a classical literature and religion.⁶⁰
But a "melting pot" society still needs an ideology to foster national

cohesion. What else could this be but the belief in a special mission? It is possible, however, to discern in the beginning of American history two elements in the American national ideology. Living in a "new world" implied not only the possibility of building an exemplary society based on individual freedom and equality, but also the idea of the "manifest destiny" of the United States to spread the American "nation" over the whole American continent.[61] But the last element lost much of its importance after the "Frontier" had reached the Pacific. Thereafter, only the idea of a special—and universal—mission of the American nation remained.[62] America should bring freedom and democracy to the peoples of the world by example, education, and influence. The American intervention in two world wars was legitimized by the belief in the American mission: see Wilson's fourteen points and, in a somewhat weakened form, the Atlantic Charter. After World War II, the American national ideology remained operative as the solid foundation on which American involvement in the affairs of the world was based. This ideological basis did not cause any embarrassment for the role of the United States in Europe, where the American commitment to defend freedom against modern totalitarianism, at least for a time, had content and significance. But the American mission to defend or bring freedom to other parts of the world is becoming rather hard to defend as the difficulty of defining American objectives in Viet-Nam has demonstrated. In a recent, more sophisticated implicit definition of the American mission, one therefore sees the replacement of "freedom" by "international stability."[63]

The idea that America is the model of a democratic society has also contributed to American support for European unification: a United States of Europe would not only be the best way to get rid of the disastrous nationalisms of the separate European powers, but would also imply the emulation of the American political system, and thus democracy. In August 1948, the State Department declared that the United States "strongly favors the progressively closer integration of the free nations of western Europe . . . it does not make sense to us to contemplate a democratic Europe attempting economic unity without political agreement."[64] Lemberg thinks that this American feeling of superiority in the postwar period has contributed to the development of a compensation ideology in Europe, to the ideas which I have called European nationalism.[65]

After World War II, the sudden global responsibility of the United States and the struggle against communist power and ideology have also led to the continuous frustration of those who took the American national ideology really seriously. The fact that America was not omnipotent, and that her superior nuclear arsenal was of very little positive use, was difficult for these people to bear. True believers always have to attribute occurrences they do not like to esoteric causes: and so the federal government, and especially the State Department, must be part of an "un-American" communist conspiracy. The supporters of the new radical right —as the McCarthyites before them—are not only extremely conservative, but also extremely nationalistic. But not only the rightist fringe suffers from frustration. Disillusionment with allies and aid is a constant and recurring danger for American foreign policy. The American national ideology implies a certain self-righteousness and a penchant for "dramatic" results. Both can be highly dangerous: the first in relations with allies and the second in the administration and the defense of foreign aid programs. To be the strongest, but probably also the most constrained, power in the world is not easy, and the American national ideology certainly does not contribute to the acceptance of that situation.

If one also defines as nationalism the unwillingness of a country to take part in supranational organizations or to accept in other ways certain limitations of sovereignty, the United States has certainly remained more nationalist than most European countries. A good example is the declaration with which the United States accepted the compulsory jurisdiction of the International Court of Justice, which contains the reservation that this shall not apply to: "disputes with regard to matters which are essentially within the domestic jurisdiction of the United States of America *as determined by the United States of America.*"[66]

Neither has the United States made it clear that it would be willing to go further than inter-governmental cooperation in an Atlantic framework. It is always being said that Congress would never accept genuine sharing of competences in the fields of economics and defense with Europe unless it were forced to do so. Because of this attitude, the unofficial conference of NATO parliamentarians could not evolve into a NATO parliamentary assembly. But there is no reason to believe that the American government is more disposed to relinquishing sovereignty, especially in the fields of foreign policy and defense.

VIII. *Some Concluding Remarks on Nationalism and World Order*

The preceding descriptions have been an attempt to demonstrate the persisting significance of nationalism—ideas, attitudes, behavior—in the group of nation-states which, according to all the typologies of development and modernization, are the most advanced. These were thought to be the most likely candidates to transcend nationalism and the nation-state; and, for some time, it appeared that they would. In the period 1961-1962—when Britain was negotiating with the EEC—it was not terribly farfetched to view EEC as the nucleus and catalyst for a process of functional international integration: European integration would lead to Atlantic partnership and to institutionalized relations between the West and various regional groups of developing nations, which would then be forced to organize themselves. More and more "interests" in integration would be created, and these would form the secure foundation for a future world order. This seemed a relevant if not a realistic utopia.

But what Pierre Hassner has aptly called "la surprise nationaliste" has proved this vision to have been an illusion.[67] But the Gaullist vision—that it would be possible to reconcile French and European nationalism through the creation of an "independent" European confederation—has also proved to be an illusion. The effect of his explicit nationalism has been to rule out political union of the Six.

To put the European example in more general terms: even when the government of a country is not led by an explicitly nationalist ideology, there are in every nation certain dominant views of the most desirable future for itself and its environment. When a group of nations agrees on establishing a "common market" with certain attributes of supranationality, not only might they do this for different reasons and with different motives, but their views of the future of the possible political outcome of such a venture might differ so radically that, instead of getting politically closer because of their common enterprise, they might be driven apart. These views of the future are connected with the respective nationalisms of the participants, which implies that it does not exactly help when one of them starts basing its policy on nationalist criteria first. When this is one of the more prominent partners, the nationalist sensibilities of the others are soon awakened too. Ultimate goals then become more important than pragmatic progress. Attitudes polarize, and progress is halted. Whether it is possible to generalize on the basis of this example or not, it does show that, for a consideration of the feasibility of alternative international or supranational structures, the precise content of the different nationalisms, namely the views of the world and the future which they imply, can be important.[68] It also shows the danger of explicit nationalism: it has a boomerang effect.

From the discussion in the above sections it seems to follow that as long as nation-states exist—or, rather, as long as states exist, since states will try to create nations out of their populations, as the new states, especially those in Africa, so clearly demonstrate—nationalism will remain alive, or at least dormant. Since nationalism wants to separate or to keep separate, it seems almost by definition disintegrative, dysfunctional, for world order. But this statement needs to be qualified. Nationalism is only one of the potential sources of international conflict. We have lived since 1945 in a world dominated by tension not so much between nationalisms as between ideologies. Ideological differences—although they have not prevented (probably as a result of the nuclear stalemate) the maintenance of a minimum world order (we survive)[69] —are still the most important potential causes of conflict, especially because they have entered into symbiotic relationships with the nationalisms of the superpowers. By disrupting ideological bloc solidarities and loyalties, the nationalisms which reassert themselves in Western and Eastern Europe alike might contribute to weakening the ideologies themselves—especially the perception of the enemy which they contain, but not necessarily the values which rule domestic politics. They then might actually contribute to strengthening the existing world order. One might express this in more general terms by saying that under certain conditions nationalism might be functional for world order.[70] From this statement it is but one step—but an unjustified one on the basis of the existing empirical material—to reassert the claims of nineteenth-century liberal nationalism in a somewhat more sophisticated form. The reasoning goes as follows:

The best possible world order humanity will be able to achieve will have to be based on states. But the requirements of legitimacy, loyalty, solidarity, and development make it necessary that states be based on nations. If this is not the case, domestic conflicts will erupt, and in the present world these have dangerous international implications. Nationalism gives citizens and political élites alike a firm sense of identity and self-respect. Stable mature nation-states, made up of stable mature individuals, will not harbor aggressive tendencies. Humanity's best chance for achieving a stable world order is, therefore, to create a world of stable nation-states, inspired by creative nationalisms. And, if some fear still remains that nation-states might not always stay stable, let each nation have its own nuclear force to deter military adventures of others; then peace will be assured.

This utopia is refuted by the historical development of nationalism. The liberal nationalist, well-intentioned though he may have been, was a sorcerer's apprentice. The development of a nationalism has never been halted at its point of "maturity," at the point when it fulfills only the positive functions of identity, self-respect, solidarity, and legitimacy procurement and none of the negative functions of being a source of international conflict (through projection of feelings of superiority, missionary zeal, desire for hegemony or spheres of influence or, at its worst, through imperialism), of oppressing other nations or minorities, and of prohibiting more rational—regional or international—forms of organization. Neither has it been proved that nationalism is the *only* way of procuring identity, self-respect, and the like. There are other forms of organization (churches, political parties, voluntary groups) and also certain kinds of activity (science, art, literature) which can, and already do, take the place of the nation in this respect. To admit the positive functions of nationalism, therefore, does not have to imply its endorsement. For this reason, I disagree strongly with Stanley Hoffmann's defense of (de Gaulle's) nationalism, which sounds so perfectly reasonable:

As long as no form of social organisation has yet appeared to replace the nation-state, or as long as the "general society of mankind," whose absence Rousseau noted, is not in sight, the only kinds of nationalism that are unquestionably evil are aggressive nationalism and a nationalism of resentment—Hitler's partook of both. Barring these, the alternative to a sane and sound nationalism of self-respect or pride is apt to be defeatism.[71]

I do not see why the alternative of functional and international integration has to imply defeatism. My own negative attitude toward nationalism is also explained by the fact that it offers no intellectual satisfaction. Nationalism nearly always implies looking for the mistakes of others and glossing over one's own faults. Discussions with nationalists are therefore usually singularly fruitless and annoying. One is often forced into an exchange of accusations, justifications, and apologies. Nationalism leads to a falsified view of the world and may therefore corrupt the best of intentions.[72]

But no matter how strongly one may disapprove of nationalism, it remains to be said that it still has much stronger assets than internationalism. The international integration ideology can offer only a utopia, a "process," and universal values (the same as are being applied within national societies) as the basis for its appeal. Nationalism as an integration ideology has a much stronger foundation in language, culture, history, assertions of independence, a sense of "home," and a richness of symbols. The regional movement that can appeal to nationalist feelings and symbols—the European movement—has better chances for success than a similar movement operating in the same setting—the Atlantic movement—which is unable to do this.

In the search for alternatives to the anarchic structure of decision-making by nation-states, we should not limit ourselves to looking for institutional solutions. We should perhaps also try to strengthen the alternatives to nationalism.

REFERENCES

1. For a useful, but deliberately confusing, survey of the most important definitions, see Karl W. Deutsch, *Nationalism and Social Communication* (Cambridge, Mass., 1954), pp. 1-14. A systematic analysis of the semantic confusion surrounding nationalism and related concepts and the ideological use made thereof is given in Frederick Hertz, *Nationality in History and Politics* (London, 1944), Ch. I.

2. Not all writers have accepted this historicist belief as given. There can indeed be made a strong case for the idea that there are strong socioeconomic and political forces at work in the European democracies leading to the acceptance of supranational institutions as a stable form of government. See Ernst B. Haas, "Technocracy, Pluralism and the New Europe," in Stephen R. Graubard (ed.), *A New Europe?* (Boston, 1964), pp. 62-89; for a thorough analysis of the relation between functional needs and institutional international integration, see Ernst B. Haas, *Beyond the Nation-State* (Stanford, Calif., 1964).

3. Gunnar Myrdal, *Beyond the Welfare State* (New Haven, Conn., 1960), p. 159. The following quotations are from an earlier version, *Economic Nationalism and Internationalism* (Melbourne, 1957).

4. For a critique of Myrdal's "functionalist utopia," see Ernst B. Haas, *Beyond the Nation-State, op. cit.*, pp. 461-464.

5. For some time it seemed as if the goal of national survival had been re-placed in the West by anti-communism, or in the positive formulation: the defense of Western values. This ideological cohesion, making a partly supranational defense effort possible, is now under severe strain. Even in a staunchly "Atlanticist" country like the Netherlands, in a recent publica-tion the question, "Why do we defend ourselves?" was, after an analysis of the possible supranational motivations, answered by stating "to maintain our national, our own Dutch identity." H. J. A. Hofland. "Waarom ver-dedigen wy ons," published by "Stichting Volk en Verdediging" (Founda-tion "People and Defense"), 1964.

6. John H. Herz, "Rise and Demise of the Territorial State," *World Politics*, Vol. 9, No. 4 (July 1957), pp. 477-493. Herz's proposition that the terri-torial state became the basic protective unit and therefore the basic political unit in Europe after 1648, because of the "hard shell of fortifications" built along the respective borders, seems to me to need historic verification. His only reference is to Meinecke's "Die Idee der Staatsraison in der Neuere Geschichte."

7. Since the United States could be penetrated by Soviet nuclear weapons, the argument that the United States would not use nuclear weapons to defend Europe has constantly been used to justify national deterrents. Ray-mond Aron has written: "Les alliances évolueront vers des communautés ou elles se dissoudront: elles ne reviendront pas aux pratiques pré-atomiques." (*Le Grand Débat* [Paris, 1963], p. 272.)

8. Florian Znaniecki, *Modern Nationalities* (Urbana, Ill., 1952).

9. Karl W. Deutsch, *op. cit.*, p. 162.

10. Stanley Hoffmann, "The French Political Community," in *In Search of France* (Cambridge, Mass., 1963), p. 35. On the thirties see especially pp. 21-34.

11. Stanley Hoffmann, "Cursing de Gaulle is Not a Policy," *The Reporter*, Vol. 31, No. 3 (January 30, 1964).

12. That stability is not de Gaulle's major goal also follows from his neglect of the problem of the stability of the French political system after his own death.

13. Citation from the translation of *L'Appel*, "The Call to Honour," (London, 1955), p. 9.

14. Press conference, July 29, 1963. *Le Monde*, July 31, 1963. My italics in this and the following quotations.

15. Alfred Grosser, "General de Gaulle and the Foreign Policy of the Fifth Republic," *International Affairs*, Vol. 39, No. 2 (April 1963), pp. 198-213.

16. Charles de Gaulle, *Le Fil de L'Epée*, Ed. 10-18 (Paris, no date), p. 39.

17. *Le Fil de l'Epée* contains a host of prescriptions for leadership, which read as descriptions of de Gaulle's present behavior.

18. There is also a definite streak of Rousseau in de Gaulle's thought. In his press conference of May 31, 1960, he cited the Rousseauan premise: "Man limited by his nature is infinite in his desires." (Cited in Edgar S. Furniss, *De Gaulle and the French Army* [New York, 1964], p. 247.)

19. Press conference, July 29, 1963. *Le Monde,* July 31, 1963. The disdainful remark against "les intérêts particuliers" is of course directed against political parties and pressure groups. The politics of the "end of ideology" is sacrilege to de Gaulle's conception of politics which for him is the art of action as guided by intuition.

20. Cited in Furniss, *op. cit.,* p. 106. Furniss goes on to explain how attractive statements like this are for the anti-Gaullist nationalists, who were bitterly opposed to de Gaulle over his "abandonment of Algeria." He cites Jacques Gagliardi: "My comrades and myself . . . passionately resisted the abandonment of Algeria. We nourish no excessive tenderness for the Chief of State. . . . But de Gaulle for some years will constitute the only obstacle to the dilution of France in a vast Atlantic market where we will only be a subsidiary of the United States." Furniss thinks that the new weapons and the new military mission, that is, "the contribution of the army to de Gaulle's European statecraft" (p. 243), have provided the French military with a new sense of purpose, thus solving de Gaulle's difficulties with the rebellious army over Algeria.

21. "De Gaulle, l'Europe et l'Alliance," *Esprit,* Vol. 31, No. 318 (June 1963), p. 1058.

22. Paris, 1963.

23. Courtin has collected thirty pages of declarations of de Gaulle concerning this "formule aveuglante de clarté" (pp. 112-142). For a recent statement of his explanation of the French attitude toward German reunification, see his press conference of February 4, 1965. (Ambassade de France, Service de Presse et d'Information, Speeches and Press Conferences, No. 216, p. 12).

24. Press conference of November 10, 1959. Cited in Courtin, *op. cit.,* p. 123.

25. For this view of the events there is support in a statement by de Gaulle which was made in a conversation with the former President of the High Authority of ECSC, René Mayer, who started to tell de Gaulle how much he had learned from his experiences in Luxemburg. De Gaulle cut him short by saying, "Eh bien! Maintenant il faut tout oublier. J'efface tout et on recommence." *Le Monde,* September 16, 1965.

26. This theory was first developed in Ernst B. Haas, *The Uniting of Europe* (Stanford, Calif., 1958). It has been refined and applied to the EEC by Leon N. Lindberg, *The Political Dynamics of European Integration* (Stanford, Calif., 1963); and by Ernst Haas himself in *Technocracy, Pluralism and the New Europe, op. cit.*

27. The metaphor of the lion and the ostrich was taken from Arthur Koestler's

introduction to the special "state of the nation" issue of *Encounter*. "Suicide of a Nation?" Vol. 21, No. 7 (July 1963).

28. Eugen Lemberg (*Nationalismus*, Vol. I [Reinbek bei Hamburg, 1964], p. 127) points to the emigration of the Puritan nationalist ideology to the United States. One could add that Mill's argument is still being echoed often in Washington.

29. Not long after the end of the Hundred Years' War, an Italian envoy to the English court observed that Englishmen "think that there are no other men than themselves; and, whenever they see a handsome foreigner they say he looks like an Englishman." Cited in Sir Reginald Coupland, *Welsh and Scottish Nationalism* (London, 1954), p. 7.

30. The Earl of Sandwich, writing in the *Observer* as part of a series of articles called "What's Left for Patriotism," January 27, 1963, states explicitly that patriotism "is not the same as nationalism" and "In fact, there is nothing 'wrong' about patriotism. It is natural and healthy. . . . But what can a man feel about a group of nations? . . . Human nature does not permit the extension of this basic emotion to a series of initials such as EEC."

31. Among those, during the period of Labour government, domestic political reasons. For the history of British relations with European unity see for the period to 1954, F. S. Northedge, *British Foreign Policy. The Process of Adjustment 1945-1961* (London, 1962), Ch. 5, "Britain and European Unity," pp. 122-167; and, for the period after 1954, see Miriam Camps' fascinating *Britain and the European Community 1955-1963* (Princeton, N. J., 1964).

32. Cited in Karl Kaiser, *EWG und Freihandelszone* (Leiden, 1963), p. 72.

33. Miriam Camps rightly considers this to have been one of the main weaknesses in the British negotiating position, *op. cit.*, p. 518.

34. For example, Kingsley Amis in the *Observer*, January 20, 1962.

35. John Mander, *Great Britain or Little England* (Boston, 1964), p. 21.

36. Cited in Nora Beloff, *The General Says No* (London, 1963), p. 140.

37. *Ibid.*, p. 141. The muddle is very well reflected in the *Encounter* inquiry among British intellectuals. "Going Into Europe" (December 1963-March 1964). Even though the result was 77 for, 17 against, and 16 indifferent or undecided, the motives for going in were often "nationalist" in the sense that only Britain was considered to be able to pull EEC away from its dangerous "inward-looking" course and to save the Continent for democracy.

38. Rupert Emerson, *From Empire to Nation* (Boston, 1962), p. 132.

39. Lemberg, *op. cit.*, p. 133.

40. As cited in Emerson, *op. cit.*, p. 430.

41. In the Berlin question, this policy found its apex in Kennedy's speech in Berlin: "Ich bin ein Berliner."

42. As has been proposed by Karl Jaspers. See for example his "Freiheit und Wiedervereinigung," in Hans-Adolf Jacobson and Otto Stenzl (eds.), *Deutschland und die Welt* (Munchen, 1964), pp. 189-197.

43. *Deutschland und die Welt, op. cit.,* p. 12.

44. They seem to have two reasons for this effort: to raise the low esteem in which the German army is held by the population at large and, paradoxically, not to let the younger generation lose interest in reunification.

45. Cited in *Die Welt,* February 7, 1964.

46. According to Albrecht von Kessel, "Zweifel oder Bewunderung," *Die Welt,* September 30, 1964.

47. See K. T. Baron von und zu Guttenberg, "NATO and the Need for a New Policy," in David S. Collier and Karl Glaser (eds.), *Western Integration and the Future of Eastern Europe* (Chicago, 1964).

48. See the remarks of Achille Albonetti, "The New Europe and the West," in *A New Europe? op. cit.,* pp. 1-37 (esp. pp. 13 and 23).

49. P. C. Geyl, *Geschiedenis van de Nederlandse Stam* (Amsterdam, 1930-37), 3 vols.

50. For the latter, see the brilliant study of I. Schoffer, *Het Nationaal-Socialistische beeld van de Geschiedenis der Nederlanden* (The National-Socialist Image of the History of the Low Countries), (Arnhem, no date [after 1955]). The Dutch Nazi leader, Mussert, hoped to become fully accepted by Hitler as "leader" of the greater Netherlands: "Then it will be possible to build something really great: The Dutch imperium, stretching from the Dollart to Kales [Dutch for Calais], with the Indies, the Congo, friend of South Africa, and cooperating closely with the big German brother."

51. With the translation of "verzuiling" into "pillarization" I follow the example of William Petersen, "A Nation Adrift, or On Which Course," in *Sociologische Gids,* Vol. II (January-April 1964), pp. 84-91.

52. When the Dutch military attaché in Berlin, Major Sas, warned the Dutch government of the pending invasion in the first days of May 1940, he was not believed by the government.

53. Cited by I. Samkalden, "A Dutch Retrospective View on European and Atlantic Cooperation," in "European and Atlantic Cooperation. The Dutch Attitude." Special issue of *Internationale Spectator,* Vol. 19, No. 7 (April 8, 1965), pp. 626-643.

54. Raymond Aron, "Old Nations, New Europe," in *A New Europe?, op. cit.,* p. 46.

55. See "Europe's Identity Crisis: Between the Past and America," *Dædalus* (Fall 1964), pp. 1244-1297.

56. Max Beloff, *Europe and the Europeans* (London, 1957), p. 24.

57. This is a means of compensation often used in the history of nationalism. After the French revolution, which gave rise to the idea of the mission of France, when Napoleon's armies crossed Europe, the difficult question of the content of German greatness was answered by Schiller's dictum, that only the "geistige Gestalt" (the spiritual and intellectual form) counted, not the political. See Lemberg, *op. cit.*, p. 131.

58. Michel Crozier, "The Cultural Revolution: Notes on the Changes in the Intellectual Climate of France," in *A New Europe?, op. cit.*, pp. 602-630. See especially, pp. 618-622.

59. Walter Hallstein, "1963, Jahr der Bewahrung," in *Deutschland und die Welt, op. cit.*, p. 331.

60. See Lemberg, *op. cit.*, pp. 250-264. Also Hans Kohn, *American Nationalism* (New York, 1957).

61. Albert K. Weinberg, *Manifest Destiny: A Study of Nationalist Expansion in American History* (Gloucester, 1958).

62. Edward McNall Burns, *The American Idea of Mission: Concepts of National Purpose and Destiny* (New Brunswick, 1957).

63. Zbigniew Brzezinski, "Peace, Morality and Vietnam," in *The New Leader*, Vol. 47, No. 8 (April 12, 1965), pp. 8-10.

64. Cited in Northedge, *op. cit.*, p. 179.

65. Lemberg, *op. cit.*, p. 254.

66. Text in *United Nations Textbook* (Leiden, 1958), p. 268.

67. Pierre Hassner, "Nationalisme et Relations Internationales" in *Revue Française de Science Politique*, Vol. 15, No. 3 (June 1965), pp. 499-528. Hassner thinks the surprise was "la rencontre entre les idéologies universalistes et le nationalisme, et la relative victoire du second," but the term may just as well be applied to the relative (or temporary?) victory of nationalism over European political integration.

68. It might in this respect be possible to push the analysis of the content of the different nationalisms somewhat further than Ernst Haas does in his "eclectic theory of nationalism that stresses ontology and developmental types" (*Beyond the Nation-State, op. cit.*, pp. 464-475), which he uses for a similar purpose, namely, of projecting the future international environment and system. Another example that comes to mind is that of Nkrumah, who has defined the mission of Ghana as bringing about African unity.

69. This is not to say that they would have caused the outbreak of a general war if there had not been a nuclear stalemate. Both ideologies claim the

enemy—imperialism or communism—is inherently militarily expansionist. In both cases these assertions have not been proved.

70. This might also be said of the nationalism of the new states insofar as they have prevented the enlargement of the ideological blocs.

71. In "Cursing de Gaulle is not a Policy," *op. cit.*

72. How this process works in an individual case can be read in the autobiography of a Hitler youth official, Melita Maschmann, *Account Rendered* (New York, 1965).

STANLEY HOFFMANN

Obstinate or Obsolete? The Fate of the Nation-State and the Case of Western Europe

I

THE CRITICAL issue for every student of world order is the fate of the nation-state. In the nuclear age, the fragmentation of the world into countless units, each of which has a claim to independence, is obviously dangerous for peace and illogical for welfare. The dynamism which animates those units, when they are not merely city-states of limited expanse or dynastic states manipulated by the Prince's calculations, but nation-states that pour into their foreign policy the collective pride, ambitions, fears, prejudices, and images of large masses of people, is particularly formidable.[1] An abstract theorist could argue that any system of autonomous units follows the same basic rules, whatever the nature of those units. But in practice, that is, in history, their substance matters as much as their form; the story of world affairs since the French Revolution is not merely one more sequence in the ballet of sovereign states; it is the story of the fires and upheavals propagated by nationalism. A claim to sovereignty based on historical tradition and dynastic legitimacy alone has never had the fervor, the self-righteous assertiveness which a similar claim based on the idea and feelings of nationhood presents: in world politics, the dynastic function of nationalism is the constitution of nation-states by amalgamation or by splintering, and its emotional function is the supplying of a formidable good conscience to leaders who see their task as the achievement of nationhood, the defense of the nation, or the expansion of a national mission.[2]

This is where the drama lies. The nation-state is at the same time a form of social organization and—in practice if not in every brand of theory—a factor of international non-integration; but those who argue in favor of a more integrated world, either under more centralized power or through various networks of regional or functional agencies, tend to forget Auguste Comte's old maxim that *on ne détruit que ce qu'on remplace:* the new "formula" will have to provide not only world order, but also the kind of social organization in which leaders, élites, and citizens feel at home. There is currently no agreement on what such a formula will be;[3] as a result, nation-states—often inchoate, economically absurd, administratively ramshackle, and impotent yet dangerous in international politics—remain the basic units in spite of all the remonstrations and exhortations. They go on *faute de mieux* despite their alleged obsolescence; indeed, not only do they profit from man's incapacity to bring about a better order, but their very existence is a formidable obstacle to their replacement.

If there was one part of the world in which men of good will thought that the nation-state could be superseded, it was Western Europe. One of France's most subtle commentators on international politics has recently reminded us of E. H. Carr's bold prediction of 1945: "we shall not see again a Europe of twenty, and a world of more than sixty independent sovereign states."[4] Statesmen have invented original schemes for moving Western Europe "beyond the nation-state,"[5] and political scientists have studied their efforts with a care from which emotional involvement was not missing. The conditions seemed ideal. On the one hand, nationalism seemed at its lowest ebb; on the other, an adequate formula and method for building a substitute had apparently been devised. Twenty years after the end of World War II—a period as long as the whole interwar era—observers have had to revise their judgments. The most optimistic put their hope in the chances the future may still harbor, rather than in the propelling power of the present; the less optimistic ones, like myself, try simply to understand what went wrong.

My own conclusion is sad and simple. The nation-state is still here, and the new Jerusalem has been postponed because the nations in Western Europe have not been able to stop time and to fragment space. Political unification could have succeeded if, on the one hand, these nations had not been caught in the whirlpool of different concerns, as a result both of profoundly different internal circumstances and of outside legacies, and if, on the other hand, they had been able or obliged to concentrate on "community-building" to the exclusion of all problems situated either outside their area or within each one of them. Domestic differences and different

111

world views obviously mean diverging foreign policies; the involve-ment of the policy-makers in issues among which "community-building" is merely one has meant a deepening, not a decrease, of those divergencies. The reasons follow: the unification movement has been the victim, and the survival of nation-states the outcome, of three factors, one of which characterizes every international sys-tem, and the other two only the present system. Every international system owes its inner logic and its unfolding to the *diversity* of domestic determinants, geo-historical situations, and outside aims among its units; any international system based on fragmentation tends, through the dynamics of unevenness (so well understood, if applied only to economic unevenness, by Lenin) to reproduce di-versity. However, there is no inherent reason that the model of the fragmented international system should rule out by itself two de-velopments in which the critics of the nation-state have put their bets or their hopes. Why must it be a diversity of nations? Could it not be a diversity of regions, of "federating" blocs, superseding the nation-state just as the dynastic state had replaced the feudal puz-zle? Or else, why does the very logic of conflagrations fed by hos-tility not lead to the kind of catastrophic unification of exhausted yet interdependent nations, sketched out by Kant? Let us remember that the unity movement in Europe was precisely an attempt at creating a regional entity, and that its origins and its springs re-sembled, on the reduced scale of a half-continent, the process dreamed up by Kant in his *Idea of Universal History.*[6]

The answers are not entirely provided by the two factors that come to mind immediately. One is the legitimacy of national self-determination, the only principle which transcends all blocs and ideologies, since all pay lip service to it, and provides the foundation for the only "universal actor" of the international system: the United Nations. The other is the newness of many of the states, which have wrested their independence by a nationalist upsurge and are there-fore unlikely to throw or give away what they have obtained only too recently. However, the legitimacy of the nation-state does not by itself guarantee the nation-state's survival in the international state of nature, and the appeal of nationalism as an emancipating passion does not assure that the nation-state must everywhere re-main the basic form of social organization, in a world in which many nations are old and settled and the shortcomings of the nation-state are obvious. The real answers are provided by two unique features of the present international system. One, it is the first truly *global* international system: the regional subsystems have only a reduced autonomy; the "relationships of major tension" blanket the whole planet, the domestic polities are dominated not so much by the region's problems as by purely local and purely global ones, which conspire to divert the region's members from the internal affairs of their area, and indeed would make an isolated treatment of those affairs impossible. As a result, each nation, new or old, finds itself placed in an orbit of its own, from which it is quite difficult to move away: for the attraction of the regional forces is offset by the pull of all the other forces. Or, to change the metaphor, those nations that coexist in the same apparently separate "home" of a geographical region find themselves both exposed to the smells and noises that come from outside through all their windows and doors, and looking at the outlying houses from which the interference issues. Coming from diverse pasts, moved by diverse tempers, living in different parts of the house, inescapably yet differently subjected and attracted to the outside world, those cohabitants react unevenly to their exposure and calculate conflictingly how they could either reduce the disturbance or affect in turn all those who live elsewhere. The adjustment of their own relations within the house becomes subordinated to their divergences about the outside world; the "regional subsystem" becomes a stake in the rivalry of its members about the system as a whole.

However, the coziness of the common home could still prevail if the inhabitants were forced to come to terms, either by one of them, or by the fear of a threatening neighbor. This is precisely where the second unique feature of the present situation intervenes. What tends to perpetuate the nation-states decisively in a system whose universality seems to sharpen rather than shrink their diversity is the new set of conditions that govern and restrict the rule of force: Damocles' sword has become a boomerang, the ideological legitimacy of the nation-state is protected by the relative and forced tameness of the world jungle. Force in the nuclear age is still the "midwife of societies" insofar as revolutionary war either breeds new nations or shapes regimes in existing nations; but the use of force along traditional lines, for conquest and expansion—the very use that made the "permeable" feudal units not only obsolete but collapse and replaced them with modern states often built on "blood and iron"—has become too dangerous. The legitimacy of the feudal unit could be undermined in two ways: brutally, by the rule of force—the big fish swallowing small fish by national might; subtly or legitimately, so to speak, through self-undermining—the logic of dynastic weddings or acquisitions that consolidated larger units. A system based on national self-determination rules out the latter; a system in which nations, once established, find force a much blunted weapon rules out the former. Thus agglomeration by conquest or out of a fear of conquest fails to take place. The new conditions of violence tend even to pay to national borders the tribute of vice to virtue: violence which dons the cloak of revolution rather than of interstate wars, or persists in the form of such wars only when they accompany revolutions or conflicts in divided countries, perversely respects borders by infiltrating under them rather than by crossing them overtly. Thus all that is left for unification is what one might call "national self-abdication" or self-abnegation, the eventual willingness of nations to try something else; but precisely global involvement hinders rather than helps, and the atrophy of war removes the most pressing incentive. What a nation-state cannot provide alone—in economics, or defense—it can still provide through means far less drastic than hara-kiri.

These two features give its solidity to the principle of national self-determination, as well as its resilience to the U.N. They also give its present, and quite unique, shape to the "relationship of major tension": the conflict between East and West. This conflict is both muted and universal—and both aspects contribute to the survival of the nation-state. As the superpowers find that what makes their power overwhelming also makes it less usable, or rather usable only to deter one another and to deny each other gains, the lesser states discover under the umbrella of the nuclear stalemate that they are not condemned to death, and that indeed their nuisance power is impressive—especially when the kind of violence that prevails in present circumstances favors the porcupine over the elephant. The superpowers experience in their own camps the backlash of a rebellion against domination that enjoys broad impunity, and cannot easily coax or coerce third parties into agglomeration under their tutelage. Yet they retain the means to prevent other powers from agglomerating away from their clutches. Thus, as the superpowers compete, with filed nails, all over the globe, the nation-state becomes the universal point of salience, to use the new language of strategy—the lowest common denominator in the competition.

Other international systems were merely conservative of diversity; the present system is profoundly conservative of the diversity of nation-states, despite all its revolutionary features. The dream of

Rousseau, concerned both about the prevalence of the general will —that is, the nation-state—and about peace, was the creation of communities insulated from one another. In history, where "the essence and drama of nationalism is not to be alone in the world,"[7] the clash of non-insulated states has tended to breed both nation-states and wars. Today, Rousseau's ideals come closer to reality, but in the most un-Rousseauan way: the nation-states prevail in peace, they remain unsuperseded because a fragile peace keeps the Kantian doctor away, they are unreplaced because their very involvement in the world, their very inability to insulate themselves from one another, preserves their separateness. The "new Europe" dreamed by the Europeans could not be established by force. Left to the wills and calculations of its members, the new formula has not jelled because they could not agree on its role in the world. The failure (so far) of an experiment tried in apparently ideal conditions tells us a great deal about contemporary world politics, about the chances of unification movements elsewhere, and about the functional approach to unification. For it shows that the movement can fail not only when there is a surge of nationalism in one important part, but also when there are differences in assessments of the national interest that rule out agreement on the shape and on the world role of the new, supranational whole.

The word nationalism is notoriously slippery. What I suggest is the following threefold distinction, which may be helpful in analyzing the interaction between the nation-state and the international system:

1. There is *national consciousness* (what the French call *sentiment national*)—a sense of "cohesion and distinctiveness,"[8] which sets one off from other groups. My point is that this sense, which tends to have important effects on international relations as long as it is shared by people who have not achieved statehood, is rather "neutral" once the nation and the state coincide: that is, the existence of national consciousness does not dictate foreign policy, does not indicate whether the people's "image" of foreigners will be friendly or unfriendly (they will be seen as different—nothing else is implied), nor does it indicate whether or not the leaders will be willing to accept sacrifices of sovereignty. One cannot even posit that a strong national consciousness will be an obstacle for movements of unification, for it is perfectly conceivable that a nation convinces itself that its "cohesion and distinctiveness" will be best

preserved in a larger entity. Here, we must turn to the second category.

2. For lack of a better phrase, I shall call it the *national situation*. Any nation-state, whether pulsing with a strong "national consciousness" or not—indeed, any state, whether a true nation-state or a disparate collection of unintegrated groups—is, to borrow Sartre's language, thrown into the world; its situation is made up altogether of its internal features—what, in an individual, would be called heredity and character—and of its position in the world. The state of national consciousness in the nation is one, but only one, of the elements of the situation. It is a composite of objective data (inside: social structure and political system; outside: geography, formal commitments) and subjective factors (inside: values, prejudices, opinions, reflexes; outside: one's own traditions and assessments of others, and the other's attitudes and approaches toward oneself); some of its components are intractable, others flexible and changeable. Any statesman, whether he is a fervent patriot or not, must define the nation's foreign policy by taking that situation into account; even if he is convinced of the obsolescence of *the* nation-state (or of *his* nation-state), the steps he will be able and willing to take in order to overcome it will be shaped by the fact that he speaks—to borrow de Gaulle's language this time—for the nation as it is in the world as it is. He cannot act as if his nation-state did not exist, however sorry its shape may be, or as if the world were other than it is. The national situation may facilitate unification moves, even when national consciousness is strong. It may prove a formidable obstacle, even when national consciousness is weak. The point is that even when the policy-maker tries to move "beyond the nation-state" he can do it only by taking along the nation with its baggage of memories and problems—with its situation. I do not want to suggest that the situation is a "given" that dictates policy; but it sets complicated limits that affect freedom of choice.[9]

3. I will reserve the term *"nationalism"* for a specific meaning: it is one of the numerous ways in which political leaders and élites can interpret the dictates, or rather the suggestions, of the national situation, one of the ways of using the margin it leaves. Whereas national consciousness is a feeling, and the national situation a condition, nationalism is a doctrine or (if one uses a broad definition) an ideology—the doctrine or ideology that gives to the nation in world affairs absolute value and top priority. The consequences of

such a preference may vary immensely: nationalism may imply expansion (that is, the attempt at establishing the supremacy of one's nation over others) or merely defense; it may entail the notion of a universal mission or, on the contrary, insulation. It may be peaceful or pugnacious.[10] It is less an imperative determinant of choice than a criterion of choice and an attitude which shapes the choices made. But whatever its manifestations, its varying content, it always follows one rule common to all the former, it always pours the latter into one mold: the preservation of the nation as the highest good. Nationalism thus affects, *at least* negatively, the way in which the freedom of choice left by the national situation will be used; indeed, it may collide with, and try to disregard or overcome, the limits which the situation sets.

The relation between nationalism and the two other factors is complicated. Nationalism (in the sense of the will to establish a nation-state) is triggered by, and in turn activates, national consciousness in oppressed nationalities; but nationalism, in colonial areas as well as in mature nation-states, can also be a substitute for a still weak or for a fading national consciousness. In nation-states that are going concerns, national consciousness breeds nationalism only in certain kinds of national situations. The national situation may be assessed by a nationalist leader exactly in the same way as by a non-nationalist one; however, nationalism may lead the former to promote policies the latter would have rejected and to oppose moves the former would have undertaken. That bane of international relations theory, the national interest, could be defined as follows:

N.I. = National situation X outlook of the foreign policy-makers.

It is obvious that the same situation can result in different policies, depending in particular on whether or not there is a nationalist policy-maker. It is obvious also that national interests of different nations will not be defined in easily compatible terms if those respective outlooks are nationalist, even when the situations are not so different. But the same incompatibility may obtain, even if the outlooks are not nationalistic, when the situations are indeed very different.[11]

II

Let us now look at the fate of the nation-states in the part of Europe occupied by the so-called Six, that is, the continental part of Western Europe, first by examining the basic features of their national situations, then by commenting upon the process of unification, later by discussing its results, and finally by drawing some lessons.

Western Europe in the postwar years has been characterized by three features which have affected all of its nations. But each of those features has nevertheless affected each of the six nations in a different way because of the deep differences that have continued to divide the Six.

1. The first feature—the most hopeful one from the viewpoint of the unifiers—was the temporary demise of nationalism. In the defeated countries—Germany and Italy—nationalism had become associated with the regimes that had led the nations into war, defeat, and destruction. The collapse of two national ideologies that had been bellicose, aggressive, and imperialistic brought about an almost total discredit for nationalism in every guise. Among the nations of Western Europe that were on the Allied side, the most remarkable thing was that the terrible years of occupation and resistance had not resulted in a resurgence of chauvinism. Amusingly enough, it was the Communist Party of France that gave the most nationalistic tone to its propaganda; on the whole, the platforms of the Resistance movements show an acute awareness of the dangers of nationalist celebrations and national fragmentation in Western Europe. The Resistance itself had had a kind of supranational dimension; none of the national resistance movements could have survived without outside support; the nations whose honor they had saved had been liberated rather than victorious. All this prevented the upsurge of the kind of cramped chauvinism that had followed the victory of World War I, just as the completeness of the disaster and the impossibility of putting the blame on any traitors crushed any potential revival in Germany of the smoldering nationalism of resentment that had undermined the Weimar Republic. There was, in other words, above and beyond the differences in national situations between indubitable losers and dubious winners, the general feeling of a common defeat, and also the hope of a common future: for the Resistance platforms often put their emphasis on the need for a union or federation of Western Europe.

However, the demise of nationalism affected differently the various nations of the half-continent. On the one hand, there were significant differences in national consciousness. If nationalism was low, patriotic sentiment was extremely high in liberated France. The circumstances in which the hated Nazis were expelled and the domestic collaborators purged amounted to what I have called elsewhere a rediscovery of the French political community by the French:[12] the nation seemed to have redeemed its "cohesion and distinctiveness." On the contrary, in Germany especially, the destruction of nationalism seemed to have been accompanied by a drop in national consciousness as well: what was distinctive was guilt and shame; what had been only too cohesive was being torn apart not by internal political cleavages, but by partition, zones of occupation, regional parochialisms blessed by the victors. The French national backbone had been straightened by the ordeal, although the pain had been too strong to tempt the French to flex nationalistic muscles; the German national backbone appeared to have been broken along with the strutting jaw and clenched fist of Nazi nationalism. Italy was in slightly better shape than Germany, in part because of its Resistance movements, but its story was closer to the German than to the French.

However, there were other elements in the national situation, besides patriotic consciousness, that also affected differently the various nations' inclination to nationalism. The defeated nations—Germany in particular—were in the position of patients on whom drastic surgery had been performed, and who were lying prostrate, dependent for their every movement on the surgeons and nurses. Even if one had wanted to restore the nation to the pinnacle of values and objectives, one could not have succeeded except with the help and consent of one's guardians—who were not likely to give support to such a drive; in other words, the situation itself set the strictest limits to the possibility of any kind of nationalism, expansive or insulating. The lost territories were beyond recuperation; a healing period of *"repli"* comparable to that which had marked the early foreign policy of the Third Republic was not conceivable either. One could not get anything alone, and anything others could provide, while limited, would be something to be grateful for.

On the other hand, France and, to a lesser extent (because of their much smaller size), Belgium and Holland were not so well inoculated. For, although the prevalence of the nation meant little in the immediate European context, it meant a great deal in the imperial one: if the circumstances of the Liberation kept national consciousness from veering into nationalism in one realm, the same circumstances tended to encourage such a turn with respect to the colonies. Cut down to size in Europe, these nations were bound to act as if they could call upon their overseas possessions to redress the balance; accustomed, through their association of nationalism with Nazi and Fascist imperialism, to equate chauvinism only with expansion, they would not be so easily discouraged from a nationalism of defense, aimed at preserving the "national mission" overseas. The Dutch lost most of their empire early enough to find themselves, in this respect, not so different from the German and Italian amputees; the Belgians remained serene long enough not to have nationalistic fevers about the huge member that seemed to give them no trouble until the day when it broke off—brutally, painfully, but irremediably. The French, however, suffered almost at once from dis-imperial dyspepsia, and the long, losing battle they fought gave rise continuously to nationalist tantrums of frustration and rage. Moreover, the French inclination to nationalism was higher because of an internal component of the national situation as well: there was in France one political force that was clearly nationalist, that had indeed presided over the Liberation, given whatever unity they had to the Resistance movements, and achieved in the most impressive way a highly original convergence of Jacobin universalist nationalism and of "traditionalist," right-wing, defensive nationalism—the force of General de Gaulle. His resignation had meant, as Alfred Grosser suggests,[13] the defeat of a doctrine that put not only a priority mark on foreign affairs but also a priority claim on *Notre Dame la France*. The incident that had led to his departure —a conflict over the military budget—had been symbolic enough of the demise of nationalism referred to above. But his durability, first as a political leader, later as a "capital that belongs to all and to none," reflected a lasting nostalgia for nationalism; and it was equally symbolic that the crisis which returned him to power was a crisis over Algeria.

2. The second feature common to all the West European national situations, yet affecting them differently, was the "political collapse of Europe." Europe did not merely lose power and wealth: such losses can be repaired, as the aftermath of World War I had shown. Europe, previously the heart of the international system, the locus of the world organization, the fount of international law, fell under what de Gaulle has called "the two hegemonies." The phrase is, obviously, inaccurate and insulting: one of those hegemonies took a highly imperial form, and thus discouraged and prevented the

creation in Eastern Europe of any regional entity capable of over-coming the prewar national rivalries. Nothing is to be gained, how-ever, by denying that U.S. hegemony has been a basic fact of life. American domination has indeed had the kinds of "domination ef-fects" any hegemony produces: the transfer of decision-making in vital matters from the dominated to the dominator breeds a kind of paternalism in the latter, and irresponsibility (either in the form of abdication or in the form of scapegoatism) in the former. But the consequences of hegemony vary according to its nature. The peculiar nature of this domination has also had unique consequences —better and worse than in the classical cases. One may dominate because one wants to and can; but one may also dominate because one must and does: by one's weight and under the pressures of a compelling situation. This has been America's experience: its he-gemony was "situational," not deliberate.

The effects have been better than usual, insofar as such hegem-ony restricted itself to areas in which European nations had become either impotent or incapable of recovery by self-reliance. It left the dominated with a considerable freedom of maneuver, and indeed prodded them into recovery, power recuperation, and regional unity; it favored both individual and collective emancipation. But the ef-fects have been worse precisely because this laxity meant that each party could react to *this* common feature of the national situations (that is, American hegemony) according to the distinctive *other* features of his national situation, features left intact by the weight and acts of the U. S., by contrast with the U.S.S.R. American domi-nation was only one part of the picture. Hence the following para-dox: both America's prodding and the individual and collective impotence of Western European nations, now reduced to the con-dition of clients and stakes, ought logically to have pushed them into unity-for-emancipation—the kind of process Soviet policy dis-couraged in the other half of Europe. But the very margin of auton-omy left to each West European nation by the U. S. gave it an array of choices: between accepting and rejecting dependence, between unity as a weapon for emancipation and unity as merely a way to make dependence more comfortable. It would have been a miracle if all the nations had made the same choice; the diversity of national situations has ultimately prevailed. To define one's position toward the U. S. was the common imperative, but each one has defined it in his own way.

At first, this diversity of domestic outlooks and external positions did not appear to be an obstacle to the unification movement. As Ernst Haas has shown,[14] the movement grew on ambiguity, and those who accepted American hegemony as a lasting fact of European life as well as those who did not could submerge their disagreement in the construction of a regional entity that could be seen, by the former, as the most effective way for continuing to receive American protection and contributing to America's mission and, by the latter, as the most effective way to challenge American predominance. However, there are limits to the credit of ambiguity. The split could not be concealed once the new entity was asked to tackle matters of "high politics"—that is, go beyond the purely internal economic problems of little impact or dependence on the external relationship to the U. S.[15] It is therefore no surprise that this split should have disrupted unification at two moments—in 1953-54, when the problem of German rearmament was raised; and in 1962-65, when de Gaulle's challenge of the U. S. became global.[16]

This is how the diversity of national situations operated. First, it produced (and produces) the basic split between those I would call the resigned ones, and those I would call the resisters. The resigned ones were, on the one hand, the smaller nations, aware of their weakness, realizing that the Soviet threat could not be met by Europeans alone, accustomed to dependence on external protectors, grateful to America for the unique features of its protection, and looking forward to an important role for Europe but not in the realm of high politics. Italy had, in the past, tried to act as a great power without protectors; yet not only were those days over, but also the acceptance of American hegemony provided the creaky Italian political system with a kind of double cushion—against the threat of Communism, but also against the need to spend too much energy and money on Italian rearmament. For the smaller states as well as for Italy, the acceptance of U. S. hegemony was like an insurance policy, which protected them against having to give priority to foreign affairs. On the other hand, Germany accepted dependence on the U. S. not merely as a comfort, but as a necessity as vital as breathing. West Germany's geographical position had turned it into the front line, its partition has contributed to imposing security as the supreme goal, the staunch anti-Communism of its leadership had ruled out any search for security along the lines of neutrality. There followed not only the acceptance of U. S. leadership but also the need to do everything possible in order to tie the United States to Western Europe. Moreover, in West Germany's helpless position, the recovery of equality was another vital goal, and it could be reached only through cooperation with the most powerful of the occupying forces. Defeat, division, and danger conspired to making West Germany switch almost abruptly from its imperialistic nationalism of the Nazi era to a dependence which was apparently submissive, yet also productive (of security and status gains) under Adenauer.

As for the resisters, they, like the West Germans, gave priority to foreign affairs—only not in the same perspective. The French reading of geography and history was different.[17] To be sure, the present need for security against the Soviet Union was felt. But there were two reasons that the "tyranny of the cold war" operated differently in France. One, French feelings of hostility toward Russia were much lower than in Germany, and, although it may be too strong to speak of a nostalgia for the wartime grand alliance, it is not false to say that the hope of an ultimate détente allowing for European reunification, for a return of the Soviets to moderation, and for an emancipation of the continent from its "two hegemonies" never died. The French time perspective has been consistently different from, say, the German: the urgency of the threat never overshadowed the desire for, and belief in, the advent of a less tense international system. This may have been due not only to France's location, but also to other elements in France's national situation. Whereas Germany's continuity with its past was both wrecked and repudiated, France (like England) looked back to the days when Europe held the center of the stage and forward to the time when Europe would again be an actor, not a stake: the anomaly was the present, not the past. Also, on colonial matters, France (more than England) often found little to distinguish America's reprobation from Soviet hostility. Two, France continued to worry not only about possible Soviet thrusts but also about Germany's potential threats: the suspicion of a reborn German national consciousness and nationalism has marked all French leaders. An additional reason for fearing the perpetuation of American hegemony and the freezing of the cold war, for hoping for a détente that would help Europe reunite, was thus provided by the fear that any other course would make Germany the main beneficiary of America's favors. Germany looked East with some terror, but there was only one foe there; when the French looked East, they saw two nations to fear; each could be used as an ally against the other—but for the time being the Soviet danger was the greater, and, should Germany be

STANLEY HOFFMANN

built up too much against the Soviets, the security gained by France in one respect would be compromised in another.[18]

There was a second way in which the diversity of national situations operated. As I have suggested, situations limit and affect but do not command choices. A general desire for overcoming the cold war and American hegemony did not mean a general agreement on how to do so. What I have called "the resistance" was split, and it is this split that has become decisive for an analysis of the obstacles to European unification. Had all the resisters calculated that the best way to reach France's objectives was the construction of a powerful West European entity, which could rival America's might, turn the bipolar contest into a triangle, and wrest advantages from both extra-European giants, the "ambiguity" of a movement led by re- signed as well as resisting forces might not have damaged the enter- prise until much later. However, there was a sharp division over methods between those who reasoned along the lines just described —like Jean Monnet—and those who feared that the sacrifice of national sovereignty to supranational institutions might entail a loss of control over the direction of the undertaking. The latter consisted of two kinds of people: on the one hand, the nationalists who, as indicated above, were still very much around, exasperated by the colonial battles, anxious to preserve all the resources of French di- plomacy and strategy in order, in the present, to concentrate on the fronts overseas and, later, to promote whatever policies would be required, rather than let a foreign body decide; on the other hand, men like Mendès-France, who were not nationalists in the sense of this paper, but who thought that the continental European construc- tion was not France's best way of coping with her situation—they thought that priority ought to go to more urgent tasks such as the search for a détente, the liberalization of the Empire, the reform of the economy.[19]

The success of the European movement required, first, that the "resisters" suspicious of European integration remain a minority— not only throughout the six but in the leadership of every one of the six, not only in Parliament but above all in the Executive, the prime decision-making force in every state: a requirement which was met in 1950-53 and in 1955-58, but not in the crucial months for E.D.C. in 1953-54, and no longer after 1958. The movement proceeded after 1958 because of the dialectic of ambiguity; however, there was a second requirement for success: that the "minute of truth"—when the European élites would have to ask themselves questions about

124

the ultimate political direction of their community—be postponed as long as possible; that is, that the cold war remain sufficiently intense to impose even on the "resisters" a priority for the kind of security that implied U. S. protection—a priority for the *urgent* over the *long-term important* as they saw it. This is precisely what was already, if temporarily, shaken by the brief period of nervous demobilization that followed Stalin's death, in 1953-54, and then gradually undermined by the third basic feature of Europe's postwar situation. But before we turn to it, one remark must be made: in French foreign policy, "resistance by European integration" prevailed over "resistance by self-reliance" only as long as France was bogged down in colonial wars; it was this important and purely French element in France's national situation whose ups and downs affected quite decisively the method of "resistance."[20]

3. The divisions and contradictions described above were sharpened by the third common feature, which emerged in the mid-1950's and whose effects have developed progressively since: the nuclear stalemate between the superpowers. The impact of the "balance of terror" on the Western alliance has been analyzed so often and well[21] that nothing needs to be added here; but what is needed is a brief explanation of how the two splits already discussed have been worsened by Europe's gradual discovery of the uncertainties of America's nuclear protection (now that the U. S. could be devastated too), and how some new splits appeared. For to the extent to which the stalemate has loosened up a previously very tight situation—tight because of the threat from the East and the ties to the U. S.—it has altogether sharpened previous differences in national situations *and* increased the number of alternatives made available to élites and statesmen. Greater indeterminacy has meant greater confusion.

First, the split between French "resistance" and German "resignation" has become deeper. The dominant political élites in Germany have interpreted the new national situation created by the balance of terror as merely adding urgency to their previous calculation of interest. The nuclear stalemate was, given Germany's position, deemed to increase the danger for the West: the U. S. was relatively less strong, the Soviet Union stronger, that is, more of a threat. Indeed, the Socialists switched from their increasingly more furtive glances at neutrality to an outright endorsement of the Christian Democratic interpretation. If America's monopoly was broken, if America's guarantee was weakened thereby, what was needed—in a world that was not willing to let Germany rearm with nuclear weapons, in a continent that could not really develop a nuclear force of its own capable of replacing America's and of matching Russia's —was a German policy so respectful of America's main concerns, and also so vigilant with respect to the Soviet Union, that the U. S. would both feel obligated to keep its mantle of protection over Germany and not be tempted into negotiating a détente at Germany's expense. German docility would be the condition for, and counterpart of, American entanglement. The German reaction to a development that could, if General Gallois' logic were followed, lead to the prevalence of "polycentrism" at bipolarity's expense was the search for ways of exorcising the former and preserving the latter. On the whole, the smaller nations and Italy, while not at all fearful about the consequences of polycentrism (on the contrary), were nevertheless not shaken out of their "resignation"; the mere appearance of parity of nuclear peril was not enough to make them anxious to give, or to make them domestically capable of giving, priority to an active foreign policy.

In France, on the contrary, the balance of terror reinforced the attitude of resistance: what had always been a goal—emancipation —but had in fact been no more than a hope, given the thickness of the iron curtain, the simple rigidity of the superpowers' policies in the days of Mr. Dulles, and Europe's inability to affect the course of events, now became a possibility; for the giants' stalemate meant increased security for the less great (however much they might complain about the decrease of American protection and use it as a pretext, their lament coexisted with a heightened feeling of protection against war in general). What the Germans saw as a liability was an opportunity to the French. Germany's situation, its low national consciousness, incited most German leaders to choose what might be called a "minimizing" interpretation of the new situation; France's situation, its high national consciousness and, after 1958, the doctrine of its leader, incited French political élites to choose a "maximizing" interpretation. The increasing costs of the use of force made this use by the superpowers less likely, American protection less certain but also less essential, Europe's recovery of not merely wealth but power more desirable and possible—possible since the quest for power could be pushed without excessive risk of sanctions by the two giants, desirable since power, while transformed, remains the moving force and *ultima ratio* of world politics. This recovery of power would help bring about the much desired prevalence of polycentrism over bipolarity.[22]

Secondly, as this feud shows, the balance of terror heightened the split over method among the "resisters." On the one hand, it provided new arguments for those who thought that emancipation could be achieved only through the uniting of Western Europe: individual national efforts would remain too ridiculously weak to amount to anything but a waste in resources; a collective effort, however, could exploit the new situation, make Western Europe a true partner of the U. S., and not merely an economic partner and a military aide-de-camp. On the other hand, those who feared that the "united way" could become a frustrating deviation reasoned that the theory of graduated deterrence justified the acquisition of nuclear weapons by a middle-size power with limited resources and that this acquisition would increase considerably the political influence as well as the prestige of the nation. The increased costs of force ruled out, in any case, what had in the past been the most disastrous effect of the mushrooming of sovereign states—a warlike, expansionist nationalism—but they simultaneously refloated the value of small or middle-sized nations, no longer condemned by the cold, bipolar war to look for bigger protectors or to agglomerate in order to assure their security. Moreover, the "united way" would be a dead-end, since some, and not exactly the least significant, of the associates had no desire for collective European power at the possible expense of American protection. Not the least significant reason for the prevalence of the second line of thought over the first has been one important element of the national situation—the army: almost destroyed by its Algerian experience, it had to be "reconverted." In the circumstances of 1962, this meant inevitably a conversion to French atomic concerns. Its success builds up in turn a vested interest in the preservation of the new establishment—and increases the difference in national situations between France and a non-nuclear Germany.

Thirdly, the new situation affected European unification negatively not only by sharpening those splits but in two other ways as well. On the one hand, until then, opposition to a supranational entity had come only from a fraction of the "resisters"; in the early 1950's the U. S. had strongly—too strongly—urged the establishment of a European defense system which was not considered likely to challenge America's own predominance in the military area. In the 1960's, the U. S. no longer urged the West Europeans to build such a system. American leadership has developed a deep concern for maintaining centralized control over the forces of the alliance, that is, for preserving bipolarity, and a growing realization that Europe's appetite would not stop short of nuclear weapons. As a result, some of the "resigned ones," instead of endorsing European integration as unreservedly as when the situation of a dependent Europe in a cold-war-dominated world did not allow Europeans to entertain thoughts of genuine military "partnership" with the U. S., now for the first time showed themselves of two minds—they were willing to pursue integration in economic and social fields, but much less so in matters of defense, lest NATO be weakened. It is significant that the Dutch resisted de Gaulle's efforts, in 1960-62, to include defense in his confederal scheme and that the German leaders, in their quest for security, put their hopes in the MLF—a scheme that ties European nations one by one to the U. S.—rather than in a revised and revived E.D.C. Inevitably, such mental reservations of those who had been among the champions of supranationality could only confirm the suspicions of those "resisters" who had distrusted the "Monnet method" since the beginning. Thus, the national situation of Germany in particular—a situation in which America's own policy of reliance on Germany as the anchor of U. S. influence on the continent plays a large role—damaged the European movement: the German leaders were largely successful in their drive to entangle the U. S., but found that the price they had to pay was a decreasing ability to push for European integration. European integration and dependence on the U. S. were no longer automatically compatible.[23]

On the other hand, even that minority of German leaders who began to read Germany's national interest differently did not really compensate for the weakening of the majority's integrating ardor. Increasingly, in 1963 to 1965, suspicions about the value of the policy of docility-for-entanglement were voiced by a group of Christian Democrats, led by Adenauer and Strauss. They still read the German situation in terms of security first; but their faith in America's aptitude to provide it was shaken, and they saw that Germany had sufficiently gained from America's support not to have to behave as a minor any longer. Their nickname of German Gaullists is however totally unsuitable. To be sure, these men are "resisters" in the sense of turning away from America; they are close to the French "integrationist resisters," insofar as they propose a European defense effort and a joint European nuclear policy (rather than a purely German one). Nevertheless, their foreign policy goals are quite different from those of all the French resisters, integrationist or nationalist. The national situation of France made most French leaders agree on a common *vision,* described above, that can be summed up as the end of the cold war and a continent reunited with a Germany placed under certain wraps. That common vision coexists with the split on *policies* already discussed—the "European" policy (in which the wraps are organic, that is, the net and bonds of integration) *vs.* the "national" policy (in which the wraps are contractual). The national situation of Germany has made most German leaders, after the Social Democratic switch,[24] agree on a common *vision* deeply different from the French—a perpetuation of the cold war, hostility to the Soviet Union, the hope for a reunification tantamount not merely to the thawing of the Eastern "camp" but to its disintegration, and with as few concessions as possible. Since 1963, this vision has coexisted with two different *policies:* the majority policy of reliance on the U. S., the minority policy of substituting a strong, tough Europe for an increasingly less reliable, increasingly détente-happy U. S. At present, "resisters" are thus split not only on methods (French integrationists *vs.* French anti-integrationists) but also on objectives (French *vs.* German).

This long discussion of the different responses to common situations has been necessary in reaction to the dominant approach to European integration which has focused on process. The self-propelling power of the process is severely constrained by the associates' views and splits on ends and means. In order to go "beyond the nation-state," one will have to do more than set up procedures in adequate "background" and "process conditions." For a procedure is not a purpose, a process is not a policy.

III

However, since it is the process of European integration that is its most original feature, we must examine it also.[25] We have been witnessing a kind of race, between the logic of integration set up by Monnet and analyzed by Haas, and the logic of diversity, analyzed above. According to the former, the double pressure of necessity (the interdependence of the social fabric, which will oblige statesmen to integrate even sectors originally left uncoordinated) and of men (the action of the supranational agents) will gradually restrict the freedom of movement of the national governments by turning the national situations into one of total enmeshing. In such a milieu, nationalism will be a futile exercise in anachronism, and the national consciousness itself will, so to speak, be impregnated by an awareness of the higher interest in union. The logic of diversity, by contrast, sets limits to the degree to which the "spill-over" process can limit the freedom of action of the governments; it restricts the domain in which the logic of functional integration operates to the area of welfare; indeed, to the extent that discrepancies over the other areas begin to prevail over the laborious harmonization in welfare, even issues belonging to the latter sphere may become infected by the disharmony which reigns in those other areas. The logic of integration is that of a blender which crunches the most diverse products, overcomes their different tastes and perfumes, and replaces them with one, presumably delicious juice. One lets each item be ground because one expects a finer synthesis: that is, ambiguity helps rather than hinders because each "ingredient" can hope that its taste will prevail at the end. The logic of diversity is the opposite: it suggests that, in areas of key importance to the national interest, nations prefer the certainty, or the self-controlled uncertainty, of national self-reliance, to the uncontrolled uncertainty of the untested blender; ambiguity carries one only a part of the way. The logic of integration assumes that it is possible to fool each one of the associates some of the time because his over-all gain will still exceed his occasional losses, even if his calculations turn out wrong here or there. The logic of diversity implies that, on a vital issue, losses are not compensated by gains on other (and especially not on other less vital) issues: nobody wants to be fooled. The logic of integration deems the uncertainties of the supranational function process creative; the logic of diversity sees them as destructive past a certain threshold: Russian roulette is fine only as long as the gun is filled with blanks. Ambiguity lures and lulls the national consciousness into integration as long as the benefits are high, the costs low, the expectations considerable. Ambiguity may arouse and stiffen national consciousness into nationalism if the benefits are slow, the losses high, the hopes dashed or deferred. Functional integration's gamble could be won only if the method had sufficient potency to promise a permanent excess of gains over losses, and of hopes over frustrations. Theoretically, this may be true of economic integration. It is not true of political integration (in the sense of "high politics").

The success of the approach symbolized by Jean Monnet depended, and depends still, on his winning a triple gamble: on goals, on methods, on results. As for goals, it is a gamble on the possibility of substituting motion as an end in itself, for agreement on ends. It is a fact that the trans-national integrationist élites did not agree on whether the object of the community-building enterprise ought to be the construction of a new super-state—that is, a federal potential nation, *à la* U.S.A., more able because of its size and resources to play the traditional game of power than the dwarfed nations of Western Europe—or whether the object was to demonstrate that power politics could be overcome through cooperation and compromise, to build the first example of a radically new kind of unit, to achieve a change in the nature and not merely in the scale of the game. Monnet himself has been ambiguous on this score; Hallstein has been leaning in the first direction, many of Monnet's public relations men in the second.[26] Nor did the integrationists agree on whether the main goal was the creation of a regional "security-community,"[27] that is, the pacification of a former hotbed of wars, or whether the main goal was the creation of an entity whose position and might could decisively affect the course of the cold war in particular, of international relations in general. Now, it is perfectly possible for a movement to feed on its harboring continental nationalists as well as anti-power idealists, inward-looking politicians and outward-looking politicians—but only as long as there is no need to make a choice. Decisions on tariffs did not require such choices. Decisions on agriculture already raise basic problems of orientation. Decisions on foreign policy and membership and defense cannot be reached unless the goals are clarified. One cannot be all things to all people all of the time.

As for methods, there was a gamble on the irresistible rise of supranational functionalism. It assumed, first, that national sovereignty, already devalued by events, could be chewed up leaf by leaf like an artichoke. It assumed, second, that the dilemma of governments having to choose between pursuing an integration that ties their hands and stopping a movement that benefits their people could be exploited in favor of integration by men representing the common good, endowed with the advantages of superior expertise, initiating proposals, propped against a set of deadlines, and using for their cause the technique of package deals. Finally, it was assumed that this approach would both take into account the interests of the greater powers and prevent the crushing of the smaller ones. The troubles with this gamble have been numerous. One, even an artichoke has a heart, which remains intact after the leaves have been eaten. It is of course true that a successful economic and social integration would considerably limit the freedom governments would still enjoy in theory for their diplomacy and strategy; but why should one assume that they would not be aware of it? As the artichoke's heart gets more and more denuded, the governments' vigilance gets more and more alerted. To be sure, the second assumption implies that the logic of the movement would prevent them from doing anything about it: they would be powerless to save the heart. But, two, this would be true only if governments never put what they consider essential interests of the nation above the particular interests of certain categories of nationals, if superior expertise were always either the Commission's monopoly or the solution of the issue at hand, if package deals were effective in every argument, and, above all, if the governments' representatives were always determined to behave as a "community organ" rather than as the agents of states that are not willing to accept a community under any conditions. Finally, functional integration may indeed give lasting satisfaction to the smaller powers, precisely because it is for them that the ratio of "welfare politics" to high politics is highest, and that the chance of gaining benefits through intergovernmental methods that reflect rather than correct the power differential between the big and the small is poorest; but this is also why the method is not likely *à la longue* to satisfy the bigger powers as much: facing them, the supranational civil servants, for all their skill and legal powers, are a bit like Jonases trying to turn whales into jellyfish. Of course, the idea—ultimately—is to move from an essentially administrative procedure in which supranational civil servants enter a dialogue with national ministers, to a truly federal one in which a federal cabinet is responsible to a federal parliament; but what is thus presented as a linear progress may turn out to be a vicious circle, since the ministers hold the key to the transformation, and may refuse it unless the goals are defined and the results already achieved are satisfactory.

There was a gamble about results as well. The experience of integration would entail net benefits for all, and bring about clear progress toward community formation. Such progress could be measured by the following yardsticks: in the realm of interstate relations, an increasing transfer of power to the new common agencies, and the prevalence of solutions "upgrading the common interest" over other kinds of compromises; in the realm of transnational society, an increasing flow of communications; in the area of national consciousness—which is important both for interstate relations, because (as seen above) it may set limits to the statesmen's discretion, and for transnational society, because it affects the scope and meaning of the communication flows—progress would be measured by increasing compatibility of views about external issues. The results achieved so far are mixed: negative on the last count (see below), limited on the second, and marked on the first by features that the enthusiasts of intergration did not expect. On the one hand, there has been some strengthening of the authority of the Commission, and in various areas there has been some "upgrading of common interests." On the other hand, the Commission's unfortunate attempt to consolidate those gains at de Gaulle's expense, in the spring of 1965, has brought about a startling setback for the whole enterprise; moreover, in their negotiations, the members have conspicuously failed to find a common interest in some vital areas (energy, England's entry), and sometimes succeeded in reaching apparently "integrating" decisions only after the most ungainly, traditional kind of bargaining, in which such uncommunity-like methods as threats, ultimatums, and retaliatory moves were used. In other words, either the ideal was not reached, or it was reached in a way that was both the opposite of the ideal and ultimately its destroyer. If we look at the institutions of the Common Market as an incipient political system for Europe, we find that its authority remains limited, its structure weak, its popular base restricted and distant.[28]

It is therefore not surprising if the uncertainty about results already achieved contributes to uncertainty about future prospects. For the very divisions among the partisans of integration make it hard to predict where the "Monnet method" would lead, if the process were to continue along the lines so fondly planned by the French "inspirator." Would the enterprise become an effective federation, gradually turning the many into one, or would it lead to a mere façade behind which all the divergences and rivalries would continue to be played out? It is at least remarkable that Gaullist and American fears should converge in one respect: de Gaulle has consistently warned that the application of the supranational method to the area of high politics would lead not to a strong European entity, but to a dilution of national responsibility whose only beneficiary would be the U. S.; incapable of defining a coherent policy, the "technocrats" would leave the decisions in vital areas to the U. S., at least by default. On the contrary, many Americans have come to believe, on the basis of some of E.E.C.'s actions in the realm of tariffs and trade, that a united Europe would be able to challenge U. S. leadership much more effectively than the separate European states ever could. The truth of the matter is that nobody knows: a method is not a policy, a process is not a direction; the results achieved so far are too specialized, and the way in which they have been reached is too bumpy, to allow one to extrapolate and project safely. The face of a united Europe has not begun to emerge; there are just a few lines, but one does not know whether the supranational technique would finally give to Western Europe the features of a going concern, or those of a Fourth Republic writ large—the ambitions of a world power, or the complacency of parochialism. The range of possibilities is so broad, the alternatives are so extreme, that the more the Six move into the stormy waters of high politics, the less not only they but also the outside powers, such as the U. S., which may be affected by their acts are willing to extend the credit of hope and to make new wagers: neither Gaullist France nor the present U. S. leadership is willing to risk a major loss of control. Contrary to the French proverb, in the process of functional integration, only the first steps do not cost much.

There are two important general lessons one can draw from a study of the process of integration. The first concerns the limits of the functional method: its very (if relative) success in the relatively painless area in which it works relatively well lifts the participants to the level of issues to which it does not apply well any more—like swimmers whose skill at moving quickly away from the shore suddenly brings them to the point where the waters are stormiest and deepest, at a time when fatigue is setting in, and none of the questions about ultimate goal, direction, and length of swim has been answered. The functional process was used in order to "make Europe"; once Europe began being made, the process collided with the question: "making Europe, what for?" The process is like a grinding machine that can work only if someone keeps giving it something to grind. When the users start quarreling and stop providing, the machine stops. For a while, the machine worked because the governments poured into it a common determination to integrate their economies in order to maximize wealth; but with their wealth increasing, the question of what to do with it was going to arise: a technique capable of supplying means does not *ipso facto* provide the ends, and it is about those ends that quarrels have broken out. They might have been avoided if the situation had been more compelling—if the Six had been so cooped up that each one's horizon would have been nothing other than his five partners. But this has never been their outlook, nor is it any more their necessity. Each one is willing to live with the others, but not on terms too different from his own; and the Six are not in the position of the three miserable prisoners of *No Exit*. Transforming a dependent "subsystem" proved to be one thing; defining its relations to all other subsystems and to the international system in general has turned out to be quite another—indeed, so formidable a matter as to keep the transformation of the subsystem in abeyance until those relations can be defined.

The model of functional integration, a substitute for the kind of instant federation which governments had not been prepared to accept, shows its origins in important respects. One, it is essentially an administrative model, which relies on bureaucratic expertise for the promotion of a policy defined by the political authorities, and for the definition of a policy that political decision-makers are technically incapable of shaping—something like French planning under the Fourth Republic. The hope was that in the interstices of political bickering the administrators could build up a consensus; but the mistake was to believe that a formula that works well within certain limits is a panacea—and that even within the limits of "welfare politics" administrative skill can always overcome the disastrous effects of political paralysis or mismanagement (cf. the impact of inflation, or balance of payment troubles, on planning). Two, the model assumes that the basic political decisions, to be prepared and pursued by the civil servants but formally made by the governments, would be reached through the process of short-term bargaining, by politicians whose mode of operation is empirical muddling through, of the kind that puts immediate advantages above long-term pursuits: this model corresponds well to the nature of parliamentary politics with a weak Executive, for example, the politics of the Fourth Republic, but the mistake was to believe that all political regimes would conform to this rather sorry image, and also to ignore the disastrous results which the original example produced whenever conflicts over values and fundamental choices made mere empirical groping useless or worse than useless (cf. decolonization).[29]

The second lesson is even more discouraging for the advocates of functionalism. To revert to the analogy of the grinder, what has happened is that the machine, piqued by the slowing down of supply, suddenly suggested to its users that in the future the supplying of grinding material be taken out of their hands and left to the machine. The institutional machinery tends to become an actor with a stake in its own survival and expansion. The same thing happens often enough within a state whose political system is ineffective. But here we deal not with one but with six political systems, and the reason for the ineffectiveness of the Council of Ministers of the Six may be the excessive toughness, not the weakness, of the national political systems involved. In other words, by trying to be a force, the bureaucracy here, inevitably, makes itself even more of a stake that the nations try to control or at least to affect. A new complication is thus added to all the substantive issues that divide the participants—one that provides them with a whole trunkful of screens and masks. Thus, the agricultural problem is one that could have been solved "technically," since the governments had previously reached basic compromises, and more or less agreed on the relations between Common Market and outside agriculture. But the way in which these accords had been reached left scars, and the nature of the agreement meant a victory for one state (France) over another (Germany). The whole issue has been reopened, due not to the states' but to the Commission's initiative. In the crisis of 1965, the Commission's overly bold proposal of a common agricultural policy (along pro-French lines) cum supranationality (against French determination) has, on the one hand, allowed some of the Six, hostile in fact to the substantive proposals, to endorse the Commission's plan and stand up as champions of supranationality, while knowing that the French would block the scheme; the French have been able to use the Commission's rashness as a pretext for trying to kill supranationality altogether; a German government not too kindly disposed toward a Commission whose initiatives and economic inspiration were hardly in line with Mr. Erhard's views has found itself defending the Commission, whose head, now under French attack, is a German; a French government anxious to get its partners committed to a protected agricultural market has preferred to postpone the realization of this goal rather than let the Commission's autonomy grow. The states have found something more to disagree about, and the Commission, in an attempt to push the car out of the bog, has stopped the motor for months. To be sure, the Commission's dilemma had become acute: either its members resigned themselves to being merely patient brokers to their quarreling clients, and letting them set the pace; or else they tried to behave both according to the ideal-type of the Monnet method, and as if a genuine community had already been established; but if prudence meant sluggishness, anticipation has meant delay. In the immediate future, the settlement of the various substantive issues—"the uniting of Europe, what for?"—is likely to be postponed while the Six try to repair the damaged machinery; in a way, haggling about the kind of grinder one wants is a polite method for appearing to want to keep grinding together, while really disagreeing completely on what one wants to put in and get out.

IV

We must come now to the balance sheet of the "European experiment." The most visible aspect is the survival of the nations. To be sure, they survive transformed: first, swept by the advent of the "age of mass consumption," caught in an apparently inexorable process of industrialization, urbanization, and democratization, they become more alike in social structure, in economic and social policies, even in physical appearance; there is a spectacular break between a past which so many monuments bring to constant memory, and a rationalized future that puts these nations closer to the problems of America's industrial society than to the issues of their own history. Second, these similarities are promoted by the Common Market itself: it is of no mean consequence that the prospect of a collapse of the Market should have brought anguish to various interest groups, some of which had fought its establishment: the transnational linkages of businessmen and farmers are part of the transformation. Third, none of the Western European nations is a world power any longer in the traditional sense, that is, in the sense either of having physical establishments backed by military might in various parts of the globe, or of possessing in Europe armed forces superior to those of any non-European power.

And yet they survive as nations. Let us go back to the criteria of integration listed above. On foreign and defense policies, not only has no power been transferred to common European organs, but France has actually taken power away from NATO, and, as shown in part two, differences in the calculations of the national interest have, if anything, broadened ever since the advent of the balance of terror. As for intra-European communications, research shows that the indubitably solid economic network of E.E.C. has not been complemented by a network of social and cultural communications;[30] the links between some of those societies and the U. S. are stronger than the links among them. Indeed, even in the realm of economic relations, the Common Market for goods has not been completed by a system of pan-West European enterprises: enterprises that find themselves unable to compete with rivals within E.E.C. often associate themselves with American firms rather than merge with such rivals. Finally, views about external issues, far from becoming more compatible, appear to reflect as well as to support the divergent definitions of the national interest by the statesmen. French élite opinion puts Europe ahead of the North Atlantic partnership, deems bipolarity obsolete, is overwhelmingly indifferent or even hostile to the U. S., and is still highly suspicious of Germany; only a minority comes out in favor of a genuine political federation of Western Europe and thinks that U. S. and French interests coincide. German élite opinion puts the North Atlantic entente ahead of Europe, believes that the world is still bipolar, is overwhelmingly favorable to the U. S., deems U. S. and German interests in agreement, is either favorably inclined toward France or at least not hostile, and shows a majority in favor of a European federation. There is no common European outlook. Nor is there a common "project," a common conception of either Europe's role in world affairs or Europe's possible contribution to the solution of the problems characteristic of all industrial societies.

It is important to understand where the obstacles lie. To some extent, they lie in the present condition of national consciousness. I mentioned earlier that there were at the start considerable differences from country to country. In two respects, similarities have emerged in recent years. There has been a rebirth of German national consciousness, largely because the bold attempt at fastening Germany's shattered consciousness directly to a new European one did not succeed: the existence of a German national situation has gradually reawakened a German national awareness, and thus reduced the gap between Germany and France in this area. Moreover, all the national consciences in Western Europe are alike in one sense: they are not like Rousseau's general will, a combination of mores and moves that define with a large degree of intellectual clarity and emotional involvement the purposes of the national community. Today's national consciousness in Europe is negative rather than positive. There is still, in each nation, a "vouloir-vivre collectif." But it is not a "daily plebiscite" *for* something. It is, in some parts, a daily routine, a community based on habit rather than on common tasks, an identity that is received rather than shaped. Thus Germany's sense of "cohesion and distinctiveness" is the inevitable result of the survival and recovery of a West German state in a world of nations, rather than a specific willed set of imperatives. In other parts, national consciousness is a daily refusal rather than a daily creation, a desire to preserve a certain heritage (however waning, and less because it is meaningful today than because it is one's own) rather than a determination to define a common destiny, an identity that is hollow rather than full and marked more by bad humor toward foreign influences than by any positive contribution.

To be sure, the negative or hollow character of national consciousness need not be a liability for the champions of integration: general wills *à la* Rousseau could be formidable obstacles to any fusion of sovereignty. However, the obstacle resides partly in the common nature of the present state of national consciousness, partly in the remaining differences. A patriotic consciousness that survives in a kind of nonpurposive complacency may not be a barrier to efforts at transcending it, but it is a drag: it does not carry forward or push statesmen in the way in which an intense and positive "general will" prods leaders who act on behalf of national goals, or in the way in which European federalists have sometimes hoped that enlightened national patriotisms would propel Europe's national leaders into building a new European community, into which those enlightened patriotisms would converge and merge. Moreover, two of the "national consciences" have raised obstacles: the French one because it remains too strong, the German one because it remains too weak. The French may not have a sense of national purpose, but, precisely because their patriotism has been tested so often and so long, because the pressures of the outside world have continued throughout the postwar era to batter their concerns and their conceits, and because modernization, now accepted and even desired, also undermines traditional values still cherished and traditional authority patterns still enforced, French national consciousness opposes considerable resistance to any suggestion of abdication, resignation, *repli*—so much so that the "Europeans" themselves have had to present integration as an opportunity for getting French views shared by others instead of stressing the "community" side of the enterprise.[31] Germany's national consciousness, on the other hand, remains marked by a genuine distaste for or timidity toward what might be called the power activities of a national community on the world stage; hence a tendency to shy away from the problems of "high politics" which a united Europe would have to face and whose avoidance only delays the advent of unity; a tendency to refuse to make policy choices and to pretend (to oneself and to others) that no such choices are required, that there is no incompatibility between a "European Europe" and an Atlantic partnership. In one case, a defensive excess of self-confidence makes unity on terms other than one's own difficult, and obliges integrationist leaders to use cunning and flattery and deceit (with often lamentable results—like the E.D.C. crisis); in the other case, an equally defensive lack of self-confidence projects itself into the external undertakings of the nation and weakens the foundations of the common European enterprise.

And yet, if the "national consciousness" of the European nations could be isolated from all other elements of the national situation, one would, I think, conclude that the main reasons for the resistance of the nation-state lie elsewhere.

They lie, first of all, in the differences in national situations, exacerbated by the interaction between each of the Six and the present international system. Earlier, we have looked at concrete instances of such differences; let us return to them in a more analytic way. One part of each national situation is the purely *domestic* component. In a modern nation-state, the very importance of the political system, in the triple sense of functional scope, authority, and popular basis, is already a formidable obstacle to integration. It is comparatively easier to overcome the parochialism of a political system which, being of the night-watchman variety, has only a slender administrative structure, whose power consists of punishing, rather than rewarding, with the help of a tiny budget, and whose transmission belts to the mass of the people are few and narrow, than it is to dismantle the fortress of a political system which rests on "socially mobilized" and mobilizing parties and pressure groups, and handles an enormous variety of social and economic services with a huge bureaucracy. To be sure, it was the hope and tactic of Monnet to dismantle the fortress by redirecting the allegiance of parties and pressure groups toward the new central institutions, by endowing the latter with the ability to compete with the national governments in the setting up of social services. In other words, the authority of the new European political system would deepen as its scope broadened and its popular basis expanded. The success of this attempt at drying up the national ponds by diverting their waters into a new, supranational pool depended on three prerequisites which have not been met: with respect to popular basis, the prevalence of parties and pressure groups over Executives; with respect to scope, the self-sustaining and expanding capacity of the new central bureaucracy; with respect to both scope and popular basis, the development of transnational political issues of interest to all political forces and publics across boundary lines. The modern Executive establishment has one remarkable feature: it owes much of its legitimacy and its might to the support of popularly based parties and pressure groups, but it also enjoys a degree of autonomy that allows it to resist pressures, to manipulate opposition, to manufacture support. Even the weak Fourth Republic has evaded pressure toward "transnationalism" and diluted the dose of "bargaining politics" along supranational lines. The civil servants' careers are still made and unmade in the national capitals. Above all, each nation's political life continues to be dominated by "parochial" issues: each political system is like a thermos bottle that keeps warm, or lukewarm, the liquid inside. The European political process has never come close to resembling that of any Western European democracy because it has been starved of common and distinctive European issues. It is as if, for the mythical common man, the nation-state were still the most satisfying—indeed the most rewarding —form of social organization in existence.[32] As for what it can no longer provide him with by itself, the state can still provide it without committing suicide, through cooperation, or the citizens can go and find it across borders, without any need to transfer their allegiance—or else there is, in any event, no guarantee that any form of social organization other than a still utopian world state could provide it. If we look at the issues that have dominated European politics, we find two distinct blocs. One is the bloc of problems peculiar to each nation—Italy's battle of Reds *vs.* Blacks, or its concern for the Mezzogiorno; Belgium's linguistic clashes; Germany's "social economy" and liquidation of the past; France's constitutional troubles and miraculously preserved party splintering. Here, whatever the transnational party and interest group alignments in Luxembourg, the dominant motifs have been purely national. The other bloc of issues are the international ones (including European unity). But here is where the *external* component of the national situation has thwarted the emergence of a common European political system comparable to that of each nation.

It is here that the weight of geography and of history—a history of nations—has kept the nation-states in their watertight compartments. It is no accident if France, the initiator of the process, has also been its chief troublemaker: for in those two respects France's position differed from everyone else's in the community, and was actually closer to England's. Historically first: for Germany, integration meant a leap from opprobrium and impotence, to respectability and equal rights; for the smaller powers, it meant exchanging a very modest dose of autonomy for participation in a potentially strong and rich grouping. France could not help being much more ambivalent, for integration meant on the one hand an avenue for leadership and the shaping of a powerful bloc, but it also meant on the other the acceptance of permanent restrictions to an autonomy that was indeed quite theoretical in the late 1940's, but whose loss could not be deemed definitive. For a once-great power, whose national history is long, and therefore used to rise and fall, inherits from its past a whole set of habits and reflexes which make it conduct its policy as if it were still or could again become a great power (unless those habits and reflexes have been smashed, at least for a while, as completely and compellingly as were Germany's); for this once-great power showed, as described above, a still vigilant national consciousness, often the more virulent for all its negativism; for the international system itself seemed to open vistas of increased freedom of action to middle-sized states. In other words, integration meant an almost certain improvement in the national situation of the other five, but for France it could be a deterioration or an adventure.[33] There is no better example than the nuclear problem: integration here meant, for France, giving up the possibility of having a force of her own, perhaps never even being certain that a united Europe (with no agreement on strategy and diplomacy in sight) would create a common deterrent, at best contributing to a European force which would put Germany in the same position as France; but the French decision to pursue the logic of diversity, while giving her her own force, has also made a European nuclear solution more difficult and increased France's distance from Germany. Moreover, a geographical difference has corroborated the historical one: France had lasting colonial involvements. Not only did they, on the whole, intensify national consciousness; they also contributed to France's ambivalence toward European integration. On the one hand, as indicated above, the worse France's overseas plight became, the more integration was preached as a kind of compensatory mechanism. But, on the other hand, this meant that integration had to be given a "national" rather than a "supranational" color, to be presented as a new career rather than as a common leap; it meant that the French consistently tried to tie their partners to the prevalence of France's overseas concerns, much against these partners' better judgment; above all, it meant that there was a competition for public attention and for official energies, between the "load" of integration and the burden of the overseas mission. The great power reflex and the colonial legacy combine today in the policy of cooperation with the former imperial possessions, despite its costs: cooperation is presented as a transfiguration of the legacy, and a manifestation of the reflex.[34]

Thus, the national situations have multiplied the effects of differences between the shapes of the various national consciences. But the resistance of the nation-state is not due only to the kind of loan of life that its inevitable entanglement in international affairs and the idle motion left by its past provide even to nations with a low national consciousness. It is due also to the impact of the revival of nationalism in France. Even without de Gaulle the differences analyzed above would have slowed down integration and kept some fire in the nation's stoves. But the personal contribution of de Gaulle to the crisis of integration has been enormous. Not only has he raised questions that were inescapable in the long run, earlier and more pungently than they would have been otherwise, but he has also provided and tried to impose his own answers. His impact is due to his style as well as to his policies. The meaning of de Gaulle has been a change in French policy from ambivalence toward supranational integration to outright hostility; from a reluctance to force one's partners to dispel the ambiguities of "united Europe" to an almost gleeful determination to bring differences out into the open; from a tendency to interpret the national situation as oppressively difficult to a herculean effort at improving all its components in order to push back limits and maximize opportunities. The meaning of de Gaulle has also been a change in the national situations of the others, leading to a sharpening of antagonisms and to a kind of cumulative retreat from integration. Each one of those meanings must be briefly examined.

Insofar as France is concerned, the key is provided by de Gaulle's concept of grandeur.[35] Greatness is a mixture of pride and ambition—the nation shall not at any point leave the control of its destiny to others (which does not mean that he does not acknowledge the existence of irresistible waves with which the ship of state must roll, lest, precisely, it fall in the hands of others who would rush to a predatory rescue or to a plunder of the wreck).

STANLEY HOFFMANN

The nation must try at any point to play as full a role in the world as its means allow. The consequences are clear: First, the kind of supranational integration which would leave decisions on vital issues to majority votes or to executive organs independent of the states is out of the question; even if the interests and policies of France should happen to prevail for a while (as indeed they did as long as the Commission, in its drive for economic integration, remained very close to French ideas), there would be no assurance against a sudden and disastrous reversal. Second, extensive cooperation is not at all ruled out: on the contrary, such cooperation will benefit all participants as long as it corresponds to and enhances mutual interests. Third, however, it is part of the very ambition of grandeur that in such schemes of cooperation which aim not merely at exchanges of *services* but at the definition of common *policies*, France will try to exert her leadership and carry out her views: the degree of French cooperativeness will be measured by the degree of responsiveness of the others.

It is true that the General is an empiricist, and that his analysis of the European situation is to a large extent irrefutable. What could be more sensible than starting from what exists—the nation-states—refusing to act as if what does not yet exist—a united Europe—had already been established, and refusing to forget that each of the European nations is willy-nilly engaged in an international competition that entails a fight for rank and power? But pragmatism is always at the service of ends, explicit or not (the definition of a bad foreign policy could be: that which uses rigid means at the service of explicit ends, as well as that whose flexible means are not serving clearly-thought-out ends). De Gaulle's empiricism is a superb display of skill, but on behalf of a thoroughly non-empirical doctrine. It is obvious that his distrust of supranational integration, which, within Europe, could submit French interests to the dictates of others, and could expose Europe to the dictates of the "hegemonists," while it is perfectly comprehensible as a starting point, nevertheless results in a kind of freezing of integration and perpetuation of the nation-state. If his chief foreign policy objective were the creation of a European entity acting as a world power, his "empirical" *starting point* would be a most unrealistic *method*. But the fact is that such a creation is not his supreme objective, and Europe not his supreme value.

His supreme value remains the nation-state; his supreme political objective is the creation of a world in which the "two hegemonies" will have been replaced by a multipolar international system, whose "first floor" would be the numerous nations, endowed with and entitled to political integrity and independence, and whose "second floor" would be inhabited by the nuclear powers, in a role comparable to that of the late European concert. Again, the implications are clear: de Gaulle's doctrine is a "universalist nationalism," that is, he sees France's mission as world-wide, not local and defensive; but this means that Europe is just one corner of the tapestry; Europe is a means, not an end. "Things being what they are," it is better to have separate nation-states (whose margin of freedom is undoubtedly smaller than when the use of force was not so costly, whose capacity to shape history is also undoubtedly limited if their size, population, and resources are mediocre, but whose ability to behave as self-determined actors on the stage is enhanced precisely by the blunting of force and by the opportunities opened to other instruments of power and influence) than it is to have a larger entity, undoubtedly more able to act as a forceful competitor in the world's contests should it be coherent, but more likely to be incoherent, given the divisions of its members and the leverage interested outsiders possess over some of the insiders. The size of the unit is less important than its "cohesion and distinctiveness," for its effectiveness is not merely a function of its material resources: if the unit has no capacity to turn these to action, because of internal cleavages and strains, the only beneficiaries would be its rivals. In a contest with giants, a confident David is better than a disturbed Goliath. This is a choice that reflects a doctrine; the refusal to gamble on European unity goes along with a willingness to gamble on the continuing potency of the French nation-state; the determination to accept only the kind of Europe that would be France writ large[36] corresponds to a conviction that French policies could be made to prevail whether Europe contributes its support or not: "with Europe if they follow, without Europe if they do not," Europe is just a card in a global game. Schumpeter had defined imperialism as an objectless quest; de Gaulle's nationalism is a kind of permanent quest with varying content but never any other cause than itself.

As I suggested above, a nationalist leader is one whose reading of the national situation is likely to be quite different from the reading other leaders would give. De Gaulle's brand of nationalism being what it is—universalist, aimed at overcoming the "two hegemonies," exploiting both of the somewhat contradictory trends that dominate the present world (the conservation of the nation as

STANLEY HOFFMANN

its basic unit, the concentration of what one might call "final power" among the nuclear states)—it is not surprising that he has altogether liquidated a colonial burden that kept France away from every one of the routes he wanted to travel, and replaced it with an ambitious policy of cooperation with the "Third World." In a way, it is true, as some critics have charged, that this policy is a kind of self-consolation prize for the failure of his European policy; but in another sense it conforms deeply to his most vital designs and to his most constant habit of never relying on one line of policy only: In the first place, cooperation manifests France's universal destiny; in the second, it aims at consolidating a system of independent, if cooperating, nations; in the third, it tries to use the prestige thus gained as an elevator to the floor of the "big five," to which access has been denied so far by the "big two." It is clear that the first two missions rule out a concentration on Europe alone, that the second prevents in any case his putting any passion into overcoming the nation-state in Europe, that the third is precisely a substitute for the "elevator" Europe has failed to provide. As a result, all that has made France's historical heritage and geographic position distinctive has been strengthened.

Every great leader has his built-in flaw, since this is a world in which roses have thorns. De Gaulle's is the self-fulfilling prophecy. Distrustful of any Europe but his own, his acts have made Europe anything but his. Here we must turn to the impact of his policy on France's partners. First of all, there is a matter of style: wanting cooperation not integration, de Gaulle has refused to treat the Community organs as Community organs; but, wanting to force his views about cooperation on partners still attached to integration, and attempting to impose his views about a "European Europe" on associates who might have settled for cooperation but only on behalf of another policy, de Gaulle has paradoxically had to try to achieve cooperation for a common policy in a way that smacked of conflict not cooperation, of unilateralism not compromise. Thus we have witnessed not just a retreat from the Monnet method to, say, the kind of intergovernmental cooperation that marks O.E.C.D., but to a kind of grand strategy of nonmilitary conflict, a kind of political cold war of maneuver and "chicken." With compromises wrested by ultimatums, concessions obtained not through package deals but under the threat of boycotts, it is not surprising if even the Commission ended by playing the General's game instead of turning whatever other cheek was left; its spring 1965 agricultural

146

plan was as outright a challenge to de Gaulle as de Gaulle's veto of January 1963 had been an affront to the Community spirit. Just as de Gaulle had tried to force Germany to sacrifice her farmers to the idea of a European entity, the Commission tried to call de Gaulle's bluff by forcing him to choose between French farmers' interests and the French national interest in a "European Europe" for agriculture, on the one hand, and his own hostility to supranationality and the French national interest (as seen by him) in the free use of French resources, on the other. Playing his game, the Commission also played into his hands, allowing him to apply the Schelling tactic of "if you do not do what I ask, I will blow up my brains on your new suit," and in the end buying his return at the price of a sacrifice of integration.[37] In other words, he has forced each member to treat the Community no longer as an end in itself; and he has driven even its constituted bodies, which still insist it is that, into bringing grist to his mill.

Second, his impact on his partners is a matter of policy as well. Here we must examine Franco-German relations. As long as he hoped that Germany would follow his guidance and provide the basis for the "European Europe" of his design, his attitude toward West Germany was one of total support of her intransigence toward the Communists. As soon as the increasing clarity of his own policy (half-veiled until the end of the Algerian ordeal and his triumph in the constitutional battle of October-November 1962) provoked German suspicion and reticence, as soon as the U.S., in response to his challenge, consolidated its ties with a still loyal Germany and even promised her substantial rewards for her loyalty, he applied to Germany the shock tactics so effectively used on Britain and the U.S. during World War II: he made his own opening to the East and gradually shifted away from the kind of celebration of a "new Germany" (heir to her greatness in her past but now willing to take her place as France's aide in the new "European Europe"), so characteristic of his German visit in the fall of 1962. He now resorts to carefully worded reminders to the Germans of their past misdeeds, of the risk which their loyalty to the U.S. entails for their reunification, and of the interest France and the Eastern states (including Russia) share in keeping Germany under permanent restrictions. Had Germany been willing to follow France, he would have given priority to the construction of a "half-Europe" that would thereafter have been a magnet (as well as a guarantee of German harmlessness) to the East. Germany's refusal leads him to put the gradual emergence of a "Europe from the Atlantic to the Urals"—indeed from the British Isles to the Urals[38]—if not ahead of at least on the same plane as the development of the "European Europe" in the West; for the containment of Germany, no longer assured in a disunited Western Europe of the Six, may still be obtained in a much larger framework. The implications are important. First, there is a considerable change in Germany's national situation. On the one hand, its external component has been transformed. Whereas for more than fifteen years both the U.S. and France carried out tacitly Robert Schuman's recommendation— "never leave Germany to herself"—the Franco-American competition for German support, the Gaullist refusal to tie Germany to France in a federal Europe so to speak for the knot's sake (that is, unless Germany follows France), America's disastrous emulation of the sorcerer's apprentice in titillating Germany's interest in nuclear strategy or weapons-sharing, in the belief, or under the pretext, of anticipating her appetite, all of these factors have contributed to loosen the bonds between Germany and the West: to the European part of the West, because of the slump in integration, and even to the U.S., because of America's failure to follow up after raising in Germany hopes that should not have been raised, but which, once raised and frustrated, are unlikely to fade. On the other hand, and consequently, the domestic component of Germany's national situation has also been affected: Still concerned with security as well as with reunification, but less and less capable of believing that loyalty to their allies will deliver any goods, the German leaders and élites may well come to feel less dependent and less constrained. Of course, objectively, the external constraints remain compelling: a policy of self-assertion may not lead anywhere; an attempt at bypassing the nuclear restrictions of the Paris agreements is not likely to make the East Europeans and the Soviets any more willing to let East Germany go; and the price the Soviets may want to exact for reunification is not likely to increase German security. But the fact that Germany's ties to Western powers are weakening means at least potentially that the capacity to test those constraints by unilateral action may well be used. To be in a cell with a chain around one's ankles and the hope of being liberated by one's jailers is one kind of situation. To be in that cell without such a chain and with such hopes gone is another situation, although the cell has not changed.

In other words, although the impact of de Gaulle on Germany

so far has not been a rebirth of German nationalism, it has been a transformation of the situation that gives to nationalism some chances—chances if not of external success, given the nature of the cell, then of being at least "tried." The temptation to use one's economic power and potential military might in order to reach one's goals and the example of one's allies competing for accommodation with one's foe are not resistible forever, especially if one's past is full of precedents. To be sure, a nationalist Germany may well find itself as unable to shake the walls or to escape through the bars as Gaullist France is unable to forge the "European Europe." But the paradox of a revisionist France, trying to change the international system to her advantage despite her complete lack of "traditional" grievances (lost territories, military discrimination, and so forth), next to a Germany full of such grievances, yet behaving in fact like a *status quo* power, may not last eternally. Of course, a less aggressively ambitious France might not have prevented Germany from trying to follow her own path one day: the possibility of someone else's imitative *ubris* is no reason for one's own *effacement;* but precisely because the "essence and drama" of nationalism are the meeting with others, the risk of contagion—a risk that is part of de Gaulle's gamble—cannot be discarded.

Thus the nation-state survives, preserved by the formidable autonomy of politics, as manifested in the resilience of political systems, the interaction between separate states and a single international system, the role of leaders who believe both in the primacy of "high politics" over the kind of managerial politics susceptible to functionalism, and in the primacy of the nation, struggling in the world of today, over any new form, whose painful establishment might require one's lasting withdrawal from the pressing and exalting daily contest.

V

This long balance sheet leaves us with two sets of questions: What are the prospects in Western Europe? What generalizations can one draw from the whole experience? As for the prospects, what precedes reads perhaps too much like a post-mortem. Is there no chance for the European Community? Is it condemned to be, at best, a success in the economic realm but a fiasco in "high politics," something like a hydra with one single body but a multitude of heads?

It would be presumptuous indeed to read hope out of court. One of the decisive elements in the movement's "spillback," de Gaulle's nationalism, may not outlive him. His successors may have a less sweeping vision and may make exactly the opposite gamble from his—that is, prefer the risks of the common enterprise, whose rewards might be high if it works, to the dividends of national action; they could indeed attempt to revive the Monnet concept of Europe, and even to overcome the deficiencies of functionalism by a leap into more genuinely federal institutions. Moreover, whereas de Gaulle has had the backing of a parliamentary majority hostile to supranational integration and has exerted the kind of rule that parties and pressure groups do not affect much anyhow, his successors may depend for domestic support and survival precisely on those parties and pressure groups which had started to weave a transnational fabric. Should this be the case, the "Europe of the Six," instead of being as close as it now is to the traditional model of interstate relations, might move again toward the other ideal-type, that of political community-building, so well described by Ernst Haas, who sees in it the wave of the future.[39]

Whereas in the case of a revival of German nationalism, the propect of failure may not be enough to deter an attempt, here I would maintain that an attempt would not be tantamount to success. In the first place, while nothing (not even the Common Market) is irreversible, no important event leaves the world unmarked, and after the event one can never pick up the pieces as if nothing had happened: this, which is true of the Common Market, is true also of General de Gaulle. It will not be easy to sweep under the rug the curls of dust he has willfully placed in the sunlight; it will not be easy to ignore the kinds of questions he has asked, even if his answers are rejected, precisely because they are the questions any European enterprise would have faced sooner or later. Second, even the passing of his nationalism might not transform the national situations of the European nation-states so deeply that all the cleavages discussed here would suddenly disappear. For, even if all the political leaders of Western Europe had once again the same non-nationalist approach, the differences in the national situations would still lead to divergent definitions of the national interests. In particular, the problem of nuclear weapons control and command in a grouping divided between nuclear "have-nots" and nuclear "haves" may prove to be as intractable, and to raise as much of an obstacle to community-formation among Western Europeans, as in the Atlantic alliance. The ideal conditions not merely for the resumption but for the success of a forward march would be a transformation of Germany's external situation and of France's domestic one. If the search for a détente should lead the U.S. to put a rapprochement with the U.S.S.R. ahead of its bonds to West Germany, and if it became clear in West Germany, as a result, both that security is neither the most urgent problem nor entirely provided any more by the U.S., and that reunification cannot be obtained from and through the U.S.; if, in addition, such disappointment with the U.S. does not encourage West German leadership to follow a nationalist path, or if an attempt by West Germany to obtain for itself from Moscow what its allies had failed to provide for her should end in frustration, then—at last—West Germany might be willing to accept a foreign policy close to de Gaulle's "European Europe" with its indifference to regimes and ideologies, its repudiation of the cold war outlook, its opening to the East, and its cautious promise of eventual reunification at the cost of border limitations and arms restrictions. In other words, on the German side, what would be required would be a "polycentric," yet non-nationalist, reading of the external situation. This would be likely to happen if at the same time France had given up her nationalist interpretation of "polycentrism," and become again more humble, more willing to trust the Community organs, more in need of adopting European integration as a goal in itself. Such a possibility would exist if, domestically, the impervious stability of de Gaulle's regime were to be replaced not merely with a political system whose Executive would lean on an "integrationist" party majority, but with the kind of instability that both prevents political leaders from acting on the world stage as if they were its managers and pressures them into seeking a European solution, or alibi, for their difficulties. Europe as Germany's least frustrating framework, Europe as the best compensation for France's domestic troubles, a Europe following Monnet's approach toward de Gaulle's objectives:[40] it may appear like a dream; it cannot be dismissed. But whether it has a chance depends essentially on *when* the General's nationalism will pass from the scene, on *what* degree of cooperation among the nations of Western Europe there will be at that time, on *whether* a new attempt by Britain to join the Community would introduce additional complications, on *what* the U.S. policy in Europe will be; the chance depends on the timely convergence of too many variables to be counted on.

Against such a chance, there is too big a range of obstacles. Here is where the European experience is of general significance.

1. A first set of remarks deals with the conditions which the national situations of the units engaged in an attempt to integrate must meet, lest the attempt be unsuccessful. Those situations ought to be similar; but a generalization of this kind is almost worthless: what matters is the nature of the similarity.

a. Insofar as domestic circumstances are concerned, two conditions are essential. The first one is obvious at first sight, much less so upon reflection: the units must be political communities, not in a substantive sense (common values and goals, à la Rousseau) but in a formal one (the existence of intense communications and of common habits and rules across regional differences as well as across the borders of ethnic groups, tribes, or classes);[41] in other words, transnational integration presupposes integration within the units.* These units need not be nation-states, in the sense of com-

---

* The distinctions I suggest are like marks on a continuum. 1. At one end, there are *cooperative arrangements* whose institutions have no autonomy from the various governments (O.E.C.D., the U.N. in most respects). Such arrangements in turn range from truly cooperative to hegemonial, that is, from representing all the members to asserting the domination and extending the will of one of them. 2. Then there are *entities* which have *central institutions* endowed with some authority, in the sense of legal autonomy from the components and legal power all over the territory of the entity, but which are *not* political communities in the formal sense, because of drastic discontinuities in communications and transactions among the components, or because the cleavages within the entity deprive in fact the central institutions of autonomy or of much effective power (that is, states such as the Congo or certain Latin American states; supranational entities like the E.E.C., and, within the limits of effective military integration, N.A.T.O.) Such entities may be astonishingly resilient if they are states, endowed with international personality and institutions that have a formal monopoly of force or at least a superiority of force over internal challenges; but if these entities are supranational (and especially when they are not merely a way of disguising the hegemony of one of the component members), they are likely to be highly unstable (see below) precisely because the entity's "central" institutions are likely to be constantly challenged by the central institutions of the component states, endowed with external sovereignty as well as with superior force. In other words, supranational entities will tend either to retrogress toward stage 1 or to progress toward stage 3. 3. Next come entities which are *political communities* in the *formal* but not in the substantive sense: that is, their central institutions have autonomy and power, there are common habits, and the rules that come from above are enforced across internal barriers, but the central institutions are not endowed with legitimacy all over the territory, and the habits and rules are not based on common values con-

munities endowed with external sovereignty under international law; but conversely, if a newly independent state is merely a shell within which there is no community yet, the cleavages that divide the population into separate communities will prove to be a decisive obstacle to trans-state integration: domestic integration is a prerequisite to the kinds of flows of transactions and of ideas which trans-state integration requires and will of necessity be the primary goal of any leader who tries to be more than the representative of the dominant sect, class, tribe, or ethnic group. This explains why, for so many countries of Latin America, Latin American integration remains a chimera, and also why it has been so difficult in Africa and in Asia to move beyond the nation-state: in many cases, the state is there, but not yet the nation.

The second condition concerns the structure of society and of the political system in units that are political communities. The students of integration have rightly stressed the importance of pluralistic social structures and élite groups in the units that try to integrate. But success depends on more than a similarity of such structures: It requires the simultaneous presence in the Executive of leaders who represent those sections of the élites that advocate union and whose power depends on the support of the integrationist élites and groups. To the extent to which many of the new states— those whose capacity to become viable nation-states is most dubious —are single-party states with so-called charismatic (or should one say authoritarian?) leaders, this internal condition for unification is missing.

b. Insofar as external conditions are concerned, what matters is not that the units be in "objectively" similar situations at the time when integration begins and while it proceeds. What matters is "subjective" similarity—a similarity that is not the scholar's assertion, but the policy-maker's conviction. The implication, which is crucial, is that one must examine more than the relation of each unit to the international system at the moment. Even if this relation is

cerning the polity; this is the case of many nation-states, which have "national consciousness" but are not political communities in the last sense. 4. Here I refer to nation-states whose central institutions are altogether autonomous, effectively powerful and legitimate, and whose society has shared values concerning the polity. These are political communities in the *substantive* sense. Needless to say, they are not legion. The difference between stage 3 and stage 4 is largely a difference in the level and scope of consensus. I would reserve the term nation to states in those two stages.

the same for all the units involved, one must go beyond: One must also determine whether the units come to this moment and place from similar origins and through similar itineraries, whether they are likely to proceed from this moment and place toward similar destinations. "Objective" similarity is disembodied—removed from time and space. The similarity that matters is a similarity in the way in which different statesmen interpret a whole historical and geographical experience and outline the future in the light of this experience. Integration means a common choice of a common future. Success presupposes two sets of conditions, one about the past, one about the present.

As for the past, integration is likely to be more successful when the voyagers' baggage is light. If the units' past international experiences have been long and heavy—long *or* heavy—if the state apparatus has developed over decades and centuries, if the state has, quite simply, enjoyed an autonomous existence on the world scene for a long time, integration will not be easy. Is it an accident if the only successful example of voluntary unification in the modern world is that of the U.S.—the fusion of units that had been colonies, not states, and in which neither the machinery of the state nor traditions of foreign policy had had the time to develop? In a sense, the shedding of overseas commitments by countries such as France and Britain should make their luggage lighter. But, as we have seen in the case of France, the old burdens tend to be replaced by new ties, the old *imperium* leaves lasting concerns, and the old responsibilities do not disappear without leaving a sense of responsibility. Moreover, even if the nations of Western Europe are less weighed down by the past than before, the present remains distracting enough.

The kind of similarity required in the present concerns the relation of the units to the international system. A first question to be asked is the degree of *involvement*. When the similarity in the national situations is one of distance or insulation from the international system, as was the case of the American states and to a large extent the case of Switzerland after the Reformation, concentration on the difficult job of unification becomes possible. A capital obstacle to integration anywhere in the world today is the loss of such distance, the impossibility of such insulation, in the echo chamber of the present international system. This obstacle can, however, occasionally be cancelled. For there is a second question: the degree of *"compellingness"* of the international system; when the national situations are similar because of an overwhelming external threat (as was originally the case with the Swiss cantons and the American ex-colonies), unification for survival or security may become an imperative. A compelling threat can make up for different pasts, and impose a common destination, when all divergencies about ultimate destinies have to be subordinated to the preservation of a chance for any destiny at all. One can argue that this was Western Europe's condition in the first ten years after the end of World War II. But the countervailing force was the combination of the different pulls of different pasts, with the different kinds of involvements in the international system: All threatened from the East, the nations of Western Europe nevertheless assessed differently the degree to which this threat superseded every other aspect of international politics. It is not an accident if the nation that deemed the menace entirely compelling was Germany, divided and literally thrown face to face with the threat at the exclusion of almost everything else. It is not an accident if France and Britain, entangled overseas and heirs to Europe's past, never let the threat from the East command their entire foreign policy in the present[42] or assumed that it would inevitably dominate their future. Moreover, Europe today is no longer compelled by the threat: Today's international system is a perverse seducer to diversity. It inflates each national situation, while it removes some of sovereignty's sting. In a way, the relative impotence of force, the postponement of the minute of truth, should reduce the significance of all differences in national situations: The mighty cannot use all the muscles they flex; the weakly can safely boast of more muscle strength than they have. But, in another way, since this is still a competitive system of fragmented states, Rousseau's iron logic applies: Each state tries to exploit whatever margin of difference it has; each state, even when its objective position in the world is not so different from its neighbor's, stresses the marginal differences above the similarities; and, since it ultimately matters much less than before, the incentive to unification in order to "pull more weight" is slim. The changes in the nature of usable power, in the relation between the uses and the achievements of power, give even to the weakest unit one asset in the contest—the power of its mere existence. The breakdown of the two polar camps, the kind of weightlessness with which restrictions on force endow the actors in the new international system, encourage the proliferation of different visions of the future or the tendency to live in the hazards and chances of a fascinatingly diverse present rather than planning too much for an inscrutable future. The rational observer, outside the contest, can preach that precisely because the stakes of the contest are more symbolic than real—barring a holocaust that would equalize through annihilation—nation-states ought to be willing to unite even at the cost of transferring for a while their energy from the intoxicating but disappointing stage of world politics to the real job of community-building; for the outcome would be the appearance of a new actor whose power, by contrast with that of each old component, could really be sufficient to make a difference. But the logic of competition operates exactly the other way; it conforms to the French proverb: one thing possessed is worth more than two things promised. In the immediate postwar system, European nations seemed obliged to choose only between separate insecurity and the Atlantic shelter. The "halfway house" of Western Europe got started, but did not progress far enough before the advent of the era in which the temptation of separateness started to smile again, and the reward for separateness was a seat in the U.N.

It is the dialectic of fragmentation and unity (a single international system, whose members may well be kicking and screaming but have an interest in the avoidance of excess violence, that is, in behaving less asocially than before) which gives to the drama of Europe so much of its pathos. On the one hand, in a "finished world" dominated by giants, in a crowded world singularly resistant to the sweep of anyone's universal mission, there is something absurb and pathetic in the tenacious persistence of separate European national wills. On the other hand, it is precisely because most of the differences between them have taken refuge in the realm of foreign affairs that integration is so difficult, despite (or perhaps because of) the fact that international politics today is more a stage on which one can parade than a battlefield that seals one's fate.

2. A second set of remarks concerns the meaning of integration. It has become possible for scholars to argue both that integration is proceeding and that the nation-state is more than ever the basic unit, without contradicting each other, for recent definitions of integration "beyond the nation-state" point not toward the emergence of a new kind of political community, but merely toward an "obscur[ing of] the boundaries between the system of international organizations and the environment provided by member states."[43] There are two important implications.

a. The first one is, not so paradoxically, a vindication of the nation-state as the basic unit. So far, anything that is "beyond" is "less": that is, there are cooperative arrangements with a varying degree of autonomy, power, and legitimacy, but there has been no transfer of allegiance toward their institutions, and their authority remains limited, conditional, dependent, and reversible. There is more than a kernel of truth in the Federalist critique of functional integration: functionalism tends to become, at best, like a spiral that coils ad infinitum. So far, the "transferring [of] exclusive expectations of benefits from the nation-state to some larger entity"[44] leaves the nation-state both as the main focus of expectations, and as the initiator, pace-setter, supervisor, and often destroyer of the larger entity: for in the international arena the state is still the highest possessor of power, and while not every state is a political community there is as yet no political community more inclusive than the state.[45] To be sure, the military function of the nation-state is in crisis; but, insofar as the whole world is "permeable" to nuclear weapons, any new type of unit would face the same horror, and, insofar as the prospect of such horror makes war more subdued and conquest less likely, the decline of the state's capacity to defend its citizens is neither total nor sufficient to force the nation-state itself into decline. The resistance of the nation-state is proven not only by the frustrations of functionalism but also by both the promise and the failure of Federalism. On the one hand, Federalism offers a way of going "beyond the nation-state," but it consists in building a new and larger nation-state. The scale is new, not the story, the gauge not the game. Indeed, the Federalist model applies to the "making of Europe" the Rousseauistic scheme for the creation of a nation: it aims at establishing a unit marked by central power and based on the general will of a European people. The Federalists are right in insisting that Western Europe's best chance of being an effective entity would be not to go "beyond the nation-state," but to become a larger nation-state in the process of formation and in the business of world politics: that is, to become a sovereign political community in the formal sense at least. The success of Federalism would be a tribute to the durability of the nation-state; its failure so far is due to the irrelevance of the model. Not only is there no general will of a European people because there is as of now no European people, but the institutions that could gradually (and theoretically) shape the separate nations into one people are not the most likely to do so. For the domestic problems of Europe are matters for technical decisions by civil servants and ministers rather than for general wills and assemblies (a general will to prosperity is not very operational). The external problems of Europe are matters for executives and diplomats. As for the common organs set up by the national governments, when they try to act as a European executive and parliament, they are both condemned to operate in the fog maintained around them by the governments and slapped down if they try to dispel the fog and reach the people themselves. In other words, Europe cannot be what some of nations have been: a people that creates its state; nor can it be what some of the oldest states are and many of the new ones aspire to be: a people created by the state. It has to wait until the separate states decide that their peoples are close enough to justify the setting up of a European state whose task will be the welding of the many into one; and we have just examined why such a joint decision has been missing. The very obstacles which make the Federalist model irrelevant to nations too diverse and divided also make all forms of union short of Federalism precarious. Functionalism is too unstable for the task of complete political unification. It may integrate economies, but either the nations will then proceed to a full political merger (which economic integration does not guarantee)—in that case the federal model will be vindicated at the end, the new unit will be a state forging its own people by consent and through the abdication of the previous separate states, but the conditions for success described above will have to be met—or else the national situations will remain too divergent, and functionalism will be merely a way of tying together the preexisting nations in areas deemed of common interest. Between the cooperation of existing nations and the breaking in of a new one there is no stable middle ground. A federation that succeeds becomes a nation; one that fails leads to secession; half-way attempts like supranational functionalism must either snowball or roll back.

b. But the nation-state, preserved as the basic unit, survives transformed. Among the men who see in "national sovereignty" the Nemesis of mankind, those who put their hopes in the development of regional superstates are illogical, those who put their hopes in the establishment of a world state are utopian, those who put their hopes in the growth of functional political communities more inclusive than the nation-state are too optimistic. What has to be understood and studied now—far more than has been done, and certainly far more than this essay was able to do—is, rather than the creation of rival communities, the transformation of "national sovereignty": it has not been superseded, but to a large extent it has been emptied of its former sting; there is no supershrew, and yet the shrew has been somewhat tamed. The model of the nation-state derived from the international law and relations of the past, when there was a limited number of players on a stage that was less crowded and in which violence was less risky, applies only fitfully to the situation of today. The basic unit, having proliferated, has also become much more heterogeneous; the stage has shrunk, and is occupied by players whose very number forces each one to strut, but its combustibility nevertheless scares them from pushing their luck too hard. The nation-state today is a new wine in old bottles, or in bottles that are sometimes only a mediocre imitation of the old; it is not the same old wine. What must be examined is not just the legal capacity of the sovereign state, but the *de facto* capacity at its disposal: granted the scope of its authority, how much of it can be used, and with what results? There are many ways of going "beyond the nation-state," and some modify the substance without altering the form or creating new forms. To be sure, as long as the old form is there, as long as the nation-state is the supreme authority, there is a danger for peace and for welfare; Gullivers tied by Lilliputians rather than crushed by Titans can wake up and break their ties. But Gullivers tied are not the same as Gullivers untied. Wrestlers who slug it out with fists and knives, prisoners in a chain gang, are all men; yet their freedom of action is not the same. An examination of the international implications of "nation-statehood" today and yesterday is at least as important as the ritual attack on the nation-state.

3. A final remark concerns the future of integration. Prospects of genuine unification would improve if the international system created the conditions and incentives for moving "beyond the nation-state." In a world in which, on the one hand, many more units had succeeded in becoming genuine nations with pluralistic structures, in which, on the other hand, a return to multipolarity had resulted both in greater autonomy for the subsystems and in a resurrection of interstate war (in the form of limited conventional war or even geographically limited nuclear conflicts), the conditions of unification would be met, at least in some parts of the world: a less universal and intense involvement, a more compelling threat, greater internal harmony might allow the nation-state to supersede itself. But even so, the result might simply be the agglomeration of many smaller nation-states into fewer, bigger ones; and there are more

things in the heaven and earth of possible international futures than in any philosophy of international relations.

REFERENCES

1. See Pierre Renouvin et Jean-Baptiste Duroselle, *Introduction a l'histoire des relations internationales* (Paris, 1964).

2. In a way, the weaker are the foundations on which the nation rests, the shriller the assertions become.

3. On this point, see Rupert Emerson, *From Empire to Nation* (Cambridge, Mass., 1962), Ch. XIX; and Raymond Aron, *Paix et Guerre entre les Nations* (Paris, 1962), Ch. XI.

4. E. H. Carr, *Nationalism and After* (London, 1965), p. 51. Quoted in Pierre Hassner, "Nationalisme et relations internationales," *Revue française de science politique*, Vol. XV, No. 3 (June 1965), pp. 499-528.

5. See Ernst B. Haas' book by this title (Stanford, Calif., 1964).

6. See on this point my essay "Rousseau on War and Peace," in *The State of War* (New York, 1965).

7. P. Hassner, *op. cit.*, p. 523.

8. Karl Deutsch, *Nationalism and Social Communication* (Cambridge, Mass., 1953), p. 147.

9. A more systematic and exhaustive analysis would have to discriminate rigorously among the various components of the national situation; if the purpose of the analysis is to help one understand the relations between the nation-state and the international system, it would be particularly necessary to assess (1) the degree to which each of these components is an unchangeable given (or a given unchangeable over a long period of time) or on the contrary an element that can be transformed by will and action; (2) the hierarchy of importance and the order of urgency that political élites and decision-makers establish among the components.

10. See Raoul Girardet, "Antour de l'ideologie nationaliste," *Revue française de science politique, op. cit.*, pp. 423-445; and P. Hassner, *op. cit.*, pp. 516-19.

11. As will be stated more explicitly in part V, what matters is not the "objective" difference detected by scholars or outsiders, but the "felt" difference experienced by political élites and decision-makers.

12. See "Paradoxes of the French Political Community," in S. Hoffmann, *et al.*, *In Search of France* (Cambridge, Mass., 1963).

13. *La politique extérieure de la V République* (Paris, 1965), p. 12.

14. *The Uniting of Europe* (Stanford, Calif., 1958).

15. See my discussion in "The European process of Atlantic cross-purposes,"

Journal of Common Market Studies (February 1965), pp. 85-101. The very success of internal economic integration raised those external issues far earlier than many expected. (Cf. Britain's application for membership, the problem of external commercial policy.)

16. The latter case is self-evident; the first, less so, since the crisis over E.D.C. was primarily an "intra-European" split, between the French and the Germans over the return of the latter to arms and soldiery. However, there was more to it than this: E.D.C. was accepted mostly by those who thought that Europe could and should not refuse to do what the U.S. had demanded—that is, rearm in order to share the defense of the half-continent with the U.S., and to incite the U.S. to remain its primary defender; E.D.C. was rejected by those who feared that the Defense Community would freeze existing power relationships forever.

17. There was, however, in France, a minority of "resigned ones," like Paul Reynaud.

18. There is an impressive continuity in French efforts to preserve the difference between France's position and Germany's: from the préalables and protocols to E.D.C., to Mendès-France's Brussels proposals, to de Gaulle's opposition to any nuclear role for Germany.

19. France's "intergrationist resisters," like Jean Monnet himself, often chose not to stress the "resistance" aspect of their long-term vision, but nevertheless aimed ultimately at establishing in Western Europe not a junior partner of the U.S. but a "second force" in the West. Mendès-France's political vision never put the nation on top of the hierarchy of values; however, in 1954 (especially in his ill-fated demands for a revision of E.D.C. at the Brussels meeting in August) as well as in 1957 (when he voted against the Common Market), his actual policies did put a priority on national reform over external entanglements.

20. It is no coincidence if E.D.C. was rejected six weeks after the end of the war in Indochina, if the Common Market was signed while war raged in Algeria, if de Gaulle's sharpest attack on the "Monnet method" followed the Evian agreements. The weight of the situation affected and inflected the course of even as nationalist a leader as de Gaulle, between 1958 and 1962. Even he went along with the "Monnet method," however grudgingly, right until the end of the Algerian War. It is not a coincidence either if the French leaders most suspicious of the imprisoning effects of the community of the Six from France were the ones who labored hardest at improving the national situation by removing the colonial burdens (Mendès-France, de Gaulle)—and if those French rulers who followed Monnet and tried to place the pride of a nation with a sharp but wounded patriotic sense in its leadership of a united Europe were the men who failed to improve the national situation overseas (the M.R.P., Mollet). The one French politician who sought both European integration and imperial "disengagement" was Antoine Pinay.

21. Especially by Henry Kissinger in *The Troubled Partnership* (New York, 1965).

22. One should not forget that the original decisions that led to the French force de frappe were taken before de Gaulle, or that the French opposition to a national deterrent came from men who did not at all object to his argument about the need for Europe as a whole to stop being a client of the U.S., and who thought that, indeed, America's nuclear monopoly in the alliance was obsolete.

23. Hence the rather vague or embarrassed formulas used by Jean Monnet's Action Committee for the United States of Europe with regard to defense in the past two years.

24. The case of Erich Mende's Free Democrats is more complicated.

25. See my previous discussion in "Discord in Community," in F. Wilcox and H. F. Haviland, Jr. (eds.), *The Atlantic Community* (New York, 1963), pp. 3-31; "Europe's Identity Crisis," *Dædalus* (Fall 1964), pp. 1244-97, and the article listed in reference 15.

26. See, for instance, Max Kohnstamm's "The European Tide," in Stephen R. Graubard (ed.), *A New Europe?* (Boston, 1964), pp. 140-73.

27. See K. W. Deutsch, *et al.*, *Political Community and the North Atlantic Area* (Princeton, N. J., 1937).

28. Under authority, I include three distinct notions: autonomy (the capacity to act independently of the governments, and particularly the financial capacity), power (control over acts of others), and legitimacy (being accepted as the "rightful" center of action).

29. Along similar lines, see Francis Rosenstiel, *Le principe de "Supranationalité"* (Paris, 1962).

30. I am using here unpublished studies done under Karl Deutsch, especially by Donald J. Puchala.

31. On this point, see Raymond Aron and Daniel Lerner (eds.), *France Defeats EDC* (New York, 1957).

32. See Rupert Emerson, *op. cit.*, Ch. XIX.

33. England's refusal to join European integration, before 1961, could not fail to increase French reticence, for integration thus meant equality with Germany, and a clear-cut difference between France's position and England's, that is, a reversal of French aspirations and traditions. England has on the whole rejected the "resignation-resistance" dilemma—and as a result, both the aspects of its foreign policy that appeared like resignation to U.S. predominance and the aspects that implied resistance to decline have contributed to the crisis of European integration: for France's veto in January 1963 meant a French refusal to let into Europe a power that had just confirmed its military ties to the U.S., but Britain's previous desire to play a world role and aversion to "fading into Europe" encouraged France's own misgivings about integration.

34. See Alfred Grosser, *op. cit.*, Ch. IV.

35. For a more detailed analysis of this concept, see my article: "De Gaulle's Memoirs: The Hero as History," *World Politics*, Vol. XIII, No. 1 (October 1960), pp. 140-155.

36. Grosser, *op. cit.*, pp. 112-113, draws attention to Prime Minister Pompidou's statement: "France is condemned by geography and history to play the role ot Europe."

37. See Thomas Schelling's *Strategy of Conflict* (Cambridge, Mass., 1960).

38. See de Gaulle's reference to England in his press conference of September 9, 1965.

39. See his essay "Technocracy, Pluralism and the New Europe," in Stephen R. Graubard (ed.), *op. cit.*, pp. 62-88.

40. As Grosser points out in his book and the presidential election campaign of 1965 confirmed, even the opposition to de Gaulle's foreign policy accepts his notion of a "European Europe" and rejects American "hegemony" (with the exception of a very few men like Reynaud or perhaps Lecanuet). There is disagreement about methods and style rather than on objectives.

41. I find Ernst B. Haas' definition of a political community in his *Uniting of Europe*, p. 5, ("a condition in which specific groups and individuals show more loyalty to their central political institutions than to any other political authority") not very helpful in the case of states marked by severe domestic cleavages; there might be more loyalty to the center than to any other political authority merely because there is no other *political* authority, and yet one would still not be in the presence of anything like an integrated society.

42. Witness France's army strength in Algeria until 1962, and Britain's extra-European troop commitments.

43. Haas, *Beyond the Nation-State*, p. 29.

44. Ernst B. Haas and Philippe C. Schmitter, "Economics and Differential Patterns of Political Integration," *International Organization*, Vol. XVIII, No. 4 (Autumn 1964), pp. 705-737, and p. 710.

45. One could argue that the entity of the Six, insofar as its functional scope is concerned (that is, the realm of welfare, which is certainly a significant part of politics) is a political community in the formal sense. My own analysis of political realities (by contrast with the law of the treaties that established the three communities) is more pessimistic; although I admit that because of the Commission's role the entity of the Six came close to being a political community in the formal sense, recent events have underlined the precariousness of the Commission's autonomy and power.

HENRY A. KISSINGER

Domestic Structure and Foreign Policy

I. *The Role of Domestic Structure*

IN THE traditional conception, international relations are conducted by political units treated almost as personalities. The domestic structure is taken as given; foreign policy begins where domestic policy ends.

But this approach is appropriate only to stable periods because then the various components of the international system generally have similar conceptions of the "rules of the game." If the domestic structures are based on commensurable notions of what is just, a consensus about permissible aims and methods of foreign policy develops. If domestic structures are reasonably stable, temptations to use an adventurous foreign policy to achieve domestic cohesion are at a minimum. In these conditions, leaders will generally apply the same criteria and hold similar views about what constitutes a "reasonable" demand. This does not guarantee agreement, but it provides the condition for a meaningful dialogue, that is, it sets the stage for traditional diplomacy.

When the domestic structures are based on fundamentally different conceptions of what is just, the conduct of international affairs grows more complex. Then it becomes difficult even to define the nature of disagreement because what seems most obvious to one side appears most problematic to the other. A policy dilemma arises because the pros and cons of a given course seem evenly balanced. The definition of what constitutes a problem and what criteria are relevant in "solving" it reflects to a considerable extent the domestic notions of what is just, the pressures produced by the decision-making process, and the experience which forms the leaders in their rise to eminence. When domestic structures—and the concept of legitimacy on which they are based—differ widely, statesmen can still meet, but their ability to persuade has been reduced for they no longer speak the same language.

This can occur even when no universal claims are made. Incompatible domestic structures can passively generate a gulf, simply because of the difficulty of achieving a consensus about the nature of "reasonable" aims and methods. But when one or more states claim universal applicability for their particular structure, schisms grow deep indeed. In that event, the domestic structure becomes not only an obstacle to understanding but one of the principal issues in international affairs. Its requirements condition the conception of alternatives; survival seems involved in every dispute. The symbolic aspect of foreign policy begins to overshadow the substantive component. It becomes difficult to consider a dispute "on its merits" because the disagreement seems finally to turn not on a specific issue but on a set of values as expressed in domestic arrangements. The consequences of such a state of affairs were explained by Edmund Burke during the French Revolution:

> I never thought we could make peace with the system; because it was not for the sake of an object we pursued in rivalry with each other, but with the system itself that we were at war. As I understood the matter, we were at war not with its conduct but with its existence; convinced that its existence and its hostility were the same.[1]

Of course, the domestic structure is not irrelevant in any historical period. At a minimum, it determines the amount of the total social effort which can be devoted to foreign policy. The wars of the kings who governed by divine right were limited because feudal rulers, bound by customary law, could not levy income taxes or conscript their subjects. The French Revolution, which based its policy on a doctrine of popular will, mobilized resources on a truly national scale for the first time. This was one of the principal reasons for the startling successes of French arms against a hostile Europe which possessed greater over-all power. The ideological regimes of the twentieth century have utilized a still larger share of the national effort. This has enabled them to hold their own against an environment possessing far superior resources.

Aside from the allocation of resources, the domestic structure crucially affects the way the actions of other states are interpreted. To some extent, of course, every society finds itself in an environment not of its own making and has some of the main lines of its foreign policy imposed on it. Indeed, the pressure of the environment can grow so strong that it permits only one interpretation of its significance; Prussia in the eighteenth century and Israel in the contemporary period may have found themselves in this position.

But for the majority of states the margin of decision has been greater. The actual choice has been determined to a considerable degree by their interpretation of the environment and by their leaders' conception of alternatives. Napoleon rejected peace offers beyond the dreams of the kings who had ruled France by "divine right" because he was convinced that *any* settlement which demonstrated the limitations of his power was tantamount to his downfall. That Russia seeks to surround itself with a belt of friendly states in Eastern Europe is a product of geography and history. That it is attempting to do so by imposing a domestic structure based on a particular ideology is a result of conceptions supplied by its domestic structure.

The domestic structure is decisive finally in the elaboration of positive goals. The most difficult, indeed tragic, aspect of foreign policy is how to deal with the problem of conjecture. When the scope for action is greatest, knowledge on which to base such action is small or ambiguous. When knowledge becomes available, the ability to affect events is usually at a minimum. In 1936, no one could know whether Hitler was a misunderstood nationalist or a maniac. By the time certainty was achieved, it had to be paid for with millions of lives.

The conjectural element of foreign policy—the need to gear actions to an assessment that cannot be proved true when it is made—is never more crucial than in a revolutionary period. Then, the old order is obviously disintegrating while the shape of its replacement is highly uncertain. Everything depends, therefore, on some conception of the future. But varying domestic structures can easily produce different assessments of the significance of existing trends and, more importantly, clashing criteria for resolving these differences. This is the dilemma of our time.

Problems are novel; their scale is vast; their nature is often abstract and always psychological. In the past, international relations were confined to a limited geographic area. The various continents pursued their relations essentially in isolation from each other. Until the eighteenth century, other continents impinged on Europe only sporadically and for relatively brief periods. And when Europe extended its sway over much of the world, foreign policy became limited to the Western Powers with the single exception of Japan. The international system of the nineteenth century was to all practical purposes identical with the concert of Europe.

The period after World War II marks the first era of truly global foreign policy. Each major state is capable of producing consequences in every part of the globe by a direct application of its power or because ideas can be transmitted almost instantaneously or because ideological rivalry gives vast symbolic significance even to issues which are minor in geopolitical terms. The mere act of adjusting perspectives to so huge a scale would produce major dislocations. This problem is compounded by the emergence of so many new states. Since 1945, the number of participants in the international system has nearly doubled. In previous periods the addition of even one or two new states tended to lead to decades of instability until a new equilibrium was established and accepted. The emergence of scores of new states has magnified this difficulty many times over.

These upheavals would be challenge enough, but they are overshadowed by the risks posed by modern technology. Peace is maintained through the threat of mutual destruction based on weapons for which there has been no operational experience. Deterrence—the policy of preventing an action by confronting the opponent with risks he is unwilling to run—depends in the first instance on psychological criteria. What the potential aggressor believes is more crucial than what is objectively true. Deterrence occurs above all in the minds of men.

To achieve an international consensus on the significance of these developments would be a major task even if domestic structures were comparable. It becomes especially difficult when domestic structures differ widely and when universal claims are made on behalf of them. A systematic assessment of the impact of domestic structure on the conduct of international affairs would have to treat such factors as historical traditions, social values, and the economic system. But this would far transcend the scope of an article. For the purposes of this discussion we shall confine ourselves to sketching the impact of two factors only: administrative structure and the formative experience of leadership groups.

II. *The Impact of the Administrative Structure*

In the contemporary period, the very nature of the governmental structure introduces an element of rigidity which operates more or

HENRY A. KISSINGER

less independently of the convictions of statesmen or the ideology which they represent. Issues are too complex and relevant facts too manifold to be dealt with on the basis of personal intuition. An institutionalization of decision-making is an inevitable by-product of the risks of international affairs in the nuclear age. Moreover, almost every modern state is dedicated to some theory of "planning" —the attempt to structure the future by understanding and, if necessary, manipulating the environment. Planning involves a quest for predictability and, above all, for "objectivity." There is a deliberate effort to reduce the relevant elements of a problem to a standard of average performance. The vast bureaucratic mechanisms that emerge develop a momentum and a vested interest of their own. As they grow more complex, their internal standards of operation are not necessarily commensurable with those of other countries or even with other bureaucratic structures in the same country. There is a trend toward autarky. A paradoxical consequence may be that increased control over the domestic environment is purchased at the price of loss of flexibility in international affairs.

The purpose of bureaucracy is to devise a standard operating procedure which can cope effectively with most problems. A bureaucracy is efficient if the matters which it handles routinely are, in fact, the most frequent and if its procedures are relevant to their solution. If those criteria are met, the energies of the top leadership are freed to deal creatively with the unexpected occurrence or with the need for innovation. Bureaucracy becomes an obstacle when what it defines as routine does not address the most significant range of issues or when its prescribed mode of action proves irrelevant to the problem.

When this occurs, the bureaucracy absorbs the energies of top executives in reconciling what is expected with what happens; the analysis of where one is overwhelms the consideration of where one should be going. Serving the machine becomes a more absorbing occupation than defining its purpose. Success consists in moving the administrative machine to the point of decision, leaving relatively little energy for analyzing the merit of this decision. The quest for "objectivity"—while desirable theoretically—involves the danger that means and ends are confused, that an average standard of performance is exalted as the only valid one. Attention tends to be diverted from the act of choice—which is the ultimate test of statesmanship—to the accumulation of facts. Decisions can be avoided until a crisis brooks no further delay, until the events themselves have removed the element of ambiguity. But at that point the scope for constructive action is at a minimum. Certainty is purchased at the cost of creativity.

Something like this seems to be characteristic of modern bureaucratic states whatever their ideology. In societies with a pragmatic tradition, such as the United States, there develops a greater concern with an analysis of where one is than where one is going. What passes for planning is frequently the projection of the familiar into the future. In societies based on ideology, doctrine is institutionalized and exegesis takes the place of innovation. Creativity must make so many concessions to orthodoxy that it may exhaust itself in doctrinal adaptations. In short, the accumulation of knowledge of the bureaucracy and the impersonality of its method of arriving at decisions can be achieved at a high price. Decision-making can grow so complex that the process of producing a bureaucratic consensus may overshadow the purpose of the effort.

While all thoughtful administrators would grant in the abstract that these dangers exist, they find it difficult to act on their knowledge. Lip service is paid to planning; indeed planning staffs proliferate. However, they suffer from two debilities. The "operating" elements may not take the planning effort seriously. Plans become esoteric exercises which are accepted largely because they imply no practical consequence. They are a sop to administrative theory. At the same time, since planning staffs have a high incentive to try to be "useful," there is a bias against novel conceptions which are difficult to adapt to an administrative mold. It is one thing to assign an individual or a group the task of looking ahead; this is a far cry from providing an environment which encourages an understanding for deeper historical, sociological, and economic trends. The need to provide a memorandum may outweigh the imperatives of creative thought. The quest for objectivity creates a temptation to see in the future an updated version of the present. Yet true innovation is bound to run counter to prevailing standards. The dilemma of modern bureaucracy is that while every creative act is lonely, not every lonely act is creative. Formal criteria are little help in solving this problem because the unique cannot be expressed "objectively."

The rigidity in the policies of the technologically advanced societies is in no small part due to the complexity of decision-making. Crucial problems may—and frequently do—go unrecognized for a long time. But once the decision-making apparatus has disgorged a policy, it becomes very difficult to change it. The alternative to the *status quo* is the prospect of repeating the whole anguishing process of arriving at decisions. This explains to some extent the curious phenomenon that decisions taken with enormous doubt and perhaps with a close division become practically sacrosanct once adopted. The whole administrative machinery swings behind their implementation as if activity could still all doubts.

Moreover, the reputation, indeed the political survival, of most leaders depends on their ability to realize their goals, however these may have been arrived at. Whether these goals are desirable is relatively less crucial. The time span by which administrative success is measured is considerably shorter than that by which historical achievement is determined. In heavily bureaucratized societies all pressures emphasize the first of these accomplishments.

Then, too, the staffs on which modern executives come to depend develop a momentum of their own. What starts out as an aid to decision-makers often turns into a practically autonomous organization whose internal problems structure and sometimes compound the issues which it was originally designed to solve. The decision-maker will always be aware of the morale of his staff. Though he has the authority, he cannot overrule it too frequently without impairing its efficiency; and he may, in any event, lack the knowledge to do so. Placating the staff then becomes a major preoccupation of the executive. A form of administrative democracy results, in which a decision often reflects an attainable consensus rather than substantive conviction (or at least the two imperceptibly merge). The internal requirements of the bureaucracy may come to predominate over the purposes which it was intended to serve. This is probably even more true in highly institutionalized Communist states—such as the U.S.S.R.—than in the United States.

When the administrative machine grows very elaborate, the various levels of the decision-making process are separated by chasms which are obscured from the outside world by the complexity of the apparatus. Research often becomes a means to buy time and to assuage consciences. Studying a problem can turn into an escape from coming to grips with it. In the process, the gap between the technical competence of research staffs and what hard-pressed political leaders are capable of absorbing widens constantly. This heightens the insecurity of the executive and may thus compound either rigidity or arbitrariness or both. In many fields— strategy being a prime example—decision-makers may find it difficult to give as many hours to a problem as the expert has had years to study it. The ultimate decision often depends less on knowledge than on the ability to brief the top administrator—to present the facts in such a way that they can be absorbed rapidly. The effectiveness of briefing, however, puts a premium on theatrical qualities. Not everything that sounds plausible is correct, and many things which are correct may not sound plausible when they are first presented; and a second hearing is rare. The stage aspect of briefing may leave the decision-maker with a gnawing feeling of having been taken—even, and perhaps especially, when he does not know quite how.

Sophistication may thus encourage paralysis or a crude popularization which defeats its own purpose. The excessively theoretical approach of many research staffs overlooks the problem of the strain of decision-making in times of crisis. What is relevant for policy depends not only on academic truth but also on what can be implemented under stress. The technical staffs are frequently operating in a framework of theoretical standards while in fact their usefulness depends on essentially psychological criteria. To be politically meaningful, their proposals must involve answers to the following types of questions: Does the executive understand the proposal? Does he believe in it? Does he accept it as a guide to action or as an excuse for doing nothing? But if these kinds of concerns are given too much weight, the requirements of salesmanship will defeat substance.

The pragmatism of executives thus clashes with the theoretical bent of research or planning staffs. Executives as a rule take cognizance of a problem only when it emerges as an administrative issue. They thus unwittingly encourage bureaucratic contests as the only means of generating decisions. Or the various elements of the bureaucracy make a series of nonaggression pacts with each other and thus reduce the decision-maker to a benevolent constitutional monarch. As the special role of the executive increasingly becomes to choose between proposals generated administratively, decision-makers turn into arbiters rather than leaders. Whether they wait until a problem emerges as an administrative issue or until a crisis has demonstrated the irrelevance of the standard operating procedure, the modern decision-makers often find themselves the prisoners of their advisers.

Faced with an administrative machine which is both elaborate and fragmented, the executive is forced into essentially lateral means of control. Many of his public pronouncements, though ostensibly directed to outsiders, perform a perhaps more important role in laying down guidelines for the bureaucracy. The chief significance of a foreign policy speech by the President may thus be that it settles an internal debate in Washington (a public statement is more useful for this purpose than an administrative memorandum because it is harder to reverse). At the same time, the bureaucracy's awareness of this method of control tempts it to shortcut its debates by using pronouncements by the decision-makers as charters for special purposes. The executive thus finds himself confronted by proposals for public declarations which may be innocuous in themselves—and whose bureaucratic significance may be anything but obvious—but which can be used by some agency or department to launch a study or program which will restrict his freedom of decision later on.

All of this drives the executive in the direction of extra-bureaucratic means of decision. The practice of relying on special emissaries or personal envoys is an example; their status outside the bureaucracy frees them from some of its restraints. International agreements are sometimes possible only by ignoring safeguards against capricious action. It is a paradoxical aspect of modern bureaucracies that their quest for objectivity and calculability often leads to impasses which can be overcome only by essentially arbitrary decisions.

Such a mode of operation would involve a great risk of stagnation even in "normal" times. It becomes especially dangerous in a revolutionary period. For then, the problems which are most obtrusive may be least relevant. The issues which are most significant may not be suitable for administrative formulation and even when formulated may not lend themselves to bureaucratic consensus. When the issue is how to transform the existing framework, routine can become an additional obstacle to both comprehension and action.

This problem, serious enough *within* each society, is magnified in the conduct of international affairs. While the formal machinery of decision-making in developed countries shows many similarities, the criteria which influence decisions vary enormously. With each administrative machine increasingly absorbed in its own internal problems, diplomacy loses its flexibility. Leaders are extremely aware of the problems of placating their own bureaucracy; they cannot depart too far from its prescriptions without raising serious morale problems. Decisions are reached so painfully that the very anguish of decision-making acts as a brake on the give-and-take of traditional diplomacy.

This is true even *within* alliances. Meaningful consultation with other nations becomes very difficult when the internal process of decision-making already has some of the characteristics of compacts between quasi-sovereign entities. There is an increasing reluctance to hazard a hard-won domestic consensus in an international forum.

What is true within alliances—that is, among nations which have at least some common objectives—becomes even more acute in relations between antagonistic states or blocs. The gap created when two large bureaucracies generate goals largely in isolation from each other and on the basis of not necessarily commensurable criteria is magnified considerably by an ideological schism. The degree of ideological fervor is not decisive; the problem would exist even if the original ideological commitment had declined on either or both sides. The criteria for bureaucratic decision-making may continue to be influenced by ideology even after its élan has dissipated. Bureaucratic structures generate their own momentum which may more than counterbalance the loss of earlier fanaticism. In the early stages of a revolutionary movement, ideology is crucial and the accident of personalities can be decisive. The Reign of Terror in France was ended by the elimination of a single man, Robespierre. The Bolshevik revolution could hardly have taken place had Lenin not been on the famous train which crossed Germany into Russia. But once a revolution becomes institutionalized, the administrative structures which it has spawned develop their own vested interests. Ideology may grow less significant in creating commitment; it becomes pervasive in supplying criteria of administrative choice. Ideologies prevail by being taken for granted. Orthodoxy substitutes for conviction and produces its own form of rigidity.

In such circumstances, a meaningful dialogue across ideological dividing lines becomes extraordinarily difficult. The more elaborate the administrative structure, the less relevant an individual's view becomes—indeed one of the purposes of bureaucracy is to liberate decision-making from the accident of personalities. Thus while personal convictions may be modified, it requires a really monumental effort to alter bureaucratic commitments. And if change occurs, the bureaucracy prefers to move at its own pace and not be excessively influenced by statements or pressures of foreigners. For all these reasons, diplomacy tends to become rigid or to turn into an abstract bargaining process based on largely formal criteria such as "splitting the difference." Either course is self-defeating: the former because it negates the very purpose of diplomacy; the latter because it subordinates purpose to technique and because it may encourage intransigence. Indeed, the incentive for intransigence increases if it is known that the difference will generally be split.

Ideological differences are compounded because major parts of the world are only in the first stages of administrative evolution. Where the technologically advanced countries suffer from the inertia of overadministration, the developing areas often lack even the rudiments of effective bureaucracy. Where the advanced countries may drown in "facts," the emerging nations are frequently without the most elementary knowledge needed for forming a meaningful judgment or for implementing it once it has been taken. Where large bureaucracies operate in alternating spurts of rigidity and catastrophic (in relation to the bureaucracy) upheaval, the new states tend to take decisions on the basis of almost random pressures. The excessive institutionalization of one and the inadequate structure of the other inhibit international stability.

III. *The Nature of Leadership*

Whatever one's view about the degree to which choices in international affairs are "objectively" determined, the decisions are made by individuals who will be above all conscious of the seeming multiplicity of options. Their understanding of the nature of their choice depends on many factors, including their experience during the rise to eminence.

The mediating, conciliatory style of British policy in the nineteenth century reflected, in part, the qualities encouraged during careers in Parliament and the values of a cohesive leadership group connected by ties of family and common education. The hysterical cast of the policy of Imperial Germany was given impetus by a domestic structure in which political parties were deprived of responsibility while ministers were obliged to balance a monarch by divine right against a Parliament composed of representatives without any prospect of ever holding office. Consensus could be achieved most easily through fits of national passion which in turn disquieted all of Germany's neighbors. Germany's foreign policy grew unstable because its domestic structure did little to discourage capricious improvisations; it may even have put a premium on them.

The collapse of the essentially aristocratic conception of foreign policy of the nineteenth century has made the career experiences of leaders even more crucial. An aristocracy—if it lives up to its values—will reject the arbitrariness of absolutist rule; and it will base itself on a notion of quality which discourages the temptations of demagoguery inherent in plebiscitarian democracy. Where position is felt to be a birthright, generosity is possible (though not guaranteed); flexibility is not inhibited by a commitment to perpetual success. Where a leader's estimate of himself is not completely dependent on his standing in an administrative structure, measures can be judged in terms of a conception of the future rather than of an almost compulsive desire to avoid even a temporary setback. When statesmen belonged to a community transcending national boundaries, there tended to be consensus on the criteria of what constituted a reasonable proposal. This did not prevent conflicts, but it did define their nature and encourage dialogue. The bane of aristocratic foreign policy was the risk of frivolousness, of a self-confidence unrelated to knowledge, and of too much emphasis on intuition.

In any event, ours is the age of the expert or the charismatic leader. The expert has his constituency—those who have a vested interest in commonly held opinions; elaborating and defining its consensus at a high level has, after all, made him an expert. Since the expert is often the product of the administrative dilemmas described earlier, he is usually in a poor position to transcend them. The charismatic leader, on the other hand, needs a perpetual revolution to maintain his position. Neither the expert nor the charismatic leader operates in an environment which puts a premium on long-range conceptions or on generosity or on subordinating the leader's ego to purposes which transcend his own career.

Leadership groups are formed by at least three factors: their experiences during their rise to eminence; the structure in which they must operate; the values of their society. Three contemporary types will be discussed here: (a) the bureaucratic-pragmatic type, (b) the ideological type, and (c) the revolutionary-charismatic type.

Bureaucratic-pragmatic leadership. The main example of this type of leadership is the American élite—though the leadership groups of other Western countries increasingly approximate the American pattern. Shaped by a society without fundamental social schisms (at least until the race problem became visible) and the product of an environment in which most recognized problems have proved soluble, its approach to policy is *ad hoc,* pragmatic, and somewhat mechanical.

Because pragmatism is based on the conviction that the context of events produces a solution, there is a tendency to await developments. The belief is prevalent that every problem will yield if attacked with sufficient energy. It is inconceivable, therefore, that delay might result in irretrievable disaster; at worst it is thought to require a redoubled effort later on. Problems are segmented into constituent elements, each of which is dealt with by experts in the special difficulty it involves. There is little emphasis or concern for their interrelationship. Technical issues enjoy more careful attention, and receive more sophisticated treatment, than political ones. Though the importance of intangibles is affirmed in theory, it is difficult to obtain a consensus on which factors are significant and even harder to find a meaningful mode for dealing with them. Things are done because one knows how to do them and not because one ought to do them. The criteria for dealing with trends which are conjectural are less well developed than those for immediate crises. Pragmatism, at least in its generally accepted form, is more concerned with method than with judgment; or rather it seeks to reduce judgment to methodology and value to knowledge.

This is reinforced by the special qualities of the professions—law and business—which furnish the core of the leadership groups in America. Lawyers—at least in the Anglo-Saxon tradition—prefer to deal with actual rather than hypothetical cases; they have little confidence in the possiblity of stating a future issue abstractly. But planning by its very nature is hypothetical. Its success depends precisely on the ability to transcend the existing framework. Lawyers may be prepared to undertake this task; but they will do well in it only to the extent that they are able to overcome the special qualities encouraged by their profession. What comes naturally to lawyers in the Anglo-Saxon tradition is the sophisticated analysis of a series of *ad hoc* issues which emerge as problems through adversary proceedings. In so far as lawyers draw on the experience which forms them, they have a bias toward awaiting developments and toward operating within the definition of the problem as formulated by its chief spokesmen.

This has several consequences. It compounds the already powerful tendencies within American society to identify foreign policy with the solution of immediate issues. It produces great refinement of issues as they arise, but it also encourages the administrative dilemmas described earlier. Issues are dealt with only as the pressure of events imposes the need for resolving them. Then, each of the contending factions within the bureaucracy has a maximum incentive to state its case in its most extreme form because the ultimate outcome depends, to a considerable extent, on a bargaining process. The premium placed on advocacy turns decision-making into a series of adjustments among special interests—a process more suited to domestic than to foreign policy. This procedure neglects the long-range because the future has no administrative constituency and is, therefore, without representation in the adversary proceedings. Problems tend to be slighted until some agency or department is made responsible for them. When this occurs— usually when a difficulty has already grown acute—the relevant department becomes an all-out spokesman for its particular area of responsibility. The outcome usually depends more on the pressures or the persuasiveness of the contending advocates than on a concept of over-all purpose. While these tendencies exist to some extent in all bureaucracies they are particularly pronounced in the American system of government.

This explains in part the peculiar alternation of rigidity and spasms of flexibility in American diplomacy. On a given issue—be it the Berlin crisis or disarmament or the war in Viet-Nam—there generally exists a great reluctance to develop a negotiating position or a statement of objectives except in the most general terms. This stems from a desire not to prejudge the process of negotiations and above all to retain flexibility in the face of unforeseeable events. But when an approaching conference or some other pressures make the development of a position imperative and some office or individual is assigned the specific task, a sudden change occurs. Both personal and bureaucratic success are then identified with bringing the particular assignment to a conclusion. Where so much stock is placed in negotiating skill, a failure of a conference may be viewed as a reflection on the ability of the negotiator rather than on the objective difficulty of the subject. Confidence in the bargaining process causes American negotiators to be extremely sensitive to the tactical requirements of the conference table—sometimes at the expense of longer-term considerations. In internal discussions, American negotiators—generally irrespective of their previous commitments— often become advocates for the maximum range of concessions; their legal background tempts them to act as mediators between Washington and the country with which they are negotiating.

The attitudes of the business élite reinforce the convictions of the legal profession. The American business executive rises through a process of selection which rewards the ability to manipulate the known—in itself a conciliatory procedure. The special skill of the executive is thought to consist in coordinating well-defined functions rather than in challenging them. The procedure is relatively effective in the business world, where the executive can often substitute decisiveness, long experience, and a wide range of personal acquaintance for reflectiveness. In international affairs, however—especially in a revolutionary situation—the strong will which is one of our business executives' notable traits may produce essentially arbitrary choices. Or unfamiliarity with the subject matter may have the opposite effect of turning the executive into a spokesman of his technical staffs. In either case, the business executive is even more dependent than the lawyer on the bureaucracy's formulation of the issue. The business élite is even less able or willing than the lawyer to recognize that the formulation of an issue, not the technical remedy, is usually the central problem.

All this gives American policy its particular cast. Problems are dealt with as they arise. Agreement on what constitutes a problem generally depends on an emerging crisis which settles the previously inconclusive disputes about priorities. When a problem is recognized, it is dealt with by a mobilization of all resources to overcome the immediate symptoms. This often involves the risk of slighting longer-term issues which may not yet have assumed crisis proportions and of overwhelming, perhaps even undermining, the structure of the area concerned by a flood of American technical experts proposing remedies on an American scale. Administrative decisions emerge from a compromise of conflicting pressures in which accidents of personality or persuasiveness play a crucial role. The compromise often reflects the maxim that "if two parties disagree the truth is usually somewhere in between." But the pedantic application of such truisms causes the various contenders to exaggerate their positions for bargaining purposes or to construct fictitious extremes to make their position appear moderate. In either case, internal bargaining predominates over substance.

The *ad hoc* tendency of our decision-makers and the reliance on adversary proceeding cause issues to be stated in black and white terms. This suppresses a feeling for nuance and makes it difficult to recognize the relationship between seemingly discrete events. Even with the perspective of a decade there is little consensus about the relationship between the actions culminating in the Suez fiasco and the French decision to enter the nuclear field; or about the inconsistency between the neutralization of Laos and the step-up of the military effort in Viet-Nam.

The same quality also produces a relatively low valuation of historical factors. Nations are treated as similar phenomena, and those states presenting similar immediate problems are treated similarly. Since many of our policy-makers first address themselves to an issue when it emerges as their area of responsibility, their approach to it is often highly anecdotal. Great weight is given to what people say and relatively little to the significance of these affirmations in terms of domestic structure or historical background. Agreement may be taken at face value and seen as reflecting more consensus than actually exists. Opposition tends to produce moral outrage which often assumes the form of personal animosity—the attitude of some American policy-makers toward President de Gaulle is a good example.

The legal background of our policy-makers produces a bias in favor of constitutional solutions. The issue of supra-nationalism or confederalism in Europe has been discussed largely in terms of the right of countries to make independent decisions. Much less weight has been given to the realities which would limit the application of a majority vote against a major country whatever the legal arrangements. (The fight over the application of Article 19 of the United Nations Charter was based on the same attitude.) Similarly, legal terms such as "integration" and "assignment" sometimes become ends in themselves and thus obscure the operational reality to which they refer. In short, the American leadership groups show high competence in dealing with technical issues, and much less virtuosity in mastering a historical process. And the policies of other Western countries exhibit variations of the American pattern. A lesser pragmatism in continental Europe is counter-balanced by a smaller ability to play a world-role.

The ideological type of leadership. As has been discussed above, the impact of ideology can persist long after its initial fervor has been spent. Whatever the ideological commitment of individual leaders, a lifetime spent in the Communist hierarchy must influence their basic categories of thought—especially since Communist ideology continues to perform important functions. It still furnishes the standard of truth and the guarantee of ultimate success. It provides a means for maintaining cohesion among the various Communist parties of the world. It supplies criteria for the settlement of disputes both within the bureaucracy of individual Communist countries and among the various Communist states.

However attenuated, Communist ideology is, in part, responsible for international tensions. This is less because of specific Marxist tactical prescriptions—with respect to which Communists have shown a high degree of flexibility—than because of the basic Marxist-Leninist categories for interpreting reality. Communist leaders never tire of affirming that Marxism-Leninism is the key element of their self-proclaimed superiority over the outside world; as Marxist-Leninists they are convinced that they understand the historical process better than the non-Communist world does.

The essence of Marxism-Leninism—and the reason that normal diplomacy with Communist states is so difficult—is the view that "objective" factors such as the social structure, the economic process, and, above all, the class struggle are more important than the personal convictions of statesmen. Belief in the predominance of objective factors explains the Soviet approach to the problem of security. If personal convictions are "subjective," Soviet security cannot be allowed to rest on the good will of other statesmen, especially those of a different social system. This produces a quest for what may be described as absolute security—the attempt to be so strong as to be independent of the decisions of other countries. But absolute security for one country means absolute insecurity for all others; it can be achieved only by reducing other states to impotence. Thus an essentially defensive foreign policy can grow indistinguishable from traditional aggression.

The belief in the predominance of objective factors explains why, in the past, periods of détente have proved so precarious. When there is a choice between Western good will or a physical gain, the pressures to choose the latter have been overwhelming. The wartime friendship with the West was sacrificed to the possibility of establishing Communist-controlled governments in Eastern Europe. The spirit of Geneva did not survive the temptations offered by the prospect of undermining the Western position in the Middle East. The many overtures of the Kennedy administration were rebuffed until the Cuban missile crisis demonstrated that the balance of forces was not in fact favorable for a test of strength.

The reliance on objective factors has complicated negotiations between the West and the Communist countries. Communist negotiators find it difficult to admit that they could be swayed by the arguments of men who have, by definition, an inferior grasp of the laws of historical development. No matter what is said, they think that they understand their Western counterpart better than he understands himself. Concessions are possible, but they are made to "reality," not to individuals or to a bargaining process. Diplomacy becomes difficult when one of the parties considers the key element to negotiation—the give-and-take of the process of bargaining—as but a superstructure for factors not part of the negotiation itself.

Finally, whatever the decline in ideological fervor, orthodoxy requires the maintenance of a posture of ideological hostility to the non-Communist world even during a period of coexistence. Thus, in a reply to a Chinese challenge, the Communist Party of the U.S.S.R. declared: "We fully support the destruction of capitalism. We not only believe in the inevitable death of capitalism but we are doing everything possible for it to be accomplished through class struggle as quickly as possible."[2]

The wariness toward the outside world is reinforced by the personal experiences which Communist leaders have had on the road to eminence. In a system where there is no legitimate succession, a great deal of energy is absorbed in internal maneuvering. Leaders rise to the top by eliminating—sometimes physically, always bureaucratically—all possible opponents. Stalin had all individuals who helped him into power executed. Khrushchev disgraced Kaganovich, whose protegé he had been, and turned on Marshal Zhukov six months after being saved by him from a conspiracy of his other colleagues. Brezhnev and Kosygin owed their careers to Khrushchev; they nevertheless overthrew him and started a campaign of calumny against him within twenty-four hours of his dismissal.

Anyone succeeding in Communist leadership struggles must be single-minded, unemotional, dedicated, and, above all, motivated by an enormous desire for power. Nothing in the personal experience of Soviet leaders would lead them to accept protestations of good will at face value. Suspiciousness is inherent in their domestic position. It is unlikely that their attitude toward the outside world is more benign than toward their own colleagues or that they would expect more consideration from it.

The combination of personal qualities and ideological structure also affects relations *among* Communist states. Since national rivalries are thought to be the result of class conflict, they are expected to disappear wherever Socialism has triumphed. When disagreements occur they are dealt with by analogy to internal Communist disputes: by attempting to ostracize and then to destroy the opponent. The tendency to treat different opinions as manifestations of heresy causes disagreements to harden into bitter schisms. The debate between Communist China and the U.S.S.R. is in many respects more acrimonious than that between the U.S.S.R. and the non-Communist world.

Even though the basic conceptual categories of Communist leadership groups are similar, the impact of the domestic structure of the individual Communist states on international relations varies greatly. It makes a considerable difference whether an ideology has become institutionalized, as in the Soviet Union, or whether it is still impelled by its early revolutionary fervor, as in Communist China. Where ideology has become institutionalized a special form of pragmatism may develop. It may be just as empirical as that of the United States but it will operate in a different realm of "reality." A different philosophical basis leads to the emergence of another set of categories for the settlement of disputes, and these in turn generate another range of problems.

A Communist bureaucratic structure, however pragmatic, will have different priorities from ours; it will give greater weight to doctrinal considerations and conceptual problems. It is more than ritual when speeches of senior Soviet leaders begin with hour-long recitals of Communist ideology. Even if it were ritual, it must affect the definition of what is considered reasonable in internal arguments. Bureaucratization and pragmatism may lead to a loss of élan; they do not guarantee convergence of Western and Soviet thinking.

The more revolutionary manifestations of Communism, such as Communist China, still possess more ideological fervor, but, paradoxically, their structure may permit a wider latitude for new departures. Tactical intransigence and ideological vitality should not be confused with structural rigidity. Because the leadership bases its rule on a prestige which transcends bureaucratic authority, it has not yet given so many hostages to the administrative structure. If the leadership should change—or if its attitudes are modified—policy could probably be altered much more dramatically in Communist China than in the more institutionalized Communist countries.

The charismatic-revolutionary type of leadership. The contemporary international order is heavily influenced by yet another leadership type: the charismatic-revolutionary leader. For many of the leaders of the new nations the bureaucratic-pragmatic approach of the West is irrelevant because they are more interested in the future which they wish to construct than in the manipulation of the environment which dominates the thinking of the pragmatists. And ideology is not satisfactory because doctrine supplies rigid categories which overshadow the personal experiences which have provided the impetus for so many of the leaders of the new nations.

The type of individual who leads a struggle for independence has been sustained in the risks and suffering of such a course primarily by a commitment to a vision which enabled him to override conditions which had seemed overwhelmingly hostile. Revolutionaries are rarely motivated primarily by material considerations—though the illusion that they are persists in the West. Material incentives do not cause a man to risk his existence and to launch himself into the uncertainties of a revolutionary struggle. If Castro or Sukarno had been principally interested in economics, their talents would have guaranteed them a brillant career in the societies they overthrew. What made their sacrifices worthwhile to them was a vision of the future—or a quest for political power. To revolutionaries the significant reality is the world which they are striving to bring about, not the world they are fighting to overcome.

This difference in perspective accounts for the inconclusiveness of much of the dialogue between the West and many of the leaders of the new countries. The West has a tendency to believe that the tensions in the emerging nations are caused by a low level of economic activity. To the apostles of economic development, raising the gross national product seems the key to political stability. They believe that it should receive the highest priority from the political leaders of new countries and supply their chief motivation.

But to the charismatic heads of many of the new nations, economic progress, while not unwelcome, offers too limited a scope for their ambitions. It can be achieved only by slow, painful, highly technical measures which contrast with the heroic exertions of the struggle for independence. Results are long-delayed; credit for them cannot be clearly established. If Castro were to act on the advice of theorists of economic development, the best he could hope for would be that after some decades he would lead a small progressive country—perhaps a Switzerland of the Caribbean. Compared to the prospect of leading a revolution throughout Latin America, this goal would appear trivial, boring, perhaps even unreal to him.

Moreover, to the extent that economic progress is achieved, it may magnify domestic political instability, at least in its early phases. Economic advance disrupts the traditional political structure. It thus places constant pressures on the incumbent leaders to re-establish the legitimacy of their rule. For this purpose a dramatic foreign policy is particularly apt. Many leaders of the new countries seem convinced that an adventurous foreign policy will not harm prospects for economic development and may even foster it. The competition of the superpowers makes it likely that economic assistance will be forthcoming regardless of the actions of the recipient. Indeed the more obtrusive their foreign policy the greater is their prospect of being wooed by the chief contenders.

The tendency toward a reckless policy is magnified by the uncertain sense of identity of many of the new nations. National boundaries often correspond to the administrative subdivisions established by the former colonial rulers. States thus have few of the attributes of nineteenth-century European nationalism: common language, common culture, or even common history. In many cases, the only common experience is a century or so of imperial rule. As a result, there is a great pressure toward authoritarian rule, and a high incentive to use foreign policy as a means of bringing about domestic cohesion.

Western-style democracy presupposes that society transcends the political realm; in that case opposition challenges a particular method of achieving common aims but not the existence of the state itself. In many of the new countries, by contrast, the state represents the primary, sometimes the sole, manifestation of social cohesion. Opposition can therefore easily appear as treason—apart from the fact that leaders who have spent several decades running the risks of revolutionary struggle or who have achieved power by a coup d'état are not likely to favor a system of government which makes them dispensable. Indeed the attraction of Communism for many of these leaders is not Marxist-Leninist economic theory but the legitimacy for authoritarian rule which it provides.

No matter what the system of government, many of the leaders of the new nations use foreign policy as a means to escape intractable internal difficulties and as a device to achieve domestic cohesion. The international arena provides an opportunity for the dramatic measures which are impossible at home. These are often cast in an anti-Western mold because this is the easiest way to recreate the struggle against imperial rule which is the principal unifying element for many new nations. The incentive is particularly strong because the rivalry of the nuclear powers eliminates many of the risks which previously were associated with an adventurous foreign policy—especially if that foreign policy is directed against the West which lacks any effective sanctions.

Traditional military pressure is largely precluded by the nuclear stalemate and respect for world opinion. But the West is neither prepared nor able to use the sanction which weighs most heavily on the new countries: the deliberate exploitation of their weak domestic structure. In many areas the ability to foment domestic unrest is a more potent weapon than traditional arms. Many of the leaders of the new countries will be prepared to ignore the classical panoply of power; but they will be very sensitive to the threat of domestic upheaval. States with a high capacity for exploiting domestic instability can use it as a tool of foreign policy. China, though lacking almost all forms of classical long-range military strength, is a growing factor in Africa. Weak states may be more concerned with a country's capacity to organize domestic unrest in their territory than with its capacity for physical destruction.

Conclusion. Contemporary domestic structures thus present an unprecedented challenge to the emergence of a stable international order. The bureaucratic-pragmatic societies concentrate on the manipulation of an empirical reality which they treat as given; the ideological societies are split between an essentially bureaucratic approach (though in a different realm of reality than the bureaucratic-pragmatic structures) and a group using ideology mainly for revolutionary ends. The new nations, in so far as they are active in international affairs, have a high incentive to seek in foreign policy the perpetuation of charismatic leadership.

These differences are a major obstacle to a consensus on what constitutes a "reasonable" proposal. A common diagnosis of the existing situation is hard to achieve, and it is even more difficult to concert measures for a solution. The situation is complicated by the one feature all types of leadership have in common: the premium put on short-term goals and the domestic need to succeed at all times. In the bureaucratic societies policy emerges from a compromise which often produces the least common denominator, and it is implemented by individuals whose reputation is made by administering the *status quo*. The leadership of the institutionalized ideological state may be even more the prisoner of essentially corporate bodies. Neither leadership can afford radical changes of course for they result in profound repercussions in its administrative structure. And the charismatic leaders of the new nations are like tightrope artists—one false step and they will plunge from their perch.

IV. *Domestic Structure and Foreign Policy: The Prospects for World Order*

Many contemporary divisions are thus traceable to differences in domestic structure. But are there not countervailing factors? What about the spread of technology and its associated rationality, or the adoption on a global scale of many Western political forms? Unfortunately the process of "Westernization" does not inevitably produce a similar concept of reality. For what matters is not the institutions or the technology, but the significance which is attached to them. And this differs according to the evolution of the society concerned.

The term "nation" does not mean the same thing when applied to such various phenomena as India, France, and Nigeria. Similarly, technology is likely to have a different significance for different peoples, depending on how and when it was acquired.

Any society is part of an evolutionary process which proceeds by means of two seemingly contradictory mechanisms. On the one hand, the span of possible adaptations is delimited by the physical environment, the internal structure, and, above all, by previous choices. On the other hand, evolution proceeds not in a straight line but through a series of complicated variations which appear anything but obvious to the chief actors. In retrospect a choice may seem to have been nearly random or else to have represented the only available alternative. In either case, the choice is not an isolated act but an accumulation of previous decisions reflecting history or tradition and values as well as the immediate pressures of the need for survival. And each decision delimits the range of possible future adaptations.

Young societies are in a position to make radical changes of course which are highly impractical at a later stage. As a society becomes more elaborate and as its tradition is firmly established, its choices with respect to its internal organization grow more restricted. If a highly articulated social unit attempts basic shifts, it runs the risk of doing violence to its internal organization, to its history and values as embodied in its structure. When it accepts institutions or values developed elsewhere it must adapt them to what its structure can absorb. The institutions of any political unit must therefore be viewed in historical context for that alone can give an indication of their future. Societies—even when their institutions are similar—may be like ships passing in the night which find themselves but temporarily in the same place.

Is there then no hope for cooperation and stability? Is our international system doomed to incomprehension and its members to mounting frustration?

It must be admitted that if the domestic structures were considered in isolation, the prognosis would not be too hopeful. But domestic structures do not exist in a vacuum. They must respond to the requirements of the environment. And here all states find themselves face to face with the necessity of avoiding a nuclear holocaust. While this condition does not restrain all nations equally, it nevertheless defines a common task which technology will impose on even more countries as a direct responsibility.

Then, too, a certain similarity in the forms of administration may bring about common criteria of rationality as Professor Jaguaribe has pointed out in his contribution to this volume.[3] Science and technology will spread. Improved communications may lead to the emergence of a common culture. The fissures between domestic structures and the different stages of evolution are important, but they may be outweighed by the increasing interdependence of humanity.

It would be tempting to end on this note and to base the hope for peace on the self-evidence of the need for it. But this would be too pat. The deepest problem of the contemporary international order may be that most of the debates which form the headlines of the day are peripheral to the basic division described in this article. The cleavage is not over particular political arrangements—except as symptoms—but between two styles of policy and two philosophical perspectives.

The two styles can be defined as the political as against the revolutionary approach to order or, reduced to personalities, as the distinction between the statesman and the prophet.

The statesman manipulates reality; his first goal is survival; he feels responsible not only for the best but also for the worst conceivable outcome. His view of human nature is wary; he is conscious of many great hopes which have failed, of many good intentions that could not be realized, of selfishness and ambition and violence. He is, therefore, inclined to erect hedges against the possibility that even the most brilliant idea might prove abortive and that the most eloquent formulation might hide ulterior motives. He will try to avoid certain experiments, not because he would object to the results if they succeeded, but because he would feel himself responsible for the consequences if they failed. He is suspicious of those who personalize foreign policy, for history teaches him the fragility of structures dependent on individuals. To the statesman, gradualism is the essence of stability; he represents an era of average performance, of gradual change and slow construction.

By contrast, the prophet is less concerned with manipulating than with creating reality. What is possible interests him less than what is "right." He offers his vision as the test and his good faith as a guarantee. He believes in total solutions; he is less absorbed in methodology than in purpose. He believes in the perfectibility of man. His approach is timeless and not dependent on circumstances. He objects to gradualism as an unnecessary concession to circumstance. He will risk everything because his vision is the primary significant reality to him. Paradoxically, his more optimistic view of human nature makes him more intolerant than the statesman. If truth is both knowable and attainable, only immorality or stupidity can keep man from realizing it. The prophet represents an era of exaltation, of great upheavals, of vast accomplishments, but also of enormous disasters.

The encounter between the political and the prophetic approach to policy is always somewhat inconclusive and frustrating. The test of the statesman is the permanence of the international structure under stress. The test of the prophet is inherent in his vision. The statesman will seek to reduce the prophet's intuition to precise measures; he judges ideas on their utility and not on their "truth." To the prophet this approach is almost sacrilegious because it represents the triumph of expediency over universal principles. To the statesman negotiation is the mechanism of stability because it presupposes that maintenance of the existing order is more important than any dispute within it. To the prophet negotiations can have only symbolic value—as a means of converting or demoralizing the opponent; truth, by definition, cannot be compromised.

Both approaches have prevailed at different periods in history. The political approach dominated European foreign policy between the end of the religious wars and the French Revolution and then again between the Congress of Vienna and the outbreak of

World War I. The prophetic mode was in the ascendant during the great upheavals of the religious struggles and the period of the French Revolution, and in the contemporary uprisings in major parts of the world.

Both modes have produced considerable accomplishments, though the prophetic style is likely to involve the greater dislocations and more suffering. Each has its nemesis. The nemesis of the statesman is that equilibrium, though it may be the condition of stability, does not supply its own motivation; that of the prophet is the impossibility of sustaining a mood of exaltation without the risk of submerging man in the vastness of a vision and reducing him to a mere figure to be manipulated.

As for the difference in philosophical perspective, it may reflect the divergence of the two lines of thought which since the Renaissance have distinguished the West from the part of the world now called underdeveloped (with Russia occupying an intermediary position). The West is deeply committed to the notion that the real world is external to the observer, that knowledge consists of recording and classifying data—the more accurately the better. Cultures which escaped the early impact of Newtonian thinking have retained the essentially pre-Newtonian view that the real world is almost completely *internal* to the observer.

Although this attitude was a liability for centuries—because it prevented the development of the technology and consumer goods which the West enjoyed—it offers great flexibility with respect to the contemporary revolutionary turmoil. It enables the societies which do not share our cultural mode to alter reality by influencing the perspective of the observer—a process which we are largely unprepared to handle or even to perceive. And this can be accomplished under contemporary conditions without sacrificing technological progress. Technology comes as a gift; acquiring it in its advanced form does not presuppose the philosophical commitment that discovering it imposed on the West. Empirical reality has a much different significance for many of the new countries than for the West because in a certain sense they never went through the process of discovering it (with Russia again occupying an intermediary position). At the same time, the difference in philosophical perspective may cause us to seem cold, supercilious, lacking in compassion. The instability of the contemporary world order may thus have at its core a philosophical schism which makes the issues producing most political debates seem largely tangential.

Such differences in style and philosophical perspective are not unprecedented. What is novel is the global scale on which they occur and the risks which the failure to overcome them would entail. Historically, cleavages of lesser magnitude have been worked out dialectically, with one style of policy or one philosophical approach dominant in one era only to give way later to another conception of reality. And the transition was rarely free of violence. The challenge of our time is whether we can deal consciously and creatively with what in previous centuries was adjusted through a series of more or less violent and frequently catastropic upheavals. We must construct an international order *before* a crisis imposes it as a necessity.

This is a question not of blueprints, but of attitudes. In fact the overconcern with technical blueprints is itself a symptom of our difficulties. Before the problem of order can be "dealt" with—even philosophically—we must be certain that the right questions are being asked.

We can point to some hopeful signs. The most sensitive thinkers of the West have recognized that excessive empiricism may lead to stagnation. In many of the new countries—and in some Communist ones as well—the second or third generation of leaders is in the process of freeing itself from the fervor and dogmatism of the early revolutionary period and of relating their actions to an environment which they helped to create. But these are as yet only the first tentative signs of progress on a course whose significance is not always understood. Indeed it is characteristic of an age of turmoil that it produces so many immediate issues that little time is left to penetrate their deeper meaning. The most serious problem therefore becomes the need to acquire a sufficiently wide perspective so that the present does not overwhelm the future.

REFERENCES

1. Edmund Burke, *Works* (London, 1826), Vol. VIII, pp. 214-215.

2. "The Soviet Reply to the Chinese Letter," open letter of the Central Committee of the Communist Party of the Soviet Union as it appeared in *Pravda*, July 14, 1963, pp. 1-4; *The Current Digest of the Soviet Press*, Vol. XV, No. 28 (August 7, 1963), p. 23.

3. "World Order, Rationality, and Socioeconomic Development," pp. 607-626.

JOSÉ LUIS L. ARANGUREN

Openness to the World: An Approach to World Peace

THE CONTEMPORARY thinker who has reflected most about conjecture is, I believe, Bertrand de Jouvenel, a Frenchman who has close ties with British and American thought. Conjecture, while it is not the same thing as looking forward (*prospective*), coincides with it in this respect: the future as it is foreseen and—if we are speaking of a real looking forward which determines events within the limits of practicability—as it is proposed constitutes a part of the present just as the past does. The past weighs upon the present and at least to a certain extent predetermines it. Similarly, from the very moment we propose a particular future, our projection begins to influence the present, to redound upon it, so to speak; in a very precise way, it has a decisive effect upon our own present.

History is not moved in a predetermined direction by a sort of Hegelian *Weltgeist* or a Marxian single cause. We ourselves are history. In passing from the abstract (history) to the concrete (ourselves) we acquire a full awareness of our responsibility—a responsibility limited by what is possible or practicable, but nonetheless a real and effective one—for the course of the world. And since my modest contribution to this inter- and multi-disciplinary symposium will be rather of an ethical nature (without, however, any overtones of moralism—I will clarify my position shortly), this *prise de conscience* of our responsibility seems a good starting

The Spanish government prevented me from taking part in the conference which was held at the Villa Serbelloni, in Bellagio, Italy, and my contribution had to be completed beforehand. This paper undoubtedly suffers from a certain monologue quality. It could not be put to the test of a direct confrontation with other positions. That initial disadvantage has been remedied in part, I trust, by the thoughtful advice of Dr. Graubard and the valuable assistance of Professor Stanley Hoffmann, who made an excellent summation of the discussions.

point. To bring about the necessary conditions for a world order, for a just order in the world, supposes a conditioning and even an operation—in a sense akin to "surgical operation"—not only upon the future but also, in accordance with what we have said, upon the past. Reality, including, to some extent, social reality, is operable, and the natural, human, and social sciences are nothing else but the subtly constructed network of those "operations." When mathematicians speak of "mathematical operations" they do so with good reason, and we must take their expression at its literal value.

Order as Peace

Order means peace and, from our point of view, international peace—peace in the minimal sense of no war, coexistence. On first consideration, this may seem to be a small thing. But it is necessary to proceed modestly and realistically, remaining content to advance step by step. In any event, compared with atomic war and its unimaginable destructive power, the present peace, precarious though it may seem, is evidently a positive good. How can we prevent war? I mean to prevent all war, for the principles of a just war are no longer valid now that any war, as soon as it becomes generalized, will always threaten to become a nuclear war. Can war perhaps be prevented through expounding and defending the abstract principle of peace? It is to be doubted. Experience has taught us that good wishes and good intentions—that is to say, morality—are not strong enough in themselves to have an appreciable effect on the course of events. We spoke before of responsibility, it is true, but of a circumscribed responsibility, limited to what was practicable. The manifestoes of intellectuals who are given to making appeals to the collective conscience, and so forth, serve as "tranquilizers" to their signatories, give a luster to that object of beauty which is their "*bonne conscience*"—and leave things exactly as they were before. The hierarchies of the spirit are always "unarmed hierarchies," and, besides, a strictly ethical-intellectual point of view is generally blind to the sociological, economic, scientific, and technical forces which condition morality.

Morality and Politics

If we grant, in accordance with an already classic saying, that war is only a continuation of politics through a different means, and consider war as the furthest extension of politics, then we may, and, I believe, should, broach the problem in terms of an essential tension between morality and politics.[1] It would be very comforting, comforting to the spirit, to possess a political ethics which was all of a piece. Unfortunately we do not even have a definitive general ethics. Morality is far more a matter of being exacting with oneself and others, an imperative, an unceasing search, than it is a quasi-medical prescription for the internal use of the conscience. Politics, in contrast, has its roots in reality, and both as individual behavior and as a structure it is made up of a series of data which are not static, but powerfully dynamic, a play of forces which it is necessary to observe and abide by if one really wants to play the game of politics.

If the two terms "morality" and "politics" are understood in this way, one immediately sees the point in question, the fundamentally problematical relation between morality and politics.[2] But the fact that it is problematical does not mean that it can be discounted. In my opinion, there is a relation, and a true one, but it is a relation always filled with tension, a dramatic relation. Man is at one and the same time *homo politicus* and *homo moralis*. He cannot cease to be either one or the other, but feels himself doubly compelled: compelled to be political-moral and compelled to be so only with difficulty. The source of the problem lies here. I have not spoken of *tragedy*, but of *drama*. Tragedy occurs when an unavoidable *fatum* hovers over us and we cannot escape it, cannot act in *any other way*. Drama, on the other hand, exists when it is possible to affect events, when there is room for sudden changes of circumstances and for freedom. It is not a matter of absolutely denying freedom, and consequently morality. It is rather that we must become aware that morality—that morality which sets itself over the humble realities of life and seeks to make them conform to its lofty aims—is something less than omnipotent. It is necessary to take upon oneself both tasks—the moral and the political—and try to make them meet without falling into political "realism"—the *Eigengesetzlichkeit* of politics, cogently portrayed in its international aspect by Professor H. J. Morgenthau—or into a moralistic Pharisaism which is all too easily satisfied, or into a righteous attitude which leaves other people to dirty their hands in politics or despairs of ever finding a solution.

If morality is to come to grips with the forces which condition our lives politically, and so economically, socially, and in other ways as well, it must function inside their frame of reference. We are not abstract men, we are always "situated." It is therefore necessary that our morality be not so much a "morality of the situation" (*Situationsethik*) as a "morality within the situation." We must take into account the concrete forces which condition us and then decide what actions are practicable. The "operation" of which we were speaking should always be carried out on the basis of an objective study of our situation.

What do I mean when I say that "we are situated"? From the international point of view, adopted here, this means that every nation now belongs to a bloc, a group, or an aggregate of nations. It means that the structure of international alliances gives rise to the conflictual character of the present world "order," which is an essentially pluralistic order, not fixed but historical and therefore unstable, dynamically changing as a result of the particular conditions of every period and even of every moment. First it is bipolar (the Eastern and Western blocs). Then it is polycentric (Soviet and Chinese subsystems at the heart of the so-called Eastern bloc; special statutes for Yugoslavia and also for Poland and Hungary; a subsystem which is supposedly forming around France, from whence "the olympian pronouncements that issue from Paris at six-month intervals"[3] are dispatched to Washington and the world at large; the "Third World" of "unaligned" nations, which in turn admits of many different configurations: the underdeveloped countries, considered apart; Black Africa; the Arab countries of Africa and Asia; the U.A.R.; and so on). Again, in the foreseeable future there may be an élitist structure imposed by an "Atomic Club." It is certainly not my intention to enumerate all the possible kinds of "crystallization," especially in view of the fact that, strictly speaking, there is no such thing as "crystallization," for the international *Gestalt* is kaleidoscopic, forever changing at more or less rapid, observable intervals. I propose to describe the factors which seem to me decisive, the relatively constant parameters of our international situation, on which—in a negative sense—the order of the present-day world depends.

Our Task

The existing order is a changing order, as we have seen, and a precarious one. Indeed, no stable order can be built upon a common ground of positive objectives, given the fundamental pluralism of the world today. We lack a metaphysics and a scale of values accepted by all. And experimental science—which is now beginning to put one particular concern, that of the exploitation of nature, over all others—is not sufficiently developed to take up the search of the old metaphysics for a single meaningful impulse behind the history of the world. Neither is economics in a position to replace metaphysics in this respect, for "development," as was shown at the conference, is not the sole value—alongside it or before it a country may try to achieve human dignity, independence, and so forth. And development may be seen as an end in itself, or as a means for achieving social justice, and it may be effected through an earlier redistribution of the existing wealth or through the creation of a socialist regime.

The precariousness of world order is never then a mere temporary, *de facto* failing, but rather follows from the current divergent conceptions of that order. Now, and for a long time to come, such divergence must appear insuperable to anyone who is at all realistic about it. If this is the case, what else can we do but take a pragmatic, day-by-day approach to maintaining an "order" which seems to imply nothing more secure than the intention to live in peaceful coexistence?

In my opinion, and this is the point of the present article, our intellectual labor on behalf of a world order should consist in absorbing the shocks, in lessening the tensions, in clearing the way for intelligent solutions by means of an open dialogue rather than in trying to achieve what is now beyond reach—universal agreement with respect to a univocal system of values on which an unshakeable ideal order could be based.

In other words, our role can consist only in working to remove the main obstacles in the way of peaceful coexistence, of a *de facto* order. In my view these obstacles arise from the hardening, the dogmatization, what in the last analysis is the *mythification* of the respective political positions. The task incumbent upon us is to try to make these positions more flexible, to render them suitable for dialogue.

The mythification of reality means especially the forging of an image which is accepted simplistically and held to be unquestionable, an image loaded with affective interest—fear, together with the drive for power and possessions, is usually the basic ingredient—which fixes our attitudes and our behavior. But in our outwardly rational world it is necessary to provide such a "mythology" with an

intellectual facade. That is the mission of both political and economic "ideologies." "Myth" and "ideology"—distinguishable from
each other only through an exercise of intellectual abstraction—are
in fact nothing but the two sides—irrational, rationalized—of a
truculent attitude which is unreceptive to the exchange of ideas
and therefore spells a constant danger for world order and peace.

This is all the more true in that myths and ideologies, far from
limiting themselves to informing—or deforming—our view of reality, turn upon it actively and transform it through a sort of praxis.
This praxis consists above all—to describe it necessarily too schematically—in "strategy" and "manipulation." And manipulation, as
far as international relations are concerned, is all too often a manipulation of fear (of the loss of life, property, independence, supremacy) occasioned by fear. Here the cycle of irrationality that was
opened by mythification is completed, and rationality is reduced
to ostensibly expounding what in truth are deep and obscure sentiments, closed off from reason.

In accordance with what we have said thus far, we shall now
treat separately the mythifying and oversimplifying function of (1)
political ideologies and (2) economic ideologies. Then we shall
speak of the modification of reality which takes place as a result of
this mythic-ideological attitude, a modification which functions primarily through (3) political-economic strategy and (4) manipulation. Fear (5) as a result of such manipulation will be the last topic
we take up, following which we shall summarize, in a few words, the
main point of this article.

Myths and Political Ideologies

The term "ideology," of course, can have diverse meanings. In
the present context it is important to emphasize one of them.
Progress in knowledge—especially in the social sciences—is always
made slowly and analytically, piecemeal, in the expression of Professor Karl Popper. But every one of our propositions has within
its purely descriptive or informative content an emotional colora-
tion and betrays a tendency to make not only judgments based on
fact but value judgments as well. This impulsive, emotional, non-
intellectual tendency to take sides, presenting one's own position
in a symbolic and graphic manner (as a myth), and also another
anti-intellectual tendency, that of impatience with detailed analytical procedures, lead people to extrapolate from their limited

fund of knowledge and accept established opinions which may be simply metaphorical, false, or only partly true, without submitting them to criticism. In this way, with an assistance from rhetoric—I mean by rhetoric a form of discourse which is not intellectual but persuasive by virtue of the very emotions it stirs up—we proceed from ideas, always colored to a greater or lesser degree by emotions, to ideology, that is, to a comprehensive synthesis which, though it is presented as philosophy and does not purport to be religious, still divides the world into two camps, a camp of Good and a camp of Evil. By a stroke of good fortune, these camps are made up of Friends on one side and Enemies on the other, all the former being virtuous and all the latter unremittingly wicked. As Senator Fulbright has said, "our national vocabulary is full of 'self-evident truths.' . . . It has become one of these 'self-evident truths' of the postwar era that just as the President resides in Washington and the Pope in Rome, the Devil resides immutably in Moscow."[4] However, the Senator continues, "now the Devil has betrayed us by travelling abroad and worse still, by dispersing himself, turning up now here, now there, and in many places at once, with a devilish disregard for the laboriously constructed frontiers of ideology." It will be seen that ideology, through this division of the world into Good and Bad, takes the form of mythology. In a fairly recent lecture, he took as his text Thackeray's question, "The wicked are wicked, no doubt . . . but who can tell the mischief which the very virtuous do?"[5] Fulbright insisted upon this point, denouncing the crusading spirit of the American people which he regards as a secular derivation of the "Puritan way of thought, harsh and ascetic and intolerant." The effect of Puritanism, he said, has been to convince many Americans that they are "God's chosen people," and that their mission is to regenerate mankind by imposing their "way of life," the only good one, in opposition to "diabolical" Communism. We have here a clear example of a myth, the American messianic myth, rationalized ideologically and wrought into a political strategy, which is a matter we shall turn to later. Fulbright objected to the commonly heard phrase "the nature of Communism": "Communism is not a living organism but a collection of ideas and premises, an abstraction. Man has an observable nature, and insofar as we are able to understand it, we can more easily understand human behavior, but I do not see how a body of ideas can be said to have a nature apart from the human nature of those who hold the ideas." And the people who hold those ideas, the

197

Communists, "are human beings with many of the same hopes and fears, sympathies and prejudices that we have."

In my opinion Fulbright's criticism in this same lecture goes further than he himself may realize. In fact, by commending a philosophy of pragmatic hedonism—"Life after all is short and it is no sin to try to enjoy it"—he argues for a way of life which, in practice, through its concern with individual consumption, approaches the theoretical and socialist materialism of Marxism: absolute primacy is given to material development. Now, apart from the increase of pragmatism and the growing priority of self-interest over merely ideological positions in politics it would seem necessary to include under consideration the existence and the force of other ideals, other objectives and goals, some of which, such as national independence and human dignity (to these we should add social justice at least), were examined in the discussions held at the Villa Serbelloni. Thinkers as different from one another as the economist Galbraith, the economist and sociologist Myrdal, the Sartrian André Gorz, and the Marxist Pierre Vilar agree, at least negatively, in their criticism of the "affluent society" with its arbitrary and wasteful enhancement of those sectors of the economy which produce individual luxury items. Services of greater social value, they point out, are relatively neglected. But this critical position, no less than that of Senator Fulbright, represents a (demythified) ideology. The question which now suggests itself, or rather which besets us, is this: can men ever dispense with ideologies? Fulbright accepts man as he is, that is, as he is in the United States, the richest and most highly developed country in the world, a country which, throughout its short history, has been made to conform to an ideology and seems, by and large, to be quite happy with it. But what of the rest of us who are dissatisfied with our reality and would welcome its transformation, how shall we move people if we cannot propose an attractive goal to them? And what are the conditions which a demythified ideology or "way of life" should meet if it is to prove valid ethically and socially? These are the two questions I have allowed myself to ask in the hope of a reply. The chairman of the seminar at Villa Serbelloni, himself an accomplished and long-standing "de-ideologizer" or "anti-ideologue" who may now have relented somewhat[6] because of a keen awareness of the dangers involved when total syntheses break down, might have been able to answer these questions better than anyone else.

Setting aside now the topic of ideologies, which, once they have been demythified, present no further difficulty than that of their (inevitable?) simplification, I should like to say a few words about the threat to world peace—and, in my judgment, it is the principal threat—posed by secular myth and mythology in our time. The struggle for demythification (and demystification) seems urgent. "Cross-cultural studies," and in France what is now beginning to be called "imageologie," point to this conclusion: it is necessary for us to make a start in understanding precisely, for the purpose of later destroying it, the web of old, established, false images, of myths, conventions, and stereotypes which prevent us from having truly human contact.

The average man's impressions of foreign countries are very fuzzy and distorted, ranging from "outlines" (oversimplified, insufficient, elementary, or stereotyped knowledge) to "myths," which, in contradistinction, are full of affective interest, positive or negative —idealization or denigration—and, generally, are much affected by ethical and political values and counter-values.[7]

Germany, Russia, and, at present, China are for Westerners the most politically mythified countries. We have previously spoken of Russia. It would seem suitable to include here some reflections on China, derived from Felix Greene's book *A Curtain of Ignorance: (How the American Public has been Misinformed about China)*.[8] Reading this book one clearly distinguishes the three or four types of images I have just mentioned: The distant, exotic, vague but benevolent image of Confucian China, peaceloving with a rich, hermetic, cultural tradition, the China of jade and marble sculpture; and a continuation of that image, the China "seen" schematically or reflected by Westerners who lived there after the Boxer Rebellion and the First World War, a China extraordinarily refined and pleasant, almost paradisiac—at least for Westerners. Finally we have the double mythification: on the one hand, the legend of Chiang Kai-shek fabricated by the "image-makers" of the "China Lobby" who succeeded in presenting the marshal and his wife to all America, in *Time* magazine, as "the man and woman of the world for the year 1937." On the other hand, the myth of the "other" China, inscrutable and sinister behind its obliging smile; the China which was a satellite of Stalin at first and came to replace him as the incarnation of Terror, the spirit of an apocalyptic destruction which she alone could survive thanks to her immense population.

199

We are studying the conditions necessary to guarantee a world order. I believe the first of these is not freedom from the influence of ideologies—which may be ultimately impossible—but rather freedom from myth and mystification, from the overly idealized or overly somber impressions which the peoples of the world hold of one another. As we said, all humans partake, in the final analysis, of the same hopes and fears, of like sympathies and antipathies. Reform in the teaching of history, correction of distorting images through education and through a constantly expanding open network of all the means of communication are surely the most effective guarantees against the fabrication of political myths.

Myths and Economic Ideologies

Economic ideologies are closely tied to political ones, and these ties grow stronger day by day, for political policies are currently far more responsive to interests than they are to principles. Political and economic demythification are inseparable.

The great myths are contained within these two words which are scarcely ever said in a tone of voice that does not betray the speaker's emotions—capitalism and communism.When these words are spoken with equanimity, it is generally because they are being considered as "abstractions," and their true significance in practice, their changing significance over a long period of time, is quite out of mind. Let us consider capitalism first. In the beginning, it depended on a terrible exploitation of human beings, but it gradually changed and now relies on the great-grandchildren of its original victims to be the satisfied consumers of automobiles and electrical appliances. The highly developed nations paid the price of their growth beforehand. Marx wrote under the painful stimulus of having witnessed merciless exploitation. Hence—in spite of himself—his work has a strong ethical, even Messianic, direction. Later, personal sacrifices were required in Russia and China as well if those countries were to develop on a similar scale. Primitive capitalism has given way to "neo-capitalism"; an ideology of "free-enterprise" has been created, which serves as a cover for the workings, which are anything but "free," of great corporations. Socialism, for its part, no longer constitutes an end in itself—especially in the "Third World." It has ceased to mean simply freedom for all mankind and it is shedding its Marxist dogma and antireligious prejudices, being now content to be regarded as the most suitable instrument for the rapid economic growth of underdeveloped countries.[9] Needless to say, an adequate analysis of "capitalism" and "communism" would have to be much more thorough, but these summary observations serve to point out the ambiguous mixture of myth and schematic abstraction which these terms have acquired.

In practice, which is to say, at a distance from myth and abstraction, there seems to be some prospect of a *rapprochement* between the "neo-capitalist" and socialist countries. In both, development has taken a place of primary importance, economic planning is commonly carried out, and industries—especially those which have only recently come into being and will sooner or later affect the whole world—are nationalized. Moreover, as a country becomes capable of greater economic growth, there is a mounting pressure for better living conditions and for certain personal liberties, such as were impossible under the regime of Stalin. A more flexible method of organizing the general economy is prevailing over the dogmatism of earlier days. Does this mean that we are headed in the direction of a world-wide integration, as Professor Duverger believes?[10] I do not know. For the present, as Raymond Aron stresses (following Rostow), each period of growth may be said to favor a certain type of political regime, but does not necessarily impose that regime. To assert the contrary would be to take Marxism, or any other theory, as a simple superstructure, and be more Marxian than the Marxists. Instead of a pure and simple integration brought about by the quasi-deterministic force of events themselves, it seems to me that one or more new ways of life are likely to emerge, which will have to be created rather than passively accepted, and could replace the two creeds which now seem to stand permanently opposed. But I must state again that I am here suggesting problems to which I can scarcely hope to provide answers. At any rate, to recognize the irrationality of myths and the abstract nature of economic ideologies with respect to the human reality of all relations between men, even those relations which purport to be strictly economic, is, I believe, to work for world order.

Political-Economic Strategy

Until now, save in a few instances, we have spoken of myths and ideologies somewhat as if they were disembodied and existed outside us. But in actuality both are always functional and they fulfill a practical role in confrontation with other myths and ideologies. The "image maker" is not, in any sense, to be described as a sort of disinterested novelist. He uses his images for the purpose of mobilizing a country, a social class, a bloc, against some other country, class, or bloc. Myths and ideologies are at the service of action; they stimulate a certain kind of collective behavior and consequently lead up to a particular strategy.

Strategy is the art of directing operations against an adversary in a previously planned way. Only in a limited sense does it refer to military operations. By an extension of the mathematical theory of games, the word "strategy" has come into common use. It seems unnecessary to say that I do not propose to present here a theory of strategy. I do not feel competent to do so, and my manner of treating the present theme is not technical but ethical, or socio-ethical. It is important, however, to make two distinctions between types of strategy, both of which lead to consequences which are, in my opinion, crucially important to the goal of establishing the conditions of a world order.

The first distinction is between open and hidden strategy. It may be advisable to mask a strategy to deceive an opponent. This was the course recommended by the (purely theoretical) political strategist Baltasar Gracián,[11] a Spanish Jesuit of the seventeenth century. For Gracián, prudence consisted in the art of calculation, in determining the extent to which one can commit oneself in pursuing a certain end. It is necessary, he believed, that we should know how to hide our intentions—or, to put it in his words, we must assume a "profound, natural unpredictability" ("incomprensibilidades de caudal") and learn to "disguise our will" ("cifrar la voluntad"). Gracián preached dissimulation, evasiveness, equivocation, reserve, and also the art of using the truth the better to deceive. For the sake of a triumph over an opponent, we should maintain a second, or even a third level of intentions in secret, and bring to bear all our skill in "seeming" and "acting." In a study of "The Political Regime of Spain in 1971," I have analyzed another example of concealed, or rather ambiguous, strategy in the form of "The Equivocation in the Relations between Francoism and the Monarchy."[12]

There is also such a thing as an open strategy, intended to make our resolution known without leaving any room for doubt: the simple act of transmitting a message with such an intention creates, so to speak, a "registered" communication; it expedites further communication, makes all sorts of negotiations possible, and even provides means for saving face and for "rationalizing" a transaction or a compromise. Even in dealings with rash and foolish men this strategy may be better than an equivocal one: "The greatest freedom of speech is the greatest safety because, if a man is a fool, the best thing to do is to encourage him to advertise the fact by speaking."[13]

A second distinction is well known in game theory. Games may be divided into those whose sum result equals zero, in which there is an absolute winner and an absolute loser, and those of variable sum, with a correlation, although imperfect, of preferences.

The current state of the world, as far as order is concerned, resembles the second class of games much more closely than the first, especially since the invention of atomic weapons. All countries have some community of interests; it is a large one if we are dealing with allied countries and restricted, but still real, in the case of antagonistic countries. We are all taking the same journey through space on a planet threatened with destruction by megaton bombs. It is true, as Aron says, that the present, very imperfect codification of the rules of international competition allows one to believe that the relations between countries are still in a "state of nature," in the Hobbesian sense. But every "state of nature" is a "historical state" in which men are "situated," as we said at the beginning.

Consequently we must realize that to adopt a strategy of open communications and to visualize politics as a game of variable sums is ultimately beneficial to world order, to peace. On a practical level, honorable behavior and a sense of fair play in international strategy follow from a close analysis, from a thorough rationality applied to the criticism of myths and ideologies.

Manipulation

In the conference at the Villa Serbelloni the theme of political planning was considered in relation to economic planning. In my view, political planning presents two different facets: there is *ad extra*, international planning in which one decides beforehand the strategy he is going to follow against an adversary, and also *ad intra*, intranational planning which involves a decision about how to control public opinion in accordance with a concept, established by the rulers, of the objectives of the community. The latter kind of

203

planning cannot be instituted successfully except through dictator-ship, or through manipulating the public so that they accept the criteria imposed by mass media as their own and do not try to take an active part in politics, but allow themselves to be governed technocratically.

Political planning—which is here somewhat different from economic planning—should not be imposed by the rulers if it is really to take root in the lives of the people. The people must be admitted as consultants and participants. Democratic political planning is necessarily presupposed by that *ethics of planning* which was discussed at the Villa Serbelloni.

It is clear that, in "manipulation," mythical ingredients are seen in sharp relief. In speaking hypercritically of it, we were as-suming an almost absolute social atomization. But, in fact, within our global society every individual is integrated into a group, which may be intellectual, socio-cultural, socio-economic, eth-nic, and so forth. That is why propaganda does not affect the basic personality so greatly as it was believed until recently; fundamental attitudes and decisions in the socio-political area with which people are familiar, that is, in internal politics, are less open to persua-sion. Western civilization, which is individualistic in many respects, and is mass-moved in other respects, is directed actively in most really important matters by the groups to which people belong. This seems certain in nondictatorial countries, where the chan-nels of communication remain open and secondary groups have not been destroyed. And even where less profound choices are con-cerned—those which may be affected by advertising and propaganda —the persuaders are really trying to anticipate—half intuitively, half technologically—what people are looking for. There is, to be sure, a reciprocal reinforcement between what we want and what we are told that we want, and advertising may influence people who do not know what they are looking for.

Where international affairs are involved, it is quite a different matter. It is impossible for one country's official opinions to have any close relation to the real conditions of life in another country, especially if the countries are separated by an iron curtain or by a curtain of ignorance. Political propaganda scarcely ever allows for distinction and contrast, and the patriotic, ideological, mythical, and emotional appeals it makes easily convey those distorting images we have spoken of, which are at the very source of our "active measures" and "acts of intervention."

All inquiries lead to the same conclusion: the essential conditions of world order and peace are an objective formulation of what is happening outside our national boundaries, especially in the "opposing bloc," and a great extension of the trustworthy means of communication.

Fear

The kind of manipulation we have been speaking of is, above all, a manipulation through fear, occasioned by fear. It consists in arousing irrational reactions and attitudes, in forcing us to make emotional rather than intelligent decisions. Fear reigns in the world today. The old "balance of power" has been replaced now by a "balance of terror."

How can we rid ourselves of fear, of terror? Terror in the collectivity is equivalent to anguish in an individual, in Heidegger's view; it is not a fear of some particular evil, but rather an emotional aura, a sort of psychic mistiness. Our real fears are abstracted and then fused in a new form which is not unlike the cosmic terror of primitive man.

Our concern is with the order, the peace of the world. We must recognize that today "order" and "peace" are founded upon fear. It seems to me, however, that the situation is changing for the better. The vague terror of that faceless monster known as Communism, the fear and indignation aroused by the contrary monster, capitalist oppression, tend to be replaced by the immense, but concrete, fear of a total atomic extermination. In centuries past, war in Europe amounted to a heroic game played, like chess, by kings and figures on horseback with the aid of mercenary pawns. Later, with the advent of mobilization and of total war, it lost its resemblance to a game and became a horrible, indiscriminate slaughter. Today, war has recovered its game-like quality in a sense: its result can be calculated in advance by applying the theory of games; or, if a mathematical formalization is not possible, it may be described as a game in which there are no victors, only losers. In any case, it is a game that it would be improper to play because either the victory would be assured beforehand or there would be no chance of victory for either side. Let us hope that good sense can prevail. To insure this, it is necessary to create states of mind so general and powerful that they can alter the course of events. In other words, we must try to reform the structures of the mind and give a reasonable meaning to our fears.

JOSÉ LUIS L. ARANGUREN

A Few Concluding Words

We have examined the conditions which seem necessary to assure order and peace in the world; on the level of attitudes, they are a demythification and relativization of ideologies and, on the level of action, a political strategy of completely open communication and a forbearance from manipulation. What is needed is a means of putting our justified fear to a rational use.

Such a transformation would evidently be difficult to bring about, and even if we do bring it about its permanence will be questionable. History will never cease as long as there are men, and history implies contrast, opposition, variance. To borrow a phrase of Maurice Duverger, we live in the time of the "impossible golden age." Even so, in the same way that we are moving toward this accomplishment on a national scale, in states of law, we must try to succeed in institutionalizing our international conflicts by having recourse to world organizations and treaties, by disposing ourselves to negotiate, bargain, and transact, whatever the cost may be.

The struggle for order and peace will never end. Stability is at best a precarious condition. No comprehensive society is fully integrated, much less an international society. What is more, the dysfunction of society plays a positive role, as the condition for development and social change, which is almost as important as its actual functions.

Observing that variance is unavoidable, we may recall that we have a need to create a variety of "ways of life" and are not obliged to choose between the two models which history now seems to be pressing upon us, which are in their own way constantly changing. History, as we said at the outset, is neither purely arbitrary nor purely deterministic. It is we ourselves—acting within our given situation to change history—who are history.

REFERENCES

1. I have treated this theme broadly in my book *Etica y Política* (Madrid, 1963).

2. Contemporary American theologians, both protestant and Catholic, Reinhold Niebuhr and J. C. Murray, for example, have seen this problem clearly.

3. J. W. Fulbright, speech given in the U. S. Senate (cf. *Congressional Record*, Vol. 110, No. 56 [March 25, 1964]).

4. *Ibid.*

5. A lecture on "Ideology and Foreign Policy," given at Johns Hopkins University, March 12, 1965.

6. Cf. the French review *Preuves* (March 1965), p. 33.

7. Concerning the use of the categories "myth" and "schematization," the reader may consult my article on "La imagen española de Alemania," published first in the German review, *Dokumente,* No. 1 (February 1957), collected later in *La juventud europea y otros ensayos* (Barcelona, 1962) which was translated into Italian: *La Gioventù europea e altri saggi* (Brescia, 1962). The essay was reproduced in the *Revue de Psychologie des Peuples,* 3rd Trimester (1964).

8. *A Curtain of Ignorance* (New York, 1964). Mr. F. Greene is also the author of the book *Awakened China.*

9. Cf. the studies of Professor Simon Jargy and the paper of Robert Badouin, "Perspective du socialisme africain," presented to the Conference Internationale de "Futuribles," Paris, April 1965.

10. *Introduction à la politique* (Paris, 1964).

11. Cf. "La moral de Gracián," an article published by the author in the *Revista de la Universidad de Madrid,* Vol. VII, No. 27 (1958) which appeared recently in French in the *Revue de Métaphysique et de Morale.*

12. SEDEIS, Serie "Futuribles," Paris, July 10, 1961. This article was included in the Italian edition of my book, *La Gioventù europea e altri saggi,* cited above, but not in the Spanish.

13. See Senator Fulbright's speech, cited above.

HELIO JAGUARIBE

World Order, Rationality, and Socioeconomic Development

I. *What Is World Order?*

Institutionalization and socioeconomic development. World order, generally defined, signifies the custodianship of the general interests of the world by means of a system of norms which are valid and enforceable on a world-wide scale. To be valid, these norms must be largely accepted by those for whom they are destined, and there must be an appropriate system for their elaboration, ratification, and observance. For these norms to be enforceable, effective sanctions against their violation must exist. This can be achieved through the establishment of agencies invested with authority to formulate and implement the norms, to inspect their proper observance, and to restrain their violation. Thus, any world order must consist both of a defined system of legal norms and of a defined system of agencies which will carry out the legislative, executive, and judicial functions necessary for the validity and enforcement of any juridical system.[1]

The totality of interests which are to be protected by this institutional system must also be considered. The possibility of adopting norms which are valid presupposes minimal conditions of agreement with these norms. The effective imposition of norms by a dominating group upon a dominated one does not succeed, *per se,* in endowing the norms with validity for the latter group. In such a case, observance depends exclusively upon the coercive capacity of the dominant group, and "norm" simply means a pattern of coercion whose formal characteristics (generality, regularity, internal consistency, compatibility with other norms, and so on) will not be sufficient to give them a juridical meaning.

The problem of establishing a valid juridical order exists in the very roots of the foundations of the State (for example, the *contrat social* and the *volonté générale* of Rousseau). According to modern theorists, this can be achieved only if there is a minimum compatibility of interests within various groups and classes and between each of these and the society as a whole. Only then is it possible to institutionalize society and insure that minimum of consensus upon which the validity of any juridical order depends. This is true even in the extreme case of the totalitarian state.

Transposed to the plane of world order, a valid juridical order must also be founded on appropriate institutional developments and grow out of a degree of compatibility among the leading interests. The world today is characterized by the greatest inequality among nations and people in their enjoyment of the fundamental goods—liberty, equality, health, education, income, and power. Any world order which did not presuppose a more equal distribution of such goods and which did not lead to a maximum increase in economic, political, cultural, and social development would not be likely to attain validity. Thus, only when a valid world juridical system has been established and socioeconomic development is generalized will it be possible to achieve the implantation of world order.[2]

It should also be mentioned that the concept of world order currently contains the implication that it will be achieved through peaceful agreement. Considered solely as an appropriate and permanent regulation of world interests, world order could, in principle, be brought about with the aid of force. This would occur, for example, if one of the superpowers gained dominance over the other and then imposed its own conception of order upon the world. World order might also be achieved if nuclear warfare, because of its increasingly catastrophic effects, imposed upon the participants the necessity of reaching some sort of agreement in order to avoid their mutual annihilation and to impede new nuclear conflicts.

The object of this study is to analyze the conditions necessary for the peaceful implantation of world order in terms which would avoid precisely the outburst of a nuclear conflagration.

Forms of institutionalization. Although any world order would, of course, involve a world juridical system, there are different forms of reaching agreement to such institutionalization. Basically, there are three possible models: the World State, the Supra-National Authority, and the International Agreement.

The World State represents the most universal form of jurisdiction and the most direct relationship between the institutional system and the people subject to it. All existing or potential states, with the exception of the World State itself, are suppressed. Only the World State is sovereign, and there is only one citizenship, that of the world, with juridical equality for all men. The legislative, executive, and judicial organs of the World State would be constituted by direct choice of all men endowed with the right to vote, independently of their previous nationality and domicile. Perhaps the most viable form of the World State would be a state such as the United States of America on an international scale.

Supra-National Authority represents an equally universal form of jurisdiction but a less direct relationship between the institutional system and the persons subject to it. According to this model, the existing states, and others that may come into being, subsist as political organizations to which their respective citizens are subject, but a supra-national jurisdiction is constituted, to which all states delegate their present sovereignty. The states retain only those powers of internal administration which are permitted by the Supra-National Constitution. The fundamental characteristic of this model is the division of the politico-juridical system into two planes: that of the national states and that of the Supra-National Authority. Only the Authority is sovereign and only it can legislate for the world in general and provide for the observance of its norms. The national states, and not the individual citizens of these states, are the subjects of the Supra-National Authority. The organs of the Authority are established not directly by the citizens of the national states, but by the states themselves. Representation of each state will probably not be merely proportional to its population, but will take into consideration other factors, such as total and *per capita* income, previous military power, and cultural standards.

The third possible model is that of the International Agreement, in which the states themselves will be both subjects and objects of world organization. National citizenships will continue, and the states will maintain their sovereignty, although it will be limited by the terms of the International Agreement and subject to the authority of the agencies which such an Agreement would provide for the execution, implementation, and observance of its norms. In this model, the jurisdiction of international norms applies to the national states and not directly to their citizens, whose relationship to the international institution is mediated through the states. This model provided the basis for the Charter of the United Nations, although with many limitations and without the approval of effective authority for the international organs provided in it. The International Agreement, therefore, may be understood as a system somewhat similar to the U.N.: all states would participate without discrimination, but effective legislative power would be given to the Assembly (probably with a weighted voting system) and power for implementing the international norms would rest with the executive body. The latter requisite would involve the necessity of abolishing national armies and of establishing an international police force under the command of the Executive Power constituted by the Agreement.

II. *Indispensability of World Order*

Cultural and historical unification. Historically, the most relevant fact of our times is the unification of the field of important political decisions, which occurred after the cultural unification of the world.[3] The latter event took place from the Renaissance to the Enlightenment, when Western culture, carried overseas by the commercial revolution, was in constant contact with other independent cultures. The more consistent operational rationality of the West condemned non-Western cultures to the dilemma of perishing either by external destruction or by internal contradiction. Toynbee applied the terms zealotism and Herodianism to this dilemma. If, when faced with the West, cultures such as the Islamic, Buddhist, or Hindu insist (zealotism) on maintaining the unity of their system of beliefs and of the practices founded upon it, they lose the ability to defend their societies from foreign domination and are destroyed from without. This happened to the Buddhists of Tibet and of Southeast Asia. If, conversely, cultures recognize the operational superiority of Western rationality and seek (Herodianism) to incorporate the science and technology founded upon it, they then face hopeless contradiction with the remaining elements of the beliefs they are trying to preserve. As a result, they convert such elements into ritualism and folklore, as is happening in Japan, India, and, more recently, China.

During the course of the nineteenth century, Western culture finally became the universal culture, the other cultures being led toward gradual but inevitable disappearance. After World War II, the field of important political decisions was also unified. Before cultural unification was achieved, different systems of references and different fields of political macro-decisions coexisted in the world. Several histories were unfolding, presided over by diverse standards of meaning and occurring in separate camps. These camps were unaware of each other, and decisions made by one had no repercussions on the others. In the interval between cultural unification and World War II, there began to be only one standard of meaning, but the many camps of political macro-decisions persisted. Nations such as Argentina and Switzerland, for example, during the last two World Wars, were neutral not only from a *de jure* point of view, but were not *directly* affected by the conflagration. Nations less involved with the Western world remained still more distant from such vicissitudes.

After World War II, with the development of nuclear energy, cybernetics, and the techniques of transportation in space, the world contracted in the same proportion as the time of communication and transportation was shortened. The fact that decisions taken in Washington or in Moscow could cause almost instantaneous destruction of enormous areas of the planet resulted in the complete unification of the world historical process. World unity today has a far more immediate and total meaning than, for instance, national unity had in the nineteenth century or the unity of a small village community had in the Middle Ages. Not only do relevant actions by the United States have repercussions in the Soviet Union, conditioning the subsequent behavior of the latter, and vice versa, but, relevant actions in any part of the world have repercussions in all regions. Even though other nations do not yet have means of action comparable to those of the two superpowers, their interests have automatically become international. It should be added that scientific and technical innovations are accessible to all peoples and that the level of nuclear-cybernetic capability is rising rapidly in Europe, China, India, and other regions.[4]

Thus, the ideal and material unification of history is an irreversible fact. The installation of a politico-juridical system of world order, therefore, represents nothing more than the institutionalization of an order which existed empirically as soon as the camps of decision were unified. It is necessary simply to convert the *de facto* order into a situation of law. The difference between the first and second stages—other factors remaining constant—is a difference in the degree of rationality. Decisions are now made with consideration of the probable repercussions in relevant sections. Moreover, the superpowers have explicitly agreed upon means for clarifying instantly the significance of decisions which might appear ambiguous or be interpreted by one of the two powers as carrying implications not desired by the other. There are, then, implicit rules of behavior and explicit forms of explaining decisions once they have been made. The conversions of the implicit rules into explicit ones would benefit both the superpowers and the world in general.

This conversion, while not altering *per se* the *status quo*, would increase the rationality of behavior and establish patterns which would insure the automatic legitimacy of those who propose to adjust to the *status quo*. The burden of immediate illegitimacy is therefore imposed upon those who violate it, and the previsibility and dependability of the system are substantially increased. Moreover, since the *status quo* is historically subject to change—much of which is desired by almost everybody—its institutionalization would minimize the social cost of change and make it compatible with the preservation of existing strategic interests.

Generalization of socioeconomic development. The establishment of a world order founded upon a more equitable and strongly progressive distribution of fundamental goods would not only constitute a formal increase in rationality but also satisfy an urgent material need. Technological advance, and the unification of history enhanced by it, created the need to generalize development. This involves not only economic progress, but also a global process which includes political, cultural, and social development.

The generalization of development is an irreversible and irrepressible need of the underdeveloped peoples.[5] The unification of history placed these peoples within the very parameters of meaning which made development desirable and possible in the West. It also drew them into the same system which determines the process of development. Whether or not the inevitable development of the retarded regions of the world will be achieved through "autonomous development" or through "dependent development" is still debatable. Autonomous development is a process based on the nationalistic mobilization of internal resources belonging to each system of nations—such as Latin America or the Arab World. This leads to an expansion of domestic demand and to an increase of the national product. Dependent development involves the complementary integration of the modern sectors of the peripheric nations with the economies of the metropolitan ones. Without analyzing, for the moment, the merits and shortcomings of each alternative, let me point out simply that the first choice is desired by the *in-*

telligentsia and by the masses of underdeveloped nations, while the second is preferred by the businessmen of developed nations and by the privileged élite of the peripheric regions.

Generalization, in addition to being an urgent need of backward peoples, is a necessity for the developed nations themselves. This correspondence of interests is unique in the course of history. Until the industrial revolution, the world was basically under the rules of a zero-sum game: whatever was won by one nation or region was totally or partially lost by another. As Max Weber has demonstrated, this was the principal cause of the decline of the ancient world. The Roman Empire established and expanded itself by capturing external booty, a process that demanded an extension of frontiers to the furthest possible military limits. Once the possibility of capturing foreign booty was spent, the implacable domestic rule of a decreasing number of persons who appropriated an increasing quantity of goods at the cost of a growing number of despoiled led to the system becoming untenable and eventually declining. This situation prevailed until the eighteenth century, when the industrial revolution made it possible to accumulate riches by the transformation of nature, rather than solely or predominantly by social appropriation. Nevertheless, until the middle of the present century, industrial profit was directly related to keeping wages down. As a result, the development of one region or sector was favored by the backwardness of others, for it was possible to maintain a high labor supply and pay low wages. In a similar manner, on a more advanced level of industrialization, the division of work between the producers of raw materials and the producers of finished goods resulted in situations which favored the latter to the detriment of the former.

This was altered radically by modern conditions of technology. Man became too important as a consumer and potential producer to be kept in ignorance and misery. Modern industry no longer requires a limitless or large supply of manual labor; it needs instead an increasing number of qualified persons who can assist in the mass production of increasing quantities of goods. This increase in goods, however, requires an equal rise in the volume of consumption, which is possible only through a corresponding growth in purchasing power guaranteed by high wages. Generalization of development and continued expansion of the process on a worldwide scale are necessary to achieve this. Thus, for the first time in history, the rich and the poor no longer find themselves in structural antagonism, for the rich can remain rich only by insuring general and increasing wealth for all.

Nuclear survival. While the formal (institutionalization) and material (generalization of development) requirements of rationality necessitate the implantation of world order, nuclear survival poses an even more compelling and urgent demand that world order be achieved. The nuclear impasse, created by the capacity of each of the superpowers to annihilate the other, whatever the outcome, whoever be the originator of the first nuclear strike, engendered a *de facto* equilibrium. Although founded upon the infeasibility of any non-suicidal use of nuclear war, the equilibrium is extremely fragile and unstable.[6] This is true because, as analysts have pointed out, it tends, over a sufficiently long period of time, to be destroyed by accident, insanity, or irreversible escalation.

With regard to the risk of accident, one should mention that there are countless opportunities for the malfunction either of the instruments giving advance warning of the attack or of the nuclear artifacts themselves. Atmospheric disturbances and other natural phenomena may, as has already occurred, cause the detectors to react exactly as if there had been a sudden advance of a fleet of missiles.[7] Nuclear bombs may have their safety devices destroyed in airplane accidents—as has almost happened—and explode in their own or "enemy" territory.[8] Once an accident has occurred, the possibility of preventing the subsequent unchaining of the nuclear hecatomb, through appropriate explanations, can be very precarious; retaliatory strategy requires that the second strike be the most immediate and automatic possible.

Nor is it completely improbable that insanity might lead to a nuclear war. Analysts, as well as some ingenious works of fiction, have repeatedly pointed out that there are maximalists—on both sides—who feel that their own governments are following a strategically or ideologically intolerable policy of appeasement. In moments of world tension, which are tending to become more frequent, certain of these maximalists could initiate a nonauthorized aggression, thereby rendering the war irreversible. Within the same realm of possibility is the risk that the increase in tensions may lead the American public or the Soviet Communist Party to elevate maximalist leaders to the supreme command of their respective nations, and that these men might senselessly initiate a nuclear holocaust.

By far the most likely possibility is that a nuclear war might be started because of irreversible escalation. As long as nations persist in employing a strategy which maximizes pressures or gains, and, in principle, goes to the brink of nuclear response—such as the tendencies of the United States in Southeast Asia and the Soviet Union in Berlin—it is inevitable that one of the parties will eventually gain an advantage over the other. In such circumstances, it might be intolerable for the other not to take action. This process of irreversible escalation necessarily leads to nuclear war because, after a certain degree of "conventional" engagement, the losing side will face the possibility of losing what it has already lost, as well as its status as a superpower and even, perhaps, its independence. To avoid this, it might use a tactical nuclear "punishment" to force the other side to a retreat and/or a surrender of the advantages gained. And so the system of escalation will be transferred from the "conventional" to the nuclear plane and, finally, from a tactical to a strategic level.

Another factor which exacerbates this problem is the fact that the atomic duopoly of some years back has already been broken. Soon France and China—and, eventually, various other nations—will be equipped with the means of originating nuclear aggression which might cause war to become general.

A rational analysis of this problem under such conditions leads to the conclusions that: (1) it would be impossible to avoid the final strategic use of nuclear arms, given the hypothesis of a generalized war, and (2) such use would lead to catastrophic consequences.[9] Equally obvious is the necessity and urgency for the implantation of a world order which would suppress the possibility of wars and provide appropriate institutional forms for settling conflicts. In spite of the uniqueness of nuclear arms, historical precedents indicate that every "quantum leap" in war technology was followed by a corresponding institutional readjustment. Thus, the transition from wars waged with metal armor to those in which powder was used led to the overthrow of feudalism and the institution of national states. The move from wars fought in battles to wars of wholesale extermination of populations resulted in the formation of the great blocs. The inevitable use of nuclear energy in any new generalized war brings one to recognize the total infeasibility[10] of such wars and the necessity of establishing a world order.

III. *Obstacles to World Order*

Despite the obvious necessity of creating a world order, there are serious obstacles to the attainment of this goal. Although progress has been made through the United Nations and through such bilateral agreements as the proscription of nuclear tests in the atmosphere, there are indications that a phase of stagnation, if not of impasse, has been reached in agreements made for that purpose. It is therefore important, even though summarily, to analyze the nature and cause of these impasses.

There are two types of obstacles to the realization of world order. The first concerns the aspirations to world hegemony which are nourished equally by the United States and the Soviet Union. The second arises from the structural imbalance of the *status quo*. With respect to the former, these aspirations are complicated even further because both superpowers fear that any reduction in their own drive for international predominance will irreversibly favor the adversary or endanger their own security. At the same time, other powers are actively promoting their own development and aspiring to maximum autonomy. This is true of France in the framework of the European system, of China among the socialist countries, and, more recently, of countries like the U.A.R., India, and Indonesia in other political systems. Such facts indicate that, in the long run, world domination by any of the superpowers is not likely to be possible. However, the same facts stimulate the superpowers to try to achieve the maximum possible short-term advantages from their present superiority.

The motivations which lead, although not expressly and often unconsciously, to an American policy pointing toward hegemony, or, at least, world predominance are not easy to eradicate. Basically, these are determined by the following major tendencies: the American desire for supremacy, its far-reaching economic expansionism, and its industrial-military complex. The desire for supremacy results from internal pressures which seek to preserve the preponderance gained by the United States after World War II and to establish a benevolent supremacy which, through persuasion rather than violence, will strengthen America's international leadership. Moralistic presuppositions, which were and continue to be so important in the configuration of an essentially equalitarian and progressive society, lead Americans to visualize international relations in terms of a conflict between good and evil. Such a point of view lends a sense of ethical or religious command to what is merely a national interest. It therefore hinders political negotiations by imposing the rigidity of fidelity to moral precepts.

Still more important is the fact that the economic and institutional structure of the nation is based on private, strongly oligopolistic and cartelized forms. These are usually, by virtue of their own system of investment, production, and sales, extremely far-reaching; they tend to transfer to a world plane the oligopolistic and cartel tendencies common at home. Without delving further into this crucial problem, one may say, in summary, that the American capitalist system is likely, by its very nature, to be incompatible with the existence of other autonomous centers of production and consumption. This forces the states that wish to maintain their own economies under the control of their own capital and agents to establish, although not necessarily or preferably through public forms, measures which will protect and stimulate the autonomy and endogeny of their own economies. This creates new obstacles for world order and new stimuli for the exercise of international hegemony by the United States.

Finally, the other internal factor which leads the United States to a policy of international hegemony is its industrial-military complex.[11] World War II, immediately followed by the cold war, caused the United States to set up the largest military machine ever built in the history of the world. In spite of the powerful civilian tradition of the United States, the installation and uninterrupted growth of that war machine led the American military establishment to assume a correspondingly greater influence in the direction of events. The necessity for permanent vigilance in order to maintain the nuclear equilibrium consolidated the ideology of national security and the policies based upon it. The increasing dependence of industry upon military contracts—reciprocated by the publicity and promotion given by the former to the latter—established an extremely solid complex of mutual interests which depend upon the continued expansion of the system. Therefore, we have the present predominance, both in the administration and in the public at large, of a point of view which emphasizes the requisites of security to the detriment of the conditions necessary to make the national American interest compatible with the interests of other nations and regions. Such a policy makes it extremely difficult to deal with negotiations pertaining to the reduction of armament and to replace the present nuclear deterrent with institutional forms for preserving the peace. It also constitutes a direct stimulus for the search for world hegemony and reinforces the current idea that disarmament negotiations and the establishment of a world authority should be taken up only after American hegemony has been consolidated. This would prevent restrictions from being imposed on American sovereignty by external forces and permit the United States to assume these limitations in the form most convenient to herself.

The factors which lead the Soviet Union to search for world hegemony and to prefer security based on its own military power are equally complex and equally detrimental to solutions which would tend, on an international scale, to institutionalize the settlement of conflicts. It is certain that the Soviets, because of their social, economic, and political system, are neither led to economic expansionism nor affected by a mutually reinforcing industrial-military complex. Both the production system and the defense apparatus are kept under the strict control of party directives. And, since the Soviet economy is based on planning toward domestic demand and on an increase of the national product, it does not operate in an imperialistic direction. In compensation, however, both the official ideology and the system of formulating and controlling power tend to be obstacles to negotiated forms of establishing world peace.

Departing from a political philosophy oriented toward the suppression of exploitation and the final abolition of the state, the Soviet Union, in fact, established a system of national development founded on state planning and management of the economy.[12] Such a regime, however, continues to base its legitimacy on the postulate of its historical necessity and the final universalization of its rule. It is well known that the sacrifices necessary for the promotion of development in capitalist regimes are concealed by apparently natural processes which permit the accumulation of investment savings through the accumulation of profits. Such sacrifices, however, are visualized in the plans of regimes based on central administration and public management. This fact leads to the formulation of political oligopolies and a party cartelization (to some extent as an alternative to the oligopolies and economic cartels of capitalism) which turn the power into a closed and restricted process. In such a system, disputes over power are not referred to social arbitration but are resolved in the ambit of the narrow governing circle, by methods of persuasion, coercion, and bargaining. Pressed by the double necessity of keeping within the internal rules of the power game and within the official doctrine of the party, the Soviet leader is not allowed to have a purely rational approach to international relations. He is obliged instead to treat international affairs in such a way that he can harmonize the policies required by events with the theoretical justifications imposed by official doctrine. Because his own domestic power depends on his ability to do this, he must present the Soviet Union as the exclusive or predominant defender of peace—and the United States and other capitalistic powers as those who threaten it. He must also maintain that time and history work in favor of the Soviets and will lead to the eschatological ruin of capitalism and the triumph of socialism.[13]

Thus, the tendency of the Soviet Union and the United States to seek world hegemony and their preference for security founded on their own military strength constitute the first category of obstacles —based on internal pressures—which impede agreement on a workable world order.

Structural imbalance of the status quo. Structural imbalances presently existing in the world constitute the second category of obstacles to the realization of a viable world order. These may be grouped broadly under three main headings: (1) the imbalance between the developed nations of the Northern hemisphere and the underdeveloped of the Southern hemisphere; (2) the imbalance between societies which have reached a continental system of integration, such as the American and the Soviet, and those which have not, such as the European, the Latin American, the Arab, and the African; (3) the imbalance resulting from the discrepancy between societies which have a population surplus, insufficiently educated, and those which bear a lighter demographic weight and are culturally more advanced.

The contrast between development and underdevelopment is an obstacle to the immediate realization of world order since the resulting discrepancies would prevent the formation of the minimum consensus necessary for achieving validity. To achieve world order it would be necessary to increase considerably the access of underdeveloped peoples to the fundamental goods—equality, liberty, health, education, income, and power. It would also be necessary to establish conditions which would lead as rapidly as possible to a basically equal distribution of these goods. Such an alteration in the *status quo* would obviously have repercussions for the present relationships of forces and interests between the two superpowers and between these and other nations, thus making a new ordering of the world difficult.

New technological conditions contribute in a double way to making the generalization of development a necessary and irreversible process: from the viewpoint both of the hopes of backward peoples and of the selfish interests of the advanced. This duality, however, characterizes only the general outlines of the process, which unfolds within numerous internal contradictions. In all advanced nations, there are some less-well-developed sectors which, in the areas of market economy, try to maintain neo-colonialist relations with the underdeveloped nations, and so conspire, even on a political plane, against their development. The underdeveloped nations themselves, in their efforts to improve their standard of living, sometimes impede generalization of development. This happens, for example, when they support redistributive processes in excess of the local capacity for saving, thereby not only diminishing the capacity for investment, but also hindering the very process of development.

The imbalance between the societies which are continentally integrated and those which are not is also a factor impeding world order, since the later would refuse to conform to a world order which might be detrimental to their future integration into larger units. Two of the models of world order mentioned earlier—Supra-National Authority and International Agreement—are substantially conditioned by the degree of integration and development attained by each participating society. In both cases, nations like the United States and the Soviet Union would tend to wield a substantially greater influence than any other single European nation and, *a fortiori*, than any single nation from underdeveloped areas. If a World State were established, this imbalance would also be evident. The advantages already held by the continentally integrated superpowers would tend to persist since their citizens would constitute articulate groups endowed with greater capacity for action and interference then the groups composed of the former citizens of the small and, especially, the underdeveloped nations.

The third structural imbalance—the discrepancy between demographic weight and cultural development—is a major obstacle to the installation of a world order. As mentioned previously, the establishment of world order would require a basically equal distribution of fundamental goods. Such a condition, however, contrasts dramatically with the present discrepancy between human quantity and quality. Greater equality among men would obviously be simpler to attain if the large populations were composed of qualified persons or if the number of unqualified persons were reduced. The initial burden which the more qualified groups will have to bear in order to furnish the uneducated multitudes with easier access to the fundamental goods—combined with the difficulties which the latter will experience in educating themselves and making their behavior compatible with the style of life of the developed nations—will constitute a powerful deterrent to achieving equality.

IV. *Conditions of World Order*

The preceding analysis demonstrated the indispensability of world order and discussed the obstacles to its establishment. However, the fact that world order is indispensable does not imply, *per se*, that it is necessary or even viable; and the fact that there are obstacles to its realization does not imply that its establishment is impossible or improbable. The following analysis will be concerned, first, with determining the viability of world order as a function of rationality in history and, second, assuming that world order is viable, with determining the prerequisites for its effective implementation.

The viability of world order. The question of rationality in history is related to the fact that man is an essentially rational being —in the sense that all men are endowed with reason—but not necessarily or permanently rational; therefore, not all human behavior is rational. An important corollary of this fundamental law is that the rationality of a process in the course of history can increase when it is not annulled, but cannot increase when it is annulled by interruptions of its rationality. Thus, the ethical improvement of humanity cannot increase—in the strict sense that each generation is able to depart from an ethical standard that is higher than the preceding—in a cumulative, continuous process, because the process of accumulating ethical rationality is annulled by each of its violations. The process of scientific and technological rationality, however, can suffer interruptions without being annulled. Thus, there has been a continuous accumulation of knowledge—which Max Scheler calls knowledge of culture and technical knowledge—since the beginning of civilization, despite various long periods of "darkness."

In the particular instance of world order, we have a form of settling world interests which is essentially rational; moreover, under the conditions of our time, it is the only rational form. World order, as a rational principle, cannot be annulled by an unsuccessful attempt to implant it. However, the best settlement of world interests —one which would spare the world of a nuclear hecatomb—would be impaired, by definition, by the outburst of nuclear war.

Viewed in these terms, it may be observed that world order is essentially viable, despite the obstacles to its implantation, but not necessarily able to be implemented. When no progress toward the implementation of world order is realized (as has been the case since the treaty banning atmospheric nuclear tests), the simple passage of time constitutes a constant exposure to the risk of a nuclear hecatomb. Diversely, all increases in stable institutions for the preservation of peace (such as the test ban treaty) constitute stages of gradual establishment of world order which facilitate the transition to the following stage. Only the last stage, which leads to the definitive implantation of world order, with the elimination of nuclear arms and the suppression of national armies, is irreversible.

Prerequisites of world order. Having established the viability of world order, let us now consider the prerequisities for its implementation. Since this article has been particularly concerned with analyzing the correlations between rationality and economic, political, cultural, and social development, it is especially important to distinguish between the theoretical and the practical prerequisites for the implementation of an effective world order.

On the theoretical plane, the problem of implementing world order involves the elaboration of a theory of world peace and development, as well as a strategy for its effective institutionalization. Only recently have the many facets of the problem of socioeconomic development been given unified treatment in the form of a general theory of development. Development was initially understood as economic progress in the restricted sense of the growth of the absolute and *per capita* national product of a given nation. The other economic implications of underdevelopment (which basically derived from the insufficient availability of natural and capital resources and the lack of influence which the underdeveloped nations had in determining their best use) were recognized only after World War II, with the work of the Economic Commission for Latin America and other United Nations agencies. Only in this decade was it understood that development is a global social process which demands change on the political, cultural, and social planes, as well as on the economic.

The problem of peace has been treated in an operational manner[14] only in very recent years, in an attempt to overcome the sterile juridical formalism of the years before World War II and the naive moralism of those who postulate the universality and superiority of their own values and claim that peace can be achieved only if the Communists or the capitalists cease to behave in bad faith. Most recent are the efforts to devise a general theory and strategy which would integrate the problems of global development with the problems of implanting an operational peace.[15]

Although it is not possible to analyze these theoretical efforts here, it is important to emphasize that they are indispensable and that we are still in the initial phases of treating a subject of enormous complexity. In view of existing obstacles to the implantation of world order, it is apparent that the motivations which naturally lead to recognition of its indispensability cannot by themselves assure its establishment. It is necessary that the theoretical clarification of the generalization of development and the achievement of peace guide the forces interested in their promotion.

It is not enough that world peace and development be viable and that the problems implied in the implementation of world order be given theoretical treatment. It is also necessary to determine the practical steps which will lead to world order, for the real forces of society must start moving toward the fulfillment of world order. These social forces—groups of interests, nations, groups of nations—will, of course, be aware of the motivations and obstacles already indicated. The problem which will arise in the course of history will be to establish the measure in which the coincidence between real interests of groups and nations and the practical prerequisites for achieving world order might help the forces of society to progress through the different stages leading to its implementation.

The indication and analysis of the stages are beyond the bounds of this work, and basically consist of a problem in the strategy for institutionalizing peace and generalized development.[16] It is important here only to emphasize that the effective implementation of each stage can occur spontaneously through decisions made by the leadership groups of the superpowers. It can also be influenced by the efforts of groups near the decision-making centers of the world. These groups can arouse strong support for world order by suggesting measures necessary to move from one stage to the next and by arousing public opinion in favor of world order, thus forcing the concerned governments to adopt the measures appropriate for each stage.

The establishment of world order depends not only on its intrinsic desirability and viability, but also on the support of men and groups who decide to dedicate themselves to the completion of such a goal. As increasing sectors of developed and underdeveloped societies begin to realize the urgent necessity of world order, the viability of its establishment, and the fact that it can be achieved by adopting measures which are reasonable in themselves, none of the governments will be able to escape public pressure for establishing world order. Only through this process does it seem possible to neutralize the established interests which favor war—for they think they can attain their objectives with good probabilities of keeping nuclear destruction within tolerable limits—or attempt to follow a policy of brinkmanship—for they think it possible to avoid the actual deflagration of war and, in the last analysis, accept this risk because they consider its effects "limitable."

The mission of the intellectuals. It is incumbent upon the intellectuals to play the decisive role in the formation of pressure groups in favor of world order. To start with, it is the intellectuals who are capable of formulating the necessary theory of peace and generalized development, as well as the strategy for establishing world order. It is the intellectuals who bear the specific responsibility for preserving and developing rationality, and they have the means and authority to overcome the parochial loyalties of groups and nations pressing for hegemony and thereby achieve a unified vision of the world. It is they, finally, who represent, in the scientific and technological world of today, the spiritual unity of men, beyond any conflict of interests, ideologies, and religions. And, if it is true that the status of "intellectual," besides being imprecise and ambiguous, does not lead anyone to overcome human limitations, it is no less true that, in the world today, there are ample groups of intellectuals who are willing to assert that there is a rational and peaceful solution for the problems of our time and who are, indeed, capable of drawing up this solution in terms which would preserve the security of each of the blocs, of all nations.

The practical problem is to convert these tendencies and ideas into articulate and coordinated movements. It is necessary that pressure groups for world order be constituted in each nation through the initiative of intellectuals and that these groups coordinate themselves internationally in order to attempt to devise a general theory of peace and development and a strategy for implanting a universally acceptable world order. It is also necessary that such groups mobilize multi-party fronts, at the level of each nation, as well as multi-regional fronts, among the various nations of the world, in order to create world public opinion in favor of peace and development. Only then will the gradual execution of the stages of implanting world order prove irresistible.

In view of the previous discussion, it seems that one could conclude this analysis with the following statement: (1) world order, understood as a system endowed with effective measures to insure world peace and development, is indispensable under the conditions of our times; (2) in spite of the serious obstacles to achieving world order, such as the conflict created by desires for world hegemony and by the structural imbalances of the *status quo*, the negotiated establishment of world order is theoretically possible and practically feasible since, in the last analysis, the probable effects of a nuclear conflagration have made war an impracticable alternative to the peaceful solution of contemporary problems; and (3) the effective reconciliation of group and national interests through the establishment of world order demands the mobilization of groups dedicated to international pressure for the gradual implantation of that world order, and it is incumbent on the intellectuals to play the decisive role in the accomplishment of this mission.

REFERENCES

1. Cf. Grenville Clark and Louis Sohn, *World Peace Through World Law* (Cambridge, Mass., 1958).

2. Cf. Amitai Etzioni, *The Hard Way to Peace* (New York, 1962), pp. 202 ff.

3. Cf. Raymond Aron, *The Dawn of Universal History* (New York, 1961).

4. Cf. Henry A. Kissinger, *The Necessity for Choice* (New York, 1962), pp. 249 ff.; and Herman Kahn, "The Arms Race and World Order," in Morton Kaplan (ed.), *The Revolution of World Politics* (New York, 1962).

5. Cf. Robert L. Heilbroner, *The Great Ascent* (New York, 1963); and Robert Waelder, "Protest and Revolution against Western Societies," in Morton Kaplan (ed.), *The Revolution of World Politics, op. cit.*

6. The effects of nuclear explosion may not be so catastrophic as was thought in the beginning. Herman Kahn, in *On Thermonuclear War* (Princeton, N. J., 1960), showed how one must distinguish, in the first place, between the types of attack—initial or second strike—and the objectives—strategic military centers, large cities, and combinations of both. In the second place it is necessary to distinguish between attacks sustained without any previous civil defense preparation, and when reasonable protective measures were opportunely adopted. In the case of a first attack concentrated on the strategic military objectives of a nation (the United States) which has adopted reasonable civil defense measures, the number of casualties, according to Kahn, may not exceed five million. The catastrophic character of a nuclear war, however, does not come from the specific and eventually

limited immediate effects of each attack, but rather from the circumstance that either the attacks are futile—and the war ends with an agreement that might have been drawn up before—or the attacks have to be escalated, in the same war or in a succession of wars, to cataclysmic levels of destruction.

7. Such an occurrence is described by Amitai Etzioni, *The Hard Way to Peace, op. cit.*, pp. 46-47.

8. Cf. Amitai Etzioni, *Winning Without War* (New York, 1965), pp. 160-161.

9. Cf. Herman Kahn, "The Arms Race and Some of its Hazards," in Donald G. Brennan (ed.), *Arms Control, Disarmament and National Security* (New York, 1961).

10. What makes nuclear war infeasible is not, as was indicated in a preceding note, the necessarily catastrophic effect of *any* attack, but the fact that the only attacks which have any decisive meaning are those which are of such power as to warrant corresponding retaliation—which tends to be projected in a more automatic form each time, as a measure of deterrence. Such retaliation has now become inevitable, since both superpowers, in order to discourage the other from surprise attack, have set up measures which assure them, in any event, an annihilating capacity of revenge.

11. Cf. Fred J. Cook, *The Warfare State* (New York, 1962). *Vide* also, although he tends to minimize the effects, Samuel P. Huntington, *The Soldier and the State* (New York, 1964), especially pp. 361 ff.

12. Cf. John Kautsky, *Political Change in Underdeveloped Countries* (New York, 1962), pp. 57 ff.

13. Cf. Marshal V. D. Sokolovsky, *Military Strategy* (New York, 1963), especially Ch. IV.

14. Cf. Amitai Etzioni, *The Hard Way to Peace, op. cit.*; and Charles E. Osgood, *An Alternative to War and Surrender* (New York, 1963).

15. Cf. Amitai Etzioni, *The Hard Way to Peace, op. cit.*; and especially *Winning Without War, op. cit.*

16. The consensual establishment of world order, under the conditions of unbending mutual distrust which characterizes the Cold War, is only viable by means of a gradualist, reversible strategy (GRIT), which would act in stages of increasing institutionalization and decreasing armament. Cf. Amitai Etzioni, *The Hard Way to Peace, op. cit.*, and *Winning Without War, op. cit.*; Charles Osgood, *An Alternative to War and Surrender, op. cit.*; and Donald G. Brennan (ed.), *Arms Control, Disarmament and National Security, op. cit.*

C. H. WADDINGTON

The Desire for Material Progress as a
World Ordering System

THE CONTRIBUTORS to this symposium have been chosen because they are "intellectuals," not because they exercise political power. Certainly, for my part, I feel it would be a waste of time for me to discuss questions of *Realpolitik* since I have no experience in that field. Moreover I take it that our purpose is not simply to describe and discuss the elements of world order which presently exist. From one point of view, any system of relations between nations, or races, or classes, or any other political unit can be regarded as an example of "order." But we are here, surely, to consider ways of improving or increasing the order that exists in the world today. The relations between the various groups of mankind are continually changing in the processes of history. Any order with which we may be concerned will not be a characteristic of a static situation but will be an order within a system which is developing.

My own technical field is that of biology, and, within that enormous domain, particularly the study of embryonic development. This is a subject which has for a long time been concerned with the problems of order occurring within progressively changing systems. An individual begins life as a fertilized egg, passes through a number of stages of embryonic existence, and eventually becomes an adult organism. Not only does this adult have a well-defined character, in which the numerous parts are related to one another in precisely orderly ways, but relationships of ordering are active in a most important way all through the whole series of changes. It is characteristic of developing biological systems that if the normal course of events is disturbed, for instance by some experimental means, the system nevertheless gets back more or less completely to its normal path of development, so that it finishes up with very little

sign that any disturbance has occurred. The series of changes leading from the egg to the adult has in fact a character which may be
referred to as a power of regulation, or of self-ordering.

Systems which right themselves after disturbance are very well
known in the physiological functioning of adult organs. For instance, if too much carbon dioxide accumulates in the blood, the
animal breathes faster, absorbs more oxygen, and removes the carbon dioxide until the normal balance is restored. The technical
term for such a restoration of the *status quo* is "homeostasis." In
development, however, what is restored is not a *status quo* but a
normal path of change. I have proposed the term "homeorhesis"
for such a situation, using a derivative of the Greek word for "flow"
to replace "stasis," which implies standing still. In considering the
order of the world at large, which will inevitably continue to undergo historical change, what we need is a system of homeorhesis
rather than one of homeostasis.

Developing biological systems are complicated; the human
world with which we are concerned is still more so. Even in an
embryo there is no one single overriding set of relations which ensures homeorhesis. There are, rather, a number of different ordering
systems, each looking after certain aspects of the total complex
process. I suggest that this is the kind of situation which we should
expect to find in human affairs. There will be not one single ordering
system, which buffers out deviations of all kinds, and restores
normality after all sorts of disturbances, but rather one might hope
that there will be a number of differing ordering systems, some
tending to restore homeorhesis after many different kinds of disturbances, others operating only within a narrow range.

There have been many partial ordering systems in the previous
history of mankind—the Pax Romana, Christendom, the Pax Britannica, the Mohammedan Empire, and many others. I think the most
powerful and the most widespread have always had a central
focus in some system of value judgments about what constitutes the
good life. This is very obvious for the numerous examples of world
ordering systems founded on religious beliefs, but it seems almost
equally true for examples such as the Chinese or Roman Empires, in
which religion, in the normal sense of the word, did not play such a
large part. It is only on the basis of some degree of consensus about
values—even about values which many of the people concerned
may consider to be partial and incomplete—that sufficient emotional
sympathy can be engendered between peoples and their repre-

sentatives to make possible a truly co-operative endeavor. I think that one of the main tasks of this symposium must be to consider what type of intellectual outlook and value system has any possibility of fulfilling this function at the present time. I shall argue that the only type of outlook which holds out any hope of being successful in this is one which holds firmly that the central focus of interest, for mankind in the next century or so, is in the improvement of the material conditions of life.

I shall present the argument rather boldly, and perhaps in a somewhat exaggerated way, partly because I feel that the main points need as much emphasis as possible in the world of today, and partly because, not being by any means an expert on or a close student of politics, I should probably go astray if I tried to go into much detail. But I should like to begin by making two cautionary points: First, "material" needs to be interpreted rather widely, to refer to such things as beautiful architecture, space, health, leisure, freedom to exercise many choices, and operate at different tempos, and not only to such banal indices as the number of horsepower or kilograms of iron per worker. Second, the material conditions of life, even if interpreted so widely, are of ultimate value only in so far as they serve to enrich the quality (and quantity, or duration) of life.

The essence of my argument is that the only possibility of reaching any agreement on how to assess the "quality of life"—and probably, in fact, the only way it can be assessed—is in terms of the material facilities available for use. Most, possibly all, other criteria, such as "freedom," "self-determination," and "spiritual profundity," either measure pseudoqualities which really are simply ways in which the many psychological pathologies of the human mind work themselves out (strivings for power, feelings of inferiority *vis-à-vis* other men or *vis-à-vis* nature) or express differences of natural modes of experience and action which should be welcomed rather than reduced to a uniform level of common agreement.

The possible alternative outlooks, other than the material conditions of life, are:

(1) *Power*. This is the basis on which the world always has been run so far. But it has never been extended over areas greater than the Roman or British Empires, and it seems improbable that it could in practice be operated on the global scale that present-day techniques have made unavoidable. The present situation is that the U.S.A. certainly, and the U.S.S.R. probably, could, if their

timing were right, extend their power over the whole globe; however, if their timing were even slightly wrong, and they knocked each other out, China's numerical resources in sophisticated manpower might leave her in a position to pick up the bits. But none of these powers—superpowers though they seem—could hope to run the whole world for more than a few decades. Britain in the eighteenth and nineteenth centuries bled itself white of competent personnel in trying to provide local rule in India and much of Africa, over which it had at that time a technological lead which no country will ever have again over the one world of today. The unification of the world on the basis of brute power is, fortunately, *impossible*.

(2) *Religion*. All the major religions—Christianity, Mohammedanism, Buddhism, Hinduism, Confucianism, Shintoism, the African religions—were developed by peoples in the pretechnological, agricultural phase of man's evolution; and it is only by sophisticated special pleading that they can be given relevance to the general problems of the world of today (important though they may be for the individual life). In so far as anyone—other than mere hangovers from the past who will rapidly diminish in numbers—still believes in the differences between them, he does so because the religions are expressions of national value systems, which are discussed in section (4). When formulated religious beliefs are influential in the world today—Mohammedanism-Hinduism in India, Mohammedanism-Judaism in the Eastern Mediterranean, Catholicism-Protestantism in Belgium—there is not only a fusty smell of people unpacking their best clothes which have been laid away in storage in camphor since the last generation, but the results have been invariably divisive and unfortunate, if not tragic. Religion, in so far as it is politically important at all, is not something which could lead to world order, but is one of the forces which a movement toward world order will have to try to get under control.

(3) *Politico-economic ideology*. There is no politico-economic ideology which can make an even plausibly convincing claim to have world-wide application. The main contestants are "Capitalism" and "Communism." The former developed a more-or-less consistent ideology first in Great Britain at a time when that country had the good fortune to find itself with a fifty-year technological lead over the rest of the world, and was therefore metaphorically sitting on a gold mine; it was developed by the United States, which, occupying an almost uninhabited and very rich continent, was ac-

tually sitting on a gold mine. The intellectual theory that emerged amounted to little more than the statement that everyone would be rewarded for doing everything he could in his own interest, and that there was room for everyone. This directed a vast amount of innate human aggressiveness into channels which were, by and large, socially constructive for a few decades. But the process of expanding into open spaces is inherently self-limiting, since the spaces are thereby filled up. And free-enterprise Capitalism soon turned itself, by its very success, into monopoly Capitalism, which has no ideology except in so far as it accepts that which I am putting forward, the crucial importance of the material conditions of life.

Meanwhile Communism, in its Marx-Lenin-Mao form, was simply a way of selling to the people—under the guise of a super-democratic political system—the need for the capital accumulation essential to a technological society in the conditions not of an uninhabited gold mine, but of a gold mine hidden under an ant-heap. Again, as soon as the gold started coming to the surface, the intellectual theory evaporated. Stalin tried to bottle it down until it blew up (and Mao is still engaged in getting up a head of steam). But it has become clear that the basic problem for the world at large is how to achieve the capital investment necessary to provide a foundation for a modern technological society, and all the stuff about "individual free enterprise," "dictatorship of the proletariat," and the like amounts to no more than a number of practical procedures to be assessed on their merits in particular circumstances. They are very far from being general principles on which the whole world could unite. (It is a waste of time to give ideological training to Afro-Asian students who come to Western Europe to study, not because they are not worthy of these profound truths, but because they will certainly see through them.)

(4) *Nationalism-Racialism-Tribalism.* This is, at the present time, by far the most serious rival to Materialism as a candidate for the position of the focus of human large-scale activity. It is serious because there is so much truth in it, and dangerous because it offers so much scope for nonsense.

The quota of "truth" there is in racialism is authentic and inescapable, being based in the fundamental nature of the human individual—who is, and always must be, a merely biological new-born infant who is converted only by his contacts with an immediate circle of elder people (parents and the like) into a fully human being and an inheritor of the human cultural tradition. All men will always feel more at home with people who remind them of their mothers and fathers—the rather low efficiency of the humanizing process results in some people feeling at home only with others who seem to be the opposite of their parents, but this is merely an inversion which proves the rule of the basic importance of parents.

For reasons of this kind, people will always "instinctively" feel that there is an in-group and an out-group. The question is, how big should these groups be and how great a gulf should be set between in and out? In most of history the in-out barrier has been sharp, but the size of the in-group has gradually grown, from the family to the village, the tribe, the collingual group, the nation. Modern transport has brought to the forefront two new types of confrontations: groups which differ in immediately recognizable visual characteristics, such as skin color; and groups, often the same ones, which differ markedly in technological knowledge (though probably not in technological capacity). The result has been to provoke two movements of feeling, which make nonsense of one another. On the one hand, there has been a wish to be able to feel that there is a real unity between all people with white skin, or more particularly with black, or brown, or yellow skins—a movement toward a super-nationalism on a continental scale; on the other, there has been a renewed emphasis on the values of a closely restricted, narrowly regional in-group, leading to a Balkanization of the nineteenth-century political groupings. If one tries, in imagination, to compare with one another a number of national-tribal groups, with respect to (a) the ways of life they consider most valuable, (b) the intellectual and technological knowledge and skills, (c) their skin color, it is easy to see what a chaotic and unilluminating—and basically boring—set of cross-currents the whole game gives rise to. Compare, for instance, the Prussian Junker society of the early 1900's, their neighbors, the Danes, the Zulu nomadic herdsmen of Chaka's time, a Rajput state in nineteenth-century India, a Bengali province of the same period, a similar colored group in Bali.

Whether there should be a political unity between all the peoples within a certain range of shades of average skin color, or between those who speak various versions of English, Arabic, or Spanish, or whether there should be Home Rule for Wales, Scotland, Tamiland, Somaliland, Brunei, Ukraine—these are empirical, local, ultimately trivial questions, which provide an appropriate outlet for people whose psychology leads them into that sort of politics.

Questions arising from feelings of racial, national, and tribal loyalties are among the brute facts of human nature that world order has to contend with—like aggressiveness and selfishness—
rather than any sort of focus around which such an order could be
organized. When a question of local "national independence" forces
itself on the world's attention—as in Southern Ireland fifty years
ago or South Viet-Nam now—the important matter should really be
not whether the political-managerial power should lie in the hands
of people defined as belonging to the same nation as those they control, but whether these powers actually deliver, or at least seem
to be in a position to deliver, the real goods of material advance.

Demands for "self-rule" are very seldom actually for that, since
it is only a tiny minority in any country who want to, or ever
do, undertake the day-to-day hard work of ruling. Such claims are
often based on the people's desire to change the government they
have, usually because it is not increasing their material well-being
as fast as they think it could be increased. Sometimes there is in addition a wish that they will be able to change governments again
in the future, but often the people are willing to settle for a change
now, even to a totalitarian regime over which they may have less
control than they have over their present one, but which is thought
to be more efficient in delivering the goods.

It is only if a climate of opinion can be produced in which everyone insists on asking, and getting an answer to, the straightforward
question—does it look as if it will pay off in material terms—that
the heat can be taken out of the pseudo-questions that now divide
the world. The bonds of common interest, which would develop
on a world-wide scale if material advancement were taken as the
main focus of interest, would be much stronger and more profound
than might appear at first sight. They would go far beyond the general sympathy which would follow from the fact that all the nations
would be concentrating on issues which everyone agreed were genuinely meaningful and worthwhile. They would have the additional strength that some of the most interesting problems to be
faced are actually the same, or very similar, throughout the whole
world. It is often thought that the "undeveloped" nations have, as
their first task, to catch up with the societies which are at present
more affluent, but this is only very partially true. The real challenge
to them is to leap, in as few jumps as possible, from their present
position to where the affluent societies will be in ten or twenty
years' time. They do not need to learn how to build early twentieth-

century industry, but how to develop late twentieth-century society; and that is something which the affluent societies themselves do not know.

What forms can the materially-good life take in a world of automated industry, mechanized agriculture, great mobility of individuals, and widely dispersed supplies of energy? There is need for great creative thinking in the domain which is becoming known as "the science of human settlements," or "ekistics," which is concerned with such questions as the organization of cities, complexes of towns and villages, roads, railways, and other communication networks, different types of land utilization, and so on. Again, mankind will have to think out afresh the kinds of economic stytems which will work effectively in a world from which the burden of heavy, time-consuming routine work has been removed. The underdeveloped nations approach these problems from the starting-point of conditions which differ from those of the affluent countries; but all societies face the same challenge to their ability to create a new type of society. In respect to the past and the present, the various societies of mankind differ widely, and in those differences there is scarcely any basis for a stable world order. It is in respect to the future that all men are equal; and it is only by concentrating their attention on the material future that mankind can discover a community of interest which could serve as an adequate basis for a world order.

IVAN MÁLEK

World Order and the Responsibility of Scientists:
A Functional as Opposed to an Institutional Approach

I

WHOEVER SETS out to contemplate world order—assuming, naturally, that he is animated by the desire to do it some service, to improve it—cannot but realize that whatever he has to say links up with the deliberations of mankind's great and representative men throughout history. In the same way our own task consists not so much in seeking new arguments, or trying to convince one another of the necessity of breaking new paths on the way to an ever better order, but rather in investigating the situation in a matter-of-fact way and deciding what can, and therefore must, be done in the present stage of mankind's development. We must consider in what ways the premises upon which we base our reasoning differ from those advanced by our predecessors. As I am anxious to focus my attention upon the present and future aspects of the issues involved, I do not intend to turn back to history in my observations. There is one great figure, however, to whom I should like to draw the reader's attention at the outset; though his efforts can, for more reasons than one, set the key to our own reflections, they are still little known to the world at large. I have in mind the life and work of my renowned countryman John Amos Comenius, the great humanist of the seventeenth century, the man who amid the most grievous hardships of the Thirty Years' War, and apart from the fight he waged to save the Czech nation from obliteration, devoted his life and his immense literary work to the question we are considering, namely, what is to be done to bring about a better order in the world. His principal work bears the characteristic title of "A General Discourse on Amending Things Human" (De rerum humanarum emendatione consultatio catholica). Equally characteristic are the views expressed in each of its seven parts: The first two introductory parts are entitled Panaugia and Panegersia respectively; the third, called Pansofia, deals with science for all; the next concerns general education (Panpaedia); the fifth examines the possibilities of an artificial international language (Panglottia); the sixth indicates and proposes ways of improving all culture and of maintaining peace among nations (Panorthosia); and the last endeavors to mobilize and encourage all those who bear the chief responsibility for planning and implementing these tasks (Pannuthesia). Putting aside those aspects of his work which were conditioned by his times, the structure of his reflections can still be accepted as quite topical. In particular what has not become obsolete is that part of his work where—as in his "Didactica" and other writings—he worked out, on the very threshold of the Industrial Revolution, principles that hold true to this day, principles of general and democratic education, indispensable and accessible to all and starting at an early age. It is this unconditional linking of educational questions with those relating to human order, and the responsibility assigned to the "wise men" (the scientists, to use the modern term), that gives positive proof of how modern his treatment of the theme really is. No doubt this is the direction which a large part of my own reflections will take.

II

What are, or rather should be, the premises on which to base *our own* considerations? The prerequisite of any discussion, particularly among men of science, is to define as clearly as possible the issues involved.

This applies equally to our topic, "world order." What meaning do we attach to this notion? Or better still, what do we lay down as a basis for discussion of this broad idea? Are we to draw up by joint effort the principles, or at least the basic outlines, of a world order that would really deserve the name of "order"? And does this include an effort to find at least some principles acceptable to all and indicating the way which would lead to a better world order? Are we convinced that we are able to agree on general principles, that we are capable of outlining *by joint effort* a world order that would be acceptable to all when we know only too well that it is exactly these and similar problems that divide the world into at least two systems, and that these two parts not only hold differing views but

actually take measures which are to a great extent mutually antagonistic?

Are we intent on finding the common denominators of these differing systems so that we can outline common objectives which
would advance humanity toward a better and more perfect "world
order" in spite of this division? And do we hold that such an effort
may yield sufficiently positive results even though these systems are
very deeply rooted in their respective institutions and in the aims
they are pursuing? The example of the United Nations and its specialized agencies seems to show that some of the problems can be
solved by joint effort, that it is possible to consult one another on a
number of problems, and even to agree on quite a few of them.
However, these have until now always been subsidiary and quite in-
significant questions. The moment the attempt is made to find a
way of solving fundamental problems relating to world order, such
as the question of disarmament, the true magnitude of these differences reasserts itself.

We are hardly inclined to think that the failure to make head-
way precisely in the most essential questions is due to lack of discussion or debate on world order; on the contrary, we are surely
aware that it is the strict adherence to the one or the other of the
two systems and to their respective aims that obstructs the way to
agreement even on those issues which are fraught with vital significance for all mankind. Thus the very fact that we are able to
thrash out the problems facing us on the basis of peaceful coexistence of the systems, and to seek what can be achieved by joint effort in spite of the differences, is to be regarded as a step forward.

Nevertheless, a mere "coexistence" would, in my opinion, hardly
provide a sufficient basis for our considerations, for it might lead
simply to an exchange of views and to getting acquainted with
our respective standpoints. What is needed is a more active approach, a positive effort to create, from the existing elements, something new that would define common aims and principles which
might lead gradually to the establishment of a better world order
and which, by being made explicit, would also provide the basis
for a critical examination of the old and outdated views held in earlier days.

To achieve this, however, we must be quite clear about those
principles we are going to insist upon as forming the basis of the
better "world order." Once we succeed in finding these and reaching
agreement on them we can proceed to analyze the impediments

that obstruct the way to implementing these principles, both in the world at large and within the respective systems. And it is this analysis that will enable us to define joint tasks which must be accomplished. To solve these will not only facilitate the creation of a better world order, but also help to remove some of the other differences, especially those springing from subjective factors, such as mutual distrust.

My own observations will proceed as follows: First, I shall try to define the characteristic features of a "world order" which all the people of this earth should seek to achieve—a world order which best conforms to the specific wants of man. Then, I shall try to discover some of the present obstacles to its implementation. Finally, I shall outline the tasks that, in my opinion, could be solved by joint effort and thereby contribute, despite all antagonisms, however acute, to the formation of the future world order. From what I have said, it should be apparent to the reader that I intend to consider the ways leading to a better world order from the functional and not the institutional point of view. For my deliberations, function is the content and institution the form. Although there is no doubt that function, that is, content, requires its form, institution, so that it can be realized, I think that at this stage it is possible to achieve success when we are clear about the kind of progress—in accord with the present possibilities and needs of mankind—we desire.

Before examining and analyzing these problems, let me express my firm conviction that today, despite everything that tends to divide the world, despite hostilities in many parts of the world, despite the enormous armaments potential which has been accumulated, conditions for reaching agreement on a number of common aims are far more favorable than in the days of the utopians who were preoccupied with thoughts of world order. The development of science, technology, and culture is proceeding at a rapid pace; the possibilities of a decent life for all men in the world are growing from day to day; the period of colonial oppression is drawing to a close the world over, and the way to full development is being opened even for that part of mankind which until recently was so humiliated; finally, man has come to understand some of the laws governing evolution not only in nature but in human society as well and thus has an opportunity to try to build a society which is in harmony with these laws.

In view of these possibilities, all those who have pondered

these goals and are trying to realize them in practice have a responsibility to show how it is possible to advance a step further. In his efforts at reforming the world, Comenius relied on the counsel of the "wise men"; their counterparts at the present stage of mankind's development are those men who base their reasoning and action on scientific knowledge. It is in this light that we, too, should view our responsibilities, and attack this problem with all the resourcefulness of scientists who do not shrink from any new views of the problems facing us and ways to solve them.

III

What, then, is that world order which we are anxious to realize? What are the imperfections of the present-day order which we are anxious to improve? We shall probably all agree that it must be an order that will ensure the well-being of all mankind, a life worthy of man for all people on this earth. But, what do these terms—well-being, a life worthy of man—imply?

For the millions of those who are still starving and enduring hardships, this no doubt means that they should be freed from hunger and disease. This must admittedly be the minimum task and program of any world order worthy of the name. It is no easy task; but, should it be undertaken as an obligation to be fulfilled by all mankind, then it is a problem which concerted efforts can solve. Of course, those countries and nations which are not starving should regard this as a duty which they are bound to perform to safeguard their own future; and they should discard the opinion that it is something outside the sphere of their own immediate interests, a question of charitable "aid," or a device designed to serve their own ends. The idea that the whole world (including people living in comparative material comfort in the so-called developed countries) can never be happy for a long time and enjoy prosperity if any part of mankind, however small, is starving and racked with disease has not yet penetrated deeply enough into people's minds. The ruling circles in many countries have not yet fully appreciated the fact that this is the essence of the problem.

While on the subject of nourishment, of freeing men from hunger (and not only subjective hunger, but also hunger viewed scientifically as a social quality), we must also appreciate that it is necessary to ensure work for all men, and work worthy of man. For many countries this task is much more difficult to accomplish than the liberation itself. We know only too well that in a majority of developing countries there is an absolute shortage of employment opportunities even for that fraction of the population who are aware that they might try to find a job.

But even this problem, when tackled by all mankind, can now be solved. The abundant manpower reserves, multiplied by the present-day possibilities of science and technology, can open new channels for the development of mankind, provided that this is undertaken as a joint effort, and that the needs of the less developed countries are considered. This, of course, certainly does not mean that the manpower reserves should be assigned work which would benefit mainly the developed countries by bringing them still more wealth and leaving the gulf between the development of the two groups of countries wide open.

As yet I have mentioned only basic minimum requirements, that is, demands affecting primarily those countries which are living on the edge of starvation, which are lagging (through no fault of their own) behind the development of the rest of mankind, their own development having been hampered by colonization. However, our reflections encompass the whole of mankind, even those sections which have already been essentially freed from starvation and from a great part of the diseases that but a few decades ago had been causing much hardship and suffering. Yet, even in many countries with a high standard of living, or even the highest (as measured by statistical average), not all these minimum facilities are equally or sufficiently accessible to all people. Thus there is certainly another, secondary, minimum requirement: that the means of freeing man from hunger or even starvation and from most diseases should be made equally accessible to all, irrespective of the position they occupy in the social scale of their country. This, too, is quite feasible; for example, some—though hitherto regrettably few—countries have introduced a system whereby the care for the health of all citizens (and not only by combating disease) is a joint, integral obligation of the whole society, as laid down by the Constitution. This, of course, includes good nutrition, admittedly one of the basic factors in health care, and applies to the way man can best arrange his life and work. Of course, we know that even this minimum is not easy to carry through and safeguard even in those countries where the general standard of living—as expressed in national income—is high enough to make it possible. The realization of this goal is obviously hampered by old habits and false ideas of individual freedom which may, of course, include freedom to starve and to endure hardships, to be socially degraded. The need to agree on this minimum is therefore imperative, since it is the absolutely essential minimum which precedes the acquisition of a whole series of belongings, large or small, which are used daily, and with which many people associate the idea of a good living standard.

Another part of the minimum, as already mentioned, is work, for today most people regard work as the very *source* of the means of subsistence and of all those other things which are considered the pleasures of life. I have already shown that this minimum requirement is not safeguarded by the order prevailing in a large part of the world today. We all know that this is true not only in the underdeveloped countries but even in many countries with a very high national income. Moreover, views are often advanced in highly developed countries that their economies benefit from having a certain proportion of people for whom such work is not safeguarded and that this requirement should therefore not be included in the minimum demands of the society. I think it of utmost importance that agreement on the necessity of safeguarding this minimum should be reached. Even today this problem affects millions of people, making them lead a life filled with uncertainty and unnecessary humiliation. In countries with a high standard of living it is absolutely inexcusable. Yet there is another reason for regarding it as an absolutely essential minimum, for the development of technology, together with automation, will reduce the need for human labor. And this development—which, by its very nature, will lead to increasing mankind's wealth and which is another step toward controlling and harnessing the forces of nature for the benefit of man—may be turned into a source of want, suffering, uncertainty, and permanent degradation of millions of people deprived of employment unless this very minimum is taken for granted by everyone. In many countries, the right to work is guaranteed by the Constitution, and society is therefore obliged to create the economic conditions which will ensure its observance. Thus the right to work must become a universal minimum of any world order which applies to all men.

General education is certainly another of these minimum demands and was recognized as such as early as the seventeenth century by Comenius, to whom I have already referred. We all know how much illiteracy still exists in the developing countries. And, today, when science increasingly permeates the life of every individual, reading, writing, and reckoning can hardly be accepted as a satisfactory minimum. It is necessary now to initiate each citizen into the present state of science, so that everyone is able, and inclined, throughout his life to follow at least the basic aspects of the progress being made in science and technology.

Do these simple minimum demands constitute a basis for a world order to which all men would aspire? Certainly not, though even these would impose many obligations on mankind. But they are undoubtedly an indispensable first step, and we shall be able to proceed only after this step is taken. Even if all these minimum requirements are fulfilled we cannot be said to have begun to safeguard the truly progressive needs of man, his truly human possibilities, his further development. Yet all of these, as I shall presently show, are capable of being extended and developed; to my mind, this is the key to a world order which would be a worthy order for man.

IV

But, for what kind of man do we want to plan the new world order? What are his fundamental qualities and basic needs? What are his true characteristics?

If we analyze the conditions that, in the history of mankind, have actually made man what he is, we are bound to reach the conclusion that the essential factor was his ability to create something new, to transform objects, as well as nature itself, in such a way that all man's needs and requirements were met in an even more satisfactory manner. The application of this capacity brought man the purest delight of having made something new, a delight that can be traced back to the most ancient relics of the past and to the creations of folk art. This long process, spread through both space and time, was by no means simple, for man achieved progress by overcoming an infinite series of obstacles and contradictions, some of which resulted from his relation to nature, while others, particularly in the later stages of mankind's historical development, resulted from the way his methods of production shaped his social relations.

To begin with, man made tools, and then increasingly complex machines that served to multiply his power in his struggle with nature. Science, and technology derived from science, gave him access to vast and ever more effective sources of energy. Yet, with the development of the industrial capitalist society, more and more people became not masters but slaves of machines which, moreover, they did not own.

In their work they were less and less subjects, that is, men with free creative ability, and became objects of machines created by man himself. I shall not enlarge upon class distinctions brought by this development into human society. I shall limit my attention to following the fortunes of creative genius, past and present, the delight of man in creating new things. Once the majority of people in a civilized technical society had actually become part of the machines, work lost the element of delight in creation, becoming merely a source of earning a living. In the course of his work man has grown alienated from his fundamental quality—his delight in creative activity—for his consciousness of this delight gradually diminished as years went by. This as a basic content of life was left only to a limited number of privileged individuals, such as scientists and artists, and to the others only after work was over. But individuals, even the privileged, were supposed to produce more and more goods not for the delight of creation, of making discoveries and conquests, but so that the results of their work might be consumed by society, and especially by those classes which earned their living by manipulating the end products of their labor. With most of these people their conception of a good life was deprived of this fundamental delight in creation which was gradually replaced by a delight in objects which could be purchased with the money earned by their passive work and which made it possible to fill, or often simply to spend or even kill, their leisure time. However, even here man was—and, in fact, still is—turning more and more into a slave of objects. He buys them because they are being offered to him, because he thinks (or is persuaded to think) that they will improve and enrich his life. To be able to own and use such objects has become a social good; not to have them is considered equivalent to social failure or even degradation. Most of these possibilities, however, are not designed to stimulate the great creative genius of man but to obliterate it more and more by this passive acceptance of things; with a large majority of mankind the process of alienation is being intensified even in leisure time. New theories and ideas are being imposed upon most people—for instance, that the creative attitude, the ability to feel delight chiefly in the process of creation, is *not* a universal quality of man and that instead only an isolated "chosen few" have this quality, while the rest of mankind is able to share only in superficial pleasures, passive kinds of work, the possession of objects of daily use, and so on. Thus man has ceased to be a creator, and has become a consumer of life and its gifts. As a result, the future society is frequently described as a consumer's society.

Let me say at once that I disagree with the theory that only a limited number of people are able to enjoy creation and need such pleasure; I disagree, if for no other reason, because it is a very cheap working hypothesis. Should I accept it (and there is of course no convincing proof that it is valid) I should be released from any moral responsibility for trying to bring about a different, better order which would make it possible to awaken and develop these creative abilities in an ever-increasing number of men and women. Should such a hypothesis be accepted by all as a creed for their work then a stagnation and disintegration of mankind would be bound to follow.

This hypothesis is far too similar to one which is unacceptable to all men trained in scientific ways of thinking: that the so-called backward nations have lagged behind because they were not capable of any other development. However, if I accept the opposite hypothesis—implying that man's fundamental quality probably is his creative genius, his delight in creating new things, in getting beyond what already exists—it becomes my responsibility to seek and create the necessary conditions, to build a new world order which would permit the development of this fundamental human quality. Even if we should discover later that we had overestimated this ability in a majority of people, that it is not possible to develop it sufficiently in all men but only in part of mankind, larger or smaller, we can be said to have made at least some contribution to improvement and progress (if only in the case of a small but significant section of mankind) and to have helped enrich what might be called the universal fund of mankind. Since we are treating of world order, and of a better world order of the future, I shall assume that our deliberations will be based on the second hypothesis.

One of the main objections raised against this hypothesis is that the Gauss distribution curve applies even to man's creative genius, since those men who are creative represent isolated cases encountered only in small, extreme parts of the curve. If genius, or the ability and urge to create new things, were a purely quantitative and simple quality then this objection might have some relevance. However, what is most remarkable in mankind is the fact that each person's basic ability and talent become manifest in different directions and forms and are devoted to a wide variety of activities and interests. Even though a distribution curve of a certain form is valid for each of these activities, it is quite certain and clear that every man appears in this series of curves in a different place with regard to his personal capabilities; thus it is very probable that every man can find a profession in which he would be in the above-average part of the Gauss curve representing talent. In other words, talent for creative work in some of the possible directions of human activities is a norm and the lack of talent a pathological state. It is necessary only to find the activity in which an individual can best apply his creative faculties.

In practice this means that the basic demand of world order must be not simply to give jobs to all men but to give them work that is worthy of mankind, work that does not merely tie man to his machine, to mechanical and uniform work, but calls forth, cultivates, and develops his best creative abilities. This implies that equal educational opportunities must be available to all men and women so that they can embark upon such a career. What this means for education and its methods will be discussed later.

Of course there is another objection that might be raised: In human society there are, and always will be, a great many working operations which require no such active approach, but, on the contrary, need just this "human machine." The objection is right only as far as it expresses the contemporary stage in the development of civilized society. But one can quite clearly discern the outlines of new possibilities: there is the scientific-technical revolution with its increasing possibilities of automating mechanical work, physical or mental, that does not call for the above-mentioned creative human approach. The question now is to make this the principal trend in automation: to try to put man back where he belongs in view of his creative abilities, to give him more and more opportunities to create new things. Is there anything the world can lose in the process? Surely not, because, for man himself, his creative genius is the greatest productive force. The more we develop this, the more people search for and find new possibilities for harnessing the forces of nature, the larger is the field we open to it, the richer is the world and thus the life of each individual man. This is just what is implied in the device: give everyone work worthy of man. That this trend is gaining is shown by the intense growth of science and of its importance and application in society, though there is no doubt that we now stand only at the threshold of future development.

In this respect we are thus at an important crossroads of mankind. The development of science and technology opens up entirely new possibilities of a genuine liberation of man, not only from hunger and diseases, but also from work that is mechanical, requires little efficiency with regard to thinking, and therefore represents but a passive extension of the machine. A new road is being opened for a growing number of people to become liberated from the stifling routine of manipulation and to embark on the active creation of new values. This opens the way to the greatest riches mankind possesses —man's creative genius—which the forms of production and the organization of human society have until now obliterated with the mire of convention, superficiality, and daily struggle for mere existence or its supposed pleasures. I think it is impossible to imagine the road to a progressive world order without searching for ways of making continually fuller use of this possibility. Moreover, it is necessary to prevent the new conditions from being directed against man's real self, against his creative genius, and to avoid a situation in which passive amusements, passive means of superficial diversions, and the like are offered to and forced upon him. I am deeply convinced that to give only "panem et circenses" is at variance with the present development of science and technology. This, of course, does not mean that I deny the importance of entertainment in man's leisure time; but it should be directed both by what he is offered and by his education, in order to strengthen the positive, truly human qualities in man, to widen his horizons, to enrich his life, to stimulate his urge to create things and to associate with people; it must not cater to man's primitive interests and so degrade him.

We are faced with the possibility that a constantly greater number of people will develop as humane personalities. I believe that all of us have to shoulder the responsibility of insuring that the opportunity of this present time is not wasted and that the possibilities given to man by the scientific-technical revolution are not turned against him, against his genuine liberty and truly human qualities.

Without going into the question of what kinds of changes this would require in the structure of society, I wish to stress my conviction that the traditional capitalist society is incapable of solving the problem satisfactorily, though it may manage to obscure, for a time, the true sense of scientific-technical revolution and the need for a more perfect world order.

V

There is another basic element which, in the interests of a better world order to come, must be developed in a new way. It is the upbringing and education of young people. As already mentioned, general basic school education is one of the first of all minimum requirements and must be realized as soon as possible.

However, today we are confronted with another task, an entirely new one, which is bound up with what I have examined in the preceding section. The general problem experienced in educating the young is compounded by the fact that there is a sharp growth in the volume of knowledge, that scientific truths valid until recently are being constantly modified, and so on. The problem is to determine how to give today's children and young people the fundamentals of knowledge about nature and the like on which they can reliably build in practical life. Moreover, the practical life itself will, as a result of the scientific-technical revolution, require a far higher standard of knowledge and level of education, particularly if we accept the principle that more and more people should be taking part in the development of mankind in a creative manner, using their truly human quality. From another point of view we can say that the question is whether in employing the modern methods of upbringing and education we shall continue to have sufficient numbers of actively creative people to meet the needs of the scientific-technical revolution.

The problem thus posed is extremely complicated and has been the subject of many discussions and exacting experiments in all the highly developed countries (such as the U.S.S.R., the U.S.A., and Great Britain). In the developing countries, too, this task involves the specific challenge of creating the foundations for an understanding of modern science. The question is on the agenda of international agencies, both govermental and nongovernmental, a prominent place being taken by UNESCO. There is no doubt that far closer international co-operation could yield much more satisfactory results. Though the problem as posed here is an arduous one, it does not seem to me to do full justice to the complicated nature of the whole matter.

It seems to me that in modern civilized society there is another very dangerous factor working in opposition to these efforts: This is the fact that children and young people continually live in surroundings which increasingly deprive them of direct contact with the reality of nature and with actual creative human work.

The number of children and adolescents who can verify and develop their capabilities of thinking and working on the basis of concrete activity and of transforming the realities in their environments is rapidly decreasing. The number of those who are confined to moving and living in a prefabricated environment which offers them very little opportunity for creative activity is growing. There seems to be less and less of what might be termed the natural polytechnical education; this type of education used to constitute the basis for the formation of categories as well as for the ability to transform the surrounding world and its objects and was a fundamental substratum in not-so-distant generations. Until recently, almost all children had their own small worlds which they helped to create. And precisely during this creation they mastered in practice the basic logical categories, such as the relation between part and the whole, structurality, and so forth. On this basis school in those days was able to instill reliable factual knowledge which became part of the active creative core of every person. Nowdays children are being guided in a more or less passive way in a world of prefabricated facts whose essence they are generally unable to grasp. Thus, contact with the facts of science becomes more or less a matter of mere memory and reproduction, and the selection of children and young people is then carried out on the basis of these, and not their creative, abilities. Modern means of education, such as films and television, though no doubt very effective in themselves, actually serve to reinforce this passive approach. School generally turns into a static affair with little active participation by the children, and thus can hardly hope to awaken the children's interest. Children and young people generally sit through more of the time devoted to their education than accords with their need for movement and active participation. Not infrequently, children with an active approach to learning, who do not find satisfaction in the existing form of education, are considered as "vexing" only because the manner of teaching does not satisfy them.

I cannot get rid of the anxiety that it is precisely here that the largest number of talented individuals get lost—individuals who, if detected and stimulated, could creatively enrich human thought and science. Perhaps even a considerable part of the difficulties which we are experiencing with a large number of young people all over the world stems from the lack of satisfaction caused by passive leading and the impossibility of active application. This also has a damaging effect on what we might call sound self-confidence, with all the consequences that can be observed in the behavior of adolescents who frequently compensate for this deficiency in a manner hostile to society. And all this goes on at a time when human society requires the development of the creative genius and capabilities which lie dormant in all individuals and which regrettably remain largely undiscovered.

I hold that from this point of view education today is at a new crossroad analogous to that in the days of Comenius. He proposed to solve it by introducing universal education, by object teaching on the basis of getting acquainted with the surrounding reality as opposed to the medieval dogmatic reproduction.

If school and the entire educational process are to afford a basis for participating in the results of scientific-technical revolution, it is not enough that they provide only a certain amount of knowledge as a basis for future occupations; what they ought to do is to call forth literally all the capabilities which are latent in children and young people. To do this, however, they must know how to awaken interest in as wide a circle of human thought and activities as possible, so that each of the pupils may find his or her own predilection, his or her ardent interest, his or her own mission. Only in this way will it be possible for students to know the pleasure of knowledge and of creation, to be able after leaving school to follow the rapid development of scientific knowledge, and thus to find their place in an active participation. This, however, cannot be accomplished by education based on mere memorization. What is required is an entirely new school in which pupils acquire knowledge by active participation.

It is by no means an easy task to work out teaching and educational methods that would be increasingly able to answer these requirements. Much is already being done by way of experiment. However, the interests of a better world order require that international co-operation should do much more in this field than has been done so far. There is no need to emphasize that such new, active, and creative schools can be built only on the basis of the widest democratization of the educational system in which all children, irrespective of social group, class, or race, are given exactly the same opportunities to develop their hidden wealth of talent.

Let us hope that even this brief outline of the tasks facing education has made it sufficiently clear that this widely democratic and active approach to education is precisely one of the fundamental sources for developing that delight in creative work which is one of the basic supporting columns of the better world order.

VI

One of the essential features of a more perfect world order is democracy—and with good reason. It cannot be assumed that any creative and satisfying work for man is possible where he is deprived of the basic possibilities to take part in deciding matters creating conditions for his work and participation in the management of society. He must be absolutely certain that the organization in which he takes part through the work he is doing is his *own* organization, that he is really participating in each of its steps, be it in his own immediate vicinity, or in wider circles. It is clear that this possibility cannot be afforded by any mere formal democracy, as represented by institutions like parliaments, by any system of two or more political parties, and so on. The reader will probably agree that a kind of "democracy" is inadequate in which the voter is free, once in a while, to express his smaller or larger measure of agreement with a given program drawn up *ad hoc* for the election period. A real democracy must consist in a system under which the whole preparation of any significant measure—whether of nationwide or regional character, or affecting one community or one institution—is carried out with all those immediately concerned taking part. Each effort to improve one or the other part of the social system must have a chance to be utilized properly. Everyone must be firmly convinced that measures are taken not only with his participation and with his knowledge but only and exclusively for his own benefit.

This, of course, serves to further the creative approach to work, leading to a situation in which individual and social benefits coincide. Man is not a mere object of measures which he more or less fails to understand, but an active subject of these. This also leads to the removal of another degree of man's alienation, his alienation within the society; the contradiction between the individual and the society, together with the resulting sadness and lack of fulfillment, would be eliminated.

Again I do not intend to go into detail. Even such demands may perhaps seem utopian. However, they are the necessary foundation for a truly human society. After all, in a number of countries serious attempts and experiments are being made to incorporate them into the very life of society. Of course, such efforts meet with distrust in many areas; they encounter passivity, the legacy of the past. Yet they are the only way toward a society whose resources consist in all human wealth and in the initiative of its citizens.

It is no doubt necessary to clear up many points on both sides, particularly among people living under differing social systems. Nevertheless, I am of the opinion that even in this respect at least some common principles can be reached and then be put into effect under differing initial conditions and consequently in differing thoughtfully conscious and determined ways.

VII

I have now dealt with the chief elements which I now consider decisive in a more efficient world order, happier for all, which it would be worthwhile to create by a concerted effort of all countries.

However, I am aware that any effort to work them out more fully and especially to put them into effect will necessarily encounter a series of obstacles. It presupposes a reappraisal of a great many values—moral, social, international, and especially material ones. I will mention only the last. After all, entirely new financial resources will be required for the active steps which must be taken, such as bringing the standard of living of all countries to the same level, implying the aid of developed countries to underdeveloped countries, new forms of education, and so forth. There can be no doubt that changes in the division of national income and different practices in laying down the basic priorities are indicated.

One of the most fundamental, and most difficult, changes is the necessary transfer of resources previously expended for armaments and wars; this can occur only after universal and total disarmament has been achieved. Though it is true that we cannot put off any active measures—especially regarding aid to the developing countries and new educational methods—until these vast resources are made available, it needs no great imagination to see what great advance could be made in the solution of all the basic questions connected with a better world order. I do not mean to enlarge upon this question; it has been much discussed in a series of international institutes, for example, the Pugwash Conferences. But I do think that a well-conceived program dealing with the questions I have mentioned might help to remove the fears felt by some people that the sudden release of men and means hitherto held together by the armaments race might lead to difficulties in some countries, such as how to employ the released manpower.

Furthermore, it is obvious that disarmament would have a number of other consequences in the moral sphere; it would increase mutual confidence and open the way to co-operation on all the fundamental tasks which, when carried out, can lead humanity to a better and happier life and thus create prerequisites for the future road toward world order. This is the reason that world order cannot be achieved unless the problems of disarmament are solved at the same time.

VIII

I am aware that much of what I have mentioned in these pages may seem a mere set of utopian slogans making deliberations on a world order as an institution unrealistic. However, in each case I have tried to prove that they are the prerequisites of a world order which might be called human in the best sense of the word and therefore might become a lasting contribution to mankind and be accepted as such.

I trust my readers will bear with me if, in conclusion, I try to demonstrate that these problems are part of a genuine interest evinced not only by ever growing numbers of scientists—who, quite understandably, can see their full significance before others do—but also by public and political personalities, and that ways are being sought and conditions created in some countries for putting them into effect.

Allow me to give a few examples from my own country. The minimum requirements I have mentioned as absolutely essential—the right to work worthy of man, the right to full protection of health, to good living and working milieu, to a general and fully democratic education accessible to all—are guaranteed by the fundamental laws laid down in the Constitution, and are therefore binding on the whole society and afforded to all free of charge. The measures safeguarding this are subject to a permanent and consistent control by the whole society, by the representatives of people's administration in the localities up to parliament and the government itself. No doubt it is necessary to search continually for ways to plan these fundamental principles in accordance with the development of science in the sense I have mentioned.

The same is true for the development of active democratic participation of all citizens in the realization of the aims of our society which is effected in all areas of administration—municipal, regional, and state—in all governmental and nongovernmental organizations, in the administration of justice. It applies equally in the solution of everyday problems of all citizens—through nation-wide discussions regarding the stages of development of the society, the management of its economy, and so on.

In addition, it applies to the problems of science and its utilization in society, as well as to the problems of culture and its being made accessible to all citizens. The greatest remaining obstacle is that a very large number of citizens are not fully aware of either their possibilities or responsibilities; it is not an easy task from the point of view of organization to determine how to concentrate opinions and activity on the solution of pressing tasks and how to harmonize individual aims with the needs of the whole society or reconcile short-term aims with over-all final prosperity.

All this is, of course, being realized not as a perfectly devised system but as a structure which is developing in harmony with the economic possibilities stemming from the development of education and culture, of industry and agriculture. This is linked to vigorous efforts to determine which elements of economic and organizational management would be most effective in ensuring the development of an entire society which would base its activities on a profound knowledge of economic laws and would be capable of utilizing all the means afforded by its national income. To a great extent these tasks of the society are new and not yet verified by practice; they involve methods of management and internal links of society which are entirely different from those that had been formed in the process of the long-lasting development of capitalist society. This, in view of the complicated character of a modern state's economy, is by no means an easy task to accomplish. Therefore shortcomings and even errors in trying to find the best ways of solving these problems cannot be excluded. I believe, however, that the new possibilities of science are creating conditions leading to more and more exact solutions of both economic and organizational problems and that the democratic principles which we are putting into effect will result in increasing activity and initiative on the part of the citizens. At the present time we are carrying out two discussions based on wide democratic principles and are trying to realize the goals deriving from them: effective methods of managing the national economy, and new forms of educating children, young people, and adults. In addition, international co-operation is being stimulated to create new values and especially to contribute to means of achieving universal and total disarmament. The necessity to assist the developing countries even at the cost of our own sacrifices is not only fully recognized, but has also become an integral part of the life of our people and is carried out in a relatively wide scope, though our country has never tried to derive any benefits, however small, from the colonization of other countries. This is the additional reason that we welcome unprejudiced discussions on all questions concerning mankind and its better future, its better world order.

IX

I hope my readers will not deem it immodest that I have used the example of my own country to try to show that the prerequisites I have mentioned above as a basis for thoughts on a world order, that is, supranational order, are entirely realistic and acceptable as a principle on the national level at least.

In the conclusion I should like to furnish proof that some of the previously mentioned principles form, *de facto*, a foundation of international, or supranational, aims, efforts, and relations, which we can describe with a certain dose of fantasy and extrapolation as an emerging world order. I have in mind the tremendous effort which thousands of scientific workers, under the guidance of international governmental and nongovernmental organizations, are exerting in an attempt to detect and eliminate disease, even in the most remote parts of the world; to search for the present and future sources of nourishment and determine how they can be activated where people are suffering from hunger; to eliminate illiteracy and concentrate efforts toward the creation of an educational system in those countries which do not yet have a literary language of their own; to improve educational methods in countries with a fully developed school system. It is certainly not necessary for me to elaborate further on the examples of such a "world order at work." I should like only to point out that it is extremely varied and polytonic, solving present problems from many different points of view and opening up new prospects. Understandably it is continually hampered by the existing "world disorder," whose sources I cannot analyze here. In essence they obstruct the efforts to solve the main tasks which were emphasized earlier. Therefore this emerging world order is in no easy position; it has the weakness inherent in the beginnings of a new undertaking but also the power of an effort which is arising out of necessity.

Here my readers can remind me of a contradiction in citing the comprehensive international effort as proof of a functional solution of the world order, although it is to a great extent connected with institutions, for example, the United Nations and its specialized agencies. However, this argument is only formal in essence: These institutions live and work in the present situation, which is full of contradictions, only because they can fulfill basic duties which correspond, however inadequately and incompletely, to the fundamental needs of the emerging world order. It is possible to envisage that their lives will be fuller and their existence stronger when they can carry out their functions more perfectly. The same applies to the great number of other far less institutional and more functional organizations and joint efforts such as international scientific programs.

This is so because the world today is divided into three entirely different systems (socialist, capitalist, and developing countries)—a fact which makes it impossible to organize institutions which can gain the confidence and meet the wishes of all except by fulfilling common and general functions in a way which does not deprive any country of its authority and which renders positive values as well. In discussions we have been facing opinions of those who proceed to deliberations on the creation of a world order by way of the establishment of the corresponding institutions. These people maintain that it is possible to start building a world order by establishing regional groups having joint planning and other functions typical of a contemporary state and then to continue by evolving into larger groupings. Such opinions seem to me unrealistic, to say the least. In the present situation, such views serve only to strengthen the barriers dividing the world. The positive results they bring within the framework of a regional grouping are usually at the cost of a further widening of co-operation. Therefore, in my opinion, they cannot be regarded as the road toward what we should like to see as a world order, perhaps with the exception of a regional grouping of several developing countries which are concerned with removing quite incidental divisions determined by the past interests of colonial powers. In my view the functional connection (when it is ripe) corresponds also to mutual relations within the framework of the future world order because it is possible to presume that many institutions—which some people consider essential to order or even a world order—will become outdated, as there will be no further need for them. The joint solution of common problems with the assistance of only those institutions and establishments which are necessary for their solution will remain the principal common road of mankind.

When this will happen is certainly a matter of conjecture, for all of us undoubtedly construct our own opinion according to how we assess the development of the system—a development in which we ourselves are sharing and about which we could argue for a long time. Such discussion and analysis are outside the framework of these deliberations, although they could help to clarify opinions about a number of problems and contradictions of this present time.

JAN TINBERGEN

International Economic Planning

The Case for International Economic Planning; Institutions Involved

IN THIS essay, *planning* will be defined as the preparation for political action, that is, action by public authorities. *Economic* planning then refers to the economic activities implied, such as governmental investments and financial, commercial, and other types of economic policy. It is characteristic for planning that it (1) tries to estimate *future activities,* while (2) setting *goals* for them and (3) suggesting the necessary *co-ordination* of the various activities involved.

Since economic policies are meant to influence the economic activities at large (including the private sector), their planning must also deal with the prospects of the economy as a whole. The goals or aims of economic policy are partly autonomous in the sense that they cannot be derived from economic knowledge alone, but also depend on the value system adhered to by the authorities. Even so the degree of concensus in this field is sufficiently high to venture the formulation of goals acceptable to all concerned. Or, to put it in other words, a compromise on these goals is within the range of possibilities. We hope to specify this later on.

The aims must be attained by the application of the means of economic policy. Their choice again partly depends on the value system of the community considered—mainly because that system may veto some means. To a much higher degree they depend on economic knowledge, that is, the knowledge of the operation of the institutions which together constitute the economic order (production units, distribution channels, tax systems, schools, group organizations, and so forth). This knowledge is far from perfect, but some main lines are available, even in operational form, that is, useful for action. Often this means that the economist is able to estimate in concrete figures the extent of a number of measures to be taken.

Economic policy and its planning are done mainly at the national and some lower levels, that is, at the state, provincial, or city levels. This is due to the high degree of autonomy national governments enjoy, often to the detriment of the world's population. This national autonomy is one of the main clashes between a complex of political facts, inherited from the past or based on emotional forces, and the requirements of an optimum of well-being. Thus, because of the autonomy of rich countries, the development of the poorer countries is less quick than planned, even though the plans are already insufficient to narrow the gap in well-being between these countries and the richer ones, a gap which will in the end menace the safety of the rich countries. This development is illustrated by the following evidence. Over the period 1960-1963, as far as figures are available, the annual percentage increases of per capita income compared with the planned figures were the following:

1960–1963 Average percentage increase in gross domestic product per capita

Country	P.	A.	Country	P.	A.
Taiwan	5	3.5	Colombia	3	2.3
Tunisia	4.5	1.7	India	3	1.1
United Arab Rep.	4.5	3.5	Korea	3	2.3
Burma	4	3.7	Pakistan	2.5	3.1
Morocco	4	1.7	Sudan	2	4.4
Ceylon	3	0.8	Malaysia	1	2.5
Chile	3	1.6			

P. = planned; A. = actual.
Source: United Nations, *World Economic Survey 1964*, Vol. I, p. 101, table 6.2.

From this table we see that for the majority of countries considered, including such an important country as India, the actual growth in production has fallen far short of the planned growth. Moreover, between 1960 and 1962 the average annual per capita income in the developed market economies increased by almost one hundred dollars, while that in the developing countries increased by barely five.[1] These few figures illustrate in a dramatic way the two types of deficiencies we mentioned.

One of the main bottlenecks to quicker development is foreign exchange, and another is the lack of qualified personnel, especially in the managerial field. Transfer of funds as well as of qualified manpower, mainly an outcome of national policies and planning, falls far short of the necessary flows, if one takes the world's interests as one's guideline. Only a world policy or, as a second best, a stronger international policy can prevent us from sliding into a complete failure of development policy and all the political consequences of such a failure. In order to discuss such a policy, we must at least have a picture of it, and this international economic planning can give us. This essay constitutes an attempt to indicate what could be done in this field in the next few years. The author believes that extension and reinforcement of international planning will be *a factor in favor of the lessening of international tensions* and *a modest contribution to the establishment of an international order.* The essay should be seen in this light. International planning will provide some basic figures needed for a technical discussion of the contributions needed from developed and developing countries. It will also create the necessary suprastructure to the planning machinery at the continental and national levels and so integrate a number of elements so far only weakly connected. At all levels it can contribute to a quiet but pertinent discussion of the hard facts and the action needed to improve them.

At present, the international scene is characterized by a very hesitating process of the creation of the necessary machinery for a more effective world economic policy, often with the open or hidden opposition of national and other pressure groups. Nevertheless, development is pressed into the right direction. We will try to give an unemotional picture of it, gratefully recognizing the action of positive forces.

In the first section a quick survey will be given of the institutions involved in such international planning and their main tasks. In the second section some recent contributions made by these institutions to international economic planning will be summarized. The third section contains a number of suggestions on the further development of that planning, whereas the fourth section adds some remarks on the implementation of the policy to be outlined in an international plan as suggested.

The United Nations Secretariat and the Specialized Agencies. Our survey of the institutions involved in some form of international economic planning almost by necessity must start with the *United Nations.* This organization is closest to a world organization, though with the deplorable nonmembership of, *inter alia,* China (mainland) and Indonesia. The activities of its Secretariat and of a number of its Specialized Agencies are based on its Charter, where in Article 1, sub 3, and in Articles 55-72 the tasks in the economic field are defined, although in very general terms only. Thus, Article 1 speaks only of "solving international problems of an economic . . . character," whereas Article 55 speaks about the promotion of "higher standards of living, full employment and conditions of economic and social progress and development" without any further specification of policies. Most of the other articles deal only with the procedures at meetings, but not with the substance of the problems.

In the U.N. *Secretariat* its Economic Projections and Programming Center is in charge of the most general activities in the field of economic planning (our definition), embracing all geographical areas and all sectors of activity involved. The Center has been operating since December 1961. Also inside the Secretariat, the U.N. Organization for Industrial Development (UNOID), headed by the Commissioner for Industrial Development, is operating, concentrating on planning and policies for the important group of sectors constituting manufacturing industry. Several bureaus inside the Secretariat supply (mostly statistical) information and analysis which is of great importance to any planning work. Another part of the general machinery of the U.N. is, in addition, the United Nations Research Institute for Social Development (UNRISD), dealing with the methods of planning for the social sectors. To these we usually count education, housing, health, and community development. In co-operation with a number of specialized agencies the Secretariat finally plays an important part in the Extended Program of Technical Assistance (EPTA), whose main contribution is in the field of the dissemination of knowledge in all sectors of socioeconomic life.

Among the *specialized agencies*, the Food and Agricultural Organization (FAO), takes care of a great variety of activities in the largest economic sector, such as the supply of information, training, technical assistance, the regulation of markets, and the planning of agricultural policies. The International Bank for Reconstruction and Development (IBRD), with the International Finance Corporation (IFC) and the International Development Association (IDA), operates mainly in the financial field, by extending loans to governments for development purposes (IBRD and IDA) or by participating in the capital of private companies and thus furthering their establishment (IFC); but it is also engaged in analyses of national economies and in training of development planners and project analysts. The oldest agency, the International Labor Organization

(ILO), finds its main task in the promotion of social legislation and the prevention (one might say) of social dumping, but more recently engaged increasingly in employment planning and, together with the International Institute of Labor Studies, social research. The International Monetary Fund (IMF) provides short-term credits to member countries with a view to bridging temporary balance of payments difficulties and advises governments on their monetary and short-term financial policies; in addition it supplies high-quality research in the field of the short-term operation of national economies and provides technical assistance in its field. The United Nations Educational, Scientific, and Cultural Organization (UNESCO) carries out projects in the field of education and disseminates information on a large scale, provides technical assistance, and engages in educational planning. The United Nations International Children's Emergency Fund (UNICEF) organizes and finances projects to increase children's welfare and recently entered the field of general development policies as far as children's interests are involved. The World Health Organization (WHO) engages in health projects, such as the eradication of malaria, and provides information and training as well as technical assistance on policies in the field and as a consequence also planning of such policies.

Because of the numerous interconnections between all social and economic fields frequent mutual consultation and co-operation between these agencies have developed, posing difficult problems of efficiency and co-ordination within the U.N. family of organizations. Problems of efficiency arise whenever the number of mutual consultations surpasses a certain level and ties up considerable numbers of highly qualified experts, who might also have worked in the field. Yet, co-ordination is necessary because of the innumerable links between the various fields. While these problems are well known already at the national levels, they become even more pressing in international co-operation.

The United Nations Regional Commissions. All the activities enumerated are spread over an enormous geographical area, requiring geographical decentralization and co-ordination also. The main machinery for this purpose is the set of *Regional Commissions,* the Economic Commission for Africa (ECA), and those for Asia and the Far East (ECAFE), for Europe (ECE), and for Latin-America (ECLA). In a way these act as the executives in each area for all United Nations activities in the economic field. Their tasks may be briefly summarized as the analysis of regional development, including planning activities, the assistance of governments in the drawing up of development plans, the organization of regional co-operation in such matters as finance, trade, river-basin projects, and training in various fields. Thus, ECLA and ECAFE have made important contributions to the development of methods of development planning; ECLA gave much attention to the possibilities of intra-regional trade and continental integration. It helped to lay the foundations of the Central American and the Latin American Free Trade Area (LAFTA). It carried out and promoted numerous studies on input-output relations and industrial complex analysis. ECAFE was among the initiators of the Asian Development Bank and the Mekong River Project. ECE devoted many studies to the comparison of East European and West European development policies and planning methods, ECA to the possibilities of co-operation between adjacent newly independent Africa countries. Each of the regional commissions now has its own training institute for planners.

Developed countries: (1) Comecon. Since international planning will have to be a process of co-operation at different levels, it is also useful to summarize some of the planning tasks assumed by international organizations covering more limited geographical areas. For obvious reasons (resources and manpower availability) it is the various groups of developed countries which so far have made the most relevant contributions to planning and the research needed for it. Among these the centrally planned economies as a matter of course are the first to be mentioned, since planning is a much more intensive and detailed activity in these countries, springing from their preference for regimented economies. The European Communist countries are all members of the Council for Mutual Economic Assistance (CMEA), also known as *Comecon;* the Asian Communist-ruled countries are observers, with the exception of Mongolia, which became a member in 1962; also Yugoslavia is an observer. In the first years after its creation in 1949, Comecon was not very active. Later on it became more actively engaged in the exchange of technological knowledge and the co-ordination of international trade in the framework of the national economic plan. Comecon has not thus far developed into a really supranational planning agency; the autonomy of the member countries is strictly recognized. Its main activity may better be described as co-ordination and promotion of research on the best division of labor between the member countries; but in view of the degree of detail characteristic of Eastern European plans this nevertheless means that fairly extensive studies have been made.

Developed countries: (II) OECD and Alliance for Progress. Western European countries had to organize themselves in order to arrive at a distribution of Marshall aid. Their organization was the Organization for European Economic Co-operation (OEEC), which has been transformed into the present-day OECD: the *Organization for Economic Co-operation and Development,* with the United States, Canada, and Japan also as full members. From the beginning OEEC has been engaged in planning operations of an indicative and macro-economic character, in order to avoid inconsistencies in the economic policies of reconstruction after World War II. The operations were indicative in the sense that they could not force upon any government a change in policy, but only recommend it. They were macro-economic in the sense of not dealing with single enterprises or projects. The type of inconsistency they were able to uncover and hence eliminate was that, for example, France would not expect higher exports to Germany than Germany expected its imports from France to be. OEEC has given particular attention to the reintroduction of multilateral trade between the member countries and the financial facilities needed for such trade; the latter were later taken care of by the European Payments Union (EPU). Two features in the procedures followed already by OEEC and taken over by OECD deserve special mention in our context. First, its Secretariat played an active role in the planning process, particularly clearly during the preparation of the 1955-1960 policies. Not only did they induce the member governments to set up plans for their countries, but they set up one themselves also, in order to be able to appraise the national plans and to suggest improvements where inconsistencies showed up. Second, OEEC developed a practice of so-called "examinations" of each member country's policies. Two other members were appointed in order to analyze critically the policies of the country under consideration; a public debate followed, finishing up with recommendations to the government concerned.

After European reconstruction was considered finished, OEEC was changed into OECD, where the emphasis was shifted to development policies, in particular policies of the member countries *vis-à-vis* the developing countries of the non-communist world. Among the instruments of policy, capital movements and scientific and educational activities came more to the fore. Thus, comparisons were made between the capital flows made available by each member country to developing countries, the conditions under which such financing was made available and the numbers of experts and teaching staff put at the disposition of developing countries.

The *Alliance for Progress* (AP) is an organization of American nations devoted to the development of Latin America, mainly by the supply of capital and by scrutinizing national development plans. Thus, the Alliance carefully analyzed the development plans of Venezuela and Colombia and on the basis of these plans, partly amended, extended financial aid to these countries.

The "European Communities" of the "Six." Within the group of Western countries a more intimate collaboration exists among the six countries of the *European Coal and Steel Community* (ECSC). *Euratom,* and the *European Economic Community* (EEC) or Common Market. The aim of the main treaty (the Rome Treaty) is to arrive at an integrated modern economy for the whole area; this implies the establishment of a common policy in several fields (trade, agriculture, social insurance, investments as far as stimulated by public financing, some types of taxes, anticyclical policies). These policies require preparation, and planning, in our sense, is therefore among the tasks of the executives. For obvious reasons the impact of this planning on the development of the Common Market economies will be more profound than other types of international planning: here a real government will develop, able to carry through a number of planned measures. Thus, part of the agricultural policies of the member countries is already based on thorough research undertaken and decisions made by the European Commission.

Some of the More Important Recent Activities

United Nations Agencies in general. Although several *United Nations agencies* have been involved in their specialized activities more or less independently, there is an applaudable tendency now to see these activities as part of the so-called Development Decade, inaugurated by document E/3613 "Proposals for Action" during that period. The Decade was solemnly inaugurated by a unanimous resolution of the General Assembly in order to accentuate the urgent need for a quicker development of the poor countries and the necessity to orient all United Nations activities to this main aim. The Proposals were drafted by the Secretariat, in close co-operation with all agencies involved. In a way this document therefore represents a frame of reference or a plan in embryo. It defines as the main aim a rate of growth of real national product of 5 per cent per annum and financial transfers from developed to developing countries of 1 per cent of the former's national income, amounting to 8 billion dollars to start with and to 12 billion at the Decade's end. In this amount private investments are included, according to the United Nations definition. The document just mentioned also sets out the action needed in the manpower, trade, and price stabilization fields as well as in various sectors.[2]

The weak spot in the "Proposals for Action" is that, in accordance with the present political situation, they constitute what national governments are at present prepared to undertake; their willingness to act is largely based on what they consider their national interest. The view taken by most parliaments still lacks sufficient broadmindedness to identify these national interests with the interest of the world as a whole. As a consequence the financial transfers and flows of technicians envisaged definitely fall short of what is actually needed to reduce the gap in well-being between rich and poor countries. Instead of some 8 billion dollars a financial flow of 15 billion will be closer to the effort needed. In addition it will be necessary to ease the terms at which these capitals are made available. In the trade field too, the needs of the developing countries must be taken more seriously, as we will set out later.[3]

Some of the Regional Commissions have also contributed substantially to such a preparation. Thus, ECAFE, for the Third Conference of Asian Planners, 19-26 October 1964, held at Bangkok, prepared a "Review of Long-Term Economic Projections for Selected Countries in the ECAFE Region," which is a Report by the Fourth Group of Experts on Programming Techniques. An important feature of this document is that it also includes projections prepared by the ECAFE Secretariat, generally less ambitious than most national plans, and running until 1980. This does not mean that these projections are better, in the sense of implying better chosen aims, than the national plans. They may be more realistic if no further changes in policy are forthcoming—policy of both the developed and the developing countries. Indeed, both have been less active than is necessary to carry out the development plans of the region's nations. The Secretariat's projections hence may be seen as a warning against such inertia.

Parallel with the projections for single countries, a report "Projections of Foreign Trade of the ECAFE Region up to 1980" was prepared. Also ECE contributed to future planning work by a chapter "Europe and the Trade Needs of the Less Developed Countries" in the Economic Survey of Europe in 1960, where projections up to 1980 were represented. Finally ECLA carried out a series of country studies in co-operation with the national governments under the general title "Analyses and Projections of Economic Development," containing, among other things, sectoral projections. All these studies contain useful elements of information and analysis which will be helpful in constructing a general international plan; they illustrate the process of a gradual widening of horizons, which must find its natural sequel in a unique, all-embracing planning activity as advocated here.

The U.N. Secretariat, and the Economic Projections and Programming Center. The *U.N. Secretariat,* in its World Economic Survey, 1964 I,[4] published a comparative study of the plans and their fulfillment of a large number of countries, entitled "Development Plans: Appraisal of Targets and Progress in Developing Countries." The study covers the period 1960-1963 as far as available; among other things it states that in most countries actual increases in per capita income fell short of planned increases (with Pakistan, Sudan, and Malaysia as exceptions). It also states that "foreign exchange scarcity is such a widespread hindrance to growth that the expansion of both aid and trade are essential" and that "the current level of aid in relation to the likely requirements of developing countries is far from encouraging."[5]

Among the recent work in the field of international planning two publications of the *Economic Projections and Programming Center* stand out. The first of these two is entitled "Planning for Economic Development" (New York, 1963) and gives a detailed survey of the methods of planning used by both Western and Eastern (Communist-ruled) countries. We will not elaborate on this since it constitutes only a preparatory orientation. It provides an excellent guide for those anxious to compare methods used and may contribute to the gradual convergence of methods. It also constitutes a step toward attaining agreement on some of the methods not yet agreed upon.

The second study contains the first piece of international planning conducted by the Center itself. In chapter 3 of this publication ("Studies in Long-Term Economic Projections for the World Economy")[6] a model is presented for the group of developing countries outside the Communist bloc as a whole, leading to an estimate, for 1970 and for 1975, of the balance of payments deficits to be expected. This represents an important contribution to real international economic planning. It brings us the first estimate of one of the most strategic economic variables in development policy, namely the need for financial assistance to the developing countries from the developed ones. For the first time this estimate has been based on a coherent and statistically tested model of the underdeveloped world (except the Communist Asian countries). It shows in what way this variable (the balance of payments gap) can be influenced either by the aims set for the development of the low-income countries or by the means applied—among the latter, particularly the means briefly characterized by the well-known question: aid or trade. For practical purposes the most important table is the one on page 69 which gives the following information:

	Estimate:	A	B
1. Level of gap in 1975 in the absence of policy measures (bln $)		20	32
2. Contribution of long-term capital flow which is assumed to reach the target level of one per cent of output of developed countries		17	17
3. Gap to be covered by additional policy measures		3	15
4. Illustration adjustment:			
a. Increase of the ratio of domestic saving to GNP from 15 to 16 per cent		3	—
b. Increase in exports if 4.2 per cent rate of growth were target		—	3
c. Additional import substitution corresponding with reduction of import to GNP ratio to 0.175			6
d. Gap remaining to be covered			6

It should be explained that estimate A is based on the savings gap approach and estimate B on the foreign payments gap approach. By the savings gap, the economist means the gap between investments needed and savings made by the countries themselves. By the foreign payments gap, he means the difference between expenditures in and receipts of foreign currency. It can be shown that the two gaps must in principle be equal, which implies that the two figures can be seen as two estimates of the same figure. But they can also throw some light on the means to be used in closing the gap, especially increments in trade facilities and in financial aid.

Information of this sort must be the hard core of any future world development policy; but it is only a modest beginning. As already observed it provides us with the single most important figure about the effort to be made by the prosperous countries in a joint development policy for the underdeveloped world.

Refinement in several directions will be needed; in particular, breakdowns with regard to sectors, to geographic areas, and to further aims and means of development policy will be needed. These will have to inform us about the industries to be developed and where to set them up, the volume of employment to be created, the needs for food, other consumer goods, and investment goods, the need for education of many types, and so on. Refinements will also be needed with regard to the reforms to be introduced, such as tax policies, facilities for small-scale industries, and training.

Comecon. In recent years the co-ordinating role of *Comecon* between the developed centrally planned economies has increased considerably in importance. The international division of labor between these countries is no longer the result of the incidental exchange of surpluses of a relatively small number of goods, but has become the subject of detailed studies in comparative costs of production between the countries under discussion.[7]

It has also gradually been understood that the custom of concluding trade agreements on a bilateral equilibrium basis is not the best way of organizing trade and that multilateral trade equilibrium is conducive to a higher level of well-being. The technical possibility of managing such a trade system has been introduced by the establishment of an international bank. Moreover, the principle is adhered to that the more developed countries should assist the less developed.

Finally it is clear that the centrally planned economies will be able, at any time, to provide abundant information about their envisaged future growth and thus may be able to join, if they so desire, any world planning activities initiated by the non-Communist countries. By so doing they may contribute substantially to the development of trade with both the West and the South, a matter we will further discuss below.

OECD, EEC, and AP. Recent activities of *OECD* of relevance for international planning consist mainly in a very thorough examination of the quantity of financial and technical assistance given by its member countries to developing countries and the conditions applied (interest charged, repayment schemes, possibly the country in which to spend the money). Part of the information collected has been published and usefully contributes to planning operations at the national level, general dissemination of knowledge, and political discussions. Unfortunately all these activities have not yet resulted in a more determined or co-ordinated development policy. One cannot help feeling that the urgency of such a policy is insufficiently realized by most of the governments concerned.

Among the activities of OECD some should be mentioned which may be important starting points of international economic planning. The so-called Summer Project 1964 of the (American) Agency for International Development (AID) deserves particular mention and praise. Essentially it applies to a number of individual developing countries a method of forecasting similar to the one applied by the U.N. Economic Projections and Programming Center, that is, the two estimates of the balance of payments deficit to be expected in 1975 are made which are the basic information needed for a future development policy. Such estimates have been made for some fifty countries, including all the major developing countries.

OECD also did some work on the development to be aimed at the member countries themselves. Thus, a rate of growth of 50 per cent in national product over the period 1960-1970 was suggested to member countries and accepted. This figure is an important basis for the estimation of the imports from developing countries to be expected in the future.

More detailed forecasts were made by *EEC* for its member countries and for the Community as a whole.[8] Under the chairmanship of Professor P. Uri, a committee of top experts from the member countries presented estimates for a series of key figures of economic development, including national income, population, and active population, consumption, gross investments, and balance of payments, subdivided into a few more categories. This constitutes a refinement and hence a more reliable estimate of part of the relevant figures needed for a world plan.

For the American continent the *Alliance for Progress*, in its rules for the appraisal of development plans for member countries, set some interesting standards for developing countries. Thus it was considered desirable that real national product rise by 5.5 per cent annually as a minimum. Among the plans approved after careful scrutiny is a Four-Year Plan for Venezuela, aiming at an 8 per cent increase per annum. These figures are significant in the discussion among economists about what rates of growth are feasible. While some skeptics doubt the possibility of pushing the rate of growth beyond 5 per cent per annum, the view is spreading that we must aim at more ambitious figures, such as 7 per cent, simply because the population explosion has changed the scene.

The U.N. Specialized Agencies. In order to arrive at an international economic plan one must go beyond the macro-economic estimates discussed so far. Subdivisions of the estimates over sectors and geographical areas will be needed. Sector plans will be needed and these have to be based on much specialized knowledge, usually better available in the *U.N. Specialized Agencies* and the networks of information they control. Thus, we must know how much more food will be required, broken down into categories; how much education and of what type is necessary. Some very promising work has been undertaken by FAO and by UNESCO.

FAO already has announced in its answer to the Proposals for Action for the Development Decade[9] that it would "undertake more accurate projections of world demands for various agricultural products." It is now engaged in the construction of a World Food Plan which will be of considerable importance to the various policy measures needed in this field. The Plan will specify, by country, the quantities of a number of different foodstuffs to be produced in the future. Needless to say, an enormous amount of analysis is needed to estimate such a coherent set of figures.

UNESCO, in the same document,[10] stated that its outlay on education planning, amounting to 3 million dollars in 1963/64, "will need to be doubled in 1965/66 and maintained at the higher level throughout the Decade." The amounts to be spent on projects of primary and secondary education (10.5 million dollars) in 1963-64 should be doubled by 1970. In the field of higher education UNESCO pioneered in its Addis Ababa 1980 Plan for Africa. In the Tananarive Conference of 1962, these figures were checked against the needs of the economies for various types of qualified manpower. In addition, proposals were formulated concerning the execution of the Plan, including proposals on the assistance from abroad.

In recent reports and courses ILO emphasized the need for the planning of employment alongside with production, because of the particularly important human and social aspects involved. Similarly, UNICEF requested specific attention, with planners, for the needs of children.[11] Since children, by the nature of things, are growing up, in the majority of cases, in large and hence poor families, they are, on the average, worse off than adults. Medical research has

271

shown that the harm done by undernourishment in the preschool years is irreversible; hence particular efforts must be made in order to improve the situation of young children in large families. On this point, general planning does not automatically further the interests of the young generation as a whole.

International planning has not been explicitly furthered by the World Bank (IBRD), but some important indirect contributions have been made by this agency. A detailed inquiry into the debt position of developing countries[12] has shown the untenable position of a number of them and the need for easier terms of financial assistance. This inquiry added up all the repayment obligations of a number of developing countries originating from loans already concluded. In a complete picture of financial flows between countries these items must also occur.

Suggestions for the Future Development of International Economic Planning

A more active role of the United Nations. Most United Nations activities have so far been hampered by the weak construction of that organization, itself a consequence of the strong preference for national autonomy. Only slowly is the awareness of the tremendous dangers of this preference penetrating into the minds of some of the leading politicians. Economists and economic policy-makers can and therefore should contribute to the education of general politicians by pointing out that a number of very pressing economic problems can be solved only if portions of national autonomy are handed over to supranational authorities. One way of convincing part of the political world at least of this truth is to show by concrete policy proposals what can be gained by such a procedure. The formulation of policy proposals is the planner's job. International economic planning thus may make a contribution, if only a very modest one, to the strengthening of the world order.

Both theoretical analysis and experience in limited areas show that a good job in international planning can be done only by an international secretariat taking initiatives itself instead of waiting for the initiatives of member governments. Fortunately, the way has finally been paved for intensified activity of the U.N. Secretariat by ECOSOC Resolution 1079 (XXXIX), adopted on 28 July 1965 in the 1392nd plenary session, requesting the Secretary-General of the U.N., the regional economic commissions, and the specialized agencies "to . . . *intensify their activities with respect to economic planning*. . . ." What is needed here has been expressed particularly well by the Government of the Polish People's Republic in its reply to the Proposals for Action during the Development Decade, where it says:

The multiplicity of forms and channels of United Nations activity makes it necessary to have active and effective centres of direction, which would fulfil two basic functions:

(1) to act as *policy-making organs* i.e. to prepare the guide-lines for the basic avenues of activity of the various United Nations bodies;
(2) to act as co-ordinating centres. . . .

The Government of the Polish People's Republic considers that these centres should be the General Assembly and the Economic and Social Council. . . .[13]

Also the reply of the Government of the U.S.S.R. emphasizes the need for intensified international planning—although in essence for the developing countries—and specifies some of the figures to be estimated.[14]

The Secretary-General of the U.N. himself states that "co-ordination becomes absolutely essential if a purposive strategy is to be inserted into the *activities of the international community* in order to hasten growth, revise flows of trade and secure higher transfers of capital.[15] Such simple statements almost seem commonplace, but their importance is in the official recognition that national autonomy, as the cornerstone of international politics, simply does not work and must be given up if the economic interests of the world's population are to be served in an efficient way.

I submit that it is the economist's task to guide politicians in the elaboration of the proper international policies and their preparation, that is international economic planning. I propose to discuss what such planning should consist in and how the implementation of some of the policies the world is in need of may be viewed.

The division of labor among agencies. An international economic plan, even if only indicative—that is, without a legal obligation for governments to carry it out—can be constructed only by a co-operation of the various agencies of the United Nations. In order that this co-operation be as fruitful as possible a logical division of labor must be adhered to. A logical *division of labor* must be based on an understanding of the interconnections between the fields these agencies are specialized in. In terms of the concepts of economic policy some of the specialized agencies represent sectors of economic life,

273

while others represent particular means of policy and still others social groups. This implies that the roles they may have to play are of a different character; this does not seem to be clearly recognized and implies some danger of duplication on the one hand and of lacunae on the other hand. To illustrate our point, FAO clearly represents a (very important) sector, agriculture. To some extent UNESCO and WHO also do. This may of course also be maintained with regard to the World Bank and IMF, but in their character the fact of representing some particular means of economic policy is more important. UNICEF and ILO, on the contrary, represent social groups.

In order to arrive at a logical scheme of co-operation among these agencies as well as with the Secretariat and the Regional Commissions, we must have in mind a method of planning. Although there are some competing methods, I venture to submit that the most useful and most usual method consists in a stepwise process, or a process of planning in stages. This is characterized by a macro phase, entrusted to the central planning body, followed by refinements, often in at least two further stages or phases; we shall call them the middle and the micro phase. The refinements may bear on a subdivision into sectors, into geographical areas, and with regard to the introduction of more means than the main means. The method is generally known in many sciences as the one of successive approximations. Its particular form in planning activities is still a matter of discussion among technicians. Apart from the question of its efficiency from a purely scientific point of view—which is a matter for debate—it has the advantage of facilitating the organization of the work and the communication with politicians.

As for the sectors, the agencies dealing with them can do their planning only if some general issues have been (provisionally) decided upon. The demand for food, to give one example, can be determined only after the general rate of growth of incomes has been chosen. To be sure, the further exploration of supply conditions may, later on, show that the demand cannot be satisfied and that perhaps the general rate of growth should then be revised. Alternatively—and this may well constitute one of our biggest problems of the near future—a particular effort may have to be made to increase the supply of food. Such revisions have to be part of the scheme and represent additional stages or steps, since they necessitate a repetition of the preceding phases.

With regard to the geographical subdivision, these estimates—

for example, the rates of growth for individual countries—can also be fixed only after the general rate of growth for the world as a whole has been (provisionally) chosen: most countries' development depends on the growth of the world market.

Again, the extent to which some of the main means (and certainly the minor means) must be used can be estimated only after the main central choices have been made. In both cases (geographical differentiation and application of means) these refinements may supply a feedback to the first provisional choice of the main parameter: the general rate of growth.

All this points to the necessity for the central planning agency to start operations. We will therefore first elaborate on that agency's task, that is, the task of the U.N. Economic Projections and Programming Center. Afterwards we shall return to the scheme of co-operation with "lower levels."

The choice of variables and geographical units. Any planning operation must start with a *choice of the "variables"* (or phenomena) to be included in its operations. For reasons of clarity and consistency such a choice is more important than its somewhat formal nature may suggest. In economic planning, it is customary to start out with a macro-economic approach, meaning that no sectors are distinguished, and the usual variables are more or less the ones already chosen in the Center's models: national income, consumption, investment, imports, exports with a possible extension to public expenditure and money in circulation. Savings are already implicit in the list, since these are equal to national income minus consumption and the deficit on current account on the balance of payments, the latter being equal to imports minus exports if properly defined. There may be scope for some more financial variables to be included, such as external debt.

A first crude subdivision into some main sectors may also be very useful; particularly a subdivision into agriculture and all other sectors, but also a distinction between national and international sectors. By a national sector we mean a sector whose products cannot be imported or exported because of prohibitive transportation costs.

Examples of such "national" or "domestic" sectors are construction, services of many kinds (retail, wholesale trade, personal services, inland transportation, government services, education), and electricity. As soon as we leave the purely economic realm and introduce social variables, employment and a number of education variables (numbers of secondary-school pupils and university students and of their teachers) are the first to be added. We may also add health services, housing, and community development. There is considerable virtue in not pushing the list too far, however, at least not in the macro phase which must be the starting point.

Contrary to what is usual at the national level, an attempt at international economic planning must from the start operate with some *geographical subdivision.* The least that can be done is exactly what the Center did, namely to distinguish between "West," "East," and "South." But a somewhat more ambitious subdivision seems indicated, for instance, the one introduced by E. S. Kirschen,[16] where each of the three main areas are subdivided, leading to a total of twelve areas.

Choice of provisional targets. Clearly a very important element in any international plan is the set of main *targets* of development policy chosen: probably all conclusions about the means to be used depend on these targets. It is precisely here that initiatives taken by the Secretariat can be of paramount importance. The disappointing results of the first few years of the Development Decade are partly due to the conflicting short-term interests of, for instance, donor and recipient countries of financial and technical assistance. National governments of rich countries cannot sufficiently back the world's interest against the short-term pressure of their own citizens, simply because they are national governments, in political competition with other groups. There is no institution except the United Nations, which can support the world interest, which coincides with the long-term interests of all nations. A subtle mixture of tact and courage must be applied to arrive at the formulation of some of the main goals for international development. I think the aims accepted by the Assembly so far are unsatisfactory and the Secretariat should suggest somewhat more ambitious aims. The results of the planning exercise will be of some help to convince an increasing number of governments that more must be done. To fix the ideas, I submit that an average rate of growth of the developed world's total real income of 4 per cent and of the developing world's total real income of 7 per cent is what should be chosen, with alternatives on the somewhat more conservative side,[17] for those not yet convinced of the necessity of the figures just quoted.

I know that many of my colleagues will consider the 7 per cent figure too ambitious. In order to avoid repetition I will add to the arguments given elsewhere only that all projections for 1980 will show in what an impossible situation we shall be if we are less ambitious and that the American and Pakistani experts responsible for Pakistan's Third Five Year Plan finish up with a similar figure. I also want to remind my readers of the necessity of a task-setting element (to all concerned) in any plan of this type: that is, going beyond what would be attained without any change in policies or efforts. This applies to business, government, and private households alike and finds widespread application in business as well as in the Communist countries.

Methodology to be used. There can be no question of dealing in detail with the *method of planning* in an essay of this kind. There is a library at our disposal on this subject. I intend only to highlight a few features which are not yet generally applied and yet seem to be useful for the task considered. Whenever a geographical sub-division appears as a main characteristic of some plan we must bring into the picture the role of transportation and communication costs. In order not to make the subject unmanageable, however, this element must be brought in in a highly simplified form. I believe the key is to be found in the distinction between international, national, and local sectors,[18] the first two already mentioned before and the third defined in a similar way as sectors in which the products cannot be imported or exported even by cities. The concepts are particularly helpful since two rather different principles should be used for planning international as distinct from the other two types of sectors. National and local sectors must grow in line with national and local demand, since there is no other way of obtaining the goods concerned than to produce them in the nation or even in the city where they are needed. International sectors, however, should be chosen so as to maximize each country's and thereby the world's income, that is, on the basis of their competitive power. To be sure this power should be estimated for a future period in which the children's diseases of the learning process have been overcome. It is a common experience that most enterprises in the beginning of their life have to go through a process of learning: to learn from errors, to integrate their activity in order to reach normal efficiency.

World planning as advocated here will supply an element of great importance, not present in the potentialities of national planning. The division of labor between the various parts of the world will be studied as a coherent problem for the world as a whole, while an individual nation can take into account only part of the evidence. Even so it remains a very difficult task on which a few more remarks will be made below.

Completing our present subject, we must at least briefly sketch the successive steps or stages mentioned above. After a first consistent set of macro figures for each of the areas considered has been estimated, the exchange of ideas with specialized agencies and regional commissions must be solicited, leading to both refinements (such as sector figures) and revisions of the macro-economic figures.

Subsequently further subdivisions, according both to sectors and to geographical areas, will be possible and necessary. Again the national and local sectors will be planned on the basis of the demand for their products and the international ones on the basis of competitive power; the latter subject will be discussed hereafter.

The scientific methods to be applied in these subsequent phases of planning are in continual development and hence far from being an established piece of science. Even so, reasonably good techniques are available.

Studies on the optimum division of labor. A substantial portion of an international economic planning effort should be devoted to the optimum division of labor between the continents and countries of the world. Studies on this subject must try to provide guidelines for governments and industrialists regarding the best specialization for each part of the world. The relevance of the subject appears from the numerous discussions about what industries to start in developing countries, what to do with the industries in the developed countries they compete with, and so on. The examples of agriculture and textiles may be used to illustrate the relevance of the subject. So far choices of this type were made by individual firms, on the basis of price-cost comparisons, in a process of competition with a number of artificial obstacles. While classical economists would have argued that this is the self-regulatory capacity of the free-enterprise system, modern economists and businessmen have learned to recognize some important imperfections in this capacity. Long gestation periods, the durability of capital goods, the effects of pressure groups on trade policies, external effects, and economies of scale all tend to make the free-competition regulation less reliable. It should at least be supplemented by scientific information and in some respects also by deliberate government policies. Information by itself can already be useful, and nobody can reasonably oppose its collection. To what extent deviations from free enterprise are needed is a more controversial question, but it can be separated from the pure information aspect. We shall discuss both in succession.

To begin with, the basic factors must be summed up which determine the optimum division of labor. Generally speaking the optimum can be defined as the state in which the total production the world needs is produced as cheaply as possible while using as many of the productive forces as possible. The most important data of the problem are the distribution of the world's natural resources, mainly soil characteristics, climate, and mineral deposits; the distribution of capital, human qualifications, and their mobility, and the costs of transportation of products. Some general principles which will influence the solution are well known from established theory of international trade. They recommend that countries well endowed with capital should specialize in capital-intensive products; countries good at research, in research-intensive goods; countries with abundance of labor, on labor-intensive goods; and countries with specific national resources, on the corresponding products. But these principles must be combined with a few additional ones; where transportation costs are considerable, they should be taken into account in order to minimize total costs; this may imply that sometimes capital-intensive goods (say fertilizer) must nevertheless be produced in capital-poor countries or labor-intensive services in countries with a labor shortage. Also, economies of scale make it desirable to limit the number of plants of some industries, so as to attain their optimum size. Finally, external effects may make a complex of industries as a whole competitive if only we make sure that they are all created in a single big city or a single region. This is typically true for industries where transportation costs are not too important, permitting an almost arbitrary choice of the spot, if only the whole complex is taken together. This latter device is particularly important if the optimum is also defined as implying an equitable distribution of new activities over various countries, whatever the precise meaning of it may be.

If we think of an optimum we must be aware of the possibility that in a somewhat more remote future production costs of young countries may be favorably influenced by a learning process and that training is an essential element of the process of development. That is, we must base ourselves on figures of estimated future costs rather than observed costs in the initial period of industrialization. Fortunately some general tendencies have been discovered which seem to govern the reduction of costs in the "infant industry" period.

The problem as a whole is so complicated that its solution can be found only approximately, in successive steps, and its implementation never by central planning alone. But already an orderly presentation of the relevant statistical and other material, the construction of partial solutions and tentative combinations of such solutions can be revealing. Also the preparation of planning schemes, containing the various elements enumerated, if only working initially with a small number of sectors and regions, will be of considerable help. The type of statistical data which can be collected on a much larger scale than has so far been the case may be illustrated by mentioning capital-output ratios (that is, the ratio between capital of an industry and its net production value), transportation costs per unit of product and distance, and optimum size of enterprises for a considerable number of industries. The latter indicates the size of an enterprise at which costs of production are at a minimum. This optimum size varies greatly among industries; it is less than one hundred workers in the clothing industry and a few thousands in steel making.

The planning procedure; co-operation with "lower levels." International economic planning requires not only a methodological effort, but also an organizational effort, or, as I will say, the creation of a *procedure*. By this I mean a succession of contacts between the agencies involved, according to a timetable, which must satisfy the conditions of (1) sufficient speed, (2) using all relevant information, and (3) democracy, that is the possibility of the most important lower levels to be heard and to have due influence on the result of the whole exercise. Some features of the procedure follow already from the scientific method of planning, set out previously. The Center should start by the preparation of a macro-economic set of target figures for the main variables and then submit these to the specialized agencies as well as to the regional commissions for comment. The latter may want to consult their member governments. After a certain lapse of time these agencies will have to send their reactions to the Center. If all member governments do not answer on time, their figures will be estimated by the regional commission. During the further elaboration, for instance according to sectors, of the plan, consultations of a similar character with sector representatives may be considered, if such representatives exist. The same may apply to the subdivision according to social categories; at a certain stage, for instance, representatives of trade unions should be consulted.

From these few indications the difficulties to be encountered will have become clear enough. These will force the Center to start out with a simpler procedure than the one ultimately to be attempted and to develop it gradually. In all probability unexpected problems will also show up and thus may influence the procedure.

An Economic Policy Program for the United Nations

An annual discussion in ECOSOC. For the economist and the economic policy-maker interested in reinforcing the international order it is striking that—as we have already observed—the United Nations Charter is very general and vague about the implementation of the economic policy aims it sets in Article 55. Any real government must be more specific about its economic policy; if eventually some elements of world government have to be created—and economic objectives are the first for which this may be possible—more specific indications about the policies to be conducted must be laid down in the members' obligations. It will, however, be better first to gain some experience with stronger forms of co-operation than exist so far, without formal obligations.

A logical beginning seems to be to change the character of the annual discussions in ECOSOC from a backward-looking to a forward-looking one. This implies, as a first step, the definition of world goals for economic policy and the recommendation, if not acceptance, of the quantitative extent of the necessary efforts. The international plan discussed in the previous section will be the ideal basis for such recommendations. Subsequently, the example of the OEEC "exams" could be taken over, if only for the main blocks of countries, in order to check actual performance with goals set by the plan. There have been similar exercises already in ECAFE and the Alliance for Progress, so we may hope that a beginning can be made.

To be sure the preparation of the debate as well as the contributions themselves will require a considerable amount of diplomacy and tact. Much will depend on the objectivity of the contributions and the skill of the chairman to channel the exchange of ideas. It should be seen, especially by the representatives of the United States and of the Soviet Union, as a real contribution to better understanding and as a form of coexistence. This does not mean that no clear differences of opinion should be expressed—on the contrary. But the level of the debate should be up to today's scientific standards.

The impact on national plans and policies. It stands to reason that the ultimate aim of the debate and the recommendations consists in possible *adaptations of national plans and policies* to the desires of the ECOSOC meeting as a whole. Among the major elements of such adaptations will be the amounts made available for foreign aid and technical assistance and changes in commercial policies. We shall discuss these at greater length in what follows.

There may also be less direct and slower adaptations in the form of a changed orientation of new investments. These may be led into the channels suggested by the study of the optimal division of labor discussed before. Other influences which may be exerted should be in the field of financial and monetary policies of the member countries in order to avoid serious dislocations: either inflationary or deflationary developments.

The impact of a United Nations plan on national policies will of course be much stronger as soon as the United Nations agencies themselves are endowed with more financial means to participate in a real world economic policy. It is a natural principle that the execution of a policy requires power, in this case economic power. Within any national economy the main policy-makers do have some power, and if the world interest is to be respected in the future it will be necessary that the institutions responsible for that world interest are endowed with more (economic) power. Hence the importance of a regular budget for development projects to be financed through taxes collected by the United Nations Secretariat. This would give the Secretariat a direct means of influencing the economic policies of member states in order to co-ordinate the development of these nations. Duplication may be avoided, or a proper choice of industries supported.

Financial policies and technical assistance. Since investments in material goods and human beings are the two primary activities needed for development, an international development policy must first of all show up in the realms of *financial policies* and of *technical assistance.* We have already seen that the capital transfers so far carried out are falling short of the needs of the developing world. One of the main targets of a more forceful United Nations activity should therefore be directed at convincing the developed countries to raise their contributions. A well-designed world plan may be one of the means to convince public opinion in these countries.

The concrete forms of financial transfers can be many and must at the same time be adapted to other emergencies, above all the difficult debt position of many developing countries. This means that IDA loans at a nominal rate and with long amortization periods must become relatively more important. One wonders whether or not a current flow of expenditure, financed from international taxes and without even the obligation of repayment, should also be added to the means. Such a means may be seen as the beginning of a new institution needed in a stronger world order, namely, a World Treasury. No authority can develop strength unless it has important financial means at its disposal. Against all political arguments raised against such an institution the economist has to point out the technical necessity, for a really efficient development policy, of such a financial center for the financing, out of current means, of development expenditures of some types.

The struggle within the Common Market around precisely this subject illustrates its importance. At the same time this struggle teaches us that it will take some time before an institution of this kind will be accepted. Not much time is given us, however, to try to solve our problems. In an attempt to push politicians in the right direction, the economist must produce his autonomous technical arguments in favor of the construction proposed.

Trade and investment policies. In this brief sketch of the policies needed to carry out an international development plan, we will consider jointly *trade and investment policies.* The reason for this joint treatment is the essential characteristic of the developing world that many of its national units are small and that all of them are hindered by a number of trade impediments. For considerable portions of the world a combination of trade and investment policies may be a good solution to overcome these difficulties. The means may be the "partial customs union with investment program." This phrase stands for an agreement between a number of neighboring countries to establish a limited number of large-scale factories, equitably distributed over the countries, and to admit mutually the products of these factories in their economies, without trade impediments. Thus, such a group of countries may reap the benefits of mass production without having to go through the difficult process of negotiating a complete customs union.

Of course this proposal does not exhaust the possibilities in the field of trade policies. In addition it will be necessary to reduce import duties on or to enlarge quotas on a number of industrial products which some of the large developing countries are able to supply for export.

Planning can play a particularly useful role when it comes to establishing large factories in such sectors as heavy chemicals and metallurgy. Here a real danger of waste exists if completely free private decisions are taken without an international co-ordination.

The World Food Program. As a consequence of both the population explosion and the slow reaction of farmers to new forms of production, a particularly pressing problem develops with regard to the supply of staple foods to large parts of the developing world. Far from being superfluous, the abundant production of food which seems to constitute a problem in the developed Western countries will be highly needed in the coming decade to avoid famine in several developing countries. Several ways of solving this problem have been proposed; a successful program already in operation is the *World Food Program,* sponsored by FAO. Surplus food is being used, together with a few other surpluses (for instance, shipping facilities) and with money, to carry out development projects implying an increased use of otherwise unemployed labor, with the corresponding higher need for food. In its first three years, an amount of 100 million dollars was the target of spending, which was almost reached, and at present almost a trebling of the target (275 million) has been favorably received by the donor countries, of which the United States is of course by far the biggest. There will be scope for a further quick development as time progresses.

Among the other projects suggested, those of Professor Fritz Baade[19] stand out. These too deserve serious consideration; one of their features is that it may be cheaper to supply the developing countries with fertilizer. One does not exclude the other, of course; and it is an important subject for further planning to find out which combination may be the optimal one.

In *conclusion* we may briefly summarize our main argument. At this moment, the development policies of the various national governments are much less co-ordinated than is desirable from the point of view of all concerned: both poor and rich countries. The process of development must be speeded up. New industries should be chosen in order to meet the increased demand for the various types of products to be expected from increased incomes and to equip each country with the industries that fit its special capabilities. Education and training, financial and commercial policies, and many specific measures should all be geared to this process. For this whole complex of activities to run smoothly a fair degree of world and continental planning will be needed. Some useful beginnings have been made, but more can be done, keeping in mind the appropriate division of tasks between all agencies involved. Such an intensified action may make a sizable contribution to the gradual establishment of a world order, at least in matters of economic policy.

REFERENCES

1. "The United Nations Development Decade at Mid Point, An Appraisal by the Secretary-General of the United Nations," E/4071, p. 4.

2. Some of these will be discussed below; here we may mention the studies made by the Center for Industrial Development ("A Study of Industrial Growth," New York 1963) and numerous documents for the United Nations Conference on Trade and Development (UNCTAD), 1964.

3. Other recent work done by the U.N. Secretariat which may be considered a preparation for planning are the World Economic Surveys of 1962 I and 1963 I entitled, respectively, "The Developing countries in world trade" and "Trade and development: Trends, Needs and Policies."

4. New York 1965, Sales No. 65 II.C.1.

5. *Ibid.*, pp. 21 and 22.

6. New York 1964, Sales No. 64 II.C.2.

7. Cf. United Nations, "Evaluation of Projects in Centrally Planned Economies," Industrialization and Productivity No. 8, 1964, p. 7.

8. "E.E.C. Commission: Prospects for the Economic Development in EEC from 1960 to 1970," Brussels 1962.

9. Replies from Specialized Agencies, et cetera, E/3613/Add. 1, 22 May 1962, p. 26.

10. *Ibid.*, p. 30.

11. UNICEF, "Planning for the Needs of Children in Developing Countries," New York 1965.

12. Cf. IBRD, "Economic Growth and External Debt—a Statistical Presentation," UNCTAD, E/Conf. 46/40, Geneva 1964.

13. E/3613/Add. 2, p. 47 (italics added).

14. *Ibid.*, p. 56.

15. "The United Nations Development Decade at Mid Point, An Appraisal by the Secretary-General of the United Nations," E/4071, p. 9 (italics added).

16. E. S. Kirschen, "Vers un modèle prévisionnel mégisto-économique," Cahiers Economiques de Bruxelles, 1962, No. 16, p. 471.

17. Cf. J. Tinbergen, *Lessons from the Past* (Amsterdam, 1963).

18. Cf. H. C. Bos, *Spatial Dispersion of Economic Activity* (Rotterdam, 1965).

19. F. Baade, . . . *Denn sie sollen satt werden* (Oldenburg-Hamburg, 1964).

JEAN FOURASTIÉ

Remarks on Conditions of World Order

THE TOPIC proposed by the American Academy of Arts and Sciences is both difficult and complex. It is impossible to attempt a total coverage of such an immense subject; all that can be done is to contribute a few bricks to an edifice that will be built over centuries to come. Or, more precisely, it is possible to reconnoiter the ground on which it may be constructed; to envisage the prerequisite work necessary to the gathering of information and to the elaboration of a scientific theory that will enable mankind to establish progressively the psychological, economic, social, political, and constitutional conditions likely to reduce excesses of violence.

For this reason, the present article will be limited to some relatively disparate and disconnected remarks that crossed my mind while following the discussions at the Villa Serbelloni. These remarks do not in any way contradict the contributions of my colleagues in this issue of *Dædalus*. My intention is neither to synthesize nor to criticize, but only to add further considerations to those that have been expressed.

The conviction I wish to impart to the reader immediately is that to deal with this subject in the context of the present moment alone, with the intention of offering radical solutions susceptible of immediate adoption, would be to run the risk of certain failure. Disorder and violence have been common to mankind for so many millennia that they form a part of our psychological foundations; they may indeed represent the extension into human thought and action of biological tensions organically linked to the evolution of life. Just as I believe that through information, conscience, and will—through the spirit of experimental science—man can progressively discipline his impulsive reflexes, regulate these, and thereby reduce savage and mortal conflicts, so I believe that this will come about only with the patient accumulation of a knowledge that remains virtually nonexistent. With this knowledge must come the slow acquisition of psycho-social reflexes and ideals presently lacking or so feeble as to have no great importance in governing our conduct.

The reader should not be surprised, therefore, to find in this essay the most general kinds of considerations together with others which are anecdotal and empirical. In the near-total darkness I find myself in, my reference points are at once the deepest attributes of life and humanity and the most elementary practical procedures useful for my purpose. The conditions of world order lie in two domains: knowledge and action.

Logically, knowledge ought to precede action. In fact, man acts before knowing. What makes this situation the more tragic is that there is presently no real alternative to this. For our knowledge of the realities more indispensable to our individual and collective life remains derisory. Notably, insofar as world order is concerned, political science spells out only partial and controversial judgments; even those few general principles on which there is wide agreement are in need of revision. The purpose of the first section of this essay will be to examine the facts we need to *know* and the theories which ought to receive priority in study and debate. The second section will deal with political *action*. It will recommend steps likely to reduce disorder and to favor an evolution toward order.

I

To outline a few directions for research, I begin with two facts about which there would be no disagreement; namely, that world order depends on complex realities, and that, among them, the personality and character of the political leaders are of the greatest importance. There is no violence without men of violence, or at least, without a leader who resorts to, or threatens to resort to, violence; conversely, as soon as men of violence appear, even if other factors favoring violence are negligible, order is threatened. We must, clearly, accord special attention to the personality of leaders in considering the causes of disorder. Among the questions that require study are the following: why do political leaders so often commit errors in their assessment of the facts? Why do they overestimate their objectives—that is, why do they perceive and depict them as more attractive and felicitous than they in fact are? Why do they underestimate the means—that is, the methods, techniques, and sacrifices that must be learned and accepted in order to attain the desired goals?

I would begin with two classic texts, both relating to the Russian Revolution; Lenin, in *State and Revolution,* wrote:

Overthrow the capitalists, crush with the iron hand of the armed workers the resistance of those exploiters, break the bureaucratic machine of the modern state—and you have before you a mechanism of the highest technical equipment, freed of "parasites," capable of being set into motion by the united workers themselves who hire their own technicians, managers, bookkeepers, and pay them all, as, indeed every "state" official, with the usual workers' wage. Here is a concrete, practicable task, immediately realisable in relation to all trusts, a task that frees the workers of exploitation and makes use of the experience (especially in the realm of the construction of the state) which the Commune began to reveal in practice.[1]

Capitalist culture has *created* large-scale productions, factories, railways, the postal service, telephones, etc. and *on this basis* the great majority of functions of the old "state power" have become so simplified and can be reduced to such simple operations of registration, filing and checking that they will be quite within the reach of every literate person, and it will be possible to perform them for "workingmen's wages," which circumstance can (and must) strip those functions of every shadow of privilege, of every appearance of "official grandeur."[2]

With such *economic* prerequisites it is perfectly possible, immediately, within twenty-four hours after the overthrow of the capitalists and bureaucrats, to replace them, in the control of production and distribution, in the business of the *control* of labor and products, by the armed workers, by the whole people in arms.[3]

This characteristic text may be likened to many others, for instance the classic text, *ABC of Communism* by N. Bucharin and E. Preobraschensky, published in 1920.

. . . But now someone will ask: "How can such a great organization be kept in being without guidance? Who will work out the common economic plan? Who will distribute labor-power? Who will reckon the social income and expenditure? In short, who will supervise the whole system?"

It is not difficult to answer these questions. The principal work of administering will be done in various counting-houses and statistical bureaus. From these places the whole field of production will be surveyed, and the quantity of goods required will be ascertained. It will also be learned where the number of workers should be increased and where decreased, and how long their working day should be. All will be familiar with the idea of common work from their childhood, and will realize that this work is necessary. They will understand that the conditions of life will be easier when everything is conducted on a well-thought-out plan, and will therefore work according to the regulations of these bureaus. There will be no necessity for having Ministers for special departments, and no need for policemen, prisons, laws, etc. As in an orchestra all the performers take their cue from the conductor, so all members of society will read the instructions of the bureaus and arrange their work accordingly. The State will exist no longer. There will be no group or class standing above all other classes. In the bureaus there will be one set of workers today, and another set tomorrow. Bureaucracy—government by permanent officials—will disappear. The State will die out.[4]

Such errors in the assessment of reality involve millions of men, entire peoples, in paths that it takes many decades to see as mistaken, ineffective, or at least less effective than other possible solutions. A mistaken assessment of the goals to strive for and a minimization of the upheavals necessary to attain them may play an enormous role in international war and in civil war, and in the various political disturbances ranging from the *putsch* to the general strike to the ministerial crisis. Such errors are particular instances of man's habitual misapprehension of reality.

Sociologists and psychologists must explain this revulsion of thought toward tangible reality—a revulsion that is being overcome only very slowly. They will find great assistance in the works of men like Edgar Allan Poe, Baudelaire, Gerard de Nerval, Stendahl, and Marcel Proust.

The human brain, the human mind, transposes reality: instead of perceiving it and describing it, the mind deforms and *idealizes* it. The mind uses reality only as food for the imagination—an "illusion to describe," to adopt Flaubert's formula. This transposition, this deformation of reality, is a law of the natural thought process (that is, thinking that is not educated and trained in the experimental method). "Our encounter with things," Proust writes, provokes within us "an inevitable deception"; only dreams satisfy us, since dream is *the reality of thought,* a reality "much more alive than the other" and tending perpetually "to take on new forms in us." This "appearance made up of imaginings and of desires . . . brings us infinitely more pleasure than [external reality] which bores and disappoints us; [it] *is a principle of action that always sets* the traveler in motion"[5]—whether this traveler be Gerard de Nerval, Proust, Lenin, Napoleon, Caesar, or Alexander the Great.

It is clear that the preceding considerations would have scant importance were it to be discovered that today's political leaders belonged to the minority (infinitesimal) of men trained in the spirit of experimental science, who found it not only their duty but also their pleasure to inquire into and to submit to reality. The violent leader with whom we are concerned is by definition a man of imagination and passion. Chateaubriand suggests that such men are of the same race as poets: speaking of Lucien Bonaparte's love of Madame Récamier, he says: "For an even-tempered man, all this is a little ridiculous; the Bonapartes lived by theater, novels, and poems; is Napoleon's life itself anything but a poem?"[6] These popular leaders, these conquerors and dominators desire to shape peoples as poets shape a verb. They dream their life and destiny, and desire to impose this dream on men and things. If they are leaders, if they possess power or control power, then they have already succeeded. Their very success encourages them in their designs; the storms that they have already stirred up and used, force them into others, and feed their desires. They recognize the real historical effectiveness of arbitrary will; they exalt their valor and the power of their own will. They divide territory as it pleases them, impose their laws, raise or reduce men.

States are always controlled by tight minorities, especially where disorder and violence are involved. These minorities are composed of men of passion who love to play. "But who does not perceive," writes Alain, "the power that collective passion, where all the angers of ambition, illness, age, are expressed too well, *with approval and glory?* Who does not also realize how imitation and modesty draw in the best of the youth, and how precocious passions draw out the worst still more?"[7]

With a man of violence, no other cause for violence is needed; nonetheless, there are many pretexts. For a peaceful man, there is no situation that cannot be resolved by an orderly evolution. Can one imagine what Jean Monnet or Konrad Adenauer might have done if he had come to power instead of Hitler, in 1933 in Germany? The man of peace wages peace as the man of violence wages war. On the other hand, with so powerful an instrument in his hands and such a docile population, any glib politician can bring on great catastrophies.

It does not follow that personality alone is important; demographic, social, and economic conditions favor the advent to power of certain types of men, and often incite these men either to orderly solutions, or to disorder and violence. In the end, there are situations that leave no other way out but revolt. These facts show the necessity of a scientific study of endurable and unendurable conditions for both individuals and groups; of ways that might be found to get out of unendurable situations; of the boundaries between the endurable and the intolerable; and thus, of the definition of order, disorder, violence, and revolt. I shall not go further into these immense and difficult problems here;[8] I should like only to inquire whether cultural diversity constitutes an intolerable condition, which is, therefore, itself conducive to disorder.

It does not appear certain that cultural differences *in and of themselves* pose a threat to international stability. Numerous historical examples prove the possibility of long coexistence (in the same city or state) of profoundly diverse and even contradictory cultural communities—such as Jews, Muslims, and Christians. The Roman Empire cannot be considered to have been a culturally homogeneous society. Conversely, there are numerous examples of culturally homogeneous populations having been torn by war and violence. I should tend to think therefore that the diversity of cultures and, even more generally, the diversity of situations and even behavior are not *in and of themselves* a cause of instability. It seems to me that instability has other roots.

Essentially, instability arises either from the refusal to prolong indefinitely an existing diversity or from the refusal to prolong indefinitely an existing homogeneity. In the first case, instability does not arise *because* of the existence of diversity, but because at least one of the various groups *rejects* diversity. The forms of this rejection may be grouped under three headings: (a) The desire to destroy, annihilate, eliminate the other, in order to remain more fully oneself. (b) The inverse desire to become the other, to be assimilated to him, to possess what he possesses. (c) The rejection of the present homogeneity, with the intention of arriving at a different situation which is deemed better. This type of refusal seems to dominate today in that nearly all the nations of the world hold economic progress as their chief goal. In such a process, the defect of homogeneity seems to be of only secondary importance, since, if the lesser-developed nations hold as their goal to be like the more-developed nations, the latter do not in the least consider that they have arrived at their ultimate goal, and on the contrary make great efforts toward further progress. The crucial element for our subject is not the existence of the desire to change, for this change is considered by all to be legitimate, normal, and ineluctable. The crucial element consists in the means envisaged to effect progress.

It is only here, but *precisely* here, that factors of disorder appear most strongly. An important number of nations believe that, or behave as if, violence alone could assure their progress; the greater number of the developed nations act as if violence is useless and detrimental.

If the attitude of violently revisionist countries can be explained by the thousands of years of human history, and especially by the facts relating to the character of revolutionary leaders indicated above, the attitude of the "peace-loving" states—in any opinion, the only scientifically correct one—seems to be dictated solely by the selfishness of the possessor. Indeed, it must not be forgotten that, until a date recent enough to be part of the life history of many alive today, Western states regularly resorted to violence. Twice in thirty years, Germany behaved as if war was the best means, or at least the inevitable means, for a great nation to compel a recognition of the rights it claimed. To be sure, these efforts failed. But if violence is condemned only because it fails, it is clear that there will always be individuals or peoples willing to take the risk that it will succeed. The recourse to violence will always be used as long as it is not demonstrated that there exist peaceful means for arriving at the desired objectives more effectively and with less risk.

Just as economic crises played a positive role in the evolution of economic structures—it has been taken over by other mechanisms since men have learned how to control these recessions—so we must recognize the *function of evolution* played by wars, disorders, and the threat of these. We must demonstrate to nations and peoples that they can obtain effectively without violence or violent claims as much as and more than through war.

It is of great importance that, in today's world, the objectives of states and peoples are open and virtually the same: that is, the improvement of the standard of living and the style of life of citizens in an industrial society. The main problem of world order is thus to identify and make known the best practical means to arrive at these objectives. Since these objectives are essentially economic, it is essential to identify the means to economic progress.

These have not been clearly discerned today either in developed or undeveloped nations. The store of general ideas on economic and social questions remains pre-scientific. They are common to the cultures both of Western countries and of the underdeveloped nations; they are also characteristic of all the dominant philosophies and varieties of Marxism, socialism, and capitalism. These general ideas consist in, first, nonexperimental conceptions of *Justice;* second, nonexperimental conceptions of *Efficacy.*

The mind of present-day man encounters a practically insurmountable difficulty in distinguishing the just from the possible; it encounters very great difficulty, too, in the concurrent problem of establishing the means and the time required to make the possible a reality. Hence, what is felt to be just is claimed to be immediately realizable, without regard to actual practical possibilities. When men today agree to think about *means,* they fall victim to grave confusions concerning *efficacy* and *power.* Schematically, *efficacy* is conceived to be the result not of an action, a technique, but of a *power;* and that power is conceived to be the result not of science, knowledge, and learning, but of a *situation,* the ownership of material or even monetary resources. It follows that the means to progress will be sought not in doing and in know-how, but in the global and instantaneous conquest of political power, ownership of the *situation.* An analysis of the dominant ideas of "progressive" ideologies and the political ideas of leftist political parties ought to be a fundamental element in the study of national and international instability.

To be sure, a correct knowledge of the process of economic and social progress has been set forth,[9] and points up the factors of evolution; but common thinking in this regard is still encumbered by ideological considerations. From the point of view of world order, it must be made clear that the fundamental cause of social and economic progress is progress in techniques of production, and, through them, of experimental sciences. The general spread of knowledge of the primary factors of desired social progress will channel the forces and steer away from sterile waste those that are still being lost today. For it must indeed be clear that order ought not to be confused with immobility, and that ends ought not to be sacrificed to means. On the contrary, the question is to reach these ends more rapidly and with less effort; man did not dominate the risks of the sea by renouncing sea voyage.

We are inclined to think that the political and social evolution of mankind is but one aspect of biological evolution. In the physical characteristics of disorder, there are traits that forewarn us;[10] moreover, and above all, the human sciences have over the past several years pointed out the correspondences between psychological and biological facts, with the result that the latter appear to us increasingly as prolongations and simplifications of the former.[11]

In any case, in the scientific theory of harmonious evolution (to be set forth), it is very probable that biological processes will occupy an important position. It is not at all an accident that the only theory of aleatory and counteraleatory processes that exists, to my knowledge, was based on biological realities originated by a doctor.[12]

Human beings and species all resolve, more or less efficiently, the problem of conciliating identity and growth, personality and evolution. Each human being sets into operation the counteraleatory processes allowing for autonomous and individual development within a nonhomogeneous milieu in which his relations are aleatory, and thus generally not adapted. There is no doubt that the scholars who will set forth little by little the future science of counteraleatory actions and "reserves"[13] in human societies will first have to consider biological processes. In the forefront of these counteraleatory techniques, to my mind, is forecasting.

It was not fortuitous that Pierre Massé, recently General Commissioner of the Plan for economic development in France, entitled his latest book, *Le Plan ou l'anti-hasard*. French economic planning is above all forecasting; it attempts to inform business leaders about the future in the same way that a road map informs drivers. By the very fact of such information, currents are channeled, storms are quieted, and conflicts reduced.

Scientists must not leave the forecasting of the future to the impulsive improvisation of men of violence. Let us admit that political forecasting is more difficult than economic forecasting. Long-term trends are less clear, objectives are generally not quantifiable, passionate and irrational factors must be taken into consideration and are not easy to integrate into rational evaluations. It must be recalled, however, that just as strong or stronger objections were made twenty years ago concerning economic planning. Nonetheless, today, it exists—very imperfect, to be sure—but progressing from year to year, and able, if not to eliminate, at least to attenuate crises to the point of reducing them to "recessions." Economic forecasting is a major factor in political planning.

The goal of political planning, like that of economic planning, is certainly not to forecast and impose an absolute evolution. It is to bring to the fore, out of all the existing possibilities, those that will yield the greatest satisfactions and the least pain. It is to demonstrate what desirable goals can be realized and by what means.

In the political domain, it is supremely important that men of action and scientists confront one another, to oblige the improvident to have foresight, and the prudent to share the fruits of their caution. Our information on reality, while remaining derisory, is beginning to be comparable to that of the little group surrounding Jean Monnet in 1946, when they began their work. In the same spirit, groups just as polyvalent should be formed having as their objective to describe the world political scene in 1985 or in the year 2000, using to that end techniques ranging from the simplest conversations to psychodramas and operational research, starting from the basis of economic, technological, and demographic predictions that already exist. Thus, we might arrive at sketching images of the future that will influence even the most impulsive men. And if a certain one of these images was to receive large support from states and citizens, it might take on a force of persuasion that would bring about its effective realization.

Perhaps the reader will find these perspectives utopian, and perhaps indeed they are today. But it is unlikely that mankind will continue for thousands of years to accept having its political life, and, consequently, its most vital interests, depend on *ad hoc* decisions, taken in the haste of dramatic crises, often provoked by impassioned, harassed, and poorly informed men. We must indeed try—at least—to rationalize and regularize international affairs as we rationalize and regularize internal markets, business affairs, the distribution of electricity and flights in outer space. Regularization and rationalization entail forecasting.

The techniques for political forecasting are practically nonexistent; they will not be revealed by a god. Like all the techniques born of experimental science, they will be formed only by observation, experience, and experiment, the confrontation of ideas with facts. We will find only if we seek. And if it takes two, three, or five centuries to form the intellectual attitudes, institutions, and techniques to regularize honorably the political affairs of the planet, is this a reason not to begin the effort at once?

In reality, we have every interest in beginning the effort now; for the first effect of even a crude forecasting will be immense: it will be to show man that a desirable future for all can be obtained more easily through order than through disorder.

II

While waiting for two or three centuries of scientific research and teaching to rationalize and regularize internal and international affairs, it is clear that man has an interest in reducing as much as possible the occasions for disordered and catastrophic reflexes. In the preceding pages, I have set forth certain directions for scientific research that would seem appropriate and useful to research centers, institutes, universities, and learned societies. I should like now to address myself to the action that might be undertaken by states, public institutions, and international organizations.

I do so with some hesitation; I am a simple citizen who has never assumed any role of responsibility either in a national government or in an international body. I am merely a spectator of a troubled epoch, and a reader of history. My Ariadne's thread is a fragile guide, tenuous, often misleading, since experimental science has not been formed for these subjects.

The effort which seems most necessary to me, and perhaps the least difficult to realize within a single century, would be to increase obstacles to the assumption of power by violent leaders of the kind already discussed—that is, of people like Hitler or Stalin, to speak only of those who have died most recently. Within this perspective, as long as associations of states exist it is natural that others in the association refuse the participation of a man who does not accept their statutes. The membership of states in international organizations might thus be conceived as the *personal* membership of the presidents and prime ministers, and thus entail an individual declaration of the leaders following each change of government. A solemn and public renunciation of offensive violence might have a certain moral effect. To be sure, one sees how easily such declarations could be violated or "twisted." But the problem is not that they be respected; it is that they be respected *sometimes;* that, *in certain cases,* however rare, but always precious, the leader be disturbed in his projects of violence by solemn declarations that he knows he has to make, or has made.

With child-like peoples, and child-like men, and in the scientific ignorance that the few who have passed beyond the stage of childhood find themselves, childish solutions must not be objected to; indeed, childish solutions are all that exist. One may, however, deem the preceding recommendation excessively naive; the following is perhaps less so: it is to gain acceptance, first in world opinion, and then in the public opinion of each nation, of the idea that no man should be allowed to come to power in a state unless he has a minimum education in social science, political science, and law. It

seems indeed certain that our descendants will weigh as a characteristic typical of underdevelopment the projection to power of an
autodidact trained by revolt alone—a ringleader, to be sure, but
not a head of state. Hence, we might envisage setting up standards
whereby only men trained in the spirit of experimental science
would be eligible for the highest political offices. For this movement to take shape, it would be necessary for the most highly
developed countries to see to it now that only such leaders are
chosen.

In this same spirit, steps toward political planning should
be undertaken in the years ahead as a part of the political strategy
of the United Nations and other national and international organizations. Useful practical consequences might follow if the American,
Chinese, Russian, Yugoslav, Tunisian, and Indian governments, for
example, were asked how they envisage the world in 1985, and by
what means they believe the evolution will take place. These are
themes conducive to training men who are scarcely trained, compelling them to think in detail about the complex realities which
they judge impulsively and to become aware of the existence of
other peoples, other needs, and other aspirations than their own.
It would introduce some long-term scientific reflection into government councils. Above all, since it would be highly inconvenient to
submit to world opinion plans based on violence, the publication
and discussion of such plans, it seems to me, would have the advantage of obliging all the heads of state in the world to seek
pacific and orderly expressions for their ambitions, however bizarre.

Thus in the next decades, political forecasting would take two
forms that would be mutually instructive, though radically distinct
in spirit, methods, and results. There would be the scientific form
we described in Part I, and the public political strategy under
discussion now. This strategy could lead to the adoption by the
United Nations of a general plan for political evolution. It would,
at the outset, serve as a procedure for the informing and training
of leaders, a means to encourage competition with ideas rather than
with guns, and to give experience of a kind otherwise unobtainable.
The United Nations already plays this role, but it must be magnified and extended. This training and informing of leaders is only
a particular example of a larger process which must be undertaken
for all citizens.

The action undertaken at the present time by international
organizations, and notably by UNESCO, falls within the outlines of

this movement. They must introduce into the consciousness of the average man an awareness of the fundamental factors of the human condition: the survival of mankind, the complexity of human societies, the diversity of their objectives, the singularity, autonomy, and originality of the individual human being.

If it be true that a large part of the present tensions arise out of the economic advance of certain countries over others, it is important to restore faith in nonoccidental cultures, and increase the prestige of nonoccidental civilizations. The fact of being in a linear race today does not imply the certainty of remaining in the lead in two, five, or ten centuries. Moreover, the evolution of mankind is not reducible to a linear race (defined by the physical volume of production or consumption). The vital vigor and the ardor to live are infinitely more precious qualities. The conceptions of the world that make mankind endure are not necessarily the same as those conducive to progress.

Would not a man who had charge of the destiny of mankind keep a large portion of the peoples alive today away from the trials and troubles, gropings, worries, and demoralization characteristic of the economically and scientifically advanced peoples? Would he not maintain this large fraction separate for several more centuries until the very long-term consequences of the mutation that the "advanced" peoples are experiencing today have appeared?

At a time when the average man in the West is rediscovering the value of art, feeling, and sensitivity, the economically retarded countries must grow aware of the great reserves of vital energy that they hold, which assure them of a preponderant place in the future of the world. In 200 years, and perhaps before then, in a perspective of peaceful evolution, a Chinese citizen will have the same culture and the same standard of living as an American or a Russian. Is it worth trying (without guarantee of success) to advance or slow down this occasion by a half-century or so, to sacrifice a quarter of mankind in war? We must demonstrate, in the words of Arnold Toynbee, the failure of *salvation by the sword.*

If it is true that, despite a reduction in the desire for assimilation which a growing awareness of the facts just enumerated should bring about, the desire for acquiring Western culture, civilization, and economic prosperity should remain strong everywhere, then we must emphasize the true means to economic progress.

We must show the average man that technical progress is the fundamental motor in contemporary economic and social evolution, that all the nations of the world were "underdeveloped" before the birth of Galileo, Newton, and Faraday; holidays dedicated to the celebration of technology must be included in the folklore of mankind. Of course, this does not exclude but, on the contrary, presupposes the development of technical assistance, which is insufficient at the present time.[14]

Mankind is discovering that the organization of space and things is more efficient than their appropriation; but statesmen will be among the last to take account of this, just as peasants accept only under constraint the procedures of consolidation of land and the use of cooperatives. Hence, men must become peace-loving before states can. It is the spirit of experimental science that will teach them how to be that.

REFERENCES

1. V. I. Lenin, *State and Revolution* (New York, 1932), p. 43.

2. *Ibid.*, p. 38.

3. *Ibid.*, p. 83.

4. N. Bucharin and E. Preobraschensky, *ABC of Communism* (New York, [1921]), pp. 59-60.

5. Marcel Proust, *Contre Sainte-Beuve*, coll. "Idees" (Paris, 1965), p. 330.

6. Chateaubriand, *Mémoires d'Outre-Tombe* (Paris, 1848), Book 29, Ch. 3.

7. Alain, *Quatre-vingt-un chapitre sur l'esprit et les passions* (Paris, 1921), Ch. 11.

8. *The Rebel*, by Albert Camus, is an important book for this aspect of the subject.

9. Cf. Raymond Aron, *Dix-huit leçons sur la société industrielle* (Paris, 1962).

10. Alain, *op. cit.*: "the trembling, the redness, the warm flashes marking the migrations of blood are signs of that state of armed peace that grows exasperated in efforts against itself. Imagination follows the same course, and goes to deliver the muscles by itself. Thus it is that a poorly controlled thought falls so easily into solutions of force."

11. André Leroy-Gourhan, *Le geste et la parole* (Paris, 1965).

12. Pierre Vendryès, *Vie et probabilité*, and more recently, "Aléatoire et determinisme dans les articulations mentales," in *Journal de la Société Statistique de Paris* (April-June 1965).

13. "Reserves" meaning "the capacity for action accumulated prior to an injurious event."

14. Cf. J. Fourastié and Cl. Vimont, *Histoire de demain*, coll. "Que sais-je?" (Paris, 1956).

JOHN W. DYCKMAN

Some Conditions of Civic Order in an Urbanized World

MODERN CITIES and the notion of a social order based on freedom grew up together. Towns developed into cities with the rise of bourgeois institutions—standardized weights and measures, uniform codes of law, and freedom from governmental restrictions. In the new society of North America, men entered the cities free of the feudal restrictions of medieval times. Self-interest was the cement of this union. The Enlightenment, in its optimism, was confident that even the constituent atoms of chemical compounds could be held together by mutual affinity. With the French Revolution, the modern urban order was founded; and the way was cleared for commercial and industrial growth in cities.

By the nineteenth century, with the maturation of what Geddes and Mumford have called the paleotechnic age, the optimism of the eighteenth century yielded to doubt, both about the city and about the stable social order based on self-interest. Now, half-way through the twentieth century, it is apparent that the transition from village to town to city has become a runaway movement in which urbanization, a powerful organizing system which merges small cities with large ones, threatens to destroy the distinctions between small and large places within metropolitan areas.

Imperfect order is a necessary companion of rapid growth. Disequilibrium is the father of change. As a group of French scholars observed recently,[1] men have paid for the advantages of larger cities with a certain number of inconveniences, which, at each succeeding level of growth, have been staunchly protested by adherents of traditional civilization. In this paper, I shall examine several characteristic forms of contemporary urban growth which are capable of upsetting the established social and political order and are likely to impede orderly transition from existing institutions to new ones.

300

Runaway Urbanization

The first threat is that of scale. The modern city came to maturity in the late nineteenth century, when the population of Europe increased from 180 to 450 millions, and that of America grew from 5 to 76 millions. This was a century in which mass politics was born, major military confrontations emerged, and the super-cities of our era began to take form. Yet none of the cities we have known has prepared us for the scale of the urban complexes which we shall soon experience. It is likely that during the next three generations the cities will have to accommodate populations at least ten times larger than those currently living in urban areas. If present agglomerative tendencies continue, they will lead to integrated metropolitan areas several times larger than contemporary New York. Harvey Wheeler expresses a common fear of this development with the observation that, "soon each of the country's ten metropolitan areas may have from 30 to 50 million people compacted into them. Traditional interventionist devices simply cannot cope with demographic dis-equilibrium on such a scale."[2]

This dis-equilibrium could take several forms. First, by overspilling old community, state, and national boundaries, metropolitan growth could require political re-ordering, threaten existing social arrangements, and upset the psychological stability of city dwellers. The elaborate technical arrangements necessary to maintain communications and the movement of persons and goods in these large service areas could become exceedingly vulnerable to sabotage or to unforeseen accidents and breakdowns. In addition, such urban growth may lead to population densities which could in time impair biological functioning.

Second, the juxtaposition of high urbanization rates and low per-capita economic growth threatens to plunge certain developing nations into financial chaos or to retard their planned national development. In the Chilean economy, for example, costs directly attributable to urbanization claim half the investment funds of the nation. In countries closer to subsistence, the drain may be felt even more keenly.

Third, urban culture, by feeding the revolutionary growth of expectations, is capable of stoking fires of rebellion and unrest. According to those who hold this view, the dense city is a source of mass discontent which may explode against almost any incidental target. In addition, mass urbanization increases the possibility of sudden floods of disquieting communication, including all kinds of inciteful rumors. Where the populations of these urban centers are compartmentalized, the danger of epidemic outbreaks, including those of social pathology, is likely to be increased.

Scale and Density

According to Wheeler, the population of the future city of 30 million might be "compacted" into dense masses. If humans living in the cities interacted like gas molecules in a closed container, or like rats in cages, increased densities could conceivably lead to over-heating, or to a volume of contact which would overload the individual's capacity for response, and result in behavior breakdown. Studies on lower animals, such as rats, suggest that this outcome is a serious possibility.[3] However, there are a number of reasons for believing that this outcome cannot be extended to humans by simple analogy.

In the first place, the metropolitan area is not strictly "closed." Though sizable regions of agricultural and village occupancy are "emptying out," and the populations are pouring into cities, the density of inhabitants in urban areas is not increasing markedly. Density is a function of the technology of transportation and of spatial organization as well as the number of persons per acre. No large residential sector of any city in the United States has population densities equal to those of the lower east side of Manhattan at the turn of the century.

Second, and even more important, humans have a capacity for creating internal order behind the protective wall of privacy. Some of the highest densities in our present urban scene are accompanied by a high degree of privacy, particularly in the areas of luxury living. It must be recognized, however, that the personal defenses which secure this internal order may at times become pathological and lead to social disorder. Privacy may be secured by de-personalization, or by withdrawing entirely into oneself. While the anomie observed by nineteenth-century sociologists is one pathological form, a kind of involuntary privacy, the self-concern of bystanders who watch murder and mayhem in a subway without intervening, is another form. A degree of insulation from social concerns may be a price which must be paid for this defense in conditions of extreme overcrowding. Thus, high densities without good transport and communication, without amenities and a means of self-protection, are capable of producing dangerous frictions. Where there are means to overcome these, high densities appear quite tolerable. Modern techniques of transportation and communication have made possible cities in the style of Los Angeles. (The Los Angeles trouble-spot of Watts, contrary to the impression created by the mass media, is not a high-density area by conventional urban standards.)

The American urban pattern, in which cities merge in great metropolitan belts, developed as a consequence of the efforts of economically free agents to maximize profits and amenities. In North America, therefore, the city is especially an economic entity. The American city is free, in an economic if not a political sense, to push its boundaries outward. It can preserve a kind of density balance in which individuals' preferences for space are accommodated and technology is used both to concentrate a high intensity of activities and to disperse places of residence. Given the extraordinary heterogeneity of the American population, it is possible that the sprawling development of American cities has actually relieved tension and reduced intergroup conflict by substituting a stratified spatial order for a genuine social accommodation. (The dangers which result from an overly rigid territorial stratification are discussed below.)

In world terms, the new metropolitan growth, with its increasing organization of economic and political life, may be temporarily disequilibrating in a number of ways. First, for poor countries or those in early stages of economic development, the rapid transfer of energies from country to city may appear to be "over-urbanization." Second, the shift from rural to urban values and styles of life may, in the absence of appropriate urban opportunities, appear as "premature" cultural transformation, or result in an over-communication of expectations. Third, the specialization of place, occupation, and roles required by urban society may lead to wasteful and dysfunctional competition. Fourth, but not least important, the communications technology of urban agglomerations in the poorer countries may not match the demands placed upon it. An organizing vacuum may be created when upward and downward communications are blocked—particularly when traditional communications channels are eliminated.

Urban Costs and Economic Development

The first friction, that of over-urbanization, is found in countries where rapid population growth outstrips economic development in the pre-take-off period. Over-urbanization is a threat to social order because (1) the demand for the minimum urban capital necessary to accommodate the population at tolerable health and efficiency levels cannot be met by scarce national resources, (2) the growth in economic and political expectations of the new urbanites rises more rapidly than their contribution to economic or political life, and (3) concentration in urban centers gives revolutionary *cadres* a position strategically closer to the management of the society and the conduct of its political life. A principal symptom of over-urbanization is the growth of squatter communities on the fringes of the established cities, sometimes accommodating as large a total population as the old cities. In the underdeveloped countries with high rural birth rates, modest growth in productivity, and a low rate of accumulation of capital, population has been moving to the city at rates comparable to those of the industrial revolution. This has happened without a corresponding growth in economic development, and in a period of improved public hygiene and higher urban birth rates. In areas having high population growth, such as Latin America and the Middle East, the swelling city populations are inadequately housed. In the words of Kingsley Davis:

By whatever name they are called, the squatters are to be found in all the major cities in the poorer countries. . . . They tend to occupy with implacable determination parks, school grounds and vacant lots . . . these areas account for about 45% of the housing in the entire city [in greater Baghdad] and are devoid of amenities, including even latrines.[4]

Though employment in cities lags behind the growth of the urban labor force, it is in the cities that the new opportunities are to be found. Success in the city is communicated to the rural areas and towns, and an over-response results. Because the rural population is increasing much more rapidly than are the corresponding employment opportunities in the villages and the country, squatters occupy land to which they have dubious legal claim, often with the tacit consent of state and municipal authorities. These squatter communities often lack even the most rudimentary water-supply and sewage systems, though the public health menace is sometimes no worse than in the corresponding slums of the established cities.

Urban Institutions under Pressure

The real difficulties are institutional and political: the squatter settlements are private governments which have set up their own administrative enclaves within the governmental process but without benefit of the usual legitimation. They are frequently anti-government (at least as far as the formal constituted government is concerned) and become centers of resistance, occasionally of rebellion. Governmental communication with the squatters is difficult; they may be outside the machinery of mobilization which can help to match people with opportunities.

Urbanization reduces the traditional violence of "feuds" but increases the chance of epidemic violence. The increasing probability of epidemic violence is not an aspect of mass urban society as such, but is a function of the character of communication in a mass society. In the past, when communication was less reliable and available channels were fewer, outbreaks of disorder were by no means uncommon. The Renaissance cities of Northern Italy were, on many counts, riotous and disorderly beyond the tolerable limits of contemporary urban life. Today we have come to depend on reliable communication, such as air-raid warnings, weather reports, and notices of school closings, for the regulation of daily city life. The possibility of manufacturing disorder through unreliable communication has increased with this new dependence. The battle for the radio station is a key feature of any contemporary *coup d'état* from Iraq to Cuba, for the radio is cheap and ubiquitous, and does not depend on literacy for its effectiveness.

Expectations of the New Urbanites

A second effect is observable where urbanization raises expectations more rapidly than it improves the means of achieving them. This is a common obstacle to developing countries striving to conserve capital for development schemes. The city is a powerful educative force in the matter of tastes because of its concentrated buying power, the diversity of consumer goods, and the highly cultivated and conspicuous forms of consumption which are evident. Migrants to the city from rural areas swiftly acquire a taste for urban consumer goods. In some countries, as the Yugoslav experience has shown, the demands of the new urbanites place heavy pressure on the supply of scarce credit. In other countries, pressure is placed on the balance of payments by the high propensity to import foreign consumer goods. The more the values of a country are organized around consumption and its growth, the more dangerous these pressures may be.

The Watts uprising in Los Angeles in the summer of 1965 may be viewed, at least partially, in this light. Pent-up resentment against deprivation of the right to participate in the urban consumption orgy exploded into attacks on stores, particularly those which practiced the lure of consumer credit and then repossessed the treasured symbols of urban dignity. In part, the residents of Watts were protesting against their inability to participate in the consumer society; in part, too, they were protesting against the terms on which participation was offered.

The social standards of urban life set these expectations. These standards are not the same in all places—for example, the acceptable or expected behavior in Berkeley, California, and Birmingham, Alabama, would be dramatically different. But in almost every case, differences between urban and rural standards within regions of the same country are greater than the differences between those regions. Until these differences are accommodated, the movement of rural people to the cities will create tension.

Segregation and Conflict

In almost every part of the world where rural-urban migration is large, behavioral and social value differentials are accommodated by detaining the migrants in segregated sectors of the city. In the poorer countries, these enclaves are virtually villages within the city boundaries.[5] In the United States, for example, racial segregation emerged as a permanent feature of urban life only after 1900, when Negroes came to the cities in large numbers.[6]

The historic occupational stratification of cities was once economically functional. The medieval city found it advantageous, even necessary, to cluster guilds in recognizable quarters, and to keep villages intact. In contemporary cities, the spatial stratification is frequently less functional. It serves the purposes of social distinction better than it does the efficient use of land, though the latter may be an element in the segregation of industrial and other non-residential uses.

Segregation is a form of order—a spatial ordering of social relations in the city. The highly developed ancient cities of the Indus Valley assigned residential quarters by occupation, an early expression of the caste system. The medieval city, of which New York is an atavistic reminder, segregated economic activities of the respective guilds. The economic and social order secured by the segregation of social groups by residence has become a source of new forms of disorder.

Rigid territorial allocations lead to fixed boundaries which are difficult to maintain. The boundaries, moreover, become the scenes at which sharply differentiated groups meet, and conflict arises. In this sense, neighborhood borders serve to promote conflict in much the way that badly defined but closed boundaries are the cause of disputes between national states. The gangs of city neighborhoods fight fiercely to protect the home "turf." The ghettos which hold populations in become barriers to movement within the city.

Segregation also leaves an area vulnerable to epidemic invasion, whether of physical or social pathology. The flow of information is accelerated by the narrowness of the channel, the homogeneity of the medium, and the absence of conflicting messages. A rumor can sweep Harlem or Watts in a fraction of the time required for it to circulate through mid-town Manhattan. It is significant that segregation has become the symbol of political and social inequality, the mark of a subject population within the larger political community. Racial segregation has bred separatist movements and has fostered the rise of conflicting nationalisms, of which the Black Muslims are a conspicuous example.

Finally, the segregation of the poor and the withdrawal of the rich to small, semi-private political enclaves have prevented the formation of integral political units at the metropolitan level. During periods of rapid urban growth, a major source of in-migration to cities is the rural poor. Thus, at a time when cities are growing large, usually by suburban accretion, they are marked by political fragmentation which combines the existing inequality in income and private consumption with a corresponding inequality in public goods provided by the respective local governments. This process hinders the acculturation and development of the in-migrants.

The Integrative City

The city is an integrating organization form. The politics, economics, religion, and the instruments of social organization and control of a society can be based on the ecology of the city, since communications are conveniently centered there. One would expect, therefore, that the city would mirror the social and political institutions of the society in which it is situated. But the process of urbanization

JOHN W. DYCKMAN

is so widespread, and the world's economy so increasingly integrated, that cities in many parts of the world reflect this international organizational growth in their structure and ecological adjustments more than they do the national traits of the society of which they are a part. India, for example, is beginning to show the suburbanization of industry characteristic of the United States and of industrially developed societies.[7] At the jet ports of the world, an international, cosmopolitan society can meet and carry on business without regard for historic differences. This is not to say that the physical or social problems of Calcutta are the same as those of New York. The former are infinitely more severe because the level of wealth, income, and technology is so much lower in India than in the United States. What can be concluded, however, is that the city intensifies the contradictions and conflicts which have been developing within the national society. Cairo is a city of villages in which the inhabitants often have lower literacy than would be found in corresponding villages of the countryside precisely because Egypt has not developed the level of economic activity required by the degree of urbanization which events have thrust upon it.

The growth of this interdependent system, in which cities are increasingly integrated into continental and world systems, responds to, and places new demands upon, technological skill. If, as Seymour Mandelbaum has maintained, a ward and precinct organization was a necessary communication channel to link the business decision-makers with the immigrant workers in Boss Tweed's New York,[8] television, extended by satellite relay, and jet planes with termini connected by expressways are technical devices for coping with the contemporary world metropolitan system. With growth in scale there is an increase in interdependence, and interdependence in turn requires an increase in discipline. In the mature metropolitan centers, this discipline has come to be ingrained and virtually taken for granted; the behavior of New Yorkers during the power blackout and transit strike showed this conclusively.

The Casualties of Efficiency

The discipline of the city dweller, moreover, is accompanied by a real loss of individual power. The forces that affect the metropolitan resident are largely beyond his control. He is a prisoner

308

of the location of freeway interchanges, the scheduling (or abandonment) of public transportation, and the accident of hundreds of historical, social, and political boundaries. In its struggle to attain a certain measure of efficiency, metropolitan organization throws off more and more individual casualties. Remedial public policy, in turn, tends to add new casualties, as is the case of urban renewal. The old and the unskilled, and particularly the Negro, are hard-hit by the selective, exacting requirements of a highly competitive efficiency system, moderated as it is by social status barriers. Even compulsory military service has had its greatest impact on the urban Negro—in this case, the young men who have minimal literacy and are most likely to be unemployed or underemployed because of the efficiency tests of metropolitan society.

The exclusion of the Negroes, the unskilled, the old, and the ideologically anachronistic small business types (who provide the recruits of the right wing) from full participation in the post-industrial metropolitan society is matched by the growing distance between the advanced industrial nations and the aspiring nations of Asia and Africa in terms of power, wealth, and influence. Not only is the gap between rich and poor nations widening, but the latter have, in the last five years, suffered some slippage in annual rates of economic growth, portending an increasing disparity between rich and poor. Indeed, the more effectively the economy is organized and rationalized, the more disadvantaged are the weaker competitors, whether they are firms, regions of a federal system, or nations in a world economy. Pockets of lagging growth find it almost impossible to catch up so long as an explicit equalization mechanism, based on other than efficiency, is not introduced. The programs of Appalachia and Mezzogiorno, not to mention the persistent problems of the southwestern and northern areas in Britain, are evidence of the difficulty encountered by disadvantaged elements of a large, thriving nation integrated into a competitive international economy. Without an industrial complex of a critical scale, investment programs poured into underdeveloped regions may suffer very heavy "leakages." The multiplier on federal investments in Alaska, for example, may be less than one. The interest payment for debt service on foreign aid returns almost half the aid of the United States. In addition to the superior returns to industrial and financial complexes, the very organization of the market for contemporary industry requires a scale of demand well beyond that provided by the poorer countries.

Anti-Urbanism on the Power Fringes

The planning and rationalization of the world and national economies on efficiency (and often profit) lines have deepened social and political divisions. The Afro-Asian bloc, and particularly China, wishes to lead an ideological foray against the increasing rationalization of the world economy by the industrial powers. In Asia, the friction between the insurgent villages of the countryside and the internationally-oriented capital cities is expressed in open conflict. Rural guerrillas are besieging the urban power centers.

In the industrially advanced countries, such as the United States, a strong "anti-organization," "anti-establishment" sentiment is to be found in almost all the dissident groups from the non-ideological left to the ideological right. The student movement, with its protests against machine education and IBM-controlled progress, but also the civil rights movement and an appreciable proportion of the so-called activist youth are seeking some way of uniting private and public issues. They feel strongly that the urban industrial scientific planning activities of the "power structure" are separating public canons of conduct from those of morality, at the expense of both. In particular, they rebel against the one-way character of communications and civic control. The message of televised political speeches is rejected in favor of the atavistic public forum of the mass meeting, the debate, and the bull session. With C. Wright Mills, whom they admire, they are seeking for "media of genuine communication . . . with the aid of which they can translate the private troubles of individuals into public issues, and public issues and events into their meanings for the private life."[9]

Control by Communication

The failure of our urban industrial society to communicate effectively with certain groups whose contribution to the control of the society and the management of its technical system is minimal leads to various types of "crises." Effective communication is essential to crisis management. Misinformation, for example, spread rapidly by rumor and other informal channels has long been recognized as an immediate occasion of many forms of civil disorder. In the long range, the most effective form of social control is control by "communication of influential messages." From one standpoint, much of the jockeying for position in foreign policy and other forms of power politics proceeds in this manner. Mobilization, displays of force, exchange of messages, and a variety of other actions can be taken as efforts to communicate strength and intentions to a rival, and to influence his behavior. As David Schwartz has observed, the "strength, range, clarity and credibility of messages"[10] are decisive aspects of communication.

The argument has been made that the management of many crises and potential revolts of the working-class population in New York City at the turn of the century was achieved by the effectiveness of the communication of the ward machine organized on Tammany lines.[11] According to this view, political organization maintained effective social control at the local level through its elaborate personal communication system. On certain issues, that control appears to be less effective in the Negro ghettos of American cities today. The most frustrating aspect of Watts from the standpoint of city officials was their inability to find local leadership through whom they could communicate with the masses of the people. One should scarcely expect to find such control in a situation in which the potential local leaders had long been excluded from the inner councils of political leadership in the city (Los Angeles) and in which the rebellious citizens had little ̃or no confidence in or communication with their nominal leaders.

Considerable attention has been given to the failure of communications media to keep pace with the great demands placed upon them in our urban industrial society. When it is simply a matter of a lag in recording stock-market changes or communicating with motorists in traffic jams, the cost of the loss of control has been tolerable. In the case of social discontent, it is much more serious. The citizens of Watts challenged the major American principle of the sanctity of private property and the civil order built upon it. When the disturbances arose, there was little time for making decisions. The main decision-makers had, moreover, failed to anticipate the situation. In the resulting crisis, they displayed a fatal inability to communicate with the aggrieved citizens. By contrast, it was possible for order to be maintained during the power blackout in New York City even with the breakdown of much of the formal communication machinery (only transistor radios were working).

These cases suggest, at least superficially, that processes of social control and social influence depend on the subjective state of those who receive information, as well as on many other factors, including trust. But they may also suggest that there is considerable risk in excluding a major segment of the population from participation, in the social and political communication processes in a society which depends so heavily on predictable individual responses in order to preserve the smooth workings of its technology. In a very real sense, our urban centers are becoming more vulnerable to civil disobedience. People can be excluded from the technical decisions, but their ability to sabotage the workings of the system suggests that communication with these citizens is lost at great peril.

The Urban Outsiders

If the city is a powerful integrating device for a society undergoing rapid social and economic change, and if the characteristic modern urban culture is rationalized, pluralistic, and dependent on highly developed communications media, those who are not "integrated" into the urban system will be more completely alienated from participating in the society than were marginal groups in pre-metropolitan areas. The degree of this alienation and its consequences for social order are functions of the rate and amount of change, the pre-urban cohesiveness of the societal values, the homogeneity of the population, and the wealth of the society. In rich societies, the "unintegrated" can be bribed not to upset the smooth functioning of the urban machinery, and their dysfunctional behavior can be made the basis of folk art, as is the case with Negro-based popular music in the United States and the expressive "mod" fashions of Britain.

Nevertheless, explosive residues of discontent are found everywhere in the world urban order. In the poor countries, it is the students, whose training has outrun the growth of opportunity in the society and whose break with the folk culture has freed them for protest actions, who form the core of the marginal society and shoulder the burden of social upheaval. The unskilled workers transported to the urban setting are, in the absence of ethnic or tribal animosities, less likely participants in these outbursts. In the rich countries, social protest explodes into mass disorder only where the marginal groups have been completely excluded from participation and communication as well as from sharing in the material benefits of their society. Yet there is evidence that a more subtle and pervasive discontent with the rationalized economic and social organization of the metropolis has penetrated many ranks of life in the most advanced industrial nations.

Traditionally, the pull of the city for small-town and village dwellers lay in social freedom, cultural variety, and economic opportunity. These pulls exist today, but appear to be diminishing in force—being replaced in part by the drive to be in the *main stream*, rather than in an exotic culture. The city is so successfully integrative that it is drying up the regional sources of cultural difference. The outsiders are fighting a rear-guard action against the very success of the city in the post-industrial Western world; they distrust the goals of the processes of integration which it represents. Their "new humanism," which is touched with Renaissance romance, insists upon an assertion of the ends of mankind, upon a release from indirect relations, from organizational discipline, and from the requirements of instrumental efficiency. Unlike their youthful counterparts in the developing countries, the Western outsiders distrust efficiency in the service of material progress.

Material progress, based on mastering the techniques of an industrial civilization, is the professed goal of almost every society in the world. Where ultimate ends diverge, material progress is accepted as a necessary means.[12] The United States has not only succeeded in achieving extraordinary material progress and storing great quantities of goods, but it has also successfully vulgarized the idea of progress. Presumably, this notion of ever-spiraling progress in material well-being should carry with it the optimism of the Enlightenment which spawned it. A sizable segment of the American community, including a preponderance of Negro members, has been imperfectly infected with that optimism. For Negroes, the promise appears hollow; for certain segments of the Right, the instrumental costs in terms of other goals have been too high; for a portion of the youth, exclusion from the decision-making processes, bureaucratic control, and de-politicalized decisions by the disciplined industrial command have bred a new kind of distrust.

The city as an artifact of our cultural development may be criticized on aesthetic grounds, may be damned for its unexpected frictions and unwelcome costs, and may be deplored for its heedlessness; but, as an instrument for the accommodation of more and more of the world's population in a single economic efficiency system, it has been effective. Dissatisfaction with urban life in the richer countries of the world stems from the fact that urban trappings are symbolic of ideals which are chimerical to the excluded minorities, and with which others have become disenchanted. To the rebels of the poorer nations, the progressive organization of the world in an urban system for economic efficiency is a symbol of the dominance of the capital-rich nations, with their monopoly of modern arms. For both groups, the technological adaptation of metropolitan life is the heraldry of triumphant, and sometimes inhuman, materialism.

The very technological dependence of the city makes it vulnerable to the resistance of dissidents within it, as events in Saigon have demonstrated. The city, moreover, is the historic incubator of ideas—the richness of its communications milieu produces change. If the city proves to be a force for the disorganization of our present world industrial order we may expect that the forces will emanate from the ideological unrest of the unassimilated groups within the city, and not from the technical breakdown of the urban apparatus as a result of increased scale, runaway growth, or indigestible communications demands. The city is a threat to our economic-technological order mainly because the inhabitants of the metropolis resist the functional demands and the personal costs of its drive for efficiency.

REFERENCES

1. *Prospective*, Vol. XI, "L'Urbanisation" (Paris, 1964).

2. Harvey Wheeler, "The Restoration of Politics," an occasional paper, Center for the Study of Democratic Institutions (Santa Barbara, Calif., 1965), p. 20.

3. John B. Calhoun, "The Social Use of Space," unpublished manuscript, National Institutes of Health (Bethesda, Md., 1962).

4. Kingsley Davis, "The Urbanization of the Human Population," *Scientific American*, Vol. 213, No. 3 (September 1965), pp. 40-53, reprinted in *Cities* (New York, 1965), pp. 3-24.

5. Janet Abu-Lughod, "Urbanization in Egypt: Present State and Future Prospects," *Economic Development and Cultural Change*, Vol. 13, No. 3 (April 1965).

6. Meyer Weinberg, "Aspects of Southern Urbanization and School Segregation," A Report for Equal Educational Opportunities Program, U.S. Office of Education (August 1965), mimeograph.

7. C. K. Jayarajan, "What is Happening to the Fringe Areas of our Cities?" *Civic Affairs* (Kanpur, India), (October 1965).

8. Seymour J. Mandelbaum, *Boss Tweed's New York* (New York, 1965).

9. C. Wright Mills, *The Causes of World War III* (New York, 1960), p. 138.

10. David C. Schwartz, "Crisis Management: On the Influence of Strategic Factors in Crisis Decision-Making," Meeting of the Association for the Advancement of Science (Berkeley, Calif., December 1965).

11. See Seymour J. Mandelbaum, *Boss Tweed's New York, op. cit.*

12. See, for example, Stanley Hoffmann's "Report of the Conference on Conditions of World Order—June 12-19, 1965, Villa Serbelloni, Bellagio, Italy," *Dædalus* (Spring 1966), p. 466.

NEVIN S. SCRIMSHAW

The Urgency of World Food Problems

DRAMATIC DIFFERENCES in health and nutrition dangerously divide the developed and technically underdeveloped countries of the world. In the developed countries, food is abundant, nutritional deficiency diseases have been virtually abolished, most children develop to their full genetic potential, and resistance to infectious disease is high. The amount of land used for agricultural purposes and the proportion of the population engaged in farming have decreased steadily, yet per capita food production continues to rise so rapidly that surpluses are helping to stave off mass starvation in a number of less fortunate nations.

By contrast, in the less developed countries malnutrition stunts the growth and development of most of the children, and infection and malnutrition interact to give mortality rates for youngsters which are ten to thirty times higher than those in the United States and Western Europe. In the rural and urban slums of the less developed areas, from one third to one half of the children born alive die before they are five years old. Infections are more frequent because of poor environmental sanitation; they often precipitate fatal nutritional diseases in already inadequately nourished children and are themselves more severe and often a cause of death because resistance is lowered by chronic malnutrition. Not only is the physical growth and development of many children in these nations impaired, but, also, according to a growing body of evidence, their mental age and learning ability may be permanently lowered.

Widespread blindness is being caused by vitamin A deficiency-induced keratomalacia, and individuals with avitaminosis A frequently die of superimposed infection. Anemias due to blood loss from hookworm disease or to dietary deficiencies of iron or B-complex vitamins weaken both children and adults. Endemic goiter causes needless disfigurement and sometimes results in mentally defective and physically dwarfed cretins. Ariboflavinosis subtly impairs health and decreases resistance; pellagra is still found in some corn-eating populations; and infantile beriberi has increased in recent years in Southeast Asia as machine milling displaces the hand pounding of corn.

Even though up to 80 per cent of their populations are engaged in agriculture, the less developed countries are losing the capacity to feed themselves. Before World War II, these regions were *exporting* 11 million tons of grain per year to the developed countries. During the early postwar years, 1948-1952, this flow reversed, as an average of 4 million tons of grain per year moved from the developed to the less developed world. As population growth rates accelerated in the 1950's, the flow increased, averaging 13 million tons annually in the years 1957-1959, and approximately 25 million in 1964.

Projections suggest that, at the end of this decade, the per capita supply of grains, legumes, roots, and tubers will be 210 kilograms in the developing countries, 470 in the Communist countries, and at least 670 in the technically developed countries of the West. Per capita food output in Asia, excluding Communist China, has dropped 4 per cent since the postwar high in 1961, and has fallen even more in mainland China. The output in Latin America has declined each year since 1958, dropping 5 per cent in five years. Reports show that per capita food production was lower in 1964 than in the preceding two years in ten of twenty Latin American countries, ten of sixteen countries in the Far East, and all four of the countries of South Asia—India, Pakistan, Ceylon, and Afghanistan. In forty-three of sixty-three countries for which data are available, per capita production of rice, wheat, and corn is currently decreasing.*

Some positive results are being achieved through the vigorous and costly efforts of many of the less developed countries to increase their food production with the assistance of the Food and Agriculture Organization of the United Nations (F.A.O.), the United States Agency for International Development (A.I.D.), the

* The data on agricultural production come primarily from publications of the Economic Research Service, U. S. Department of Agriculture, especially the publications "Man, Land, and Food" and "Increasing World Food Output" by Lester R. Brown.

Rockefeller Foundation, and other agencies. There has been a rise in total food production in nearly all of the developing nations except those torn by civil strife, war, or attempts to collectivize agriculture. But they are not able to keep pace with the needs of the world's growing populations.

The death rates in the less developed nations, although still shockingly high when compared with the rates in industrialized countries of the West, have been falling steadily since the 1930's as a result of public health measures, modern medicine, and the control of mass diseases. There has been no corresponding decrease in fertility, and high rates of population growth are inevitable until efforts to lower the birth rates are effective.

The consequences of a continuing decrease in per capita food production in the developing countries cannot—for political, economic, and agricultural reasons—be avoided indefinitely by ever-increasing food shipments, largely from the United States. Yet, these must be continued at present since the only immediate alternative is further political unrest, administrative chaos, and in some cases mass starvation. It is evident that the rapidly deteriorating world food situation can be permanently improved only if there is a more rapid increase in food production in these regions and a less rapid increase in population.

We cannot, of course, countenance demographic control by a return to higher death rates. Nor should we blame successful public health programs and preventive medicine for the dilemma or lessen our efforts to improve health and reduce mortality in the developing countries. On the contrary, only a well nourished and healthy population can learn readily and achieve high productivity. Unless parents can be assured of living offspring, they cannot be expected to practice family planning. Fertility control is more readily accepted where medical services are effective, and health programs are needed to help disseminate the means of such control. It should be remembered also that we live in a shrinking world and that the return of many of the diseases which once kept death rates high would be a threat to the developed countries as well.

We should not delude ourselves that food shortages will provide a natural check on the increase in the world populations. If we ever allow this to happen, we will destroy virtually all hope of ever narrowing the dangerous gap between the developed and under-developed nations before we are engulfed in a world catastrophe. Morally we cannot permit a return to high mortality rates, and politically it would be suicidal. There is no rational or acceptable alternative to a reduction in the present high birth rates of developing countries. Fortunately, there are many indications that progress is at last being made in the development and application of effective and acceptable means of limiting family size. It should be a matter of grave concern to all of us that there has not been corresponding progress in increasing agricultural yields.

In the developed countries, yields have more than doubled in the last twenty-five years, while they have increased only about 8 per cent in the technically underdeveloped areas. Most of the growth in food production of the latter regions has resulted from an increase in the land area being cultivated, and not from the introduction of more efficient farming methods. Many countries are now running out of good agricultural land without showing any sign of the yield take-off achieved several generations ago by the present industrialized countries and more recently by Japan.

The factors limiting food production in the developing countries are primarily social and economic rather than physical. These include the illiteracy and inadequate education of the rural populations, long-standing customs, limited agricultural training, inadequate storage and distribution facilities, lack of fertilizer, pesticides, and mechanized equipment, poor seeds and animal breeds, and lack of money or credit.

The effort required to improve the knowledge and productivity of rural workers and to make available the material requisites of modern agriculture far exceeds the present international, bilateral, foundation, industrial, and private aid being offered to the less developed nations. Technical assistance has been too spotty and too limited. Although we may sometimes speak with pride of a single fertilizer factory, milk or fish-flour plant, or set of silos constructed in some country a decade or more ago, we should not lose sight of the fact that hundreds of such projects must be carried out every year for years to make significant inroads into the problem. Obviously, the nature and scale of past efforts both within the developing countries themselves and from outside sources have been inadequate to cope with the situation. This is indicated by the fact that the food gap is still increasing alarmingly, demographic projections are staggering, poverty and social unrest are the rule, and low-income countries are becoming trapped by growing dependence on external sources of food and money.

During the past year historic progress was made by A.I.D. and

Food for Peace programs in formulating sound statements of the problem and new policies for dealing with it. Their implementation must not be allowed to falter. They can buy the world valuable time, as can the programs of the U.N. specialized agencies, F.A.O., W.H.O., and UNICEF. There is no doubt that present efforts are insufficient in themselves to reverse the current unfavorable per capita food trends.

The industrialized countries as a group must soon come to recognize that the application of scientific and technical knowledge in the developing nations requires a concerted and sustained effort equal to that being made to conquer space or a substantial portion of that devoted to armaments. If a revolutionary breakthrough is not achieved in the application of knowledge in these regions, the time will not be far off when we must all face the consequences of widespread starvation in many of them.

It is clear that the present—*and* future—populations of most of the developing countries could be fed by their own agricultural production of conventional crops if only there were time for crop yields to catch up with their needs and the economic situation improved sufficiently for the people to be able to purchase food. Since neither of these conditions can be met today, we must look to less conventional means to solve part of the food problem.

The major limiting factor in the food supplies of developing countries is the inadequate supply of protein of good quality, although in most cases more calories are needed also. Fortunately, there is no fixed nutritional requirement for the relatively costly sources of protein—milk, meat, and eggs. Legumes and oilseed meals are acceptable alternatives, as is fish protein concentrate. One third of a properly processed oilseed meal combined with two thirds of a cereal grain gives a mixture whose quality and concentration of protein is adequate for all human needs, even those of the infant and young child.

A low-cost, protein-rich vegetable mixture, Incaparina, was developed on this principle by the Institute of Nutrition of Central America and Panama (INCAP). Over three million pounds of Incaparina were sold in Colombia and Guatemala last year to make a drink with the protein value of milk at one fifth the cost; it is now being test-marketed in Venezuela, Brazil, and the rest of Central America. Similar mixtures are available in India, South Africa, and Hong Kong and can be developed to suit the local agricultural resources and food habits of any developing country.

Eighty-three million metric tons of oilseeds were produced in the world in 1964, of which only a small fraction was used directly for human consumption. Extraction of the oil leaves a cake containing 50 per cent protein which costs only three to five cents per pound. Thus oilseed meals offer by far the largest and cheapest new source of good quality protein for human consumption, and they must be used for this purpose in the future to a much greater extent than at present.

A recent research breakthrough at Purdue University, the discovery of a gene in corn which can be introduced into any variety and which nearly doubles the quality of the protein, should also be mentioned. Corn contains about 9 per cent protein, but in ordinary varieties less than half of this can be used either by nonruminant farm animals or by man to meet protein needs. There is every reason to believe that similar genes will be found which can improve the protein value of wheat, rice, and other cereal staples such as millet and sorghum.

Last year the Bureau of Commercial Fisheries perfected a process for manufacturing fish protein concentrate from whole lean fish. The resulting powder has a neutral taste and odor and contains 80 per cent protein of high quality. The cost of this concentrate, when it is produced in quantity, should be similar to that of dried skim milk. The process should be of great help in providing protein to countries with good fisheries potentials.

Oilseed meals and fish protein concentrate have been developed to the point where they can now be used on a wider scale to satisfy world protein needs; in a few years, this will also be true of cereal grains having higher nutritive value. Unfortunately, the excellent, newly available synthetic foods made from textured soy protein isolate and the revolutionary freeze-dried foods which are light to transport, keep well, and are highly palatable are far too costly at present to help solve the problems discussed. Ionizing radiation, however, seems likely to make a contribution to the conservation of food even in the developing countries.

Other innovations lie ahead which eventually may relieve some of the pressure for agricultural land. Intensive industrial research into microbial protein grown on petroleum and other substrates is being undertaken both in this country and in France. Photosynthesis can be applied to algae more efficiently than to higher forms of plant life. An increasing number of nutrients are becoming available at low cost in synthetic form. Palatable, wholly synthetic foods, although not now economically feasible, are well within the reach of modern technology.

There is a real danger, however, that we will count on these new developments to solve the basic problem of world food supplies rather than concentrate sufficiently on the indispensable task of raising the yields of conventional crops. We need have no concern about the potential ability of agriculture, aided by science and technology, to feed the future world population if only the rate of increase becomes a reasonable one. But, anyone who expects that the important new agricultural and food developments mentioned above assure easy solutions to world food problems is unjustifiably optimistic. Experience to date demonstrates the vast difference between the availability of scientific and technical solutions and their effective application. I can see no substitute for massive assistance which will enable the developing countries to improve their own yields of cereals, legumes, oilseeds, poultry, meat, and eggs and to utilize oilseed meals, better cereals, fish protein concentrate, and other new developments.

This assistance must be unprecedented both in its magnitude and in its emphasis on providing health, motivation, and training for the individuals actually involved in food production, processing, and conservation. It must be flexible enough to adapt to varying social, biological, and physical environments, to give responsibility to the local people, and to make readily available to them the tools, improved seeds, chemicals, and other material requirements of modern high-yield agriculture. The basic productive work must be done by the citizens themselves and not by teams of experts assisted by national counterparts who serve merely as translators, handymen, or companions. The experts must know how to do the technical job, but their role should be largely educational and social. Such assistance can succeed only if the local population is properly fed and protected from disease. It will be difficult unless illiteracy is also overcome.

The principle which should be emphasized is that development depends on the efforts of people and is exemplified by people—and not by material things per se. The finest roads, dams, power plants, school buildings, and hospitals will all be to no avail unless the technical knowledge, motivation, and working capacity of the individuals in a population are improved.

There is, of course, no simple formula that will guarantee success —many different approaches will be required simultaneously, and these will vary greatly from country to country. Furthermore, governments, specialized agencies of the United Nations, private foundations, and private groups all must participate. Essential and too often neglected is the crucial role of private industry both in supplying the seeds, chemicals, and machinery which modern farming requires and in producing and marketing the new low-cost, protein-rich foods which the developing countries need.

Even if the industrialized countries are willing to give of both their material and human resources for this purpose on a scale hitherto unimagined, the task will not be easy and will take many years. We still need to learn *how* to share with the less developed nations the benefits of modern agriculture, medicine, education, and industrial technology. The widening food gap attests to the fact that our present efforts are failing to do this.

For our own future and that of the entire world we must soon begin to succeed, or it will be too late. We have a little more time, but not much more. I believe that governmental and private agencies in the United States are now on the verge of leading the world in an effort which can ultimately eliminate the differences in food, health, and opportunity which now so dangerously divide the privileged and underprivileged nations. The goals have been set, but the deeds must still follow.

This article is based on an address by Professor Scrimshaw to the Annual Meeting of the American Freedom from Hunger Foundation on October 18, 1965, in Washington, D. C.

Notes on Planning for the Future

IT WOULD be no exaggeration to claim that we owe the modern phase of the industrial revolution not so much to the advances in the natural sciences as to the rationalization of their technical and economic application. What appears to me to characterize our epoch is not the surprising control of nature we have achieved, but the development of scientific methods to guide the life of society. Only with this achievement has the victorious course of modern science, beginning in the nineteenth century, become a dominant social factor. The scientific tendencies of thought underlying our civilization have in our time pervaded all aspects of social praxis. Scientific market research, scientific warfare, scientific diplomacy, scientific rearing of the younger generation, scientific leadership of people—the application of science to all these fields gives expertise a commanding position in the economy and society.

And so the problem of an ordered world assumes primary importance. The old problem of simply understanding the existing order of things is no longer the issue. It has given way to the difficulties of planning and creating an order not yet in being. But, is the question germane: Should something that does not yet exist be planned and implemented? It is quite apparent that the kind of world order one would like to see governing international relations does not exist. This, in part, is due to the various ideas about what constitutes the right world order, ideas so incompatible that the over-all solution has been suspended in favor of resigned coexistence. But the slogan of coexistence, substantiated by equivalence in nuclear arms, predicates a threat to the problem as posed. Does talk of creating a world order still make sense if, from the start, we are faced with irreconcilable ideas on the constitution of a right order? Can one plan according to a standard of world order if one is ignorant of the end toward which all mediating and possible steps proceed? Does not all planning on a world scale depend on the existence of a definite mutual conception of the goal? Certainly, there are encouraging advances in such fields as world health, international communication, and possibly even world-wide distribution of food stuffs. But, can we simply proceed along the course of these successes to expand progressively the scope of uniformly and rationally applied directives, ending up with a universally regulated and rationally ordered world?

The concept of world order necessarily assumes a substantive differentiation corresponding to the guidelines of the kind of order that is proposed. This is manifest methodologically by taking such a concept and contrasting it with the possible forms of its negation. For it lies in the nature of things that our ideas of right and good are less exact and definite than our notions of wrong and bad. Consequently, the concept of disorder, with whose elimination we are concerned, is always more easily defined; it facilitates the understanding of different meanings of order.

But is it legitimate to transpose those areas of life where disorder dominates and where order should be established on to the whole problem of creating a world order? Let us take the example of economic disorder. The domain of economics allows for an easy conception of rational systematization. Every set of conditions which hinders economic rationality may be termed disorder. In the concept of general well-being there certainly are to be found differing interpretations of an economy on a universal scale which cannot be simply reduced to the idea of rationality entertained by a single, large world factory. For instance, we have still not resolved whether exceptionally large profits are justified as advancing the standard of living, or whether we should prefer, on the basis of socio-political considerations, a nationalized and correspondingly bureaucratized economy even though it is characterized by a lower degree of performance.

This reflection, however, indicates that it is not possible to separate the economic from the political point of view. Can one define a condition of political disorder whose elimination would make possible a rational consideration of political order with the same certainty as one speaks of economic disorder and a rational universal economic system? One could claim that the prevention of global self-destruction poses the same unequivocable standard for international politics as does general well-being for a world economic order. But, is this a genuine parallel construction? Can one actually derive from it workable concepts of political systems which would achieve a reasonable amount of unanimity? If one says, for example, that the preservation of peace is the purpose of all politics, then the meaning is severely restricted as long as we are dealing with conventional wars. Taken literally, it means: the *status quo* is the international order to be preserved—a conclusion made possible and meaningful today by the pressures of nuclear equivalence which tend to constrict the latitude for changes in international politics. But, is that a meaningful standard for politics? Politics presupposes the changeability of conditions. Nobody would want to dispute that there are political transformations which are "right" and which could serve the "right" system of universal political order. But according to what criteria is such "correctness" measured? According to a political vision of order? Even when such reasonable political ideals of order are at issue (as, for example, the unification of Europe as suggested by Lord Gladwyn), the standard becomes quite elusive. Would such a Europe be "right," that is, represent a progressive step toward the administration of the world? Would it be "right" even if international business and political concentrations were disturbed, for instance, if the cohesion of the Commonwealth were broken? Would the result be greater order or more disorder?

The problem can be formulated more basically. Is it possible to think of one precise political arrangement which would not provoke all the very opposite of ideas of world order? Are political visions of order conceivable which do not favor one political system and that only when it is detrimental to the other? Should one assert that the existence of contradictions among power interests constitutes disorder? Is not such a condition itself constitutive of the essence of political order?

It is common to consider the existence of underdeveloped nations as a condition making for disorder, and to call the elimination of such disparity a "politics of development." Here we immediately confront concrete issues amenable to rational solution, for example, the kind of politics dealing with population or with nourishment. In this context it is evident that a population explosion, or, on the other hand, the waste of food stuffs, the nonutilization of natural resources, the destruction of food sources, represents disorder. But all such particular conceptions of order are so enmeshed in international politics and so subject to manifold standards of measurement that it appears impossible to secure agreement. Furthermore, there exists no rational basis for believing that the expansion of those areas in which rational planning and administration is successful would bring a reasonable world-wide political system any closer to realization.

One could with equal justification arrive at the opposite conclusion and admit to the growing danger posed by the application of rational directives to irrational ends, such as is implied in the slogan: "Guns before butter." And one would have to inquire more fundamentally whether it is not precisely the overdependence on science in our business and social life—keeping in mind opinion research and the strategy of opinion shaping—that has increased the uncertainty regarding the intended goals, the content of a world order as it should be, by first subjecting the design of our world to scientifically informed and guided planning, while obfuscating the uncertainty which surrounds the standards. Is the task wrongly posited? Though scientific and rational approaches characterize the advances in innumerable fields of endeavor, can one actually consider the organization of world affairs as a subject of such rational planning and execution?

The question we pose goes completely against the grain of the unquestioned belief in science so characteristic of our age. It has to be asked because it goes further back in time. The problem must be viewed in a more general context, as a broader question posited with the inception of modern science in the seventeenth century and unresolved since then. All reflection about the potential ordering of our world must proceed from the deep tension which exists between the asserted authority of science and the ethics and customs of national forms of life transmitted by religion. We are by now familiar with the tensions which underlie the problems arising from the contact of the ancient cultures of Asia, or those of the so-called underdeveloped nations, with European civilization. But they represent only special aspects of this more general problem. It seems to me less urgent to find ways of reconciling occidental civilization with alien traditions in distant lands and bringing them to a fruitful symbiosis, than to evaluate the significance of the civilizing progress, made possible by science, in terms of our own cultural heritage and to discover ways of reconciling such progress with our moral and religious traditions. For that in truth is the problem of the world order which occupies us at present, because, by virtue of the civilizing achievements of European science, the problem has been raised to a uniform level of importance throughout the world. One glance at the history of the past few centuries shows clearly that the scientific ideas, which were first implemented in the seventeenth century, and the universal possibilities which they contained, unfolded in a hesitating and gradual manner. With the single exception of nuclear physics, we can assert that the developments exhibited by our contemporary industrial revolution rest on the scientific discoveries of the nineteenth century. This is to say, scientifically speaking, that they were possible even then. But even the liberal nineteenth century hesitated in applying them because of the extent to which such ideas were contested by the persisting influences of Christian and moral norms. I refer to the resistance which Darwinism had to overcome. Today these restrictions seem to be diminishing, and the technical possibilities of our scientific discoveries have been correspondingly liberated. The expert makes the possibilities inherent in his field of science available to the public; and popular consciousness, in having to decide on the feasibility of such possibilities, demands nothing less than another science to pass judgment. Here too the exception proves the rule. We need think only of the possibilities of applying genetics to the breeding of the human species, in regard to which man still entertains unresolved elemental fears.

There have been a sufficient number of warning voices that have made themselves heard during the past century in the form of a pessimistic cultural critique, predicting the West's impending collapse. In spite of the reverberations they have enjoyed among social strata threatened with extinction—especially among the nobility, the *haute bourgeoisie*, and the cultured middle class— they carry little conviction, if only because they are themselves immersed in the civilization produced by modern science. I recall the memorable onslaught Max Weber once made upon Stefan George's romantic esotericism. This, however, does not mean that these prophetic voices are not in themselves of documentary value. What they testify, however, is not what they pronounce. They attest to a certain disproportion between a diminishing body of values of disappearing traditions and the continuously self-justifying belief in science. I find it ominous that modern science should revolve only around itself, that it is concerned only with those methods and possibilities which are necessary for the scientific control of things—as if the disparity between the realm of attainable means and possibilities and the norms and goals of everyday life did not exist. But that is precisely the inherent tendency of scientific doctrine: to make superflous the scrutiny of ends by successfully providing and "controlling" the means at one and the same time.

Thus the question concerning the forms of ordering our contemporary and future world can be posed in scientific terms. What can we accomplish? What must be changed? What must we take into consideration so that the management of our world will become continually frictionless and better? The idea of a perfectly administered world appears to be the ideal to which the outlook and the political convictions of the most advanced nations are committed. Moreover, it seems significant to me that this ideal is presented as one of perfect administration and not as a vision of a future with a predetermined content. It is not like the state of justice in Plato's utopian republic, nor does it endorse the dominance of one people or race over another. Contained in the ideal of administration is a conception of order which does not specify its content. The issue is not which order should rule, but that everything should have its order; this is the express end of all administration. In its essence, the idea of management incorporates the ideal of neutrality. It aspires to smooth functioning as a good in itself. That the great powers of our day would prefer to confront each other on the neutral basis of this administrative ideal is not, in all probability, such a utopian hope. From here it is hardly a big step to consider the notion of world administration as the form of order peculiar to the future. In it, the idea of making politics concrete and mundane would find its fruition. Is this formal ideal of world administration the fulfillment of the idea of a world order?

It has all taken place once before. The initiate in the Platonic dialogues knows that in the age of Sophist enlightenment the idea of expertise was given a similar universal function. The Greeks knew it as *techne,* an art, skill, craftsmanship—a science capable of perfectibility. The *idea* of the object to be manufactured constitutes the perspective to which the whole process conforms. The choice of the proper means, the selection of the right materials, the skillful execution of the individual phases of the work—all these allowed themselves to be raised to an ideal perfection, giving credence to Aristotle's dictum: *Techne* loves *tyche* (fortune), and *tyche* loves *techne.* Nevertheless, it is in the essence of *techne* that it does not exist for its own sake or for the perfectibility of the object, as though the latter existed for its own sake. What pertains to the nature and appearance of the perfectible object is wholly dependent on the use for which it is intended. But, regarding the utility of the object, neither the knowledge nor the skill of the craftsman is master. The faculties of the craftsman do not guarantee that the object will be used according to its requirements, or, more decisively, that it will be used for something which is right. It appears that an additional expertise is required to determine its correct utilization, that is, the application of the means to the right ends. And since our whole consumer world is obviously a sacerdotal mixture of such means-ends relationships, the idea of a superior *techne* is appealing—a special expertise competent to order all other faculties, a kind of regal expertise: the political *techne*. Is such an idea sensible? The statesman as the expert of all other experts, the art of statecraft as the ultimate expertise? Naturally, what in ancient Greece was called a state was a *polis*, and not the world. But since Greek thought about the *polis* deals solely with the order in the *polis*, and not with what we understand as the great politics of interstate relations, this is merely a question of degree. The perfectly administrated world order, in our terms, corresponds precisely to the ideal *polis*.

Meanwhile, the question we face is whether this all-inclusive expertise, which Plato calls political craftsmanship, is anything more than Plato's critical rejoinder against those contemporary politicians whose ignorant diligence ruined his native city. Does the ideal of *techne*, the teachable and learnable expertise, satisfy the demands confronting man's political existence? This is not the place to speak of the range or limits of the idea of *techne* in Platonic philosophy —not to mention the problem of how Plato's philosophy serves distinct political ideals, which could not possibly be ours. But, in recalling Plato, we can help clarify our own problems. He makes us doubt whether the increase in human knowledge could ever encompass and regulate the whole of man's social and civic existence. Perhaps one must say that the Cartesian juxtaposition of *res cogitans* and *res extensa* has correctly appraised all possible modifications of the basically problematic application of the field of "science" to the sphere of "self-consciousness." Only when we start applying science to society, which Descartes with his "provisional moral" postponed as a distant possibility, do we confront the full seriousness of the problem. Kant's talk of man as the "citizen of two worlds" adequately expresses the dilemma. That man in his being could become a mere object, susceptible of being reconstructed and manipulated in all his social relationships by another man; moreover, that there would exist an expert other than himself, able to regulate him and all others while being himself managed in his administrative capacity—a suggestion of this kind invites such notorious implications as to render the idea of expertise an ironic caricature, even though it be acclaimed as a technicolor inspiration, a vision of a transcendental divinity or virtue.

Even setting aside the question of the position to be occupied by the planner responsible for a reasoned, systematic world order and the rational administrator of that order, it is evident that the complications would prove insoluble if the idea is to apply "science" to the concrete life situation of people and the practical exercise of their commonsense rationality. Here, too, Greek thought seems to be extremely relevant. It is the Aristotelian distinction between *techne* and *phronesis* which clarifies these complications. Practical knowledge which recognizes the feasible in concrete situations of life does not allow for perfection in the same way as does expertise in *techne. Techne* is teachable and learnable, and its performance is manifest independent of the quality of man morally or politically. Yet, the practical knowledge and reason which man employs to guide and illuminate life situations are not thus independent. Surely, we recognize here that general knowledge, within certain limits, is applied to concrete cases. When we speak of human nature, of political expertise, of business acumen, we tend to make analogies, inexact, to be sure, to a body of general knowledge and then infer its application. If this were not so, then that philosophy which Aristotle designed for his *ethics* and *politics* would be impossible.

Nevertheless, the logical relations of universals and particulars are not at issue. Neither are the corresponding scientific calculations and predictions of events, the features of modern science. Even if one were to outfit the utopian ideal with a physics of society one could not extricate oneself from the Platonic dilemma which elevates the statesman, the practical political activist, to the rank of supreme specialist. For the knowledge of a supposed physicist of society might make possible a technology of society, but it would not guarantee a wise choice, on the part of the social physicist, from among the technological possibilities open to him. Aristotle devoted much thought to this problem and decided to call practical knowledge, which concerns itself with concrete situations, a different kind of knowing. This is no hollow irrationalism to which he gives expression. Rather he identifies the clarity of reason which, in a practical political manner, is always able to discern the feasible in a given situation. Every practical life decision is obviously constituted by a selection of possible alternatives which satisfy our aims. Since Max Weber, the social sciences have justified their scientific legitimacy on the rationality employed in the selection of means. And today they stand on the verge of concretizing and banalizing an increased number of areas which heretofore belonged to the domain of political judgment. But if Max Weber tied the pathos of his value-free sociology to a likewise pathetic adherence to the "God" whom everyone must choose for himself—is it still permissible to abstract, as social science does, from the established ends?

There is no doubt that the prospects of agreement are greater among experts than statesmen. One is always tempted to attribute responsibility to the political directives issued by governments for the breakdown of agreement at international conferences of so-called authorities. But, is this really the case? Undeniably, there are particular concerns in which the rationality of means is unambiguous; on such issues the experts can agree without difficulty. But how seldom are such pure matters of fact really brought up for debate. What an immense amount of self-control a judge must exercise to confine his legal opinion to those aspects of the case for which he, by virtue of his particular expertise, is responsible. The court expert who would be of such extreme scrupulousness would be short of being unfit for the court. The necessity to weigh judgments, which exists for the courts, shows repeatedly that courts deal with assessments whose irrefutability is by no means certain. And it is not only circumstantial evidence that is uncertain. The more the dominant social and political prejudices are brought into play, the more fictitious the pure expert becomes and with him the notion of a scientifically certified rationality. It might hold true for the whole spectrum of modern social sciences that they are unable to control means-ends relationships, without, at the same time, implying a preference for specific ends. If, in my opinion, one were to trace the inner determinacy of this implication to its logical conclusion, the contradiction between timeless truth, which is sought after by science, and the temporal condition of those who utilize science would be made manifest. For what is feasible is not simply what is possible or, within the realm of the possible, the purely advantageous. Moreover, every advantage and preference is weighed according to a definite standard which one posits, or which has already been established. It is the aggregate of what is socially admissible: the norms, evolved from ethical and political convictions and fortified by training and self-education, which determine this standard.

This should not be misconstrued to mean that there are no ethical or political ideals other than conformity to the established social order and its standards. To do so would be to succumb to another set of inverted abstractions. Meaningful criteria are not simply those posited by society—or those of our ancestors—applied as law to a given case. Rather, every concrete determination by the individual contributes to socially meaningful norms. The problem is similar to the one of correct speech. There too we find undisputed agreement on what is admissible, and we subject it to codification. The teaching of languages in schools, for example, makes it necessary that the schoolmaster apply these rules. But language continues to live, and it thrives not according to a strict adherence to rules, but by general innovations in spoken usage, and in the last instance from the contributions of every individual.

Among the philosophies of our century, some of these truths have been represented by the much-maligned school of Existentialism. The concept of "situation" has played a particularly significant role in the rejection of scientific methodology of the Neo-Kantian school of thought. Indeed, according to Karl Jaspers' analysis, the concept of "situation" encompasses a logical structure which transcends the simple relation of universal and particular, of law and case. To find oneself in a "situation" involves an experiential moment which the objective cognition cannot fully grasp. In such a context people are obliged to resort to metaphor. They claim that they must "put themselves in the situation" before they are able to recognize the really expedient and possible from many alternatives. "Situations" do not possess the characteristics of a mere object which one meets face to face; consequently, certainty does not arise from the simple understanding of objectively existing phenomena. Even the adequate knowledge of all objectively given facts, such as are provided by science, cannot fully encompass the perspective as seen from the standpoint of a man involved in a particular situation.

The result of these reflections seems to be that the idea of *making and craftsmanship,* as it has been passed down for ages, represents a false model of cognition. The tension between a formal knowledge available to everyone, as it is associated with the concept of a teachable science (for example, *techne*), and the knowledge of what is practical and good for oneself, is, in itself, quite old and familiar. But, it is quite obvious that before the inception of science it had not been raised to a real antinomy. Aristotle, for example, sees no problems in the relation between political science and political sense (*techne* in relation to *phronesis*). The whole corpus of knowledge in which all forms of knowledge participate provides *techne* with a standard as well. *Techne*, in a fundamental sense, is that branch of knowledge which fills the gaps nature left for human skill. That is how things were in the old days. Today, in contrast, the magnificent abstraction with which the methodological ideal of modern science isolates and encloses its subject has ensured a qualitative differentiation between the infinitely expanding knowledge of science, on the one side, and the irretrievable finiteness of actual decisions, on the other. The specialist and the politician are respective embodiments of this rift. A rational model seems unable to define the knowledge necessary for a statesman. Max Weber's exaggerated differentiation between value-free science and ideological decisions makes this failing obvious. Perhaps one could remedy the difficulty by substituting the old *model of piloting*, or steering, for the model of making. This model has the advantage of being able to account for two integral notions: the maintenance of equilibrium, which oscillates in a precisely set amplitude, and guidance, that is, the selection of a direction which is possible within the oscillating equilibrium. That all our planning and execution transpires within an unstable equilibrium, which constitutes the determinations of our life, is quite evident. The idea of equilibrium is not only one of our oldest political concepts of order that limits and defines the degree of active freedom, but it appears to be a structural determinant of life as such, to which all indeterminate, not yet established, possibilities of life are relegated. A man of our technological and scientific civilization can free himself from this restriction no more than can any other living being. Yes, perhaps the actual determinations of man's freedom are to be found here. Only where the forces of equilibrium are maintained can the factors of human volition and desire be of any consequence. To acquire freedom of action presupposes the establishment of an equilibrium. Even in modern natural science we confront something similar. We are increasingly devoting ourself to discovering the regulative systems of nature. Correspondingly, we are leaving behind the naive belief that the crude means we possess can assist the self-corrective systems of living organisms. And yet, all our research, to the extent to which it provides us with information and understanding, makes—increasingly less crude—interference possible.

And so, the cognitive model of piloting, compared to the idea of planning and making, acquires greater significance. However, this model also cannot hide the kinds of assumptions—knowledge of goals and directions—which are necessary for piloting. Plato also thought that the skill of the pilot illustrated the limits of all skill. He transports all passengers securely to land. But was it good for them that they had arrived? It is possible that Agamemnon's pilot succumbed to doubt after he saw that his master had been murdered.

Perhaps there is no better example to illustrate the present problem than the situation of the doctor. For here the dilemma is experienced in the relationship of science to its practitioner, whose humane function must not be subserved by the merely "scientific." The coexistence of dual faculties in one occupational activity defines the physician's problem. Analogous complications occur wherever a learned profession must strike a balance between practical activity and science, as with lawyers, psychiatrists, and teachers. But the example of medicine epitomizes the conflict. Here modern science, in all its magnitude and promise, collides directly with the historic role of the healer and the assumptions underlying his compassionate activity. In itself, the problem of medicine is old: How much is "science," a practical science, to be sure, a *techne* and, consequently, an art? While every other creatively pragmatic knowledge verifies its "knowledge" in the results it achieves, the task of medicine remains irreducibly ambiguous. In each case of its intercession it is debatable whether the measures taken by the doctor resulted in the cure, or whether nature came to its own assistance. Therefore, the whole art of healing—quite in contrast to other branches of *technai*—has, since antiquity, required a special apologia.

This is doubtless due to the vagueness of the concept we call health. It is a norm defying clear definition. We might better call it a condition, which, since time immemorial, has been characterized by the concept of balance, or equipoise. Balance, however, has the attribute of a certain set of oscillations which equalize each other to keep the whole in equilibrium. When the bounds are exceeded the balance is offset completely and, if at all possible, must be corrected by a new expenditure of effort. Consequently, the re-establishment of equipoise is nothing more than the reintroduction of an oscillating equilibrium. This attributes to "interference" a special set of limitations. Or, to express it in more general terms, a fundamental tension exists in the connection of "knowing" to "doing." Particular relations can be studied in terms of a causal analysis proper to the natural sciences. However, the organism as a whole can be understood, as Kant has shown, only from a tele-ological point of view. In this respect, modern medicine shares the general difficulties being investigated by contemporary scien-tific biology. The tremendous advances achieved in this sphere, especially by what is called information theory and cybernetics, have reduced to feasibility what appeared utopian to Kant: the aspiration to become the "Newton of a blade of grass." Nothing said here affects the validity of morphological methods, and there seems to be no reason that a morphological approach should not be compatible with causal analysis. The behavioral sciences, for ex-ample, apply certain preliminary morphological assumptions in interpreting the behavior under observations as being not merely the result of a mechanical cause-effect relationship—although there would be nothing inconsistent in considering the existence of such a relationship. Should it eventually become possible to create living organisms in a test tube, it will not be senseless to study the *behavior* of such constructed organisms. The idea of science justifies the use of both methods and directs them to the same end: to explore a realm of experience scientifically and to open it up for useful pur-poses. To make something available does not mean simply to re-construct it. It also entails the ability to predict the course of sponta-neous development which, for instance, a living organism might undergo under specific circumstances.

But precisely here the specific difficulties of medicine prove in-formative. And, I believe, the medical dilemma is closely analogous to the one we face in discussing the theme of world order. The tremendous advances made by modern medicine in dealing with really critical illnesses lay bare problematic complications which the subscribers to the Hippocratic oath will have to take into ac-count. Obviously, the practical demands of helping and healing do not alone bear the burden of responsibility for the fact that the purely technical use of science is too restricted a model. Certainly, it is also the level of our knowledge and, consequently, its limitations which necessitate in the end that the doctor trust his tactile sense and his intuition, and, when these do not suffice, that he revert to simple experimentation. Meanwhile, there appears to be no contradiction in contemplating a perfect biology, which would also raise medicine to a scientific perfection of a scope we cannot yet imagine. But precisely then, I should think, those complications we are beginning to perceive at the present early stage would become explicit. Take, for example, the prolongation of life which contemporary medical technology is attempting to realize. The identity of the person, who as patient confronts the doctor, has no place in such a scheme of things. Similar difficulties posed by controlled genetics have already been mentioned. It seems that the circumscribed and finite nature of life makes the conflict that exists between the glorious promises of natural science and man's understanding of himself unavoidable.

Let us apply these reflections to the state of affairs of the modern world and to the tasks we face. Here we will not make scientific suggestions toward a scientific mastering of the problems of global order. In this respect, we should stress that science still has a tremendous future, even though it is not certain that occidental civilization will proceed without resistance eventually to displace and suffocate all other human forms of order. But that is precisely the problem. The creation of a technically uniform civilized man, who acquires the use of a correspondingly uniform language—and English is far advanced in filling that role—would certainly simplify the ideal of a scientific administration. But the relevant question is precisely whether such an ideal is desirable. Perhaps developments in linguistics can provide us with an insight into how the leveling process will work itself out in our civilization. The system of sign notation, which both requires the services of a technical apparatus and makes it possible, develops a dialectic all its own. It ceases to be simply a means for the attainment of technical ends, since it excludes the data which the apparatus does not identify or transmit. The perfect functioning of an international language of discourse is subject to the limitations imposed by the information to be communicated.

The attempt to perfect a logical and perfect universal language of theoretical cognition for use in science, as the advocates of the "Unity of Science" movement are to do, would meet the same fate. Were it perfected, it might successfully eliminate all imprecision and ambiguity in interhuman understanding. We would not even have to wait for the invention of a future world language. It would suffice to incorporate all living national languages into a system of transliterated equations so that an ideal translating machine could guarantee a uniform intelligibility. This is all possible and perhaps quite near. But here again it might be unavoidable that the universal means would become universal ends. Therefore, we would not have acquired a means to say and communicate everything imaginable; we would, however, have obtained a means— and we are on the way to achieving it—which would ensure that only the data assimilated in the programing would be communicated, or even thought. The forbidding possibility of speech control, which has evolved with the growth of modern mass media, expresses clearly how the dialectic of such means and ends operates. In our own day this dilemma is reflected in the confrontation of the cold war antagonists: What in one part of the world is called democracy and freedom appears only as a convention of speech which in the other part of the world is interpreted as a device for mass manipulation and domestication. But that demonstrates only the incompleteness of the system. The manipulation of language has permeated everything and has become an end in itself. In the process it has concealed itself and passes unnoticed.

One should keep such extreme possibilities in mind in order not to lose light of certain features which are characteristic of all elemental life experiences. To say that the language in which we become immersed as we grow up is more than just a set of symbols serving the needs of a civilizing apparatus should not be misinterpreted as a romantic idolization of a mother tongue. It is indisputable that every language has a tendency to schematization. As a language is learned, it creates a view of the world which conforms to the character of the speech conventions that have been established in the language. A thing is defined by the words one uses. The genial speech habits of a two- or three-year-old child are terminated by the demands of communication made by the environment. Nevertheless, it seems to me that in contrast to every artificially devised system of signs, the living aspect of language perfects and develops itself in association with the living traditions that encompass historical humanity. This secures for the life of every language an inner infinity. The boundlessness is preserved still more when man, while learning a foreign language, steps into an alien system of meanings and, by comparison, experiences the wealth and poverty of his own speech. Man's irreducible

finitude is displayed here too. Everyone must learn to speak for himself and in the process establish his own history. And, should even
the most farfetched mechanization of society be successful, man
will not lose this uniqueness. The age of *post-history* into which we
are now proceeding will find its limits in this distinctiveness of man.
(Cournot)

In conclusion we must inquire what significance this type of
rumination can have in the face of the overwhelming trend toward
a scientific form of civilization. That the popular critiques of
technology share the insincerity of all other forms of culture-
criticism has been mentioned earlier. One should certainly not
expect that, by becoming cognizant of the factors which set limits
to the technological dream of the present, we could or should be
able to influence the measured advance of progress. All the more
reason for asking what the awakening of consciousness is to achieve.

The answer to it will not be the same in all situations. The
possibilities of conquering nature will have a different significance
and a higher esteem where nature is still largely uncontrolled, and
where people continually struggle with physical deprivation, poverty, and sickness. The élites of countries characterized by such
backwardness will fully endorse and support scientifically pro-
gramed planning. They will also be sensitive to the retarding effects
of religious influence on social norms. If the execution of the plan
requires a high level of morale and strict discipline, then it will be
seen to that political qualifications and a consciously worked out
ideology are brought into play to secure the success of the plan.
In the highly developed nations it is unlikely that we will oppose
the imaginative planner who promises to increase human well-
being. Here too, one will have to fight the obstacles which are embodied in property relations and profit incentives. But, the more we
liberate ourselves from external needs and excessive labor, and,
if it ever becomes possible, the more we modify the life tempo of
our modern industrial society, all the less will we expect salvation
only from scientific planning of the future.

The differences among the economically developed countries are
not crucial here. The idiosyncrasies of ancient cultural traditions also
rise to the forefront of consciousness in a compressed world. Consequently, the task of making consciousness aware of extant differences
between peoples and nations assumes a priority in a world where
planning and progress seem to guarantee the satisfaction of all
desires. Such an awakening of consciousness, however, is now

hardly ever performed by science. It is more readily a result of a critique of science. Its greatest effect is education to tolerance. Attested ideas of orderly civic life, as, for example, the ideal of democracy (either in the Western or Eastern sense), will develop an inner consciousness of their own requirements, while economic progress, though equally desired in all parts of the world, will not have the same meaning throughout.

With justified anxiety one may ask what the awakening of consciousness to these problems, as long as they remain confined to small intellectual circles, is to accomplish. To demand more than the sharpening of our understanding of these problems, to expect that the solution of the inclusive difficulties of international politics will be provided by some kind of brain-trust, would be ridiculous. Meanwhile, contact among nations increases and leads them in greater measure to the awareness of what it is that separates them or unites them. The problem of intellectuals is a problem in itself. But, what is mirrored in their understanding—their naive superiority notwithstanding—can become the conscious property of everyone.

In conclusion it might be permissible to inquire into the role philosophy plays in solving the dilemma we have described. Does it still possess a relevant function in a scientific culture attaining to perfection? First, we must reject certain widespread assumptions about philosophy in addition to views which philosophy itself entertains. To require that philosophy be some kind of super-science, able to provide an all-encompassing framework for the specialized sciences, is scientific dilettantism. This is no longer practicable; it is an obligation philosophy set for itself in classical times when it indeed constituted a comprehensive science. Furthermore, to expect philosophy to be the source of doctrines of logic and methodology is no less frivolous. The various specialized scientific disciplines would gain nothing from this, for they have long since borrowed methods and systems of notation from each other, assimilating to their own needs what seemed appropriate. The philosophy of science is certainly a legitimate task of philosophy. But to the question, whether philosophy still functions as a universal agent of awakening consciousness, theory of science is unable to reply. On the contrary, it assumes to answer before it has fully understood the question. To awaken a consciouness of what *is*, necessarily supposes the awakening of consciousness as to what science is. But it equally includes preserving the openness of one's own consciousness, and to be cognizant of the fact that not everything that *is,* is or could become the object of science.

In contemporary philosophical discourse we can find essentially two answers to justify the awakening of consciousness. In the first instance, it sharpens and radicalizes the understanding of what really exists. To this task belongs the destruction of all romantic illusions regarding the good old days and the snug security provided by a Christian cosmos. It must also heighten the awareness that God has been obscured for us (Martin Buber), and that the question of being has fallen into forgottenness as our metaphysical tradition sinks into the realm of science (Martin Heidegger). Philosophy would then recognize itself as a kind of secularized eschatology, possessing a kind of expectancy which takes pride in expecting nothing definite, but being, as it were, a kind of challenge. He who subordinates himself to that which *is* and refuses to deal with the ensuing consequences demands by default that the future should pursue its own course irrespective of direction.

But there is another possible answer concerning the purpose of awakening consciousness, which appears to me to be in full accord with our own desire to know. It could be that the technological dream entertained by our time is really just a dream, a series of changes and transformations in our world, which, when compared to the actual realities of our life, has a phantom-like and arbitrary character. To be awakened to consciousness could also mean to become aware of how little things change, even where everything appears to be changing. What is involved is not a plea for the preservation of the existing order. The concern is simply with a readjustment of our consciousness. The conservative, like the revolutionary, seems to me to require a similar rectification of his understanding. The unavoidable and unpredictable realities —birth and death, youth and age, native and foreign, determination and freedom—demand the same recognition from both groups. These realities have measured out what men can plan and what they can achieve. Continents and empires, revolutions in power and in thought, the planning and organization of life on our planet and outside it, will not be able to exceed a measure which perhaps no one knows and to which, nevertheless, all are subject.

PAUL MUS

Buddhism and World Order

At the Conference on Conditions of World Order, held in Bellagio, Italy, Raymond Aron enumerated several possible meanings of the term "world order." He suggested that the seminar concern itself with one of them, half descriptive and half normative—"order as the minimum condition for coexistence"—rather than with the purely normative one—"order as the conditions for the good life." The latter would too easily have been interpreted to mean "the good life as the condition for world order," which would have resulted in each participant supporting his own conception of that life. This, according to Professor Aron, could lead "only to platitudes or to acrimonious reproduction of the conflicts of values that exist in the world."

Under that cautious guidance, we avoided such dangers and reached substantial agreement "on the importance of the nuclear stalemate and on the continuing dynamics of development as the bases of world order." In contrast with this basic agreement, the seminar "reflected quite well the present state of affairs" in that it flatly disagreed "on the extent to which the new forms of interdependence would create not only the 'minimum conditions of coexistence,' but also a genuine community of values and of power" as a prerequisite to the endorsement of these conditions.

The quotation from an ancient Chinese author, Mo-ti, selected by Professor F. S. C. Northrop as an epigraph for his book, *The Meeting of East and West* (1946), still retains its relevance: "Where standards differ, there will be opposition. But how can the standards in the world be unified?"

What can a philologist hope to contribute to the kinds of issues raised at our Bellagio meeting? A letter from the Editor of *Dædalus* specified the initial intention. He wrote:

In a world in which we increasingly think of people only in economic terms . . . we ought to realize that there are other criteria for categorizing them also. Not the least of these criteria is the one provided by religion. . . . The existence of certain religions in the East is as important a factor in determining the attitude of these people as any other single factor. We in the West tend to ignore such factors and to think that what really separates one society from another is simply the level of economic development. It is well to be reminded that such categories as *developed* and *underdeveloped* are not the only important ones.

The obvious advantage of convening a seminar on "The Conditions of World Order" essentially among political scientists and economists, some of the latter "in charge of economic planning in their respective countries," East as well as West, was that the procedure, directed by a thinker and debater of Raymond Aron's class, simply could not have gone astray. It was a professional matter for that group of participants. The fact that eminent natural scientists were also invited to the conference to advise or arbitrate from the point of view of the latest scientific methods did not raise any problems and helped us to make our way toward the solution of a few.

With all the diffidence that befits a layman confronted with such technicalities, I must confess that to my mind the term "world order" seems to imply, besides planning, a broader inquiry which considers the appeal of such planning to the interested parties, that is, to the vast intercontinental areas markedly differentiated—as Mr. Graubard rightly observed—not only by their economic development, but also by deeply diverging trends in their conception of the world as a whole. In its widest implication, I would take the term not in any abstract sense but in a definite sense, what linguists call a *pregnant* sense, connoting, in the present case, some model of an order and also ways of implementing it.

I am thus at one with Stanley Hoffmann when he admits that our seminar reflected serious misgivings in this matter. Wherever planners do not secure or are denied solid ground on which to pursue the application of their propositions, planning reminds us of Aristophanes' satire of the great Socrates. In the light of what was to follow, one may think that the author of *The Clouds* unintentionally passed judgment not so much on the Sage of Sages as on those, including himself, who did not recognize him as such: History took charge of carrying out the sentence. The lesson is thus that a *plan* for world order, no matter how well-devised and realistic, may not even constitute a step toward world order if it provokes a sufficient amount of opposition—even unfounded opposition.

Religions, especially in Asia, represent, even today, more than "folkloristic residues," as they were tellingly described in one of our sessions. Moreover, no great Asian religion, whether Hinduism, Buddhism, or the popular Chinese mixture of Confucianism, Taoism, and Buddism, may be categorized among "single factors." For these traditions, world order is not, as it is for us, a matter to which they may sometimes turn their attention. It is not, according to Professor Northrop's penetrating analysis, a *postulation*, a prospective and provisional scheme which we formulate, check against experience, and more or less successfully try to improve upon. It asserts itself as an autonomous, continual, and all-embracing process in which we find and may more effectively insert ourselves. The total, not the individual, comes first—a mode of thinking coinciding with Durkheim's much discussed but fundamentally sound description of society as an organic whole rather than as a mechanical addition of parts and circumstances.

Many centuries before the Stoics elaborated the idea of world order along lines still largely accepted by the Western world— though in a quite different spirit because of the penetration of Christian values—world order was generally conceived, throughout a wide cultural area extending from Egypt to China, not as a more or less direct religious preoccupation. On the contrary, it was religion itself, in its highest and impersonal expression, reflected on earth and personalized in a Pharaoh, a King of Kings, a Son of Heaven, or a King of the Wheel.

This can be seen, for instance, in Joseph Needham's suggestive *aperçu* of the Chinese version of the Pattern of Patterns:

The highest spiritual being known and worshipped was never a Creator in the sense of the Hebrews and the Greeks. . . . The Chinese world-view depended upon a totally different line of thought. The harmonious cooperation of all beings arose not from the orders of a superior authority external to themselves, but from the fact that they were all parts in a hierarchy of wholes forming a cosmic pattern and what they obeyed were the internal dictates of their own nature.

Under various formulations, this high level of temporal and religious organization seems to retain, though with obvious differences, something of a previous, more primitive period, when divine powers may have been less directly conceived as personal figures.

The outcome is often called Asian pantheism—a term which should be accepted only with the reservation that, as in the previous stage, the site was more divine than the genius, often theriomorphic and especially ophidian, that haunted it. In the same spirit, now, the total image of the world and of world order remains more divine than the pantheism it accommodates.

Such considerations will not be easy to reconcile with the notion so deeply embedded in our religious traditions that God has meant our surroundings to be, in the last resort, a Valley of Sorrow through which we gain a new life in the hereafter, once this world of ours comes to its end and final judgment is pronounced on us according to whether we have or have not succeeded in redeeming ourselves from its iniquities. Such a world is much more closely connected with the notion of an ordeal than of an order. However, many Westerners would not endorse such ideas today. Among those who would endorse them, many would not be fanatical about them, as was true in previous times. This is why Raymond Aron thought it possible to ask us to forget our personal and often irreconcilable conceptions of "the good life."

But, from another point of view, would it not be possible for our modern world, insofar as it is not totally satisfied with Newton's understanding of the laws of nature as given by a personal God and Creator, to find inspiration in the descriptive, naturalistic, and rational principles underlying China's classical philosophy? It is well known that such was the feeling of certain of our eighteenth-century thinkers, even though the interval was one of at least two thousand years, and of a society half a planet away. Joseph Needham's illuminating study, *Human Laws and Laws of Nature in China and the West,* Professor F. S. C. Northrop's *The Meeting of East and West,* and the collective volume published under his general editorship, *Ideological Differences and World Order,* give a sufficient idea of how large the gap remains.

The comparative approach may occasionally lead to suggestive conclusions, even though our current documentation on ancient and medieval Asian institutions derives mainly from religious or purely literary sources. Professor Needham's analysis of the Chinese cosmic pattern could, for example, help us to discern on our own side some very special stresses and trends during the Nazi venture—that most devastating attempt of ours at an authoritarian ordering of the world. Although lip service was paid to a God of its own, the Nazi machinery did not work fundamentally through divine command or through rational principles, but through the fanatical application of a pattern—the Pattern of Patterns, that of the "tall, blond, dolichocephalic Aryan race"—established, much more emotively than in the Chinese system, as the supreme reference. This earth had already been given a foretaste of its reign during an Aryan semi-mythical Golden Age. It was to be reestablished, and this time for thousands of years. The prophecy was somewhat curiously echoed each morning, though in quite different cultural surroundings and with different racial connotations, in the greetings of the Japanese to their emperor and the dynasty: *Banzai*, "Ten thousand years!" East and West thus demonstrated their ability, if not to meet, at least to build between themselves the two extremities of an axle uniting either the most or the least commendable elements in both—a factor to be kept in mind when planning for world order.

Asian Order and the Westerners' Inroads

China, as early at least as Ch'in Shih Haun-ti, had built herself more than just theoretically into a self-contained and self-assertive world. Is it not symptomatic of that "Middle Kingdom" that the Dutch Sinologist De Groot should have summed up his elaborate interpretation of the popular Chinese syncretism of Confucianism, Taoism, and Buddhism in the specific term *Universism?* In a less centralized but equally effective way, India, culturally, reached a similar position. In the eyes not only of her own "teeming millions" but also of her Southeast cultural dependencies, India became not just a large part of the world but the central expression of a world order. As already indicated by the famous message of Prince Shō-toku to the Sui Emperor, Yang-ti: "The Emperor of the Rising Sun to the Emperor of the Setting Sun . . ." (607 A.D.), the Japanese line long followed the same direction, although it was somewhat distorted, for a while, by its connection—without adequate ethical compensation—with modern Western power concepts.

How, then, can we expect such cosmic, self-vindicating systems, still powerful at the popular level, to put aside their traditional assertions about themselves in order to adopt our own set of values? This would be a self-denial unlikely to appeal to them since it would mean their joining us, under our leadership, in our desperate endeavors to establish some minimum of world order in the teeth of an impending destruction. The Afro-Asian nations see the present situation as proof 'that our system leads to destruction far more directly than to order. Are we, in the West, sufficiently aware that if the Russo-Japanese War offered evidence to Asians that they might emulate the West, the First World War (not to mention the Second) came as a warning that they ought not to do so? Something else had to be found: a Western-sponsored United Nations Organization may not be in a position to overcome this handicap; it will look dangerously like a stopgap.

We have not fully realized the implications of the fact that the major Asian civilizations view world history as essentially cyclical. In contrast with our own Western conception of an open, indefinite progression, they recognize progress and regress—that is, an alternation, at the cosmic level, of general improvement and deterioration of world order, bringing us periodically back where we began, thus to start all over again.

As a result, each of these different traditions considers that the Golden Age existed when their own patterns of thought and collective as well as private behavior were naturally followed all over the world. The notion that things could have been otherwise does not even arise. Degenerescence—whatever be its final reason—began when an increasing number of people went astray. This is a view which Westerners often do not understand, but which it is essential for us to know. How can the Asian civilizations fail to hold us and our activities responsible for the ever deeper obscurity of this Iron Age, where the leading powers in the world appear to have lost their bearings so that we not only openly expect—and dread— Armageddon, but prepare for it with all our might?

The first Asian impulse, a distinctly conservative one, would be to go back to its own traditions. This mood derives its strength partly from the preceding considerations, partly from the belief in transmigration—always so difficult for us to grasp—according to which Westerners and all that they represent and bring with them, *problems* rather than *solutions,* do not belong in the East at all. If they did, they would have been reborn there as natives.

This does not mean that belief in *karma* and transmigration discourages travel and communications—quite the contrary. In the usual, flexible, and highly pragmatic application of the doctrine, the contacts between the local people and visitors, sailors, traders, temporary guests, or even colonizers show that there must be enough in common in their respective retributions for these people to meet in the East. However, in contrast with the case of the natives destined by their merits and demerits to be born there and nowhere else, the force that brings alien elements to their countries operates peripherally; they will *come* but they do not *belong* there.

In good doctrine, to hear of Burma, or Cambodia, or Viet-Nam, then go there, and finally be born there, but as an alien, constitutes a regular progression. As these are Buddhist countries where one may get acquainted with the Master's teaching and his church, this progression allows the classification of the corresponding "destinies" as an escalation of rewards. But, as a Vietnamese friend told me once very seriously, to be entitled to a share in the administration and, consequently, in the revenue of the country, a person must wait until karmic retribution has moved one step further, making him a Burmese, Cambodian, or Vietnamese, as the case may be, by right of birth. Otherwise, there will be a perversion of the world order and commensurate punishment. "Why are you in a hurry?" asked my friend. "You are already so close to us, you and some of your compatriots. It *must* come!"

I confess that such speculations are a far cry from our quiet and productive Bellagio meeting; but perhaps this is one reason that a brief mention of them should find a place here. The road to international peace will *also* have to pass by Mandalay and Bangkok, by Phnom Penh and Saigon.

The age of Western colonial domination has come to an end. Since my early years in Viet-Nam and for nearly half a century, the Vietnamese never ceased to expect the final French withdrawal and to speculate on the time it would take. They considered it a natural and inescapable issue. They had reason to know: With the Chinese, occupation went on, once, for eleven centuries, time enough to build up two or three local Joans of Arc. This is not a country where the spirit of resistance wears off easily.

All this suggests that we should pay attention to the steady propaganda that feeds the newly liberated nations with the fear that colonization is not over, that a less overt but no less efficient form of neo-colonialism has taken its place. The criterion of transmigration, so remote from our usual way of thinking, is destined to play a not inconsiderable role in the opinions that the Southeast Asian masses form of the situation at home and abroad. Twenty years after the event, I see little to change in the conclusion of a report sent to General de Gaulle after a clandestine contact, in his name, with the Indochinese "underground" under the Japanese occupation: "nothing will grow any more in Viet-Nam except on the deepest local roots."

This is certainly not to say that Viet-Nam, Cambodia, Laos, or their sister-nations of the culturally "Anglicized" half of Indochina will fall back on their old customs and superstitions, as may happen at first in some backward areas. The world is moving; they know it, and do not want to lag behind. They will need to be equal participants this time in the common venture. Token industrialization, screening their role as essentially purveyors of raw materials, will never do. To go to Tokyo and visit exhibitions displaying German, French, English, and American counterfeits or allegedly "inferior" copies of Japanese cameras, recorders, binoculars, and the like is to see what Asian industrialism can be. I would not say that such a goal is near for the Southeast Asian nations; nor do they believe it. But whoever does not understand that industrialism is at least one of their goals, and why it is, will find them difficult to handle. It is natural that they are sensitive about the management of their internal affairs. They will go abroad and learn, but the time of the foreign adviser is over.

To say this, of course, is to enter on highly controversial ground, and the objections can easily be anticipated. First, a question: "Does it apply to Northern Viet-Nam too, with its Russian and Chinese advisers and technicians?" Yes, given time, for we have to take into account that circumstances and perhaps a better understanding of the local psychological conditions have allowed the "obtrusion" to be lighter and less self-assertive there. But the more forcible exception will be that, in view of all that is at stake in Viet-Nam, with the prospect of an escalation of American expeditionary forces from two hundred to four or even six hundred thousand men in the near future, and the issuance of official statements suggesting that "We are reaching the stage when we shall not lose any more"—the whole picture of Vietnamese sensitivity to karmic interference of Westerners and their expectations may sound obsolete and somewhat childish.

One ought not, however, to regard as negligible the liminal and often subliminal approach of the Asian masses to this kind of situation. If they are to be expected eventually to shoulder a sizable share of the program devised for them, they must first of all be made to feel at home in it, to become aware, in terms closer to their way of thinking, that they belong in it. But how can they experience such a feeling and awareness if they do not initiate the program themselves? Is this a vicious circle? If so, the first step should be to recognize it as such.

Buddhist Concern in This World: Historical Background

Since the Geneva Agreement of 1954, which marked the end of the Colonial period in what was once called French Indochina, many new political factors have come to the fore in the whole of Southeast Asia. None has taken our experts more by surprise than the role played in many tense circumstances by the various schools of Buddhism in Mahāyānist Viet-Nam, as well as in the countries of Theravāda obedience, Cambodia, Laos, Thailand, and Burma, all of which claimed Ceylon as their religious metropolis. Although Buddhism there was recognized as having deep roots, governing peoples' lives and behavior, it was reputed to be non-political.

I have attempted to explain elsewhere that this erroneous assessment of the political influence of the Doctrine of the Elders (Theravāda) derives from data, texts, translations, and exegesis mainly established through the sustained activity of the Pali Text Society, first in Ceylon and later in Burma. The British Raj had put an end to the local Buddhist dynasties in these two countries in 1802 and 1885 respectively. In both cases, this left a kind of rump Buddhist society deprived of the vitally important support of the faith which the temporal authority is canonically in charge of. This temporal Buddhism was based on the commemoration and cult of the Master, with the Church, for its part, entrusted with the perpetuation of his teachings.

No critical account seems to have been taken of this grave mutilation. Our vision is of a Southern Buddhist monasticism that has turned its back to the world in quest of an egoistic, personal salvation, to be fulfilled in a monastic career extending over several lives, in accordance with the basic belief in transmigration.

When viewed in this manner, Buddhism becomes a complete enigma. How was it possible for a religion so lamely equipped doctrinally to conquer half the world? In his well known book on *The Religion of India,* Max Weber, noting that the Buddha's teaching gave birth to "one of the great missionary religions on earth," inserts this mystified comment:

This must seem baffling. Viewed rationally, there is no motive to be discovered which should have destined Buddhism for this. What could cause a monk who was seeking only his own salvation and therefore was utterly self-dependent to trouble himself with saving the souls of others?

According to Hermann Oldenberg, our most authoritative expert, "princes and nobles, Brahmans and merchants, we find among those who 'took their refuge in Buddha, the Law and the Order,' i.e., who made their profession as lay believers; the wealthy and the aristocrat, it seems . . . exceeded the poor." Were such people attracted by "the giddiness of annihilation" and by the final negation of self and soul, fading away in the unfathomable vacuity of Nirvana?

Oldenberg asserts that the belief in transmigration had put the last touch to the dreadful picture of the condition that the thought of India, exposed to the woes of a tropical climate, was convulsing itself into. Elaborating on the vedic hymns, most of which concerned, according to him, the legacy of happier times, Oldenberg says that the ritualists

on all sides . . . descried gloomy formless powers, either openly displayed or veiled in mysterious symbols, contending with each other and like harassing enemies, preparing *contretemps* for human destiny. The tyranny of death also is enhanced in the estimation of the dismal mystic of this age; the power of death over men is not spent with the one blow which he inflicts. It soon comes to be averred that this power over him, who is not wise enough to save himself by the use of the right words and the right offerings, extends even into the world beyond and death cuts short his life yonder again and again; we soon meet the conception of a multiplicity of death-powers of whom some pursue men in the worlds on this side and others in the worlds beyond.

Thus, even death, the supreme recourse of the unfortunate in case of extreme misery, failed the degenerate and endarkened scions of the "tall, blond, dolichocephalic" race that so valiantly had entered the country a few centuries earlier.

In fact, and quite apart from such mistaken ideas of ours, the philosophy and *Weltanschauung* of the Vedas, reflecting the impact of the Indo-European tribes in India, had very strong positive characteristics. To the variegated and at first disconcerting appearance of the Indian world and its denizens, they opposed, as a deliberate counterweight, the massive unity of an ideal world. This world was bolstered by endless sacrifices, the soul and repository of which were to be found in the vedic texts. The epitome of Indo-European traditions and values thus became the cultural program of the invaders. In the course of the centuries, it had to cope with indigenous and mixed traditions and products, such as the belief in local spirits and gods and, above all, transmigration. The outcome was Hinduism, in which the positive values, previously built on sacrifice (*yajña*), were transferred to a more personal devotion (*bhakti*) to a personalized cosmic power, Ishvara "The Lord." Ishvara was seen as the Lord of the Universe and, pantheistically, as that universe itself. The self (*ātman*) of the devotee, once built on his sacrificial achievements (*karma*), was now more and more authenticated by, and at the same time finally reabsorbed in, the omnipresence and omnipotence of these Ishvaras (Shiva and Vishnu). The world, in such a perspective, tended to become a mere picture, an illusion (*māyā*), supreme religious values being everywhere. For the initiate, it was a refuge from the real world and its problems.

This is precisely what the Buddhist revelation sweeps out: the whole mental construction is shattered and with it the prestige and profits which the Brahmans derived from it. At the same time, it becomes less surprising that the new doctrine should have rejected the notion of the person (*ātman*), and yet presented itself, to all objective assessment, as the most rigorous "personalism." It builds each individual entirely on himself and his own actions, without ritual alibis or escapes by atonement. Thus, the conventional self of the Hinduistic rites and devotion was definitively eliminated, leaving everyone to face his own responsibilities: "none but the doer of the deed will reap the fruit of the deed." It was a reformation of a kind. The days of the indulgences were past.

The real innovation was to reject final identification with the obscure and unpredictable notion of the cosmic total and to assert that the truth of the transient substantive "states" (*beings*) lay in their very transience, determined by their moral—instead of their ritual—actions (*karma*). Hence the interest shown by early, basic Buddhism in the temporal world. For these early Buddhists, there was (in contrast with the Brahmanical views) no other world on which to rely in order to reach liberation from this one. It is the way in which we handle this world of ours, reducing its beings and finally our being into ways and means of action (*karma*), that leads, thanks to the Buddha's illuminating disclosures, to the "way out" (*nirvana*).

Cosmic Law and World Order: The Burmese Experiment

But was this sufficient to justify a temporal Buddhism, which was overseen by faithful kings and tended to maintain and develop not only order, but prosperity and even abundance in this world—a remarkable anticipation of our "continuing dynamics of development" as the basis for world order? How can such an anticipation of our concept of the Welfare State, with which the historical Maurya king, Ashoka (3rd century B.C.), has been especially credited, be reconciled with the strict doctrine of personal action and retribution, clear of all indulgences, recourses to "others," and alibis?

What is a king, but a figurehead in the inexorable, though not fatal, process of transmigration, in which everyone may count on his own actions, and on nothing else whatsoever, to improve his future conditions?

Professor Emanuel Sarkisyanz, in his remarkable exposition of *The Buddhist Backgrounds of the Burmese Revolution,* has found solid reasons for denouncing local attempts at re-enacting the great Maurya king's *saga* as tragically inconsistent with the ethics and teachings of the Master. Under the pretext of emulating Ashoka, whose glory is to have replaced the drum and weapons of war by the weapons and drum of the Law—the sound of which was the signal of his moral conquests—Burmese historical sovereigns ended in a bath of blood their unfruitful attempts to extend their power over their neighbors. One of them went so far as to boast of having built pyramids of heads. If the Buddhist Cosmic Law is, as canonically described, a peaceful, all-embracing ordering of the world, what has it to do with such cruel and unfortunately too authentic stories?

The notion of cosmic law can be derived from several sources in which the proportion of observation and positive verification, in contrast to pure theorizing, varies greatly. The Brahmanical sacrificial approach of pre-Buddhistic times, centering essentially on the typical Aryan family and its head (*pati*), was related to the ultimate abstract power of the sacrificial formula (brahman), in harmony with the seasons of the year. However, the Buddhist mode of salvation took into consideration a finally impersonal sequence of actions and retributions (*karmaphala*), which was mistaken by "unawakened" (lit. "childish") minds for a "self" or "soul" (*ātman*).

In early Vedic times, the ritualistic approach, with its extensive and strict pattern of sacrificial procedures (*karma*) which covered and authenticated all actions and circumstances of human life, could harmoniously organize that society to meet the short-range interests and elements of routine existence. They developed a hand-to-mouth, autarkic economy. There were, of course, occasional wars against the aborigines, the results of which, as the outcome demonstrates, were usually favorable.

But as soon as we transpose the problem from the simple, comparatively uneventful schedule of a *grihapati*'s life, ancient-style, to what befalls a kingdom, its population, and its cities, especially during the uncertain and agitated centuries that followed the advent of Buddhism, an oversimplified and ritualistic conception of cosmic law and world order can no longer work satisfactorily.

Max Weber, following Oldenberg, appears to strike the right note when he stresses the fact that "rural surroundings, cattle and pasture were characteristic of the ancient Brahmanical teachers and schools, at least in the early times of the Upanishads, whereas the city and the urban palace with its elephant-riding kings were characteristic of Buddha's time." This applies, of course, to Hinduized India as well as to Buddha's time.

Wars, invasions, and political and religious revolutions obscured what had been, for a while, a clear and somewhat monotonous conception of world order as the frame of a prosperous "Aryan" life. The final effect was that all Indian religions from then on had to accommodate themselves to a more intricate, more rhythmic, and broader vision of the world—the theory of the recurrent ages— which might well have originated in the Middle East in connection with early astrology and astronomy. It told of a vanished Golden Age. The turn taken by contemporary history, especially in Northern India, thus announced the cataclysmic approach of an end of the world. Early Buddhism associated these ideas with belief in a gradual recession of the Buddha's teaching, leading to the disappearance of the Doctrine of the Church. It found comfort, however, in the expectation of a new Golden Age, to be brought back to earth by the coming of a new Buddha, Maitreya. Though evidently unfounded scientifically, this way of thinking comes remarkably close to what we would call the graph of a periodic phenomenon— in this case, the phenomenon of phenomena, that is, the phenomenon of the world or worlds as a whole.

If such a graph were known with perfect accuracy, we would be able to predict effectively the turn that our lives and the world's affairs would be expected to take. However, no Indian system has ever claimed this degree of accuracy, least of all Buddhism. It was essential to its doctrine not to submit to any fatalistic predestination: the act (*karma*) was to build the world in accordance with the full responsibility of the actors.

Thus, the Buddhists, in the pangs of the present Iron Age, were bound to attach ever greater importance, just to be able to see ahead of themselves, to the exact position of our world as shown on its graph. This made sense of the royal power, of its social activities, its attempts at a peaceful conquest of the earth, establishing a Welfare State that would take charge of the entire world, an ideal nearly attained by Ashoka. Such a reign was a check and, in the case of success, a signal: It meant that the Buddha to come was not indefinitely deferring his coming. There might still be many centuries to wait, but a turning point must have already been reached as things seemed to be improving instead of growing worse. The psychological value of such speculations is not to be slighted. We have recently had ample occasion to appreciate the deep impression made on the Buddhist world by the conviction that we have reached, with the 2500th anniversary of the Buddha's birth, the precise point when we could consider ourselves halfway between his "revelation" and his expected successor, Maitreya.

The West cannot remain indifferent to the fact that so many millions of our contemporary "fellow men" look in that direction in their expectation of an oncoming world order.

The massacres perpetrated by the Buddhist kings who tried to emulate the Maurya Emperor thus make more sense—if a dire and forbidding one. They should be understood as a kind of test or ordeal. Such wars were initiated as a check of the point reached by world affairs on the graph of the ages of the world. The history and, even more clearly, the legend of Ashoka's reign established the pattern of such an experiment. Whatever his final relation to the oncoming Buddha, a point which, in the present state of our documentation, cannot be clearly assessed, after a bloody beginning, a moment had come when—because of his past merits and the accumulated merits of all men and of his contemporaries—the latter spontaneously turned to him and submitted to his sway without further resistance. Such is evidently the signal that the Burmese conquerors sought—and that finally did not come.

There would be great profit in reading Professor Sarkisyanz's remarkable book in the light of such preconceptions, still alive among the masses. This would make it easier to understand why U Nu, commonly taken in 1960 to be the impersonation of the King of the Wheel (*cakravartin*) that forebodes the coming of the Buddha, or even as the "incarnation" of the Buddha himself, should have been quasi-unanimously borne to power, and nevertheless failed in the eyes of his fellow countrymen and found little support among them against General Ne Win, when the latter deposed him in 1962. U Nu had remained short of the expected "signal": bringing around the Communists to his charisma. This political or, more accurately, cosmic test had, to all appearances, failed.

Conclusion

Relying largely on Professor Sarkisyanz's admirable analysis of the Buddhistic backgrounds of the Burmese crisis, I have tried to show how difficult it is for Westerners to comprehend a vision of the world and world order which is neither *normative* nor purely *objective*, but, shall we say, *prospective*. Still deeply affected by their traditionally half-Buddhistic, half-folkloristic approach to such problems, the masses bet heavily on what they imagine will or might happen—their stakes being themselves. The closest analogy with our modern methodology would be Claude Bernard's famous *Expérience pour voir*. U Nu has been given precisely that chance and has not lived up to it—his achievements as well as his failure offer a remarkable illustration of both sides of the question.

Thus, far from considering "lay" Buddhism, Ashokan style, as a mere pragmatic accretion to the Theravāda faith, a closer study of its intimate connection with the doctrine will help to reconstruct a more human and convincing picture of both the social and political expansion of the Southern School and the eventual grounds for its reconciliation on such matters with the much more open and active leanings of the Mahāyānist or Northern School which prevails in Central and Eastern Asia, Viet-Nam included.

If, before the arrival and interference of the Westerners, a kind of political, quasi-national Buddhism was established on authentic Theravāda and Mahāyāna values, it would seem possible to build, at least between the various Indochinese denominations, a new covenant on that strong and lasting foundation: the Buddha's message.

DAVIDSON NICOL

Toward a World Order: An African Viewpoint

INTERPLANETARY COMMUNICATION, intraplanetary travel, and a visual impression of a revolving world with its continents and oceans —as seen from space ships by millions on television—have all been powerful incentives for the average person to realize the necessity and, in fact, the present reality, however imperfect, of a world order.

In the United Nations there has been an obvious, practical, but incomplete attempt to achieve this order—incomplete because of the significant absence of nations such as Israel and China.

However, unity has been sought by different countries in many different ways. For geographical convenience, the ocean frontier which creates continents has been used in this effort, undoubtedly because migrations and movements are easier within a land mass than without. This continental principle has been recognized in the formation of the Organization for European Unity (OEU), the Organization of American States (OAS), and the Organization for African Unity (OAU). Furthermore, for either economic or military reasons, regional blocs have come into being. Sometimes, as in the case of the Southeast Asia Treaty Organization (SEATO), such a bloc will represent not just an area but also nations which have interests in the region.

Other attempts to achieve unity have been based, sometimes unconsciously, on a racial principle. The alliance of the Arab countries is based partly on race and partly on religion. The North Atlantic Treaty Organization (NATO) is both a regional and a racial organization. Its racial basis is clearly demonstrated by the insistence that Turkey be included as a white, European, and non-Asian country while Tunisia—with a better claim to membership than Turkey—is excluded. Until recently when China joined them, the nuclear powers were another select, racial group, although accidentally so. The Afro-Asian bloc is primarily a regional grouping, but it also happens to be nonwhite. It is likely that if

Australia had been completely peopled by colored races it would have been invited to join it.

There is a political principle involved also. The NATO, SEATO, and Warsaw Pact countries are not only regional but also strongly political blocs. In fact, their political ties are sometimes more important than their regional boundaries. Then there are ideological groupings, the most important of which is that of the Communist countries. Yugoslavia, Albania, and China have created rifts, but, in spite of this, international Communism represents the largest number of people in the world, outside of those who belong to one or another of the great religions, who are held together by the force of ideas and a belief in a particular way of life.

Finally, we must note, for those of us with intellectual concerns, the importance of the international meetings of scientific and professional societies. The potential influence of these groups as national societies or, as in the case of the Pugwash conferences, as individuals is important; it has never been exploited to the full, perhaps because such groups lack the inclination, power, and organization to go on global strikes.

It is of interest, on the basis of this cursory survey of groups which might form units in a world order, that only the nuclear powers and the professional societies constitute groups based on intrinsic intellectual achievements.

The movement toward world order is hampered by great barriers. Some of these are being overcome; others remain difficult to surmount.

Language is one of the most obvious barriers, but it is being minimized by mechanical devices and translating machines. The invention of speedy and easy methods of learning languages has also been helpful. However, these are merely instruments. The first necessity is the desire to learn a language. At present this happens mostly for economic and sometimes political reasons. It should become ideological.

Historiography, with a wrong national or racial emphasis, is another barrier. The true greatness of figures like Napoleon, Lincoln, or Lenin is obscured for millions of young intellectuals by the way in which their writings or actions are misinterpreted in countries or sections historically opposed to them. For example, the question of the motives that led to the abolition of slavery is now very confused because for so long it has been described solely and patronizingly as an act of charity and nobility. Yet, it is clear, as Dr. Eric Williams of Trinidad and Dr. Kenneth Diké of Nigeria among others have forcefully shown, that capitalistic and economic motives for abolition were also present.

The childhood fears instilled in homes, institutions, and societies, which are racially homogeneous in a world that is racially heterogeneous, lead to still another barrier. One of the great unnoticed barriers which keeps individuals, nations, or races from realizing the necessity of a world order is an equally human failing. It is the sense of individual pride and fulfillment that comes from attributes we have not achieved individually but which we have inherited. For millions, being white, Anglo-Saxon Protestant, Brahmin, or Samurai, or descended from the daughter of the prophet Mohammed, is tremendously important for morale and forms an effective obstacle to normal communication and easy friendship with others.

In order to achieve a world order, we must first examine how its subunits, that is, nations, are formed. We can see this most clearly in the formation of new nations. The United States of America is perhaps the greatest of the new nations.

The older and more settled parts of the United States, such as New England and the South, still exert great influence over the rest. It seems, at least from outside, that a significant proportion of those who provide the drive to advance are immigrants or the descendants of recent immigrants. That part of the country which was built up largely during this later period can provide a lesson on the forging of nationhood. For example, a common language was imposed as well as, with the aid of mass media, a common orthography and a recognizable accent. A common history was taught, and certain figures were made to appear heroic and exemplary. Myths were invented or adopted. However, enough maneuvering was allowed within the units of the nation to provide scope for those local ambitions and prejudices which did not affect the integrity of the whole.

In a smaller, more recent but not less significant way, Israel demonstrates another attempt at building a new nation from disparate groups. A common language has been imposed; a common heroic and racial history has been and continues to be taught. In addition, sufficient scope for activity is permitted to diverse groups of either religious or racial origin.

A few years ago, in a realistic statement, the leader of an African state with a population of about six million people doubted the wisdom and viability of any state that had less than three million inhabitants. This announcement was passionately and angrily denounced by leaders of states smaller than this, clearly illustrating that the question of national sovereignty is of tremendous importance to African politicians.

It is easy to continue indefinitely to blame the former colonial powers for the political and economic ills now besetting the African nations. But this exercise is not completely profitable since it detracts from the energy available for positive and forward thinking and adds to a general defeatism in the necessary business of striving for improvement and change. Nonetheless, those critics who blame African leaders for their intransigent attitude and unwillingness to federate into larger and more economically viable units must be prepared to add that this results from one of the major failures and historical legacies of the colonial powers.

The usual imperial policy of divide and rule did not initially lead to fragmentation. In the nineteenth century the British tried very hard to govern the West African *coastal* settlements (chiefly Nigeria, Ghana, Sierra Leone, and Gambia) together from one headquarters in Sierra Leone. They failed twice before the difficulties of communication and the egocentricity of the divisional British administrators forced them to give up entirely. Later, however, when the active conquest ("pacification" it is sometimes called) of the interior took place, it became convenient to break up such large and viable units as the empires of Samory, Dan Fodio, and the Mossi kings. When necessary, those Africans who through fear or ambition were willing to co-operate with the conquering colonial powers were appointed as the leaders of the fragmented units. Any instance in which there was a federation of units had very little to do with nation-building. It seemed inconceivable that in the near future there would be any independent African nations, given the general contempt with which Africa was regarded by Europeans in the latter third of the nineteenth century and in the first half of the twentieth century. A federation of African units or an enlargement of existing units became possible only when existing rulers were weakened or sufficiently vassalized. This followed in the wake of active European soldier-administrators.

The boundaries of the various European-controlled areas in Africa were crystallized and formalized in Berlin in the eighteen-eighties and were maintained by bilateral treaties as further conquests in the interior took place. The interior areas were usually related to the nearest coastal cities or coastal provinces and named after them. The formation of larger units was on a strictly pragmatic basis. The lands of the Mendis, Temnes, Limbas, and other groups were attached to what was then a few square miles of the coastal colony of Sierra Leone and were then taxed to pay for the administration of the territory, a task the home government in Great Britain was either unwilling to do or tired of doing. It is said that, after he conquered it, Sir Frederick Lugard joined Northern Nigeria to Southern Nigeria, that is, chiefly Lagos and the other commercially important ports, in order to be able financially to maintain the administration of all the conquered territories.

Occasionally the need to preserve and safeguard trade routes to Europe was the determining factor in the establishment of territorial boundaries. Any tendency toward interdependence or understanding among various groups of Africans which might have led to a supra-territorial outlook in Africa was suppressed, deliberately or accidentally, by the dominant European powers. Because of this, the influences of different European countries could make themselves felt in a single individual, or on the members of the same family or tribe, or on neighboring tribes. A Susu might be French or British, a Bakongo might be Belgian or French, a Somali might be Italian, French, or British. Within a single lifetime a Togolese could experience the influence of German, French, and British culture, law, and customs—perhaps, in addition, Portugese, if he was of Brazilian slave ancestry. It is clear that when single tribes or neighboring tribes have been introduced to world culture and politics through such diverse channels—with their separate cultures overlaid by the differing outlooks of their European masters—the possibilities of different African tribes or nations coming together voluntarily are remote. Given this situation, the measure of achievement and agreement that is represented by a federation like Nigeria or by countries like Somalia and Kamerun is surprising.

It is sad but evident that for the cohesion of a unit, whether nation, race, or continent, the presence or invention of a common threat is necessary. In the United States, this is Communism; in Western Europe, Russia; in the Arab Countries, Israel; in Russia, first the West and now China; in India, China; in China, America; and so on in a sorry circle. The newest nations in the world are in Africa, and the common threat they recognize is neo-colonialism, or the return of white domination by the United States, Western Europe, or Russia through economic or clandestine political means. This fear is evident in the periodic expulsions from different African nations of individual diplomats from these countries. The repeated slogans of Africanization, nonalignment, and positive neutrality may be the direct consequences of this fear.

Let us now further examine the position of the African nations and the contribution they can make toward the establishment of a world order. Every African nation must face up to two kinds of unity—Pan-African unity and internal unity.

Writers like George Padmore and Colin Legum have ably dealt with the subject of Pan-African unity. All African nations and leaders subscribe to this almost as an article of faith. When he was selected to lead his country, one of the most recent and dynamic of African prime ministers, Albert M. Margai of Sierra Leone, made this the central theme of all his speeches.

In the three great language groups of Africa, there have been three chief protagonists of Pan-African unity during the past decade in which most African states have gained their independence: Nasser in the Arabic sector, Sekou Touré in the French-speaking territories, and Kwame Nkrumah in the English-speaking areas. Their impassioned writings and declarations about African unity have dominated the scene, in addition to the two venerable father figures, Haile Selassie, Emperor of Ethiopia, and Dr. William V. S. Tubman, President of Liberia, who are symbolic not only in their persons but also in the historical priority of their countries' independence.

Statements on political philosophy have been made largely by the leaders of states which were formerly in the French colonial empire. This applies not only to Africa but elsewhere, probably because the tradition of humanities has had more influence on the French educational system than on the British. As a result we note the unusual combination of politics, philosophy, and poetry which has been produced by national leaders like Sekou Touré of Guinea, Leopold Sedar Senghor of Senegal, Ho Chi Minh of North Viet-Nam, and Aimé Césaire of the Antilles.

In contrast, the African leaders from the English-speaking nations have written memoirs and collections of speeches which give interesting and shrewd accounts of the growth and development of their political parties, and of their individual parts in the struggle for freedom and independence. These range from the restrained account of the Zambian leader, Kenneth O. Kaunda, to the firm statements of the late Ahmadu Bello, Sardauna of Sokoto and Premier of Northern Nigeria. Then there are two leaders, still very active, who three decades ago wrote scholarly accounts of the African scene—one in political science and one in social anthropology. They are, respectively, Dr. Nnamdi Azikwe, former President of the Republic of Nigeria, and Dr. Jomo Kenyatta, President of the Republic of Kenya. Both outline on a firm academic basis the situation as it was then in their territory. More recently, Senghor and his temporarily estranged colleague, Mamadou Dia, from Senegal have made cogent statements of African socialism.

The writings of these leaders must be studied by any serious student of the African political scene. The dearth of African journalists and political commentators leaves these as the main sources available at present for an indication of the direction in which events are moving or will move in Africa. It is also important, in spite of the prevalence of one-party states, to study the statements and views of opposition leaders, whether they are in exile or not.

The conferences of the OAU have provided a forum for the hopes and ideas of African leaders. Such conferences have been held in Addis Ababa, Cairo, and Accra. The OAU is not racist in nature. No two people can look as different as a Tunisian and a Congolese. Moreover, two of the most politically active states, Tanzania and Kenya, have white cabinet ministers; and, in some technical meetings dealing with nonmilitary matters, white Frenchmen, in the service of French-speaking states, sometimes act as their representatives. Portugese Africa, Rhodesia, and the Republic of South Africa are excluded from the OAU because the governments of these countries do not represent their population. No matter how long the governing groups may have been in these countries (and some of the Portugese and Afrikaners have been in Africa for three centuries) they are wrong to maintain an attitude of permanent white supremacy. They make no provision and provide no outlet for the hopes of the struggling black majority except, perhaps, to allow an illicit racial dilution over the course of several generations, or to call for the total acceptance of European culture at the price of a complete and shameful renunciation of all that is good in African culture. The only answer of these countries to the African situation is one of racial absorption and cultural genocide.

Furthermore, the OAU is of tremendous importance in the creation and maintenance of world order. It has demonstrated its usefulness in the containment of border conflicts in Africa, and in the ceaseless and often unnoticed negotiations of the foreign ministers of African countries. True, disturbing antagonisms appear regularly at OAU meetings, but this is to be expected because there is no common agreement about the nature or timing of a complete federation of African states. Many states have tasted and enjoyed independence for too short a period to be ready to surrender their sovereignty to a union of African states. However wrong and mistaken their idea may seem, such a union does not appear to them to be any different from the colonial rule of a European power. But, fortunately, there has never been any open division along racial or religious lines in the OAU and, whatever internal differences there are, they are not irreconcilable. The external view of the organization in most instances, with one or two notable exceptions such as the U.S. view, has been reserved and lacking in enthusiasm.

There are, however, certain powerful forces which tend to oppose political Pan-African unity and which lead to a continued attachment to national sovereignty. Since independence has come in such piecemeal fashion to the various nations, there can be little hope that it will be quickly surrendered in favor of supranational sovereignty. Great importance is attached to diplomatic representation and a seat in the United Nations. This is one of the only means individual African nations have of making their individual voices heard. There are other factors of equal importance that are not so immediately evident. For many of the different communities which are now nations, to be an individual nation is a new idea. Originally the nation may have existed only as a colonial and administrative unit; it was part of a civil service which owed its allegiance to a metropolitan power and was naturally subordinate to it. When this power left, there was inevitably a fragmentation of some units, as small as some of them already were. Even though, as we have previously mentioned, larger federal units should have been formed earlier, it is to the credit of the last colonial governors that in many instances they resisted the pressure of regional and tribalistically inclined African politicians who, on the eve of independence, pressed for the further carving up of the existing national units.

The importance of individual national sovereignty with its diplomatic representation, seat in the United Nations, prime minister and cabinet, flag, postage stamps, and national anthem is that *within* the national territory itself it indicates to the different communities for the first time that they are one, free people. Such sovereignty is a very necessary preliminary for unification of great importance to people whose immediate loyalty has always been to a village unit or tribe. These people can now recognize within their government's cabinet persons with whom they share a recognizable identity. They can visit or reside in a capital city and get to know each other better. Their children can begin to go to the same school and, more important, to such postschool institutions as universities or technical and professional institutes, which will make them full members of one nation. All this must happen before these Africans can be expected to broaden their loyalties and intellectual horizons to encompass a supranational Pan-Africanism and a supracontinental world order. A Scotsman and a Cornishman must feel a common identity as British before they can become European; a Provencal and a Norman must be French before they can become European; a Pennsylvania Dutchman, a Minnesota Swede, a Boston Irishman, and an Alabama African must be brought together effectively under a national flag with national traditions and myths before they can be useful as U.S. members of the OAS.

The members of any African state must have time to feel that they constitute one nation before they can adopt supranationalism or internationalism. However, these processes need not be consecutive; they can be concurrent. The important factor is one of time. It is our contention that if this process of education had been begun earlier by the colonial powers in the large units they first encountered, or if they had formed larger units and carried on such education, our present tasks would be less difficult and take less time. It must be the duty of Africans to work for African unity in the same way that Europeans are now seeking European unity.

Nevertheless, looked at from another angle, the proliferation of African states has not been without advantage. It has enabled Africa to make its voice heard in a multiple and effective way in international conferences and has provided powerful numerical strength in voting. It may well be that without plural representation at this critical juncture in African affairs, Africa might not receive the attention it needs for its wrongs to be righted.

Of more individual advantage to particular states, is the fact that when it comes to financial aid, donor countries are more interested in channeling their contributions directly to a specific African country or group of countries, as they choose, than to a region of the continent or to the continent at large. Sometimes the choice is the result of past colonial ties; sometimes it reflects strategic considerations or ideological encouragement; sometimes it may be simply because the donor country wants to direct its aid to a single unit so that it can more readily measure its effectiveness. In the case of countries with past colonial ties an element of sentimentality and warmth may be present, although a nationalist African probably regards such aid simply as the continuation of the commercial interests of the metropolitan country.

The disadvantages of the balkanization of Africa are chiefly economic. Many African countries are not and never will be economically viable unless oil or uranium is discovered in them. The prospect of becoming another Kuwait is like a mirage in the desert; it encourages the maintenance of national sovereignty in many small states which might otherwise consider early federation with their neighbors.

The shortage of skilled manpower with its uneven distribution is another severe disadvantage. Although temporary in nature, this shortage is serious because it slows down the making and the implementation of decisions at this most formative period in the existence of the African states. The advantage of multiple African representation at the United Nations has been mentioned; we must mention also that tying down so many of our skilled Africans at innumerable international or interterritorial conferences several times a year removes them from the effective internal development and administration of their territories. In any one territory the few technically proficient and professional Africans may be away for many months voting on important but occasionally vague resolutions. Then, when they return home, routine administrative duties keep them tied down to their desks; or, if they are involved in politics, they may have to start campaigning for the next election. It can thus happen that most of the important developmental operations and decisions in a country are directed by foreign personnel or by international civil servants while the country's leading citizens are away or busy with other things. At the present time, it is necessary to have expert foreign personnel; it is wrong, however, for them to replace local leadership in all projects. The development of local leadership must be part of the national goal. Local schemes can sometimes be robbed of their correct orientation by frequent absences abroad of national representatives, sowing seeds of misunderstanding and future allegations of neo-colonialism, when leadership is left to foreigners.

The question of the shortage of skilled personnel must lead to a consideration of means for improving this situation. There have been three notable conferences which have discussed the problems of higher education in regional and continental Africa. Their findings and resolutions have been repeated in the other conferences which are still being held on this topic. It is our contention that it would be more sensible and realistic to proceed with the implementation of these suggestions than to continue the debate with still more experts.

The Freetown Seminar of 1961, which was held under the auspices of the Congress for Cultural Freedom and Fourah Bay College (report published by Ibadan University Press, Nigeria, 1962); the 1962 UNESCO Tananarive Conference on Higher Education in Africa; and the 1963 Khartoum Conference of Heads of African Universities (report published by the International Association of Universities, Paris, 1964) have all stressed some salient points in African university education. All African experts and intellectuals who wish to use their skills effectively in the African environment in technology or in the humanities need a sound grounding in African studies. The exchange of students and staff among universities, the positive measures needed for the training of much-needed African academic staff, and the key position of libraries and university presses in the African framework are all important. With regard to the latter we note that European and American journals and publishing houses are often crowded and have long waiting lists for the publication of their own material. This makes it necessary for some publishing to be done in Africa. In addition, rare manuscripts and expensive publications cannot be obtained by every university library in Africa so that there should be a constant interchange among all universities. However, each library should certainly have its own distinctive local collection of Africana in books and archives, and the existence of each collection should be made known to scholars in every African university.

The relevance of the education of African students to their effectiveness in the development of the continent has been the subject of much discussion recently. The foreign structure of African universities—French, English (that is, London and Durham largely), Belgian, and American—provides a foundation on which African scholars and others on the university scene can now build institutions more useful and apposite to the main requirements of African development.

African universities can become foci of unity in Africa; they can forge friendships and bring to bear influences which will be very important in the future. Al Azhar in Cairo is a meeting place for Muslim students from all over the continent. On a more regional basis, Fourah Bay College in Sierra Leone has been a meeting place for English-speaking West Africans for several generations, while for the past three decades Dakar in Senegal and Makerere in Uganda have served the same purpose for French-speaking West Africans and English-speaking East Africans.

In addition, we must remember that for many years London, Paris, and New York have had concentrations of African students which have greatly contributed to African unity. Recently, a new and more positive attempt to provide a meeting place for African students outside the continent has been made by the Patrice Lumumba University in Moscow, where the university is actually run for Afro-Asian students and staffed by leading Russian professors. On a smaller scale, Israel is attempting something similar, although naturally there are not very many Africans from Arabic-speaking countries enrolled.

It may not be wasteful to establish new universities and colleges in the new countries if attention is paid to the principles of cooperation that have been carefully worked out in the past few years. It must not be forgotten that a university in an African country can be the repository of local culture, a center for local economic research, and, when so allowed, an island of free and independent thought.

The economic sphere appears to be the one in which there may be the earliest move toward unity. There is very little intra-African trade as compared with overseas trade. The poor intraterritorial communication and the markedly centripetal routes toward the shipment of goods from African coastal cities to established markets in Europe and America—encouraged by the road and railway systems designed for this purpose in colonial times—all contribute to the continued extraterritorial export of raw material and commodities.

Some countries such as Guinea, Liberia, Sierra Leone, and the Ivory Coast are combining together to form a free trade area. The territories bordering on the River Niger have combined in a group to exploit the river's usefulness. But, on the other hand, the East African Common Services Organization that linked Kenya, Uganda, and Tanzania in the economic sphere has ruptured. This may be disappointing, but it is not surprising. Most of the unions formed in British Africa among different territories have tended to come apart after the territories have achieved independence, probably because Great Britain did not continue to finance them heavily. Usually such unions are helped briefly and then encouraged to become self-supporting. The first sign of trouble usually appears over the allocation of finances. It is a different story with the heavily subsidized unions of the French-speaking states which appear to be more successful, although the rupture of the Senegal-Mali union is an unfortunate exception. It may be that the economic unions which come into existence following independence, on the basis of voluntary negotiations, under present ECA guidance, stand a better chance of continuing success. It would be most helpful if donor countries like the United States were to encourage existing unions rather than concentrate on individual states.

In summary, the position of national sovereignty in Africa is the following. The desirability of supranationalism is admitted by all and is made manifest in the OAU. However, the retention of certain elements of national sovereignty is useful; it contributes to nation-building and internal homogeneity. The proper training for the achievement of a supranational goal and the nature of its leadership are questions which will be debated and disputed for some time to come.

The extracontinental impact of African independence has some relevance in our considerations. Africans remember gratefully that there have always been some individuals and some groups in both Western and Eastern countries who have held firmly to a belief in African freedom. These people regarded the liberation of the African continent as a personal achievement and fulfillment. It took place after years in which they had been helping and encouraging African students and leaders openly and clandestinely, and in which they had been faced with loneliness and unpopularity in their metropolitan countries because of their faith in the potentialities of the African.

In the view of many, the appearance in rapid sequence of over thirty African countries in the United Nations has changed and added to the effectiveness of the organization. The effect of these countries has been more studied and documented than the influence of any other region in that body. It is unnecessary to study it in great detail here. A few brief remarks will be enough.

By the equalization of destructive power, the East-West conflict has reached a nuclear stalemate. It is clear from an economic point of view that both blocs are building up or have built up a standard of living which rightly they do not wish to lose. Both are aware of and are afraid of the destructiveness of nuclear warfare. Members of the Afro-Asian bloc and the Latin American bloc have to some extent started, or are continuing, to fight each other—but always with conventional weapons. They are sometimes imbued with a philosophy of despair and fatalism, feeling that because they have so little, they have little to lose. It is likely that for some time there will have to be peace-keeping operations in these areas. The big power blocs watch these conflicts with interest; they encourage with arms and advisers those who share their ideology, but by tacit agreement they confine the struggle to African and Asian areas which are well outside their own metropolitan countries. The success of the United Nations will be measured by its persuasiveness and its ability to halt these localized wars, which in an ideological sense are colonial wars. In these cases the Afro-Asian bloc sees it as one of its special duties to intervene forcefully in the international forum.

The emotional impact of the advent of so many African states seems to have been felt relatively less among the colonial powers, probably because, in the immediate postwar period, experience with India, Indochina, and Indonesia prepared imperial Europe to accept the approaching independence of black and brown men. Under the militant leadership of Nkrumah, Azikiwe, Kenyatta, Touré, Bourguiba, and others, and the wise acknowledgment of the situation by Great Britain and France, most of nonwhite Africa was liberated in about a decade. At least political independence was acknowledged, although considerable control of the disposal of African exports and raw materials still remains in European hands.

In the coming decade, we will see more clearly the impact of African independence on Western Europe and America. There will be an intensified struggle over commodity prices, the ownership of plantations and mines, the extent to which business firms in the metropolitan powers will allow processing and industrialization in Africa, and the establishment of trade agreements which may be deleterious or hostile to individual European and American interests.

In Eastern Europe African independence was hailed as a victory over imperialism and capitalism, at the same time that it exposed the prevalent ignorance of Africa in this area—an ignorance which scholars like the late Ivan Potekhim worked hard to overcome. With the exception of an isolated incident, for example, Poland's colonial ambitions for Liberia in the thirties, Eastern Europe has the advantage of not being tainted with a colonial past. Before independence, the main contacts between Eastern Europe and Africa were through trade, as for example between Czechoslovakia and Africa.

In the beginning it was felt that Africans needed or were looking for extra-African political guidance, which would most likely be supplied by the Communist governments. Now, both the latter and the Western world realize that they were mistaken. There are still very few African embassies in the Communist countries. The main African residents in these countries are students whose political activities have sometimes been an embarrassment to their hosts. The vitality, ability, and sheer resistance or nonchalance to political indoctrination of these students have been significant. These students, at present, meet increasingly with kindness and respect, and not patronage. It has been realized that they have minds of their own and independent points of view on political questions.

This is also the case in a different setting—in the geographically Eastern countries where the Afro-Asian brotherhood of the U.N. delegates' lounge in New York is put to the test by the presence of Africans in Asian universities and hotels. After a period of preliminary trauma, this has led to better understanding on both sides.

The echoes of African independence also have reached as far as Australasia, where anticolonial manifestations in New Guinea have been a consequence of the African revolution, not the Asian one.

Another area in which African independence has had a most powerful effect is in the Americas and the Caribbean, where there are many citizens of African descent. In both places it has led to a tremendous increase of self-respect and a stiffening attitude against racial prejudice. To know that black men from less-developed countries could be in seats of power, courted and entertained by white leaders in America, while, figuratively at least, colored and sometimes better-educated Americans still have to use the back door, has sharpened the mental attitude of many. African resentment about incidents of racial prejudice in America has, in the view of some observers, speeded up domestic policy in this area in the United States. However, the pride of the colored American in African independence does not necessarily lead to a desire to emigrate to Africa any more than pride in Israel has led to the mass emigration of American Jews to that country. Instead it gives the American Negro a confidence in his background which prepares him psychologically for high positions in America.

African independence has had another important effect in the United States. It has led to the tremendous amount of scholarly research now being undertaken into African matters, and to the economic and political interest that the United States now displays in independent African countries as compared with the colonial period when entry into these countries was restricted for Americans.

Finally, the increasing number of African students and visitors in the United States means that a wider African audience can now appreciate the fact that individual states like Texas and Vermont, comparable in size and population to some of their own countries, have been able to join in a federation of united states. This has been a catalytic agent in the movement for a united Africa.

African countries need the skills, technical abilities, and drive which have led the United States to its present position. At the same time they reserve the right to determine the political framework within which these skills should be used. They feel rightly or wrongly that these factors can be separated.

A still wider unit than the OAU has come into being. This is the unit which contains both African and Asian nations and which first met in Bandung ten years ago. Since Bandung, it has had meetings of committees and groups on several occasions and it has formed a consultative bloc in the United Nations.

The Afro-Asian bloc is important in several ways. It contains the largest, the most rapidly expanding, and the hungriest populations in the world. Its young people are more idealistic and more restless than any others in the world, except perhaps in South America.

Among its members, the Afro-Asian group has experienced

the longest periods of suspended government in the modern world. By this we mean an interruption and rearrangement of sovereignty. Most of Western Europe went through a period of suspended government during the German occupation. That this government was in some cases said to be efficient did not justify it. However, the period of suspended government was only five years. In Afro-Asian countries the period of occupation and suspended government varied from sixty years in the case of Nigeria to more than two or three centuries in some parts of Indonesia. One of the most common mistakes observers make is to imagine that the Afro-Asian countries exercised power for the first time when they were recently granted independence. It is forgotten that they governed themselves, sometimes with great success, before they came under colonial domination. Without any doubt they made economic gains, although this was sometimes incidental, by their contact with Europe. A homogeneous kind of law and order was spread over a wide area by a colonial power, and persecuted minorities were protected. The seat of indigenous authority was changed, sometimes for the better, sometimes for the worse. Even in Japan, which had only about ten years or less of colonial occupation, changes were carried out. The great loss, however, suffered by some of the Afro-Asian nations was the quality of experience in the exercise of power and in the making of decisions, especially in cases where new indigenous groups replaced previous traditional and indigenous authority. This temporary loss of power to govern after experiencing a suspended government is matched by the experience of the chaotic governments in liberated Europe immediately following the war. Nonetheless, they recovered, and undoubtedly the Afro-Asian countries will recover good government and economic prosperity, given time.

It is important for this matter to have been examined so fully by analogy in order to avoid the prevalent feeling that the new Afro-Asian nations have an intrinsic lack of the ability to achieve good government. It is important in considering their role in the creation of a world order to know that these nations can achieve eventual stability.

No one country has bid definitely for leadership in the Afro-Asian group, partly because each member is too individualistic, and partly because in both Africa and Asia the domination of foreign powers has been too recent. Russia, because it contains a large Asian element, attempted to become a member of this group. At first its attempt may have seemed entirely justifiable. However, Russia is a federal union with its capital firmly in Europe.

Peking has made definite moves toward establishing a claim as the guiding force. Its vast population, its political dedication, and the fact that by possessing the nuclear bomb it has removed total control of this weapon from the solely non-Afro-Asian powers are all very much in its favor. The warmth of the Chinese reception to visiting Afro-Asian dignitaries, trade-union workers, and professional groups has been notable. The drawbacks to the Chinese bid for leadership are the reports of aggression in India, the lack of integration of its immigrant and commercially successful communities in other Southeast Asian countries, the reports of the dissatisfied students who have returned home from China, and the friendly overtures of the Taiwan Government with its successful work in agricultural and other fields in various African countries. Further, the absence of Peking from the United Nations, where most Afro-Asian diplomats meet and talk regularly, is one of the greatest stumbling blocks in the path of the influence which the People's Republic of China wishes to exert. On the other hand, the recognition of the Peking regime by France, a country with great influence in Africa and the Middle East, has done much to enhance the prestige of Peking in Afro-Asian circles.

The influence of Tokyo among the Afro-Asian nations is steadily rising. There is great admiration for the advances in industrial skill and technology which have taken place in Japan since the war. The commercial enterprise of the Japanese is evident in nearly every country. Their presence is felt in the numerous commercial delegations sent to the Afro-Asian countries; and their fishing trawlers are scattered along the coast of Africa. Naturally, their influence is greatest in Asia. Their wartime activities are gradually being forgotten and forgiven. They are better known to African ex-servicemen than any other nation in Asia, apart from India. The recent invitation to Japan from a Malaysian leader to assume leadership in Asia is significant, even when judged against the political background in which it was made.

The most ubiquitous Asians in Africa are those from the Indian subcontinent. They have not exerted much influence on the West Coast; in East Africa, after the British departed, their influence waned considerably. Nevertheless, their commercial power in all parts of Africa, including the South, is still quite considerable. However, India appears to have great internal problems which continue to keep it preoccupied and which limit any attempts it might wish to make to pursue a leadership role in Afro-Asian affairs, particularly so now, with the towering father figures of Gandhi and Nehru absent from the scene.

It is in the United Nations particularly that Afro-Asian activities have found their most cogent expression.

We must appreciate and repeat again that this decade marks the first time in which the majority of Afro-Asian nations have had the opportunity of making their views known to the world at large. For this reason alone their interventions need careful audience and a full analysis. Yet few of the great powers have done this. The majority have simply noted whether a given state was on the side of the Western powers or of the Communist bloc in voting. Sometimes this consideration has determined the giving or withholding of financial aid. Yet, if in situations where the Afro-Asian powers have differed from the Western powers, the Western powers were to reverse roles, they would probably see clearly that they have wanted the non-European powers only to be satellites in their power bloc. These Afro-Asian powers, especially the African ones, are not credited with the ability to make independent decisions and to adhere to a declared neutrality and nonalignment.

The representatives of the African states at the United Nations are men of distinction who can hold their own equally well in European or American society. A cursory view of the heads of the Afro-Asian delegations reveals lawyers; civil servants who have gained eminence in the service of their countries under the British or French in competition with the best citizens of these colonial powers; scholars educated at the Sorbonne, Oxford, or Cambridge; international jurists; and often men of letters of great experience. It is absurd that the behavior of men of this caliber should be described, as has been done, as childish or obstructionist when they decide to take a firm stand on matters that involve the peace and stability of their own continents or of the world. A mistake made most often by great powers is that they do not, either in public or private, declare the extent of their financial or political interest in certain matters about which Afro-Asians feel strongly. Rather, they sometimes insist on maintaining their position on moral or legalistic grounds. For example, the feelings of the Western powers on questions involving Portugal, such as Goa, Macao, Angola, and Mozambique, are strongly influenced by the value to the West of military bases in the Azores and by the consistent anti-Communist record of Portugal in the East-West struggle. If everybody was open, some modus vivendi on the Portuguese question could be found. In the same way, the powerful Western financial interests in the Republic of South Africa, involving not only wealthy men but also the life-savings of many small investors, ought to be acknowledged openly and early. This background, together with the consanguinity of the white citizens in the Republic and Central Africa with Great Britain and other European nations, should be explained to the Afro-Asians as a starting point for an attempt to solve the latter's hostility to South Africa. Openness of this kind would prevent accusations of hypocrisy which form the negative attitude sometimes displayed by Afro-Asians to the West at the United Nations. Finally, in this connection, it should be acknowledged that the views of the Afro-Asian bloc or of its individual members on international affairs can sometimes be correct, while those of other powers can sometimes be wrong. The assumption that those who possess nuclear weapons have a monopoly of common sense or of wisdom in international affairs is as dangerous as the missiles themselves.

These various observations on the activities of Afro-Asians are necessary, since it would be quite impossible for there to be any unification into a world order without a thorough understanding and appreciation of the Afro-Asian viewpoint.

The responsibility of the great nuclear powers to exercise tolerance and understanding has never been more important than at the present moment in history. The positive achievements of Great Britain, France, America, and Russia in transforming empires into commonwealths and satellites into independent states are acts of confidence and faith which they have all performed in varying degrees in the past decade. Have they enough courage to continue this, or can they only allow sycophancy among our countries? If they see us only in the role of faithful supporters, they will lose the opportunity of considering solutions for urgent world problems which may be offered by black and brown men from nonnuclear countries, and from civilizations which may be both old and wise. The solutions of such black and brown men, at this time of transition in the regaining of their countries' independence, reflect the interaction of two civilizations—the one in which they were born and the one in which they were educated. They can thus bring to international matters an interpretation of particular force and significance which few from Europe and America can match.

NOTES ON CONTRIBUTORS

Notes on Contributors

JOSÉ LUIS L. ARANGUREN, born in 1909 in Avila, Spain, is former Professor of Sociology and Ethics at the University of Madrid. Among the books he has written are *Etica, Etica y Política, Catolicismo y Protestantismo como formas de existencia, El Protestantismo y la Moral, La juventud europea y otros ensayos, La Etica de Ortega, La Filosofía di Eugenio d'Ors*, and *Sociología de la Comunicación*.

RAYMOND ARON, born in 1905 in Paris, is Professor of Sociology at the University of Paris. His many publications include *Introduction to the Philosophy of History; The Century of Total War; The Opium of the Intellectuals; France, Steadfast and Changing: The Fourth to the Fifth Republic; Main Currents in Sociological Thought;* and *The Great Debate: Theories of Nuclear Strategy*.

GODFRIED VAN BENTHEM VAN DEN BERGH, born in 1933 in The Hague, is Research Associate of the Europa Instituut of Leyden University. He is the author of *The Association of African States with the European Economic Community* (1962), and has written various articles on European integration and politics. During the academic year 1964-1965 he was Visiting Scholar at the Center for International Affairs of Harvard University and during 1965-1966 he was Research Associate at the Institute of International Studies at the University of California, Berkeley.

JOHN W. DYCKMAN, born in 1922 in Chicago, is Professor of City and Regional Planning and Chairman of the Center for Planning and Development Research at the University of California, Berkeley. He is the co-author of *Capital Requirements for Urban Development and Renewal* (1960), and a contributor to *The Future Metropolis* (1962) and *Explorations in Metropolitan Spatial Structure* (1964). He has written numerous articles in the fields of urban planning and economics.

JEAN FOURASTIÉ, born in 1907 in St. Benin d'Azy, France, is Professor at the Conservatoire National des Arts et Métiers and President of the Labor Commission of the French Plan. Among the books he has written are *The Causes of Wealth, Le Grand Espoir du XX° Siècle*, and *Les Quarante Mille Heures*.

HANS-GEORG GADAMER, born in 1900 in Marburg, Germany, is University Professor of Philosophy at the University of Heidelberg. His principal books include *Platos dialektische Ethik* (1931), *Plato und die Dichter* (1934), *Vom geistigen Lauf des Menschen* (1949), *Wahr-*

heit und Methode: Grundzüge einer philosophischen Hermeneutik (1960, 1965), and *Dialektik und Sophistik im Siebenten platonischen Brief* (1964).

LORD GLADWYN, born in 1900 in Firbeck Hall, Yorkshire, England, is Director of S. G. Warburg and Co., Ltd., President of the Atlantic Treaty Association, and Liberal spokesman on foreign policy in the House of Lords. He is the author of *The European Idea* (1966), *Power and Super-Power, 1948-84* (forthcoming), and various pamphlets on the cold war and the balance of terror. He is former British Representative to the United Nations (1950-54) and Ambassador to France (1954-60).

STANLEY HOFFMANN, born in 1928 in Vienna, is Professor of Government and Research Associate of the Center for International Affairs at Harvard University. His publications include *Contemporary Theory in International Relations* (1960), *The State of War* (1965), and, as co-author, *In Search of France* (1963). He is the author of numerous articles on international affairs which have appeared in academic and professional journals.

HELIO JAGUARIBE, born in 1923 in Rio de Janeiro, is Visiting Professor in the Government Department at Harvard University. He is the author of "For a Policy of National Development," in *Cadernos de Nosso Tempo* (1956), *Philosophy in Brazil* (1957), *Nationalism in the Brazilian Actuality* (1958), *Economic Development and Political Development* (1962), and "The Dynamics of Brazilian Nationalism," in *Obstacles to Change in Latin America* (1965).

HENRY A. KISSINGER, born in 1923 in Fürth, Germany, is Professor of Government and Faculty Member of the Center for International Affairs at Harvard University. He is the author of *A World Restored: Castlereagh, Metternich and the Restoration of Peace, 1812-1822* (1957), *Nuclear Weapons and Foreign Policy* (1957), *The Necessity for Choice: Prospects of American Foreign Policy* (1961), and *The Troubled Partnership: A Reappraisal of the Atlantic Alliance* (1965). He has written numerous articles on American foreign policy and related subjects.

IVAN MÁLEK, born in 1909 in Zábreh-na-Moravě, Czechoslovakia, is Director of the Institute of Microbiology and member of the Presidium of the Czechoslovak Academy of Sciences and Professor of Microbiology at Charles University of Prague. He has written over two hundred scientific papers in various fields of general microbiology and several textbooks on microbiology. He is a member of Parliament of the Czechoslovak Socialist Republic.

PAUL MUS, born in 1902 in Bourges, France, is Professor of Civilizations of the Far East at the Collège de France in Paris and Professor of Civilizations of Southeast Asia at Yale University. He is the author of *Barabudur Esquisse d'une Histoire du Bouddhisme* (1934), *La Lumière sur les Six Voies: Tableau de la Transmigration Bouddhique*

(1939), *Viêt-Nam: Sociologie d'une Guerre* (1952), *Le Destin de l'Union Francaise de l'Indochine à l'Afrique* (1955), and *Guerre sans Visage* (1962)

DAVIDSON S. H. W. NICOL is Principal of Fourah Bay College, the University College of Sierra Leone, West Africa; he was formerly Fellow of Christ's College, Cambridge, England. He has served as a member of the Sierra Leone delegation to the Organization for African Unity Defense Commission, with UNESCO Higher Education Committees, and in the WHO General Assembly.

D. P. O'CONNELL, born in 1924 in Auckland, New Zealand, is Professor of International Law at the University of Adelaide, South Australia. His publications include *Law of State Succession* (1956), *International Law* (1965), *Law in Australia* (1965), and contributions to various journals of law, politics, and affairs.

NEVIN S. SCRIMSHAW, born in 1918 in Milwaukee, Wisconsin, is Professor of Nutrition and Head of the Department of Nutrition and Food Science at the Massachusetts Institute of Technology. He is the author of many articles on nutritional biochemistry, protein-rich foods for human feeding, nutrition and infection, and other aspects of clinical and public health nutrition. He is a member of the Nutrition Advisory Panel of the World Health Organization and Chairman of the Committee for International Research of the National Institutes of Health.

JAN TINBERGEN, born in 1903 in The Hague, is Professor of Development Planning at the Netherlands School of Economics in Rotterdam. He is the author of *Shaping the World Economy* (1962), and *Economic Policy: Principles and Design* (1958). He was Director of the Dutch Government Central Planning Bureau from 1945 to 1955.

CONRAD H. WADDINGTON, born in 1905 in Evesham, England, is Buchanan Professor of Animal Genetics at the University of Edinburgh. His publications include *How Animals Develop* (rev. ed., 1962), *Introduction to Modern Genetics* (1959), *Organisers and Genes* (1940), *The Scientific Attitude* (1941), *Principles of Embryology* (1956), *Strategy of the Genes* (1957), *The Ethical Animal* (1960), *The Nature of Life* (1961), *New Patterns of Genetics and Development* (1962).

INDEX

INDEX

Abu-Lughod, Janet, 314
Addis Ababa 1980 Plan, 271
Adenauer, Konrad, 91, 128
Administrative structure. *See* Bureaucracy
Adul, Mr., 15
Africa: colonial domination of, 32, 360–362, 364, 373; Indian influence in, 374–375; national sovereignty in, 8, 364–365, 369; Republic of South Africa, 363, 376; and the Western nation-states, differences between, 6. *See also* African states
African independence, extracontinental impact of, 369, 370–372
African statements on political philosophy, 362–363
African states: conferences on education, 367; continental integration, 220, 221, 263, 357 (*see also* Integration); disruption of southern, 73, 74; East African Common Services Organization, 369; economic disadvantages, 366; economic unions, 368–369; financial aid to, 366; local leadership, 366–367; manpower shortage, 366; national sovereignty of, 8, 364–365, 369; numerical strength of, 365; open declaration of Western interests in, 375–376; Organization for African Unity, 357; 363–364, 369; and Pan-African unity, 362, 364; regional commission, 262–263; representation in the United Nations, 364, 370, 375–376; threat of neo-colonialism to, 362. *See also* Developing countries

African students abroad, 371
African universities, 367–368
Afro-Asian bloc, 357, 372–375; bids for leadership in, 373–375; localized wars, 370; period of suspended government, 373; representation in the United Nations, 375–376; view of the international system, 346–347
Agency for International Development (AID), 270, 317, 319–320
Agriculture. *See* Food
Alain, on political leaders, 290, 299
Albonetti, Achille, 107
Aleatory and counteraleatory processes, 294, 299
Algerian war, 40, 105, 161
Alliance for Progress (AP), 265, 270, 281
Amis, Kingsley, 106
Anarchical order of society, 25–26
Anti-Americanism, 96–97
Appalachia, 309
Appropriation process, 11
Arab alliance. *See* United Arab Republic
Aranguren, José Luis L., 191
"Arising ends," concept of, 14, 15
Aron, Raymond, 1–21 *passim*, 25, 104, 107, 160, 162, 201, 203, 226, 299, 342
Asia: anti-urbanism in, 310; concepts of world order, 15; domination by force, 32; industrialism in, 349; Southeast Asia Treaty Organization, 357, 358. *See also* Afro-Asian bloc
Asian belief in transmigration, 347–348, 353

385

Index

Asian Development Bank, 263
Asian pantheism, 345
Atlantic Alliance, 85
Atlantic Charter, 98
Atlantic cooperation, 89, 100; Dutch view of, 95, 107; reason for the lack of appeal of, 103; U.S. involvement in, 99. *See also* European integration movement
Atlantic Society, 75
Atomic taboo, 43–44. *See also* Balance of Terror; Nuclear weapons
Attlee, Clement, 89
Austin, John, 55
Australia and the Afro-Asian bloc, 358
Azikwe, Nnamdi, 363

Baade, Fritz, 284, 285
Badouin, Robert, 207
Balance of Terror, 205; an encouragement to the independence of nation-states, 69; and the Franco-German foreign policy split, 125–127; maintenance of, 41, 68
Bellagio conference, 1, 342–343; balance of achievements and failures, 22–24; "builders and critics," 21–22; fragmentation of knowledge in, 21
Bellicose peace, 35, 39
Bello, Ahmadu, 363
Beloff, Max, 96–97, 108
Beloff, Nora, 90, 106
Ben Bella, 12
Berlin in the Cold War, 36, 39
Biological evolution, political and social evolution, one aspect of, 293
Black Muslims, 307
Bos, H. C., 285
Brennan, Donald G., 227
Brugmans, Henri, 97
Brzezinski, Zbigniew, 108
Buber, Martin, 341
Bucharin, N. and E. Preobraschensky, *ABC of Communism,* quoted, 288–289, 299
Buddhism, 350–356; belief in transmigration, 347–348, 353; zealotism, 211
Bureau of Commercial Fisheries, 321
Bureaucracy, 11, 140–141, 167–174; effect on diplomacy, 172–174; in revolutionary periods, 172–173

Bureaucratic-pragmatic leadership, 175–179, 185
Burke, Edmund, 165, 190
Burns, Edward McNall, 108

Cairo, 308
Calhoun, John B., 314
Camps, Miriam, 106
Camus, Albert, 299
Capitalism, 200–201, 218, 231–232, 247
Carr, E. H., 111, 160
Castro, Fidel, 183
Central America and Panama Institute of Nutrition, 320
Césaire, Aimé, 362
Charismatic leadership, 182–186
Chateaubriand, on Napoleon, 290, 299
Child malnutrition and infection in less developed countries, 316–317
Child welfare, 262, 271–272
Chilean economy, 301
China: admission to the U.N., 72; American images of, 199; bid for leadership in the Afro-Asian bloc, 374; Communist ideology, 182 (*see also* Communism); debate with the Soviet Union, 182; food supply, 317; Herodianism in, 211; membership in *Comecon,* 263–264, 269; nuclear power of, 36, 47; power rise, 4, 22, 47; and the problem of "two Chinas," 53; religion and behavior, 15; world view, 344, 346. *See also* Communist states
Cities: alienation of the unintegrated in, 312; and anti-urbanism, 310; crisis management in, 310–311, 315; discipline in, 308; epidemic violence in, 305; of the future, 301–302; integration into world systems, 308; interdependence, 308; migrant expectations, 305–306; occupational stratification, 306; over-urbanization, 303–304; political fragmentation, 307; population densities in, 301–302; privacy and de-personalization in, 302; rise of, 300; spatial stratification in, 306; urban renewal in, 309
Civil rights movement, 310
Clark, Grenville, 226
Clausewitz, 39, 44

Index

Index

tion, 91, 128; foreign policy, 92, 122–128; interpretation of the Balance of Terror, 125–126; nationalism, 90–93, 118–119, 138, 139, 150–151; nineteenth-century leadership, 174; policy toward the EEC, 93; postwar resignation, 122–123, 128; rearmament, 122, 161 (*see also* European Defense Community); rebirth of national consciousness, 138–139; relations with France, 105, 123–124, 147–149, 161; reunification issue, 71, 86, 91–93, 105, 151; weakening ties to the West, 148

Geyl, Pieter, 93–94, 107

Ghana, mission of, 108

Girardet, Raoul, 160

Gladwyn, Lord, 4–9 *passim*, 22, 66

Glaser, Karl, 107

Gorz, André, 198

Governmental structure. *See* Bureaucracy

Gracián, Baltasar, 202, 207

Graduated response doctrine, 41

Graubard, Stephen R., 16, 21, 103, 162, 163, 191

Great Britain: African rule, 360–362, 364; entry into the EEC, 71, 89–90; and European integration, 88–90, 106, 162; foreign policy, 162; nationalism, 87–90; nineteenth-century leadership, 174; nuclear force, 36, 90

Great-Netherlands, 93

Greene, Felix, 199, 207

GRIT, 227

Grosser, Alfred, 82–83, 104, 162, 163

Guerrilla warfare, 32–35, 40

Haas, Ernst B., 103, 105, 108, 150, 160, 163

Hallstein, Walter, 97, 108, 131

Hassner, Pierre, 100, 108, 160

Haviland, H. F., Jr., 162

Health, 240–241, 335; in less developed countries, 316–317; World Health Organization, 262, 320

Heidegger, Martin, 205, 341

Heilbroner, Robert L., 226

Herodianism, 211

Hertz, Frederick, 103

Herz, John, 79, 104

Hinduism, 351–352

Historical unification, 211–213

Historiography, a barrier to world order, 358

Hitler, Adolf, 166

Hitler youth official, autobiography, 109

Ho Chi Minh: nationalism, 76; political statements, 362

Hoffmann, Stanley, 1, 4–12 *passim*, 17–20 *passim*, 81, 96, 102, 104, 110, 160, 191, 315

Hofland, H. J. A., 104

"Homeorhesis," 12, 229

Hotline, 38

Hunger and disease: freedom from, 240–241; in less developed countries, 316–317

Huntington, Samuel P., 227

Ideological differences, 167, 173–174, 345

Ideological type of leadership, 179–182, 185

Ideologies: evidence of the death of, 23; institutionalized, 169, 182; and myths, 196–202, 207; in the nation-state, 6; political, and myths, 196–200; Puritan, 87, 106, 197; role in foreign policy, 167; and world order, 12, 101, 108–109, 200

"Image maker," 202

Incaparina, 320

India: border disputes, 33, 73; a future nation-state, 4; Herodianism in, 211; influence in Africa, 374–375; nuclear capability, 73; Pant on the economy of, 13; religion and behavior, 15; sub-urbanization, 308; world view, 346

Indochina, war in, 40, 161

Indonesia, political association, 73–74

Institutionalization, 6–9, 208–209, 213, forms of, 209–211

Integration, 70, 103, 201; conceptual basis of, 87; continental, 220, 221, 263, 357; disruption through diversity, 121–130; domestic, 152–153; economic (*see* European Economic Community); essential conditions for, 152–156; European (*see* European integration movement); functional method, 131–132, 134–137, 157–158; future of, 159–160; goals, 131; meaning of, 156–159; Monnet method of, 7, 17, 124, 128, 129–

Index

Kohn, Hans, 108
Kohnstamm, Max, 162
Korea demarcation line, 33

Language: a barrier to world order, 358; international, 337–339
"La surprise nationaliste," 100, 108
Latin America, 152; food production, 317; integration, 153 (*see also* Integration); localized wars, 370; Organization of American States, 67, 74, 357; regionalization, 74
Le Fil de l'Epée, 82, 104
Leadership, 5, 174–186; aristocratic, 174–175; bureaucratic-pragmatic, 175–179, 185; charismatic-revolutionary, 175, 182–186; educational standards of, 296–297; ideological, 179–182, 185; personality of, 287–290; violent, 290, 294, 296
League of Nations, 68
Lecanuet, 163
Legum, Colin, 362
Lemberg, Eugen, 91, 98, 106, 108
Lenin, 173, 288, 299
Lerner, Daniel, 162
Leroy-Gourhan, André, 299
Lindberg, Leon N., 105
Lugard, Sir Frederick, 361

Macmillan, Harold, 90
Making and craftsmanship, 333–334
Malaysia: political association, 67, 73–74; war of liberation, 40
Málek, Ivan, 6–10 *passim,* 236
Malnutrition, 316–317
Mandelbaum, Seymour, 308, 315
Mander, John, 89, 106
Manipulation through fear, 196, 203–205
Marx, Karl, 22
Marxism, 180, 200–201; theory of coexistence, 60
Maschmann, Melita, 109
Mass, problems of, 22
Mass media: effect on world peace, 6; rebellion against, 310
Massé, Pierre, 294
Material progress, 313; the common goal, 11–13, 230, 234–235; and human dignity, 13; "operational rationality" in, 10–11, 222; ways and means to, 9–11, 292–293, 298–299. *See also* Economic planning

Mayer, René, 105
Mazzini, 6
Medical dilemma, 335–336
Mekong River Project, 263
Mende, Erich, 162
Mendès-France, Pierre, 124, 161
Messina Conference, 95
Mezzogiorno, 309
Middle East, common Muslim sentiment in, 73
Mill, John Stuart, 87–88, 106
Mills, C. Wright, 310, 315
MLF, 125
Mollet, 161
Monnet, Jean, method of European integration, 7, 17, 124, 128–131, 140, 161, 295
Montesquieu, 88
Morality: ethical-intellectual view of, 192; and politics, 192–194
Morgenthau, H. J., 193
Morison, 10, 14–15, 20
M. R. P., 161
Mumford, Lewis, 300
Murray, J. C., 206
Mus, Paul, 15, 342
Myrdal, Gunnar, 77–79, 103, 198
Myths and ideologies, 195, 202, 207; economic, 200–201; political, 196–200

Napoleon, 166, 290
Nassau conference, 90
Nasser, Gamal Abdel, 362
National consciousness, 115–119, 138–140; French, 139; German, 138–139
National interest, 117
National self-abdication, 114
National self-determination, 112, 114
National situation, 116, 117; diversity in, 117, 140–143, 160; and European integration, 121–122, 124–128, 152–156
National sovereignty, 26, 30, 60; and the argument of emancipation, 6, 57–58, 63; transformation of, 158–159
National survival, 79, 104
Nationalism, 76–77, 116–117; liberal, 101–102; and national consciousness, 117; semantic confusion surrounding, 103; suggested distinctions among, 6; temporary demise of in Western Europe, 118–120; of

Index